JEWEL OF THE DESERT

JEWEL OF THE DESERT

Japanese American
Internment at Topaz

SANDRA C. TAYLOR

UNIVERSITY OF CALIFORNIA PRESS
BERKELEY   LOS ANGELES   OXFORD

University of California Press
Berkeley and Los Angeles, California

University of California Press, Ltd.
Oxford, England

Library of Congress Cataloging-in-Publication Data

Taylor, Sandra C.
    Jewel of the desert : Japanese American internment at
Topaz / Sandra C. Taylor.
        p.   cm.
    ISBN 0-520-08004-1
    1. Japanese Americans—Evacuation and relocation,
1942–1945. 2. Central Utah Relocation Center.
3. Tanforan Assembly Center (San Bruno, Calif.) 4. World
War, 1939–1945—California—San Francisco Bay Area.
5. Japanese Americans—California—San Francisco Bay
Area—History. 6. San Francisco Bay Area (Calif.)—
History.   I. Title.
D769.8.A6T39   1993
979.4′61004956—dc20   92-27669

Printed in the United States of America
9 8 7 6 5 4 3 2 1

To the brave people of Topaz

Contents

Illustrations

Photographs follow page 164

Maps

Figure

Preface

On October 9, 1990, Attorney General Richard Thornburgh distributed checks for $20,000 and letters of apology signed by President George Bush to the nine oldest living Japanese Americans who had been interned in concentration camps during World War II. The ceremony was picturesque: Thornburgh knelt as he presented the checks to the six Issei, all over one hundred years old, who were well enough to receive them in person. It was a dramatic end to the official history of relocation, a story that began with the evacuation of 110,000 Japanese Americans from the West Coast in the spring of 1942. Yet the memory of the experience has not been erased for those whose lives were affected directly, and relocation continues to have a strong meaning for many third- and fourth-generation Japanese Americans, as a continuing reminder of what it has meant to be a member of a minority group in America. By 1991 interest in relocation had grown slightly because of the redress movement, but the general public was not necessarily better informed about it. Although the travails of Japanese Americans became the subject matter for a romanticized Hollywood film, *Come See the Paradise,* this fictionalized account did not enlighten but rather perpetuated a vague image based on stereotypes and some factual errors. Certainly it did not suggest that the need for research had ended.

The United States' war in the Persian Gulf gave new meaning to the entire concept of evacuating and resettling "potential" internal enemies. Japanese Americans suffered because they had the faces, but not the minds, of the enemy. In 1991 Arab Americans found themselves in a similar dangerous situation. Although they came from many national groups, they were easily lumped together and identified with the Iraqi enemy, and the fragile tolerance that Caucasian America has always held for its inhabitants who do not share the ethnicity, religions, or culture of the white majority began to be replaced by the hatreds that war fever produces. Fortunately, the Gulf conflict was brief enough that this minority group was not persecuted by the federal government, although individuals did suffer discrimination and acts of hostility as a result of their appearance and customs. Even though, in the case of Japanese Americans, the paying of redress suggests that at least one generation of politicians was willing to admit the existence of injustice and make a token gesture toward restitution, a newly victimized group might find that public officials quickly forget the past in their desire to pander to popular demands and hysteria.

Although the subject matter of relocation and redress is thus timely, it needs to be addressed in a fresh manner. This book analyzes the Japanese American experience through the framework of community, the network of associations and institutions that held together a group of people who were set apart from the majority by their ethnicity.

I use the word community in full awareness that it is controversial, even "loaded," in the context of today's deconstructionist idiom. My definition draws on two sources: the literature on community studies, which has a rich bibliography, dating back to the early 1950s; and the more specific meanings given to enclaves and small settlements of Japanese Americans by those who have previously studied them. In its sociological sense, Colin Bell and Howard Newby defined the term in 1956 as containing "some or all of the following: a territorial area, a complex of institutions within an area, and a sense of belonging";[1] this description, although old, is still useful. The definition given by Thomas Bender twenty years later is more complete: "A community involves a limited number of people in a somewhat restricted social space or network held together by shared understandings and a sense of obligation. Relationships are close, often intimate, and usually face to face. Individuals are bound together by affective or emotional ties rather than by a perception of individual self-interest. There is a 'we-ness' in a community; one is a member. Sense of self and of community may be difficult to distinguish."[2] Between the two definitions lies a copious literature, and arguments rage even today over whether the term is useful, valid, or even appropriate.

If we leave the debate about the general meaning of the term to sociologists, social historians, and demographers (ignoring entirely the concept of community studies as a form of fiction) and turn to the term as used among historians who have studied specific groups of Japanese Americans, we find that it has a more specific meaning, which continues to be useful today. S. Frank Miyamoto noted in the mid-1930s the tendency of Japanese in western America to concentrate in three centers, Los Angeles, San Francisco, and Seattle. He stated later, in a revised edition of his earlier work, "Within these areas of concentration they invariably build numerous little communities. Since Japanese immigrants are seldom found adjusting to American life except in groups, to consider their problems without the relief of community background is to distort seriously the picture of their adjustment."[3] In a 1969 study of Los Angeles, John Modell used the term *community* to describe "a group with spokesmen, with differentiation of function within, with characteristic enterprises rather than jobs which by chance fell to its members."[4] More recently, in a book published in 1991, Timothy J. Lukes and Gary Y. Okihiro accepted this notion of community while emphasizing the role of racism in the treatment of the Japanese of the Santa Clara Valley and the determined resistance of the community to it.[5] Miyamoto noted two distinct aspects of community: the "totality of Japanese living within the civic boundaries [of a place] who feel a common bond with all the rest of their nationality; and the central area within which all of their major activities are carried on."[6] His definition certainly applies to my usage of the term to describe both the Japantown that existed "within the civic boundaries of San Francisco," and the outlying communities around the bay where economic and social activities took place. Sucheng Chan contributed an extremely useful addition to the concept of community as it applied to Japanese Americans before World War II: these were not "normal" communities demographically, since most of their inhabitants were men, some of whom, in the case of San Francisco, moved about in search of work. Because women were prohibited from immigrating after the National Origins Act of 1924, the Japanese American communities were marked by an unusually large number of unmarried men, as well as a large age gap between the husbands and the wives and children.[7] Chan's work, published in 1991, supported the concept that *community*, as applied to Japanese Americans, has a specific meaning and is a useful term. In *Japanese American Ethnicity: The Persistence of Community*,[8] Stephen S. Fujita and David J. O'Brien showed the continuing validity of the term, at least for a certain group of scholars.

This book borrows the term *community* from all these sources. It refers to Japanese Americans who lived in a specific area (San Francisco, the peninsula, and the East Bay); had a common point of origin (four prefectures of Japan); shared a common tongue (which was less well known by the second generation); and were linked through various organizations (specifically, before World War II the Japanese Associations, the prefectural associations, and—although less for the Nisei—the Japanese American Citizens League). They were bound by a network of occupations and trades to which they were restricted by the racism of the dominant Anglo-Saxon culture, and they attended the same churches and temples and schools. They were people who knew one another—or knew of one another—more than in other ethnic communities because once emigration from Japan ceased in 1924 the community's growth was primarily internal. This sense of polity was particularly important in the years before World War II, when the status of Japanese Americans as members of a hated minority and objects of racism and discrimination drew them especially close together. The residents of Japantown, Nihonmachi, in San Francisco and its offshoots in the smaller localities on the peninsula south of the city and in the East Bay typified this solidification of community, as larger Japanese American settlements did in Seattle and Los Angeles.[9]

This book differs from the many studies of Japanese relocation that preceded it: it focuses on the effects of the evacuation of these Japanese Americans from their California homes and their subsequent resettlement first in the assembly center at Tanforan and then in the concentration camp at Topaz, Utah; it also treats briefly their dispersal and resettlement after the war. Consequently, it examines the camp experience through a different lens.[10] Its purpose is to show how a particular group of Japanese Americans made the transition from immigrants to residents of the Bay Area, how they functioned in the larger Caucasian society, and how they suffered discrimination before as well as during the war. The book also analyzes the complex interaction between whites and the non-white interned people of the new settlements created by the evacuation: Tanforan and Topaz. It concludes with a brief examination of the disintegration of the old Bay Area community and the creation of a new one in postwar northern California. Since many former residents did not return, it also studies those who rebuilt their lives independently, outside the framework of the past, in locations where there was less a sense of community than one of ethnic identity.

As a Caucasian I feel compelled to clarify my position in relation to a piece of American history about which no one can be neutral today. I start from a belief that the policy of the federal government in uprooting the Japanese Americans of San Francisco and the West Coast was unjust, unnecessary, and illegal. The internment was a trauma that became the center point of the lives of those who endured it, and the experience left visible and invisible scars. The redress movement has amply confirmed the judgment that federal government policy was in error, and both the executive and legislative branches have apologized and agreed to pay compensation. But to identify relocation as an evil does not mean that all who were interned were victimized in the same way, or that those who administered their confinement were necessarily evil men and women who sought to harm them. Many Japanese Americans did not allow themselves to become victims, either physically or psychologically. Some were resilient and determined, and their successes in postwar America bear testimony to the stupidity of incarcerating them.

Others suffered tremendously and still bear scars. The experience of internment shattered their world, and its reconstruction took place individually and internally, in many parts of the United States and Japan.

This study attempts first to reconstruct the community that Japanese Americans built in the San Francisco Bay Area, from the time of their arrival in the 1880s until Pearl Harbor. The bulk of the work is concerned with their wartime experiences, particularly in the camp at Topaz. Perhaps no single author can fully assess the price these victims of racism paid for official ignorance, prejudice, and intolerance or understand the many kinds of recovery demonstrated by Japanese Americans of the Bay Area and other places where the former Topazeans settled. Nevertheless, that is my goal.

☙

This book draws on a rich historiographical tradition but differs from other works in several dimensions. The history of the internment of Japanese Americans has often been told. Its chroniclers were first social scientists and the displaced themselves, who established the University of California Japanese American Evacuation and Resettlement Study, directed by Dorothy Swaine Thomas. Thomas's two works, *The Spoilage* (written with Richard S. Nishimoto) and *The Salvage*, discussed aspects of evacuation, the repatriation movement, and case histories of people interned. Although the JERS study has been strongly criticized for its lack of historical focus and because of the connection between the researchers and the federal government, it set the tone for the highly critical accounts that followed. It also provided a rich body of documentation, available in the Bancroft Library at the University of California in Berkeley, and it serves as a counterweight to the voluminous documentation left by the War Relocation Authority at the National Archives in Washington. There were also early works by Japanese interned at Topaz, most notably Miné Okubo's *Citizen 13660*. The history of the evacuation was popularized by Audrie Girdner and Anne Loftis in *The Great Betrayal: The Evacuation of the Japanese-Americans During World War II*. Roger

Daniels published a number of accounts of Japanese American history that are as critical of internment as their titles imply: *The Politics of Prejudice: The Anti-Japanese Movement in California and the Struggle for Japanese Exclusion; Concentration Camps, North America: Japanese in the United States and Canada During World War II*, which was published earlier as *Concentration Camps, U.S.A.: Japanese Americans and World War II*; most recently *Asian America: Chinese and Japanese in the United States Since 1850*; and scores of articles and book chapters. All these works decry evacuation and internment; in fact, the only apologists have been the War Relocation Authority itself, especially its *Final Report* (Washington: 1944),[11] and some of the Caucasian participants, notably Dillon Myer in *Uprooted Americans*. Even the U.S. government reversed itself as the passage of time, civil rights, and the redress movement demonstrated beyond a doubt the naked racism of internment. In 1982 the researchers of the Commission on Wartime Relocation and Internment of Civilians published a report entitled *Personal Justice Denied*.

If anything, recent works have been even harsher and more condemnatory. Michi Weglyn's *Years of Infamy* and Richard Drinnon's *Keeper of Concentration Camps* are almost polemical in their criticism of the camps. The focus seems to have shifted from the federal government's policy to the interned, in studies that consider to what degree Japanese Americans acquiesced in or resisted internment, and how passive or active resistance was implemented.

This work shares with its immediate predecessors the conviction that the internment of the West Coast Japanese Americans was racist, illegal, unwise, and highly destructive to the people involved. It differs from the works that preceded it because it centers on one specific community that was displaced. While it does not condone the outrageous treatment of the Japanese Americans, it is not a polemical attack upon administrators of a bygone day, who were neither Adolf Eichmanns nor universally evil. The story of Topaz is the story of Japanese San Francisco and the Bay Area's Japanese American community, its origins, development, dissolution, and rebirth. The closing of Topaz in October 1945 meant the dispersal of many of its inhabitants, but some 60 percent eventually found

their way back to the Golden Gate and even those who did not still
maintain ties with camp through visits to the Bay Area, class and
camp reunions, and correspondence. What the experience of internment did to them—what it meant for their lives and their
community—is the focal point of this book.

Many of the sources for this history are found in the records of
the War Relocation Authority, which administered the camps for
the Department of the Interior. The materials gathered for the study
conducted by Thomas and her associates in JERS form another
important part. Secondary works and newspapers were also used.
The most important source for this book, however, consists of oral
histories of nearly fifty Japanese Americans, Nisei and Issei, residents of San Francisco, the Bay Area, or Sacramento who were
evacuated from their homes, incarcerated in Tanforan, and then
moved to Topaz. These interviews do not constitute a random
sample of the still-living population of the camp. I was directed to
the Topaz community in New York by Michi Kobi, while Fumi
Hayashi and Daisy Satoda put me in contact with many people in
the Bay Area. Carole Hayashino of the San Francisco Japanese
American Citizens League also searched diligently for names and
addresses of former Topazeans in San Francisco, and of course one
person often suggested another. I attended a reunion of the Topaz
High School Class of 1945 and made many contacts there: hence,
its members may be overrepresented. Issei were hard to locate, and
often language barriers hindered good communication. Lack of
time and money prevented me from interviewing people in the
Midwest. The interviews cover the respondents' experiences of
camp life and stories of their parents' immigration, life in prewar
California, and the impact of Pearl Harbor. Even though it has been
forty-five years since these people lived in Topaz, the relocation has
been the focal point of their lives. It shattered their sense of community and replaced it with another one, a somewhat prisonlike
existence where they lived under Caucasian domination. That community was more "Japanesy" for most than their prewar lives had
been, for everyone in camp except the administrators and their
families was Japanese American. The interviews reflected the diversity of experience of the former residents, and the time they

required—from a few minutes to more than four hours—in some way expressed the degree to which the respondents had been harmed by the internment and how deeply its scars were embedded in their psyches.

Topaz, the "jewel of the desert," lived an ephemeral existence. The War Relocation Authority tried to resettle its charges as quickly as possible, to destroy the West Coast ghettos and farming communities that aggravated the Caucasians by their very success, and to disperse the residents across America. It succeeded only to a limited degree. Interviews with former Topaz residents in New York and New England help explain how the former community died and what the disintegration did to the lives of former residents who were spun far from its source. But a majority did return. Tomoye Takahashi could never forget the beauty of the San Francisco skyline illuminated by the setting sun as she and her family took the ferry across the bay to rebuild their lives in San Francisco. The financial success of the Takahashis is a rebuke to those who ordered them away. The new community that she and many others helped to build is no ghetto, but rather a jewel in the crown of multi-ethnic San Francisco; it is also a diverse ethnic group scattered throughout the Bay Area, intermingled with the society around it. Its people are proud to be Americans and proud of their Japanese heritage as well.

This book would not be complete without my special thanks to the people who provided expertise when it was most needed. For assistance with oral history, I thank Floyd O'Neil of the American West Center and Gregory Thompson of the Western Americana Division of the Marriott Library, University of Utah. The Helen Z. Papanikolas Fund provided assistance with transcribing the oral tapes. I also acknowledge the financial assistance provided by the Research Committee of the University of Utah and the Career Development Committee of the College of Humanities. I must give special praise to Betsey Scheiner of the University of California Press, without whose careful editing this final version would not have come about. And last, I give special thanks to my husband, Russell Wilhelmsen, whose computer expertise and patience saved me from a world of grief.

Chapter One

Japanese San Francisco

The young Tomizo Fujita arrived in San Francisco in 1906, the year of the great earthquake and fire. He made port on August 13, just four months after the catastrophe that left 4,000 dead and more than 100,000 homeless. His son, Tad, recalled eighty-one years later that his father had told him that "all the city was leveled and it was too late to return" to Japan.[1] In view of San Franciscans' racist treatment of Japanese Americans, it was truly ironic that Japan subsequently contributed $244,960.10 to rebuilding the devastated city, more than half of the total amount raised from all sources outside the United States. But Tomizo Fujita foresaw none of this; he was naive, optimistic, and full of faith in the future. He brought his young wife to a hostel run by another Japanese family, where they resided in a packing shed. Tad was born there three years later,[2] a native San Franciscan and a Nisei, a citizen of the United States of Japanese ancestry.

The Fujitas joined a growing community of emigrants from Japan who had settled in San Francisco and other parts of the Bay Area as early as 1860.[3] Another member of the community, Tomoye Nozawe Takahashi, told a similar story. Her father arrived a few years before the earthquake and set himself up in partnership with his cousins in the laundry business, where he took care of the steam pipes, the mechanical washers, and the ironing mangles the young business required. In a few years, despite the disaster, he was able to go out on his own.[4]

California was a new world of fresh hopes, governed by a constitution that promised freedom, equality, and justice for all before the law, but it was also a land steeped in prejudice against Asians. This bias was the product of hatred against people of color generally and a suspicion of Asians nurtured throughout the nineteenth century in encounters with Chinese immigrants; anti-coolie clubs were organized in San Francisco as early as 1862, and the anti-Chinese issue was among the most important political issues in the state of California in 1870.[5] But the first Japanese immigrants knew little of this heritage of racism.

The Japanese government had long maintained a ban on emigration, which it formally lifted in 1884. A few Japanese subjects had left earlier—primarily shipwrecked seamen. The first official Japanese immigrants came to work in Hawaii in 1868: these were the *gannenmono,* or "first year people," 141 men, 6 women, and 2 children.[6] A year later colonists founded a silk farm in California, and in 1870 the Japanese government opened a consulate in San Francisco.[7] San Francisco, a thriving seaport community, was a natural location for travelers from Asia to the North American mainland, and a small community developed there about the same time Japanese Americans were establishing toeholds in the Pacific Northwest and in the Los Angeles area.[8] The first Japanese settlers were often upper-class students or other travelers, some of whom were just passing through. They were a "select group," permitted to leave by officials of the new Meiji government because they were viewed as healthy, literate, and upstanding people who would reflect well on Japan's national honor.[9] In succeeding years the emigrants were much more diverse.

◈

Significant numbers of Japanese began to arrive in 1886, when the Meiji government allowed legal emigration to the new world for the first time, and more arrived in the decade that followed.[10] They were a different population from the first small group, coming primarily from Hiroshima and three other *ken,* or prefectures: Gumma, Yamaguchi, and Fukuoka. They were primarily agricultural

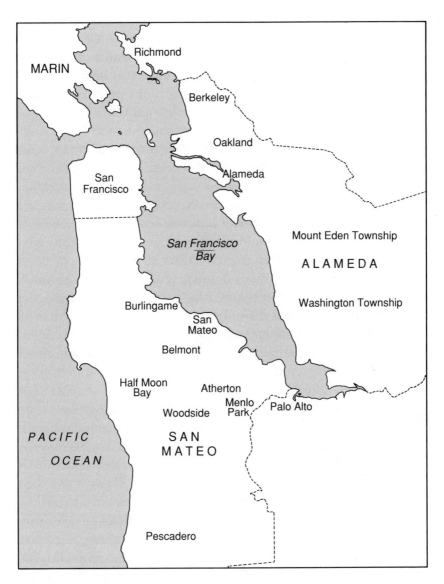

1. Prewar San Francisco and the Bay Area

people dislocated by the social upheavals accompanying the modernization of the Meiji period; they left home in search of economic betterment and the opportunity to own and farm land. Others—students, second sons of landed gentry, and the venturesome—sought the challenges to be found in a foreign land.

Many who settled in San Francisco resided first in Hawaii, laboring in the sugarcane fields, but they, like earlier migrant laborers there, found the work hard and the rewards few. After 1898, Hawaii's annexation by the United States made further migration possible, so for the next decade many Japanese moved on to the mainland.[11] Most of the original Japanese settlers intended to save their money so that they could return to Japan quickly and buy land there, and a large number did so, following the pattern of other immigrant groups.[12] But many found that work was hard in America, and the rewards meager, and they gradually accepted the fact that the new world, not the old, would be their home.

Not all sought an agricultural life. Included among the immigrants were urban people who made their living as shopkeepers, professionally trained men, and a few women brought in to serve as prostitutes in this highly male society. Those who settled in San Francisco resided in all parts of the city. The largest group set up shops on Chinese-dominated Dupont Avenue (present-day Grant Avenue), living among the Chinese until they were displaced by the earthquake of 1906. From there they moved to an area called South Park (Second and Third streets to Brennan and Bryant), and then to Polk Street and north to Bush Street, in an area known as the Western Addition. Others settled on O'Farrell Street near Mason, and some on Stevenson Street, around Second. Most worked first as domestics, the easiest job for someone who knew little English to obtain. Others occasionally toiled as laborers in the Central Valley during harvest season and wintered in the city.[13] Aspiring businessmen ran cheap hotels or restaurants that their fellow countrymen patronized; these were usually located near piers 34–36, where their ships had docked, or near the Southern Pacific railroad depot, which was also close to the waterfront. The immigrants were young, usually male, mainly under thirty-five, and they made little money, about \$25–\$30 a month, scarcely enough on which to return home.[14]

❧

Like members of other ethnic groups, these immigrants brought some religious institutions with them from Japan and acquired others through missionary work in the community. Japanese Americans accepted both the Buddhist and the Christian faith. Devotion bonded the new residents and gave them solace, which was especially necessary in a Caucasian community that did not welcome these "strangers from a different shore," as historian Ronald Takaki has termed them.

Most Issei (first-generation Japanese Americans) were Buddhist, the predominant faith at that time in Japan, but their institutional ties were not strong. Miyamoto suggested that Buddhism's fatalistic approach, accepting the world as it is, was not as well suited to life in America as Christianity was, which enjoined its members to struggle to improve life on earth as well as to prepare for the world to come. In Seattle this approach had produced a predominantly Christian Japanese American community by the mid-1930s,[15] and San Francisco seems to have followed a similar course. Protestant Christian missionaries were working as early as the 1870s among isolated Japanese students, bringing them together in friendship as well as faith. There were numerous Christians among the new arrivals; the faith had attracted a very small but elite minority in Japan since its official toleration began in 1873.[16] Methodists carried out the first missionary work in San Francisco, approaching the Japanese as an offshoot of their work with the inhabitants of Chinatown. The Japanese Gospel Society was founded in 1877. Church historian Lester Suzuki documented that the first immigrant Japanese to be baptized was Kanichi Miyama, who became a minister and firmly established Methodism among San Francisco's Japanese American community. Miyama later inaugurated mission work among the Japanese of Hawaii. He and Kumataro Nakano were both converted by Dr. Otis Gibson, a missionary to the Chinese; they were the "first harvest of Japanese mission work in America in Chinatown, San Francisco."[17]

The pattern in San Francisco was similar to religious work in Japan, where Caucasian missionaries spread the Gospel but converts quickly organized their own houses of worship, ordained native ministers, and proselytized as well. In the case of the immigrants, evangelism was mixed with social services, which met other needs of the newcomers. The Gospel Society, which met weekly on Saturday nights, charged a fee of twenty-five cents; its members studied the Bible, but they also practiced public speaking.[18] The society made English lessons available to its members and found temporary lodging and employment for them. It soon moved to larger quarters in the basement of the Chinese Methodist Mission on Stockton Street. In 1881 the Gospel Society split, and an offshoot was organized on Tyler Street (later called Golden Gate Avenue). The Tyler Gospel Society became the Japanese YMCA, and from it the Japanese Church of Christ was formed. In 1884 the original Gospel Society was recognized as part of the Methodist Mission; two years later, it became the Methodist-Episcopal Mission. The Stevenson Gospel Society, which had begun its operations on Stevenson Street, merged with the Tyler group a few months later. These small mission efforts led to the formation of the Pine Methodist Church in 1886. A subgroup became the organized Church of Christ Presbyterian. Thus, all Japanese Christian groups in Northern California emerged from the same mother body, the Japanese Gospel Society.[19]

Japanese Protestant churches slowly spread throughout the Bay Area. Under the leadership of Dr. Ernest A. Sturge, the Presbyterians organized their first church for the Japanese in San Francisco in 1885; it became the Christ United Presbyterian. The Protestant Episcopal Church established churches in San Francisco in 1895, and the Reverend Joseph Tsukamoto served the city for many years. The Sycamore Congregational Church was founded in Oakland in 1904 by the Reverend Shinjiro Okubo. The Free Methodists (who were, at this time, separate from other Methodists) established churches in the Berkeley-Richmond area and Redwood City; the Methodists united in 1939. The Reformed Church also located in

San Francisco. The Seventh Day Adventists founded churches in San Francisco and Oakland, and the Salvation Army, Japan Division, established a corps in San Francisco in 1918, led by Major Masasuke Kobayashi. During the 1930s it built a home on Laguna and Geary streets, to which the emperor of Japan donated money; his action stimulated donations among many Issei.[20] These denominations and others soon spread among the immigrant Japanese communities throughout America, linking them to the broader Christian world and to some degree to the Caucasians who shared their faith, if not their houses of worship. Bay Area churches and missions encompassed the first significant numbers of Japanese Christians outside Japan.

The Buddhists were not far behind the Christians in extending religious work to the immigrants. They began missionary work in San Francisco in 1898, and a year later were founding groups throughout the Bay Area and in other places where Japanese had settled. The Berkeley Buddhist Church, founded in 1911, held its first services in private homes. It then moved to a hotel and finally dedicated its house of worship on Channing Way on February 13, 1921. The Buddhists—both those of the Buddhist Churches of America (BCA), who followed the Jodo Shinshu way, and those of the Nichiren sect—maintained closer ties with Japan than the Christians did, because they required ministers to be trained in Japan. Tom Kawaguchi recalled that although the largest Buddhist church in San Francisco was affiliated with the Nishi Honganji in Kyoto, there was also a Nichiren Buddhist church located on Pine Street. There was a Soto Zen temple in Japantown, and a Shinto shrine a few blocks away.[21] The Buddhist Church of America began a training program for English-speaking ministers in 1930. Within a few years it had opened a headquarters in San Francisco and begun a program of lectures and correspondence courses to prepare prospective priests for study in Japan. Its mother temple was the Nishi Honganji in Kyoto.[22] Like the Christians, the Buddhists established youth groups and Sunday schools to serve the growing Nisei population; in the 1930s the BCA sponsored an annual climb of Mount Tamalpais, across the Golden Gate in Marin County.[23]

The location of the various churches gave evidence of the wide dispersal of the Japanese population in San Francisco: the YMCA was on Haight Street, the Methodist Episcopal on Pine near Larkin; the Fukuin Kai Gospel Society on Bush near Hyde, and the Buddhist on Polk near O'Farrell. By the time of the evacuation in 1942, Buddhist and Christian churches had been established in San Francisco, Oakland, Berkeley, Alameda, South Alameda County, and San Mateo, as well as further south on the peninsula, in the Central Valley, and Los Angeles. Shinto was also represented, but to a much smaller degree.

Kenjinkai, or prefectural associations, were also very important to the growing Japanese American community. They met social needs, serving as self-help organizations and instruments of social control. Tom Kawaguchi, who grew up in prewar San Francisco, recalled that when a Japanese ship docked, the sailors from Hiroshima Ken were entertained by the Hiroshima Kenjinkai; other associations did the same.[24]

⁂

The early residents in San Francisco were a mixture of merchants, traders, and students. "Schoolboys" were students who made their living as domestics while attending classes. Many of the schoolboys came as bona fide workers, but there was an increasing number of students and *shosei,* pseudo-students "who came [only] to learn English and 'the ropes.'"[25] Some of these were refused entry into the country after they were identified as political radicals by the local Japanese consul, who feared they could bring disrepute upon the Japanese American business community. The students, whatever their political orientation, came from a higher class than the laborers. Seizo Oka, a historian of the San Francisco Nikkei community, proposed that the arrival of an increasing number of less cultured laborers had much to do with the rise in prejudice against the Japanese. The early students were an elite and usually politically moderate or conservative group, and they were inoffensive, few in number, and unobtrusive.[26] The relative lack of discrimination they encountered may have been due simply to the modesty of their numbers: there were only 148 Japanese in America according to the census of 1880. As the numbers grew, the dedication of the Japanese to education diminished. As few as 900 of the 6,395 Japanese in the United States who came as students between 1867 and 1902 may actually have been studying.[27]

These numbers are significant only when one realizes how few Japanese immigrants there were in America altogether. The following census figures give a picture of ethnic Japanese (who did not intend to be permanent immigrants) resident in the United States:[28]

	United States	*California*
1880	148	86
1890	2,039	1,147 (590 in San Francisco)
1900	24,326	10,151
1910	72,157	41,356
1920	111,010	71,952
1930	138,834	97,456

Drawn together by their common heritage, Japanese immigrants to San Francisco began to form a separate ethnic district of the city as early as the 1880s. Miyamoto pointed out that most Japanese Americans on the Pacific coast before World War II either lived in or were "in some fashion bound to a Japanese community and were significantly influenced by the affiliation,"[29] and those in San Francisco were no exception. This grouping focused on businesses and services. A core group lived in the central area (which, as we will see, shifted over the years), but the population was somewhat dispersed, usually as a result of employment: newcomers who worked as domestics often resided with their employers.

Family structure was an essential component in the creation of a permanent ethnic culture. Like other immigrants, the Issei viewed America through the cultural perspective of their homeland, where family ties held society together. Neither Caucasian San Franciscans nor the Japanese immigrants favored intermarriage, which was, in any case, illegal. The Japanese government encouraged women to emigrate, in order to discourage men from resorting to prostitutes, but few women actually left Japan unless they were already betrothed or married. In 1905, 22 percent of the Japanese population in Hawaii was female, in contrast to 7 percent of the mainland population.[30] This unequal sex ratio (which included many males who were married but had either left their families in Japan or were awaiting their arrival in America) made for many lonely men, even among those who intended only to be "birds of passage," returning to Japan when they had earned enough money.

One solution to the problem was to import prostitutes. A 1910 Japanese study noted that there were 913 Japanese prostitutes in Honolulu and 371 in San Francisco. In countries such as the United States, where prostitution was theoretically illegal, these women were often smuggled into the country in barrels.[31] Their lives were harsh in the extreme. Usually coerced into the practice or even sold by their parents, they were accepted by neither the white nor the traditional Japanese culture. The trade in prostitutes was supposedly ended with the Gentlemen's Agreement of 1908, which allowed only spouses, parents, and children of Japanese Americans to immigrate to America. After that year, Seattle at least had begun to disperse its colony of prostitutes; some were deported, while others went into the countryside. The situation in San Francisco is not as clear, but certainly by the 1920s the community had begun to develop a family-centered culture, entering the "settling period," as Miyamoto described it.[32]

Between 1911 and 1920 women represented as much as 39 percent of all Japanese immigrants. Many came as picture brides; others were married conventionally either before the husband emigrated or while he was on a trip home. Picture brides entered into marriages that were arranged by exchanging photographs. The picture bride institution, which continued until 1921, was not unusual in a culture that commonly used a *baishakunin* (go-between) to negotiate between families that wanted to establish a marriage. These brides might accompany their husband to America or travel alone to meet him there, but whatever the circumstances, they found a new and unexpected world where the streets were not paved with gold and life was not easy. Often the spouse they met on arrival was neither as good-looking nor as wealthy as they had been led to believe, and they entered upon a life of very hard work, especially if they had married a farmer. Their process of adjustment was as difficult as their husband's had been, if not more so.[33]

The new brides were often considerably younger than their husbands, for men could not send for a wife until they themselves were financially established. Married Issei women's options were even more limited than the men's. Traditional Japanese culture dictated their inferior status in society, and little in their new circumstances conspired to change that. In the rural areas, as well as in the outlying nurseries and fields of the Bay Area, they often worked with their husbands, and couples in domestic work were both wage earners. As a couple, they earned little, but the woman brought in far less than her husband. Still, the women's primary tasks were to maintain the home and raise the children.

The family home attested to their presence. Miyamoto described how Issei Seattle homes combined American and Japanese elements, and the same was true of Nisei homes I visited in San Francisco in the late 1980s. Although Japanese was no longer the family tongue unless an elderly Issei grandparent lived there, Japanese foods, shoji screens, floral arrangements, and pictures were as evident as family shrines had been for an earlier generation. American appliances and luxuries came with increasing wealth and were more apparent in the 1980s than in the 1930s.[34]

For many Issei women learning English was almost impossible, because they had no time to go to school and no regular contact with native English speakers. This situation tied them to their family and ethnic community for their entire lives. But it did not necessarily mean unhappiness: Chitose Manabe, an elderly Issei woman who resided in Berkeley not far from her daughter Fumi Hayashi and son-in-law Tad in 1988, could speak only broken English, but her life as mother, wife, and partner of a lay Christian leader, and even her camp internment, seemed to have brought a great sense of inner peace and contentment.[35]

Children and parents also crossed the Pacific, creating a more normal family situation for many of the Issei males who now called America home.[36] Some families came together; Bob Utsumi recalled that his grandfather on his father's side immigrated in 1901 with his wife, infant son, and daughter. The two children returned to Japan for their education but came back to the United States, where Bob's father entered the University of California. The grandfather on his mother's side immigrated to Alameda in 1898, joining cousins who had come in the mid-1880s. He married a picture bride who came from the same prefecture in Japan. This long family history in the United States gave Bob the somewhat unusual distinction of being one of the few teenaged Sansei (third-generation Japanese Americans) to be interned at Topaz.[37]

⚜

The Nisei, the first generation born in America, were U.S. citizens. They rapidly took their places in the ethnic world of San Francisco's Nihonmachi, which had established itself along Buchanan between Geary and Pine.[38] Bilingual at least in part, they lived in a Japanese world of restaurants, Christian and Buddhist churches, public and Japanese-language schools, prefecture associations,[39] and a growing Japanese business community filled with shops, hotels, newspapers, and other enterprises. Since Alameda County had become a flourishing nursery area, San Francisco developed a floral exchange; these flowers, sold on street-corner market stands, gave San Francisco its distinctive appearance. John Modell noted that restaurants were the first Japanese businesses to be opened in Los Angeles, and that may well have been the case in San Francisco.[40] They usually served Japanese, Chinese, and American food, and catered to the Japanese community as well as other residents of the area.

Because the young Nisei often lived near or went to school with Caucasian children, their worlds were less segregated than those of their parents, but they too suffered the effects of discrimination by their peers. Tomoye Takahashi, who grew up in prewar San Francisco, recalled that she was never invited to class functions such as birthday parties or "anything that happened after school." She could still remember how lonely she was as a little girl. Even though she was allowed to bring a long jump rope to school, she could only turn the rope but not jump. She lived near Twin Peaks, not in

Japantown, and for her going to Japanese school after regular school was a joy because it meant being with other Nisei children.[41]

The Nisei were truly Japanese Americans, growing up with one foot in each culture. For some their identity was determined by the degree to which they spoke Japanese and could communicate with parents who spoke little English, but other factors were also important: where in San Francisco they lived, what church they attended, and how much contact they had with white children. Racism was always present, but it affected the Nisei in different ways. For some it did not really become apparent until they had completed higher education and found that their job prospects were entirely limited to their ethnic community.

The Issei remained Japanese citizens, prohibited by the American government from becoming naturalized.[42] Citizenship, once reserved for whites, had been extended to African Americans in 1870, but repeated challenges by Japanese aliens, including four who had served in the American armed forces in World War I, had been denied. The ultimate decision, rendered by the Supreme Court in Ozawa v. U.S. in 1922, was in the negative. No degree of Americanization, no amount of participation in the duties of a citizen, could override Berkeley resident Takao Ozawa's place of birth: Japan. This judgment was an expression of contempt born of the racism that eventually led to exclusion and the camps, but during the 1920s it was just something to be tolerated, like the Alien Land Laws. As Frank Miyamoto stressed, alien status not only made the Issei subject to economic hardship but also gave them a sense of being unwanted, unwelcome, permanent outsiders.[43] Lack of citizenship was not, in the 1920s, an occasion for fear or outrage— rather, it was an aggravation. Fear came later.

Especially important to the lives of the Issei was the local Japanese Association, which was founded in San Francisco in 1900 and quickly spread to other major population centers.[44] Later very controversial, the associations were originally established for the purpose of self-help and to intercede between the Issei and the

Caucasian world, particularly as racism and discrimination developed in northern California. The Japanese Associations were never nationally coordinated. At one point there was a national headquarters in San Francisco, several branches called "central bodies," which corresponded to the territorial boundaries of the different Japanese consulates, and a myriad of local associations.[45] As John Modell pointed out, these were "expressions of solidary communal resistance to white hostility."[46] Roger Daniels concluded that because of their very close ties to the Japanese government, they should be considered semiofficial organs of it,[47] but their function was usually bureaucratic rather than governmental. The local association issued a certificate enabling an Issei to bring his bride (whether proxy or conventional) to the United States (before 1924), but it was also involved in issues as mundane as obtaining Japanese-language driving tests. The central body of the Japanese Associations met periodically in San Francisco. It occasionally protested to Japan that the $800 in savings that the Japanese government demanded an emigrant possess before it would issue a passport was exorbitant, but the organization was ineffective in changing this stipulation. The associations also attempted to protect immigrants against discrimination by whites. They served as agents of acculturation as well, urging Issei to become "Americanized" so they could keep a low social profile and not attract hostility.[48] The importance of the Japanese Association in San Francisco did not diminish even as Issei developed more contacts with the Caucasian community, because it and the local East Bay associations continued to play an important role between the Issei and Japan.[49]

Japanese San Francisco followed a pattern similar to the Nihonmachi in Seattle and Los Angeles, the other major West Coast urban centers where Nikkei (Americans of Japanese ancestry) settled. As in those communities, the many *kenjinkai* met to provide friendship and reinforce ties based on a common prefectural origin. The urban dwellers were increasingly a minority of their ethnic group in America, most of whom lived in rural areas and pursued an agricultural life.[50] To outsiders the community appeared a crowded ethnic enclave, but to those inside it was safe, familiar, and secure. One resident after World War II recalled the old days, when

Nihonmachi had a "ghetto mentality" centered on the Japanese school and the churches: "We couldn't think beyond; the white world was completely beyond our understanding."[51] To those who could have afforded better, it must have been confining as well as comforting, but for most it was simply home.

⚜

From the beginning of the twentieth century, San Francisco became increasingly the hub of Japanese America, and the economic institutions of the community grew apace. Most Japanese entered America through its port, and its Nihonmachi quickly became the most important. The Japanese consul general was headquartered there.[52] Two Japanese banks, the Japanese American and the Golden Gate, were opened in 1905, only to fail the next year after the earthquake. The population before the earthquake has been estimated at over 10,000, but it dispersed considerably in the months that followed.[53] Those who did not live in Japantown—perhaps half the population—were live-in domestic servants, residing in servants' quarters in such luxurious areas as Pacific Heights, but they too shopped, attended church and language schools, and frequented the Japanese Association in Nihonmachi. There were also Japantowns in Oakland, Alameda, Berkeley, and Richmond. Until 1907 the Bay Area, Sacramento, and the upper San Joaquin Valley were the areas where the Japanese population was growing most quickly, but after that year more people moved to the south because of growing discrimination against Nikkei in northern California.[54]

Hotels were perhaps the most important business establishments serving the Japanese pouring into San Francisco, since a place to stay was essential. The first, constructed between 1885 and 1890, consisted of a few small boardinghouses on Stockton Street in the Chinatown district. Somewhat larger boardinghouse hotels were built next; they served the many single men in the community. Proximity to the waterfront was an asset for businesses that catered to the new arrivals, but after Chinatown was destroyed in the earthquake and the fire, new hotels were built in the South Park district, a block south of Market Street yet still near the waterfront. It became, as Karl Yoneda recalled, a thriving little Japantown with many hotels and stores, the former filled in winter with single male farm workers who wintered in San Francisco until the spring planting began.[55]

One family that successfully established a hotel in Chinatown was the Kitanos. Years later Chizu, one of the daughters, recalled that her father, Motoji, immigrated in 1905, when he was eighteen, just in time to see the earthquake and fire. Because he came from a very poor family and wanted to send money back to Japan, he was willing to work hard. After farming in different northern California communities, he finally leased a hotel in San Francisco and in 1913 was successful enough to marry a picture bride, who was chosen for him by his family in Japan. Kou Yuki Kitano was twenty-three when she arrived in San Francisco. Kou was at first discouraged to see how different Motoji was from his portrayal of himself as a successful businessman. Her life was hard, and it did not become easier as the family grew to include five daughters and two sons. The Kitanos remained in Chinatown after other hotel owners moved on. The parents knew little English, and their children interceded between them and the white world. Motoji learned enough English to get by, but Kou, who remained at home with the children and hence had little interaction with Caucasians, learned very little. The children acted as intermediaries between their parents and not only the Caucasian community but also the Chinese world around them.[56] Chinese resistance kept most Japanese from returning when Chinatown was rebuilt after the fire: the Kitano family was a rather rare exception.

Most other Japanese residents moved to South Park and then to the Fillmore district, which soon became the heart of the Japanese colony in the city. This area was described by one former resident as "set apart from the surrounding area by its overhead, dome shaped main street lights extending the whole length of the town for nearly twenty blocks."[57] By 1922 most of the stores and hotels that catered to the Japanese community were in the Fillmore; South Park died out when Japanese immigration ceased in 1924 with the passage of the National Origins Act.[58] In 1940 Nikkei operated sixteen hotels and nineteen apartment houses in the district. They also had five hotels in the Chinatown area and nine in South Park. In general, the facilities were spartan; only the Yamato Hotel was an exception, for it catered to wealthy visitors from Japan. Most of the guests were poor young men, anxious to earn money for their families in Japan, and often San Francisco was just a way-station to the rich agricultural areas of the Central Valley.

❧

Although the hotels and restaurants served a basically Japanese clientele, they were usually leased from Caucasian owners. The leaseholders made little more than a subsistence income from them, but their presence was vital to the Nikkei community in the city. They not only provided food and lodging; those along the water-front and on the fringes of Chinatown also served as general employment agencies for the immigrants, as boardinghouse operators did elsewhere in the country.[59]

The proprietors obtained jobs for farm laborers and railroad workers, but they also hired out young men for schoolboy jobs as domestics. These youths worked for board and room with families while they attended school and learned English. By 1909 there were an estimated 2,000 Japanese domestics in San Francisco, most of them schoolboys. This number was half what it had been a few years earlier, but the more mobile and ambitious moved on to better jobs as soon as they could.[60] They were succeeded by immigrant wives, who similarly took jobs in homes to learn American ways as well as English. Male domestics continued to work as servants and cooks. Those who "lived in" made $75–$85 before the evacuation, and those who had their own residences earned $125 a month or more. Women received about $10 less than men. Gradually the workers became specialized, washing windows, cooking, tending children, or doing laundry work. Morgan Yamanaka recalled that his parents had worked as domestics and lived in with a wealthy family in the Pacific Heights section of San Francisco. Their place of residence was of some benefit to Morgan and his brother Al, who were able to attend Lowell High School. To him the scholastic standards of the high school partially offset the discrimination of his white classmates.[61] Other Issei worked by day or took work to do at home. The schoolboy or schoolgirl worker still persisted, doing three or four hours of work while attending school.[62]

Domestic work was one of the most common forms of labor available to the new arrivals. Issei had only to be clean, neat, and reliable to win the favor of their employers. Not everyone could do it, however. Wakako Adachi recalled that her husband, Isaburo, who immigrated to San Francisco in 1897 at the age of twenty-five, took a job as a houseboy. He had worked in a bank in Tokyo before his departure and knew nothing of housework. Hired as a cook, he was asked to bake some biscuits. "Those that didn't turn out were enough to fill a sack," Mrs. Adachi related; when Isaburo realized the enormity of his failure he left the house at night "like a robber," carrying the sack full of inedible biscuits over his shoulder. The incident became a fond memory for the Adachis years later when they were successfully operating a nursery in El Cerrito.[63]

Most Issei were very successful as domestics. Their value as employees was acknowledged by many employers who wanted to get "their" Japanese back from camp when the war ended. Many Caucasians regarded the Japanese they knew from a lifetime of good service as an important commodity, especially in a world where domestic workers were increasingly scarce or, if available at all, African American. The employment service manager of Topaz estimated in 1945 that 20 percent of the prewar adult Issei population of San Francisco had done domestic work of some kind, living with a Caucasian family, and another 20 percent had been engaged part-time or by the hour. However, this labor was almost exclusively an Issei occupation, for the Nisei were better educated and generally very ambitious, and neither they nor their parents wished them to continue in such a low-status or low-paying job.[64]

Since the Japanese quickly gained a reputation for reliability, they were soon also in demand as chauffeurs, chefs, caterers, and gardeners.[65] Gardening, in particular, was prized, for working with the soil had status in Japanese culture. The Japanese gardener, who was skilled and creative, became a feature of California life that continued after the war. Most gardeners worked on the peninsula, where estates had large gardens; few residences in San Francisco had enough land to support a full-scale garden.

⚜

It was not gardening, however, but domestic service by schoolboys that caused problems. In 1893 the San Francisco School Board resolved that Nisei school children should attend the segregated Chinese (or Oriental) school. Since Issei working as domestics resided all over the city with their families, this decision caused much hardship. The officials were ostensibly concerned because the "schoolboys" domestics were occasionally much older than the other students in the class and were attending solely to learn English. After the Japanese consul, Chinda Sutemi, protested, the order was quietly rescinded. There were too few Japanese in San Francisco at the time for their numbers to be really noticeable or to provoke a serious outbreak of Japanophobia. But that situation quickly changed.

The numbers of immigrants began to increase dramatically at the turn of the century, and local politicians seized the issue. On May 7, 1902, a large anti-Japanese meeting was held in San Francisco.[66] It was the first major outpouring of racist sentiment; the disaster of earthquake and fires in 1906 brought another. White gangs assaulted Japanese shops and stores, despite the aid given to earthquake victims by Japan.[67] Out of such racist incidents arose the beginning of the movement to remove the community from San Francisco, the jewel by the bay, to Topaz, the concentration camp known sarcastically as the jewel of the desert.

⚜

The rest of the Issei community also developed around a service-oriented economy. Between 1900 and 1909, the number of Japanese businesses in San Francisco grew from 90 to 545, the vast majority of them small. A survey of Japanese enterprises in California in 1909 revealed that 58 percent had capital investments of less than one thousand dollars, and 55 percent of the proprietors operated without hired help.[68] The Nikkei met their own needs by producing specialty products like tofu (bean curd) or miso (soybean paste), and occasionally groceries for the larger Caucasian community. Issei who moved beyond the domestic work force were limited by the hostility of the all-white labor unions toward nonwhite workers. Their fears were expressed in terms of concern about the willingness of the newly arrived to accept lower wages, but primarily they arose from racism, pure and simple. Prohibited from joining unions or entering industry, Japanese had either to become self-employed or to work for established Issei businessmen.[69] Ronald Takaki identified the creation of a separate Japanese economy and community as a process that made "America a society of greater cultural diversity."[70] It may have been, but progress up the economic ladder was slow or nonexistent, for the competition of the white community effectively squeezed them out.

The laundry and dry-cleaning businesses, which were established in the decade between 1910 and 1920, demonstrated such a pattern. The laundry industry began in 1895 in Tiburon, across the Golden Gate in Marin County, where an Issei established the first Japanese laundry in the state. After four hard years the owner moved to the Mission district of San Francisco. He competed with both Caucasians and Chinese, but the former were the more insidious. They formed the Anti-Jap Laundry League to challenge him, and for several years before the earthquake he was imprisoned weekly for violating an ordinance regulating the operation of steam boilers. Although the anonymous Japanese laundryman apparently helped his Caucasian neighbors by letting them draw water from his well after the disasters, he did not earn their friendship.[71]

Within a few years other Japanese laundries had sprung up, but harassment by Caucasian competitors did not cease. The number of Chinese laundries, also victims of persecution, dropped from 300 in 1900 to 100 in 1920. Japanese laundries were penalized by an obscure city statute requiring block residents to sign a petition supporting the efforts of an enterprise to locate there. The pioneer laundryman found that even those who had enjoyed his water would not sign his petition. However, he was able to borrow money and buy a new location in the business section of the city. He survived the Depression and his future seemed secure. Then came the evacuation, and the loss of all he had gained.[72]

Japanese also went into the dry cleaning and dyeing business, some as early as the end of the nineteenth century. It was at first a sideline for laundries and tailor shops but became a separate operation, ideally suited to established Issei and their newly arrived wives. The Japanese Dry Cleaners Association, which dated from the earthquake and developed out of an earlier, looser-knit organization, was one of the most influential and powerful Japanese business organizations at the time of the Panama Pacific International Exposition in 1915. It functioned in economic matters, setting prices and maintaining harmony with Caucasian cleaners and American labor unions, and it also controlled the number of Nikkei dry cleaners in the city, keeping the membership "in the family" of the Japanese American community. Even the few businesses not part of the association apparently abided by its strictures.[73] The Issei favored this occupation for several reasons. It required only a limited knowledge of English, since conversations with customers were not extensive and good service and a cordial manner were more important than language ability. The business did not require a large initial capitalization, especially as shops were often acquired from close friends or relatives.

As the older generation retired, the Nisei gradually moved into the trade. The membership of the association was 40 percent Nisei by 1941. Like laundries, dry cleaning establishments were usually family-run. The cleaning was sent out to a wholesaler who did the actual cleaning, while the shop owner did the ironing and often sidelined in tailoring, alterations, and mending. As the Nisei took over they expanded the businesses, most of which had a steady Caucasian as well as Nikkei clientele. In the years just before World War II, most of the wholesale cleaning for association members was done by a Japanese wholesaler in San Francisco and one in San Mateo.[74] The Japanese Americans built a solid business based on good service and a willingness to do a bit more for their customers than the Caucasian cleaners did, and they prospered from it.

⚜

The experiences of the laundries and dry cleaning shops were duplicated in the other businesses in which the Japanese residents of San Francisco specialized. Perhaps the most outstanding Nikkei enterprise was the plant nursery. The damp, moist, and temperate climate of the Bay Area was ideally suited to flower cultivation, and the growers produced flowers for both the adjacent rural areas and the city, where they were sold on street corner stands and shops. Kenji Fujii recalled that his father immigrated in 1909, when he was in his late teens. Although he came from a wealthy family, his father was a second son, and his prospects were not auspicious. After working for a well-to-do Caucasian family near San Jose, he acquired enough money to return to Japan to find a wife and married someone known to his family (they actually passed each other on the Pacific and only married after he returned to America). The Fujiis went into the nursery business in Hayward and were able to buy land despite the Alien Land Laws because of the assistance of the lawyer Guy Calden, who helped them put it in the name of a family corporation.[75]

⚜

Flower vendors were not the only businesses whose merchandise appealed to both the white and the Asian community. During the 1910s trading companies were established, along with curio shops and art goods stores.[76] These dealers handled dry goods, chinaware, toys, lacquer wares, vases, rugs, ornaments, and other curios. Few Caucasians were aware that the four blocks of Chinatown adjacent to the entry to Grant Avenue were owned by Japanese Americans until the evacuation. The shops in this section sold high-quality art goods, antiques, and Asian clothing. During the prewar years the Japanese section of the street was considered the most picturesque, in contrast to the rest, which was filthy and dangerous.[77] Japanese merchandising in Chinatown dated to 1890, when several stores were leased by Japanese who located there because of its proximity to the piers where ships from Asia docked. Since most Issei merchants left the street after the earthquake, by the time of the Panama Pacific International Exposition of 1915, only about twelve Japanese art goods stores were located there. Two of the oldest were Daibutsu and Shiota.[78]

The Japanese in the art goods business competed constantly with both Caucasians and Chinese. However, the Nikkei sold mainly to tourists, while Caucasian department stores that handled such merchandise cultivated the local white clientele. Chinese and Japanese merchants on Grant Avenue were highly competitive with each other. Chinese merchants even resorted to picketing the Japanese stores in an effort to drive patrons away, but to no avail.[79] Both ethnic groups suffered in the Depression, but after that setback the profitable trade resumed.[80]

⚜

Commercial fishing out of San Francisco was one of the least known but most profitable enterprises conducted by Nisei and some Issei.[81] Although it was not as large or significant as in Los Angeles or Monterey, it employed 150 Nisei before the war, assisted by some of the Issei who had begun it during the 1920s. The season was year-round, limited only by the weather, which cut it to fifteen or eighteen days a month. The Issei had originally leased boats, but by the 1930s they owned them outright. Unlike other Japanese American industries, the fishing industry was unionized. The Nikkei belonged to the Congress of Industrial Organizations, which was more sympathetic to them than the American Federation of Labor (both unions were involved in this trade). The Japanese were too few in number to arouse Caucasian fishermen's hostilities. The only real competition was with the mainly alien Italians, who were even lower on the social scale than the Japanese. The losses of the fishermen during the evacuation were substantial.[82]

Other small enterprises kept the less virtuous entertained. Gambling was a frequent diversion for Japanese laborers, especially in the countryside, and in the city pool halls provided much pleasure. There were forty-one in San Francisco in 1912. Japanese bar-restaurants also entertained lonely men; there barmaids "served them familiar foods and spoke Japanese with charm and traditional deference."[83]

Japanese-language newspapers were important to the community as sources of information for the Issei and a means to hold the dispersed population together. In 1925 Kyutaro Abiko began publishing English-language news in the *Nichi Bei,* and a year later he began publishing the *Japanese American Weekly.* These papers and the *Shin Sekai* communicated news of the Nikkei in the city and reported in Japanese on political developments, such as the alien land ownership controversy, that affected their readers. The Nisei organization that preceded the Japanese American Citizens League published an all-English semimonthly publication, the *Nikkei Shimin,* which soon became the *Pacific Citizen.* It has published continuously since the 1930s, as a voice for the citizen Nisei and as a statement of the intensely pro-American views the JACL would adopt. The *Shin Sekai* went bankrupt during the Depression and closed before the war. The *Nichi Bei* was the only Japanese American paper to publish continuously until the evacuation; Nisei editor Yasuo Abiko was arrested by Federal Bureau of Investigation agents immediately after Pearl Harbor, but they allowed him to continue publishing the paper so the government could communicate its instructions to the Nikkei until they had all been removed.[84]

During the 1920s the community was modestly prosperous. Oscar Hoffman noted in a report to the War Relocation Authority in 1943 that "real estate men sought Japanese clients. American banks sought Japanese customers. The Anglo California National Bank was the first to employ a Japanese. The Bank of America and the

American Trust Bank opened branches in Fillmore Street to give accommodations to Japanese."[85] Hoffman also reported that the Salvation Army Building, the YMCA, the YWCA, and the Buddhist Church were constructed during this time, signs of community prosperity. The population was estimated at around two thousand families.[86]

Economic ties between the Nikkei and the Caucasians were very important, but there were also institutional connections. Young Japanese Americans became involved with the work of the American Red Cross, the Community Chest, and the Boy Scouts of America. Participation in a Boy Scout troop was very significant in the lives of many Nisei youths, and as they grew older they themselves led troops. Tad Hayashi of Berkeley and Tom Kawaguchi of San Francisco not only participated in scouting but led Scout troops themselves when they returned to the Bay Area after the war.[87] Support for the Red Cross, which continued even when the Nikkei were interned, was both a social outlet and the indication of a desire to be responsible members of the community.

Education was very important to the community, for Issei expected their children to do well and viewed schooling as a means of economic and social advancement. Some parents became involved in the Parent-Teacher Association, which helped them to aid their children's progress in school. The language barrier prevented many from taking such a role, however, since the teachers were all Caucasian.[88] Many Nisei attended local colleges and universities. Chizu Kitano Iiyama remembered how important education was for her family; her parents urged all the children to do their best in school, and they spent many hours in the local public library.[89]

The Japanese American community was stratified according to economic achievement, religion, intellectual interests, prefecture of origin in Japan, and other factors. The white-collar workers topped the pyramid, followed by shopkeepers, farmers, and semiskilled and unskilled workers. In differentiating on the basis of religious preference, recreational activities, political beliefs, and place of origin, the Nikkei were scarcely different from the larger Caucasian community.[90] Even as early as 1927 Karl Yoneda had noticed that agricultural workers were "at the bottom of the totem pole in the Japanese community."[91]

⚜

This rosy picture was not the only side of the story, of course. Discrimination against the Japanese began almost as soon as the first immigrants landed on American shores. San Francisco had been a focal point for prejudice against the Chinese, and it spread easily to the Japanese. In July 1870 the first large anti-Asian mass meeting in the nation was held in the city, preceded by a torchlight parade and followed by speeches against the Chinese. The labor movement that grew out of the anti-Chinese agitation was for many years the most outspoken group in its racism. Throughout the decade of the 1870s there were anti-Chinese mass meetings and a series of discriminatory ordinances were passed. The Working-men's Party, headed by Dennis Kearney, campaigned on the slogan "The Chinese Must Go."[92] The agitation culminated in the passage of the Chinese Exclusion Act in 1882.

Prejudice against the Issei began where that against the Chinese had left off, but there were few incidents before 1900. Yamato Ichihashi recorded one episode in 1887 and another in 1890, when fifteen Japanese cobblers were attacked by members of the shoe-makers' union; this forced the Japanese to leave the trade. White workers demanding the renewal of the Chinese Exclusion Act, which was due to expire in 1902, quickly extended their hatred to the Japanese and urged Congress to ban them as well. This new "yellow peril" was even more threatening than the earlier version, for the Issei had partially adopted American economic practices and hence were perceived as more competition to whites than the Chinese were. The California state government also responded to Caucasian agitation, urging Japanese exclusion as early as 1901. The Asiatic Exclusion League took up the cry, and the rhetoric of hate escalated.[93]

San Francisco Mayor James Duval Phelan was a major figure in the campaign against the Japanese, launching a tirade of abuse in the spring of 1900 that he continued for some thirty years. He claimed the Japanese, like the Chinese before them, were inassimilable, "not the stuff of which American citizens [could] be made."[94] As Frank Miyamoto pointed out with respect to Seattle, the exclusion of the Issei from various economic opportunities as well as their residential segregation had the effect of producing a close-knit community that might well appear to outsiders as "inassimilable."[95] Widespread protest against the Nikkei soon spread throughout San Francisco, based on racism with an economic motivation as well; laborers feared that the Japanese would take jobs from lower-class whites and work for next to nothing. The outcry against the Japanese raged for a few years; they nearly became targets in the drive to renew the Chinese Exclusion Act but then were ignored for tactical reasons. The agitation briefly died down, reappearing in 1905.[96] Since San Francisco was the largest urban center of the state's Japanese population, the hostility was labor-based and virtually restricted to the city, with the lone exception of Fresno, in the Central Valley, where Chester H. Rowell of the *Fresno Republican* also took up the cudgels.[97]

Overt discrimination also began against the very few Japanese American children in the public schools.[98] A local school board crisis extended beyond its original scope because of the implications it had for American relations with Japan. The latter nation had become a power to contend with in the Pacific, particularly after its victory in the Russo-Japanese War in 1905, and its citizens abroad commanded attention from Tokyo, which was concerned that they be treated with respect. On October 11, 1906, the San Francisco School Board, responding to local pressures, tried to force Japanese, Chinese, and Korean students to enroll in a segregated school. President Theodore Roosevelt attempted to assure the Meiji government, which championed the rights of the Issei, that he disapproved of San Francisco's position. But the president, almost as racist as the Californians, had to pacify both Japan and the San Franciscans. He scolded the latter and deployed federal troops in the city to protect the Japanese; and he also urged Congress to accept the Japanese. But even though he asked for the same fair treatment that was due European immigrants, he himself believed that the whites were, in fact, a superior race. The school board's desire to segregate a few students was basically a call for immigration restriction, and it did force Roosevelt to act. The president began to negotiate an agreement with Japan contingent upon a cessation of discriminatory legislation in the state. Each house of the California state legislature passed anti-Japanese legislation in 1907 aimed specifically at Issei land ownership, but no one piece was approved by both houses. Roosevelt tried to deter the Californians from passing legislation even more offensive to Tokyo because he realized the necessity of heading off a crisis. By skillful and delicate negotiations he concluded the Gentleman's Agreement in 1907–8.[99]

The agreement was the product of more than one and a half years of painstaking diplomacy. The Japanese agreed not to issue passports for workers to go to the United States (in return for which America agreed not to let U.S. workers emigrate to Japan). It did not prohibit Japanese Americans from returning from visits to Japan, and wives (whether picture brides or other), children, and parents could still immigrate. Thus, the agreement "served to irritate further the already raw nerves of the Californians and by its very nature was almost bound to do so."[100] Since it did not totally exclude the Japanese, it was unsatisfactory to the xenophobic Californians. The Exclusionist League continued its agitation, and the *San Francisco Examiner* and the other newspapers owned by William Randolph Hearst picked up the issue. But the focus of anti-Japanese agitation moved from San Francisco to the rural areas of the state, and the emphasis shifted from schoolrooms to immigration and land ownership. Immigration was an issue that festered for nearly two decades, but the issue of land ownership seemed resolved by California's passage of the Alien Land Law of 1913 and subsequent legislation.[101]

Japanophobes suggested simple solutions to the legal issues of land ownership and immigration restriction. They favored the enactment of legislation on either the state or the federal level that would prohibit aliens ineligible to citizenship (thus, Japanese, by definition) from owning land. The legislation provoked considerable protest from the Issei community and the Japanese government, but the Nikkei soon found ways around it. The Issei initially had to accept three-year leases and move from property to property, but later they put their land in the names of corporations in which they held substantial interest, until their children came of age (as with the Fujii family of Hayward). Then the land was held in the names of their Nisei children. The alien land law was renewed in 1920 in a much harsher form, outlawing the leasing of land or its acquisition by minors, and a subsequent amendment made farming even more difficult, but the Issei were not without friends. Sympathetic Caucasian lawyers like the Fujiis' friend Guy Calden assisted them by purchasing shares in land they held.

Immigration, however, was a federal matter. The exclusionists saw many defects in the Gentleman's Agreement, but the time was not ripe to reopen the issue. During World War I, Japan was allied to Great Britain and associated with the United States in fighting the Central Powers, Germany, Austria-Hungary, and their allies. Legislation against the Issei would have been awkward, given the nation's preoccupation with winning the war as quickly as possible. But the determination of West Coast Japanophobes to remove the Nikkei from the United States was only dormant, not dead.[102]

The year 1920 was an election year, and once again Japanese exclusion surfaced as a major issue. A reorganized Japanese Exclusion League mobilized its forces and a stronger alien land law was passed in California (although not necessarily enforced). Temporary restrictions had been enacted in 1917 and 1920 to bar Asians other than Japanese from immigrating, but the exclusionists desired a permanent solution—not the elimination of Asians in America but the elimination of "economic gain through Asian migrant labor and dependency."[103] They were led by central Californians, including former senator Hiram Johnson and former publisher V. S. McClatchy.[104] The negotiation of the "Ladies' Agreement" in 1921 ended the entry of picture brides. In 1922 the Supreme Court ruled in the case of Takao Ozawa that Japanese, regardless of their qualifications, were aliens ineligible to citizenship.[105] With the principle of the seeming inferiority of the Nikkei now established by the highest court in the land, the exclusionists were strengthened in their convictions and determined to end the matter forever by barring further immigration from Japan.

The unhappy story of the 1924 immigration bill has often been recounted. The legislation originally postulated a quota system, long advocated by Japanophile Sidney L. Gulick and others, to be based on the number of immigrants of that nationality residing in the United States in 1890. Under such a system Japan, which at that time had only 2,039 nationals in America, would have been eligible for some 100 immigrants a year, a minimal and negligible allowance, yet one that would have allowed the proud nation to save face. It seemed that the bill would pass in that form when a disaster occurred. Secretary of State Charles E. Hughes asked the Japanese Ambassador Hanihara Masanao to write the U.S. Senate about Japan's reactions, and his response was misinterpreted by that body as an insult. Japan's warning that exclusion would have "grave consequences" became a club with which Senator Henry Cabot Lodge bludgeoned the quota system to death.[106] The National Origins Act of 1924, an act of "studied international insolence," had grave consequences indeed.[107] In addition to its effect on international relations, it relegated all Japanese, both Issei and Nisei, to a seemingly permanent inferior status in the United States.

❧

Oscar Hoffman, writing the history of Japanese American enterprises in San Francisco and the Bay Area for the edification of the War Relocation Authority's second director, Dillon Myer, did not comment on the passage of the National Origins Act of 1924. Instead, the Topaz community analyst noted that the period 1920–41 was a time "when Japanese capitalized on the fruits of their earlier labor and savings." However, he did not hesitate to call the Japanese American area of San Francisco a "colony," and he seemed amazed at how many churches were located there. He pointed out that the thriving Japanese catered to the "American" trade with curio and arts stores, laundries, restaurants, florists, and embroidery shops.[108]

Nisei historian Ronald Takaki painted a more accurate picture of Nikkei life after 1924. Embittered, despairing, and angry, the Issei turned inward. Some returned to Japan. Others became stoic, muttering *shikata ga nai,* it can't be helped. Those who had not married before 1924 now found that there were no available spouses; they could not bring wives from Japan, and almost no unmarried Japanese women were left. The very successful few, such as the "potato king" George Shima, recognized that their lives and fortunes were tied to California. Even George Shima was discriminated against, despite his wealth, when he bought housing in a wealthy area of Berkeley in 1909. The less prosperous realized that their success was bound to that of their children, who could be educated and Americanized and act as their intermediaries. Nisei had become the majority of the Nikkei population by 1930.[109]

The legislation of the 1920s only governed the larger issues of Japanese American existence in the Bay Area. Daily examples of racism were not affected by it, for these had occurred from the very beginning. For example, even as they were recovering from the 1906 earthquake some San Franciscans physically attacked individual Japanese. They did not distinguish between local victims and distinguished travelers and even stoned a group of visiting Japanese scientists inspecting earthquake damage.[110] In the decades that followed, discrimination and prejudice took a slightly more subtle course. Racial covenants prevented the Nikkei from moving out of the various Nihonmachi throughout the state. Farmers in the East Bay and on the peninsula were often unable to obtain any but the most undesirable land to cultivate, which they often converted with great effort into level and productive gardens. Japanese were charged exorbitant rents, even though they often improved the owners' orchards by intercropping the land, planting vegetables between the rows of trees.[111]

Discrimination hurt most the educated and the enterprising. The Nisei often excelled in school, spurred on by eager parents like the elder Kitanos, but graduates found that even advanced degrees from Stanford or the University of California would not qualify them for positions higher than running a fruitstand. Only 25 percent of the 161 Nisei graduates of the University of California between 1925 and 1935 found employment in the professions for which they had been educated.[112] Those who became businessmen were subject to harassment, intimidation, and ruthless competition. The only ones spared were the very young, who lived in a Nikkei world where their playmates were just like themselves.

⚜

The Depression struck San Francisco and the Bay Area as it did the rest of the nation. For people at the bottom of the economic ladder, it was apparent in small ways: less call for domestic workers, fewer buyers for flowers, less work for farm laborers. As Roger Daniels noted, the Depression was not as severe for Japanese America, in part because the Pacific coast states were not as hard hit as the rest of the country. Since many businesses were small and owner-operated, they were able to survive. Japanese who worked for the American branches of Japanese trading companies also were secure, but they had long been relegated to positions at the bottom of the ladder and denied economic advancement by the Japanese, who considered them second-class and refused them positions in management. A few Japanese Americans had been able to secure jobs in civil service, and they also had secure employment.[113]

But the greatest change during the 1930s was in the nation's rising perception of Japan as a growing military threat. John Modell noted the rise of nativism in Los Angeles, which was manifested in a fear of fifth-column activities rather than the previous fear of economic competition. He cited as an example the passage of a law in 1931 forbidding the employment of aliens on public works.[114] Most Americans sided with China in the Sino-Japanese War of 1937, and many joined in a boycott of Japanese-made goods.

On the surface San Francisco's Nihonmachi looked calm, even prosperous—much more so than Los Angeles' beleaguered community. On January 1, 1989, the *Hokubei Mainichi* (called *The Progressive News* before the war) published a special supplement entitled "A Walk Through Japantown—1935," which gave a detailed picture of life in prewar Japanese San Francisco. Based on a

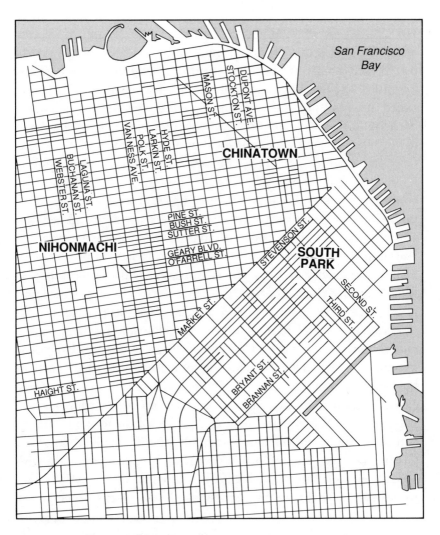

San Francisco Bay

CHINATOWN

NIHONMACHI

SOUTH PARK

DUPONT AVE.
STOCKTON ST.
MASON ST.
HYDE ST.
LARKIN ST.
POLK ST.
VAN NESS AVE.
LAGUNA ST.
BUCHANAN ST.
WEBSTER ST.

PINE ST.
BUSH ST.
SUTTER ST.
GEARY BLVD.
O'FARRELL ST.

STEVENSON ST.
SECOND ST.
THIRD ST.

MARKET ST.

BRYANT ST.
BRANNAN ST.

HAIGHT ST.

2. Japanese Towns of San Francisco
Based on maps prepared by Seizo Oka.

1935 survey of ethnic minorities by Paul Radin, an anthropologist at the University of California, the lengthy but anonymous article traced each block of Japantown, identifying all the stores and shops by trade and even supplying owners' names when it could. The title called the area "Japantown," since that is the name by which it has been known since the 1950s, but the text referred to it as "Japanese town," the name by which the local population knew it. A detailed map accompanied the story. The types of Japanese businesses differed little from those of the 1920s, but some details about the community were particularly interesting. A grocery store, the Dupont Company, on Geary Street, was run by a widow and her son, who delivered to all parts of the city, serving customers who were scattered and preferred to order by phone. Other shops on Geary included a jewelry and dry goods store that had been in business for twenty-five years, a coal yard, a beer parlor, a hotel and rooming house, and a confectionery store called Benkyodo that sold Japanese sweets, which had made all the tea cakes sold by the Japanese concession at the Chicago Century of Progress World's Fair. Benkyodo was owned by Sueichi Okamura, who also had been in business for twenty-five years. There was a garage run by a Caucasian, a laundry, a dry cleaners, and then a beer parlor—a particularly "notorious place"—next door to a transfer and draying company run by S. Hikoichi Shimamoto and his younger brother, George Gentoku Shimamoto. George was a college graduate who specialized in Japanese architecture and whose talents would help to beautify both Tanforan and Topaz. A few blocks down was a newspaper, *The New World,* one of three Japanese newspapers in San Francisco, which all suffered from competition with one another. Next was the Candy Kitchen, whose owner was the only Japanese maker of Western candy. Then there was a pool parlor owned by a Caucasian, a Japanese barbershop, and a restaurant featuring parties and sake, "wine, women and song." The author noted it had been hard-hit by the Depression. The restaurant was next door to a bird store that had recently been raided by narcotics agents, who found a cache of drugs there. The *Hokubei Asahi Daily News* was nearby, staffed in part by workers who had walked out on strike from the *Japanese American News.* A row of tenements was followed by a tailor and a store selling fishing rods. At Webster Street, the Japanese district ended.[115]

There were non-Japanese establishments in the area, but very few. Ace Restaurant was run by a Japanese but catered to African Americans and some whites. A Chinese laundry existed next to a Japanese drugstore. At the end of Webster Street was a chimney-cleaning shop, a "Negro" church, a restaurant, a Japanese gymnasium, and a grocery store. A Filipino barbershop was next to a "shady" hotel, Nishikawa Rooming, "with its unmistakable red sign reading 'Rooms.'" Further down was a restaurant specializing in fresh eel from Japan. A fish store was run by Kiichiro Murai and legally owned by his son Hajime; it did a thriving business. Down the street was a dry goods store, Nichi Bei Bussan, owned by Shojiro Tatsuno. Nakagawa's Shohin Kan was across the street; Tatsuno and Nakagawa once had been partners but had become competitors after a misunderstanding. A small vegetable store was tended by Mrs. Nakata while her husband delivered his wares all over the city. A landmark of the area then and now, fifty years later, was Soko Hardware, owned by Masayasu Ashizawa. Both Nichi Bei Bussan and Soko Hardware survived the evacuation because sympathetic property owners helped the Japanese proprietors reestablish their businesses.[116]

There were also carpentry businesses, the office of the night police patrol, jewelry shops, chop suey houses, camera stores, a printing shop, doctors' offices, a bookstore, a bath house, opticians, and pharmacies. The author of the *Hokubei Mainichi* article noted that a cash grocery in the area deliberately kept prices low on its non-Asian merchandise to keep customers from going to the nearby Fillmore shopping district, a major competition for small ethnic businesses.[117]

Geary and Post were the main shopping streets, but Sutter, Bush, Pine, Laguna, Buchanan, and Webster, the cross streets, also held a number of Japanese businesses. The American Fish Market was an important location, and so was the employment office. There were many flats on Sutter Street, as well as a new YWCA; Japanese tenants shared rooms with African Americans and Filipinos, and further down Japanese and Caucasians were neighbors. The Japanese Language Institute and the new home of the *Japanese American News* also were there, but the largest Japanese-language school in the country was on Bush Street. One of the largest goldfish hatcheries in the region, Nippon Goldfish Company, owned by Tadayasu Murata, was nearby. The new Zenshu Sokoji Buddhist Temple was on Bush, occupying a building that was formerly a Jewish synagogue; it was the first formal temple the Buddhists owned in San Francisco. On Pine Street were two smaller Buddhist churches, a Nichiren and the San Francisco Buddhist church affiliated with the Nishi Honganji. Mixed in were Japanese and Caucasian residences, and according to the reminiscences of Tom Kawaguchi, a few modest houses of prostitution. The Japanese Catholic Church was on Octavia, and it included a school, an auditorium, and a residence. The Christ United Presbyterian Church was also located on that street. On Laguna Street was the office of the Japanese Association of San Francisco; further down was the office of the Japanese Association of America, not far from the Japanese Salvation Army. Buchanan was the busiest street, next to Post; it held a full complement of shops, including candy stores, restaurants, the Seiko Kai church, a bookstore, and a Japanese nightclub. A large vacant lot on the street was the projected site of the Japanese branch of the YMCA.[118] There were also branches of Japanese import-export firms as well as branches of Japanese banks. This was urban Japanese America, a far cry from the stoop-labor communities of the rural ethnic West.

⚜

The pattern of Nikkei prosperity, if such it was, was uneven. The description of Japanese town in 1935 in the *Hokubei Mainichi* contained few references to the economic crisis of the 1930s, except to note the occasional restaurant or shop that had failed. John Hada's father's art and dry goods store folded in the early 1930s, and he went to work for the Oriental Department of Gump's department store.[119] Other businesses, such as the laundries—especially those that were perceived as threats by the Caucasian community—had to cope with intense competition throughout the period. There were twenty-eight sizable laundries in the Bay Area at the time of the evacuation, the two largest located in Oakland. They did wholesale work for fifty Chinese laundries and serviced hospitals, restaurants, and hotels. The Oakland operations did more work individually than the two largest Japanese laundries in San Francisco did jointly. Their work forces were unionized in 1939 without any ensuing labor problems.[120] The dry cleaners also prospered, grossing over $1 million of business annually.[121]

The art and curio dealers on Grant Avenue seemed to thrive despite bad times, but their employees were paid wages as low as $50 to $60 a month for a ten- to fourteen-hour day. They had not tried to organize. Since the clerks lacked job opportunities outside the Nikkei community, their chances for alternate employment were poor. The firms, on the other hand, did well. An average-sized store with about five employees usually grossed more than $15,000 a month. The largest firm was owned by several partners, who ran a chain of about a dozen throughout the country. The largest strictly wholesale firm, Nippon Dry Goods, grossed around $500,000 a year. All the Japanese stores in the city probably totaled over $3 million.[122] Japanese San Francisco was becoming a middle-class community before the Depression; it felt the impact, but it slowly recovered from the crash in the ensuing decade.

For families uncertain of their situation in a time of economic distress there was the option of sending one or more children to Japan for a few years of education. With this goal in mind, they insisted their offspring learn the language in Japanese schools in America. (The language schools also helped cement community bonds.) If times worsened and opportunities appeared too limited, these children could always return to Japan to live. Japan-educated Nisei, or Kibei, returned to America as strange hybrids, almost as "Japanesy" as some of the Issei and very different from the Americanized Nisei.[123]

⁂

The Japanese American community soon extended across San Francisco Bay. Nikkei on the peninsula and in the East Bay were primarily agricultural; city children were often sent to the fields in the summer since only there could they find work. Orchards, floral nurseries, strawberry fields, and truck gardens were the primary Issei endeavors. Many of the nursery and agricultural products were sold in the wholesale produce markets of Oakland and San Francisco, some sent to canneries, others shipped to the East Coast. There were about 1,300 Nikkei in Mount Eden and Washington townships in southern Alameda County in 1940. Fewer than 25 percent of the farmers were landowners, but they had over a million dollars invested in nurseries, farms, and homes. Practically all of them leased their land but owned their homes, equipment, and trucks, the easiest arrangement under the Alien Land Law of 1920. Truck farmers raised two or three crops a year, including strawberries. The labor involved was intensive, and usually the whole family participated. The floral nurseries received the largest capital investment, from $15,000 to $300,000.[124] This network of production and marketing as well as the practice of sending city children to the countryside helped strengthen the ties between the hub of the Japanese American community in San Francisco and its satellites around the bay.

Mount Eden and Washington townships were organized socially like the other Japanese towns in the area. People from the same prefecture tended to settle together, as S. Frank Miyamoto noted, and they formed an important component in the solidarity of the Japanese community.[125] Several *kenjinkai* provided the focal point of social life for the Issei in Mount Eden and Washington townships, whereas churches and school activities predominated for the Nisei. The Nisei held dances and skating parties as well as a yearly community banquet to which leading Issei and even some Caucasian community leaders were invited. The Japanese American Citizens League, founded in 1930, had a few local members, but it had limited support in rural areas before World War II. There were also the usual athletic events to entertain people.[126]

The community of Alameda was a residential area of 35,000, of whom about 800 were Nikkei. Most were small businessmen, independent and conservative. In the Alameda Nihonmachi were floral shops, laundries, a garage, an art shop, groceries, cleaners, and the like. Many Japanese Americans lived in Alameda because of its good schools and commuted to work in San Francisco. Social events followed the same pattern as in southern Alameda County. One of the Japanese florists, Harry Kono, was well known by everyone in town; he belonged to the Rotary Club and the Merchant's Association, and he took a group of Japanese and Caucasian children to Japan each year to play baseball. Everyone got along well, so that it was painful to all the residents when Alameda was among the first localities to be evacuated because of its strategic location near ports and airfields.[127]

The East Bay floral industry, dominated by Japanese, was relatively prosperous before the war. Issei had begun to grow flowers in this region from the time of the earliest Japanese settlements, leasing land they could not purchase, and they numbered more than one thousand by 1941. Three wholesale flower markets were established in San Francisco, the largest operated by Japanese, another by Italians and other Caucasians, and the third by Chinese. Some of the land used for growing flowers was very valuable, hence out of reach of the modest resources of the Issei, and greenhouse acreage within the city was quite expensive. Leasing property, required by the Alien Land Law, was not only necessary but also practical, since greenhouse soil wore out rapidly, particularly if—as Fumi Hayashi of Berkeley recalled years later—the Issei grew Chinese asters or had bad luck with plant diseases. Relations with Caucasians in the floral industry were generally good and characterized by cooperation. The Japanese American flower growers periodically gave good-will parties to which the whites and other ethnic groups were invited, and these were considered to be "some of the biggest social affairs of any sponsored by the Japanese."[128]

The town of San Mateo was the center for Japanese who lived in the northern peninsula; about 600 Nikkei resided there. The towns of Belmont and Burlingame contained most of the Japanese in San Mateo County, although there were a few in Half Moon Bay and Pescadero. Many had worked as domestics in San Mateo for thirty years or more, having moved south at the time of the earthquake. Masako Tsuzuki recalled that her parents had lived on the third floor of a large home, where her mother worked as a cook and maid and her father cared for the grounds and in the afternoons taught in the Japanese school. She, an only child, remembered being rather lonely, growing up in such a setting.[129]

Of the 100 Nikkei living in San Mateo, 34 Issei owned their own homes. The community was modestly prosperous by Japanese community standards, even though most still worked as gardeners and domestics. In addition, Issei operated four laundries, three cleaning and dyeing shops, two grocery stores, two nurseries, and two florists. Nisei also ran an additional half dozen enterprises. Belmont held many nurseries, as did San Mateo, all but two of which were leased from Caucasians.[130]

The communities of Menlo Park, Atherton, and Woodside on the southern peninsula had a Japanese population of only about 250. Atherton and Woodside were towns of the wealthy, and the Japanese were primarily located in Menlo Park, where they were in great demand as domestics and landscape gardeners. Other Nikkei ran nurseries or farmed, and a few were in business. One family owned one of the largest grocery stores in Menlo Park. Social interaction with Caucasians was high, in part because of the relatively liberal influence of Stanford University. The social center of the area was Palo Alto.[131]

By 1940 the older Nisei of San Francisco and the Bay Area were beginning to take their places in the adult world. As in Los Angeles, some were beginning to work with or replace their parents as managers and proprietors of small businesses.[132] Kenji Fujii was working with his father, running the family nursery in Hayward. Lee Suyemoto was in junior high school.[133] Hiromoto Katayama was attending the University of California on a scholarship and holding down a job; his widowed mother worked as a domestic. She and he were pleased that he was preparing to graduate and planning to attend graduate school.[134] San Franciscan Tomoye Nozawa had graduated from the University of California, where she had made the acquaintance of many other Nisei from around the state as well as Japanese graduate students who had come to California for their education. Graduating in 1937, in the depths of the Depression, she found employment nearly impossible. She did some volunteer work, but when work opened at the Golden Gate International Exposition she was easily employed, since her double major—ecological studies and Oriental languages—had equipped her with excellent Japanese as well as a knowledge of Japanese arts and crafts. Further volunteer work brought her romance as well: she met a young journalist named Henri Takahashi. They were married in July 1941 and set up housekeeping in a home on Arguello Street.[135]

Many other younger Nisei, like Lee Suyemoto, were still in secondary school. Fumi Manabe was studying in Berkeley, and so were Mari Eijima and her sister Hanna; Bob Utsumi was in school in Oakland. Many Nisei who had completed school were having considerable trouble finding employment, and their parents had endured economic hardship during the Depression. But for many young urbanites life was still as Tomoye Takahashi remembered it years later: they worked hard in both American and Japanese school, associated with other Nisei in Christian or Buddhist churches and related youth groups, participated in evenings of amateur entertainment that included Kabuki and plays, and celebrated Japanese festivals such as the Bon dance and Buddha's birthday. Their world and that of their parents came to an abrupt end on December 7, 1941.

Chapter Two

From Pearl Harbor to Evacuation

By the eve of Pearl Harbor, most Issei families in San Francisco and the Bay Area communities had achieved a level of modest prosperity, certainly outstripping the economic position they held when they immigrated to the United States. A larger proportion of Issei than of the general U.S. population owned farms and businesses, but theirs were self-insulated communities whose achievements were outside the realm of white America. Discrimination had made the Issei "more insulated against Americanization than were most contemporary immigrant groups."[1] Their ethnicity— their Asianness—separated them from white culture, and its racism conspired to keep them out. Racism reinforced the sense of community the Issei felt, but it did not create it: that they had done intentionally, through the web of institutions that held the Nikkei together, wherever in the city or the Bay Area they happened to reside.

Their children, the American-born Nisei, had many traits in common with other second-generation immigrants. Much younger than their parents and often limited in their ability to communicate with them, they tended to adopt certain elements of the Caucasian culture in which they were growing up. Although every day after public school they attended Japanese school to learn the language of their parents, for most it was a difficult tongue to master. Their instruction was uneven in quality, as was their motivation, and many spoke only enough to communicate with elderly relatives, who often had little command of English.[2] The teenagers wore bobby socks, played baseball, jumped rope, and dressed as other American teenagers did. Those who lived in Nihonmachis attended church and school with other Nikkei, but those who resided in other parts of San Francisco associated, although not as equals, with Caucasian classmates. Only Tomoye Nozawe Takahashi recalled being accepted as an equal, and she went to the exclusive Girls' High School, which had many diplomats' children. Many Nisei went on to higher education; their average educational level was two years of college.[3] Despite their achievements, few held civil service jobs or became teachers, and professional positions were impossible outside the Japanese community. Their isolation had become increasingly clear during the 1930s. When the Sino-Japanese War broke out, some 60 percent of Americans sided with China while only one percent supported Japan; 36 percent of Pacific Coast residents favored boycotting Japanese-made goods, compared to 21 percent nationwide. John Modell pointed out that "awareness of a military threat recalled to Californians the racial threat at their doorstep."[4]

Some Nisei sought an outlet in politics, forming Japanese American Democratic clubs in San Francisco, Oakland, and Los Angeles. They were "progressives," generally liberal, sometimes radical, but supporters of the New Deal and advocates of racial toleration. Others joined the Japanese American Citizens League, which expanded between 1930 and 1940 to fifty chapters; its goals were "conservative and accommodationist strategies of enterprise and self help." They believed they could achieve acceptance in white America by outspoken patriotism, not confrontation.[5] Racism limited their options as their faces identified their ethnic roots; what differed was the strategy competing political groups chose to become part of white society. Yet they did not aspire to assimilation. The prewar Nisei never abandoned the Japanese American community; very few even married outside it. To do so was not only illegal, it was not acceptable among their peers.[6]

Generational lines did not clearly delineate the stratification within the Nikkei community. The older Kibei operated on the fringes of the Nisei world. They were often liberal or radical, marked by the intellectual currents that swept Japan in the 1920s and early 1930s, while the younger Kibei, who were there later, were usually influenced by Japanese militarism. The Kibei found it difficult to cope with life in the United States or to interact with other Nisei, since they were so much less Americanized, and the Nisei frequently found them hard to understand. The relocation was especially painful for this group.

❧

The shock of Pearl Harbor was almost overwhelming for Issei and Nisei alike. While the community had not expected such an abrupt introduction to war, the Issei at least had considered the possibility, for relations between the United States and Japan had deteriorated since the Manchurian Incident of 1931–32. By 1940 the two nations were clearly on a collision course. Nevertheless, few really expected conflict to come, especially at the time and in the manner it did. The Issei knew that as aliens ineligible for citizenship they might face incarceration, but their children were citizens, and parents felt that this status would protect them. They did take the precaution of obtaining birth certificates for their American-born children, but this was not enough. The attack on U.S. forces in Hawaii touched off a tornado that swept away the West Coast Japanese American community.

A wave of anti-Japanese sentiment followed the attack, and the Issei remained indoors, following orders from Japanese Association secretary Joseph Hikida to stay out of sight.[7] Many of their children did also, at least for a few days. The JACL promptly declared its loyalty and condemned Japan for the outrage. Nonetheless, there were economic repercussions against the Nikkei community and isolated acts of aggression in the city. Japanese Americans were ordered to turn in contraband articles such as shortwave radios, weapons, ammunition, dynamite, and cameras,[8] and their travel was restricted. Violence between Japanese Americans and Filipinos broke out Christmas week, following Japan's invasion of the Philippines. When Manila was bombed and subjected to a reign of terror despite its proclaimed status as an open city, the Filipino ethnic community grew outraged and retaliated against the Nikkei.

Immediately following Pearl Harbor the Federal Bureau of Investigation began to round up "suspicious aliens," and by Tuesday, December 9, thirty-six Japanese had been incarcerated at the U.S. Immigration Service building, according to the *San Francisco Chronicle*. One of those arrested was Don Nakahata's father, arrested on December 8 because he was working for the newspaper *Shin Sekai*; the fact that he had suffered a stroke and was partially disabled might have alerted the FBI to the unlikelihood that he was a spy, but such was not the mood of the times. He was an educated man and a community leader, and that was enough.[9]

By the week's end 370 Japanese, 1,002 Germans, and 169 Italians had been arrested throughout the nation, according to *Time* magazine on December 22. These were people whose names had been identified by the FBI as much as a year previously as potentially dangerous.[10] For most the charges were never specified, and families were left to fend for themselves without the men who had held them together. Don Nakahata's father remained in custody and the family never saw him alive again. Don's maiden aunt Faith Terasawa, and his grandfather, a retired Episcopalian minister, became the heads of the family. Since his grandfather was ill, Aunt Faith took charge. By the end of December 1,291 Japanese in the Bay Area had been taken into custody.[11] The assets of Japanese banks were also seized, impoverishing many people. In Los Angeles the fishing fleet was an immediate target for seizure, but San Francisco's Japanese Americans had few assets in this vulnerable category.[12] Those who were fishermen did indeed lose their boats. For the rest, their property problems came later.

After the attack the Caucasian community was full of rumors of a fifth column, but by the end of the first week public opinion began to calm down. The beginning of the new year saw a change in the public mood. Stirred up by the press, a wave of fear emerged, created by Japan's quick string of victories and new rumors about the culpability of Hawaiian Japanese Americans for Pearl Harbor. Anti-Japanese organizations from the old days revived their racist charges, despite efforts of the Fair Play Committee, a liberal Protestant group primarily located in Berkeley, to counter them.[13] Politicians, ever eager to heed the public, listened to agricultural

interests; the advocates of Japanese removal from the West Coast
began to be heard in Washington. Registration of enemy aliens was
ordered because of the supposed military danger that the Nikkei
posed. It began January 6, 1942.[14]

Yet despite these warning signs it was still a shock to the Nikkei
community when President Franklin D. Roosevelt concurred with
the demands for exclusion being made by hysterical racists in the
Western Defense Command, led by Lieutenant General John L.
DeWitt, abetted by Washington-based Colonel Karl Bendetsen,
chief of the Aliens Division, and Provost Marshall Allen W. Gul-
lion. On November 7, 1941, Roosevelt had received an independent report written by Curtis B. Munson, a wealthy Chicago businessman with impressive State Department credentials. Mike
Masaoka, who talked extensively with him, concluded that Munson was part of "President Roosevelt's personal intelligence network" and that he was conducting a thorough investigation of the
JACL. Munson reported that the West Coast Nikkei posed no
threat to American security either by sabotage or by espionage. In
fact, his findings concluded the Nisei were "90 to 98 percent loyal
to the United States, if the Japanese-educated element of the Kibei
is excluded."[15] DeWitt, who was headquartered at San Francisco's
Presidio, was a lifelong hater of Japanese Americans; in 1923, as
a colonel, he had worked on an army plan to defend the island of
Oahu that called for the internment of both alien and citizen Japanese on the grounds of military necessity—nearly twenty years
before Pearl Harbor. Gary Okihiro concluded that this project
might well have influenced DeWitt's "perception of the 'Japanese
Problem' within the Western Defense Command" some nineteen
years later.[16] DeWitt was not impressed with the Munson Report.
Nor did he concur with the Justice Department that individual
suspects could easily be located and confined without the necessity
of mass removal. Concluding in his notorious words, "A Jap's a
Jap," the general urged the president to remove all Americans of
Japanese ancestry from the West Coast on the grounds of "mili-
tary necessity." Roosevelt had received the Munson Report on
November 7, 1941. Nevertheless, on February 19, 1942, he signed
Executive Order 9066, entitling the army to designate military
areas to which any person could be denied access. Roosevelt was

following the recommendations of Secretary of War Henry L. Stimson; he was also influenced by Assistant Secretary John J. McCloy's beliefs about who should be excluded from areas deemed militarily sensitive, primarily the West Coast and later interior California, central Oregon and Washington, and western Arizona. Although Japanese Americans were not mentioned by name, Executive Order 9066 was clearly aimed at them. German Americans and Italian Americans were not visibly different from the mainstream Caucasian population.[17]

Fear of Japan's intentions seemed warranted when on February 24 a submarine surfaced off the coast of Santa Barbara and shelled American soil. This event touched off a new wave of hysteria, which only began to recede when the army announced that all Japanese Americans would be removed from the West Coast.[18] Half a century of racism had finally borne fruit.

Since the wording of the executive order was somewhat vague, Congress deemed it necessary to educate the citizenry about its meaning. Beginning on February 21 a congressional committee headed by Representative John H. Tolan of California conducted a series of hearings. Created before Pearl Harbor, the Tolan Committee's official purpose was to investigate "National Defense Migration," but its charge had been extended to include the "problem of evacuation of enemy aliens and others from prohibited military zones."[19] Nisei were encouraged to think that the vagueness of the mandate meant that perhaps their fate, if not their parents', was still undecided. The committee moved like a "traveling medicine show," from San Francisco to Portland to Seattle and back to San Francisco, assessing public opinion from whites as well as Japanese.[20] Most Caucasians who spoke were strongly anti-Japanese, reflecting not only the shock of Pearl Harbor but also the indigenous racism of the West Coast. The first witness, for example, was the Italian American mayor of San Francisco, Angelo Rossi, who was certainly unlikely to denigrate the loyalty of his fellow Italians.[21] The Nikkei hoped that their Caucasian friends would support them, and some church people like YMCA leader Galen Fisher of Berkeley and members of the Committee for Fair Play did. A few Nisei also spoke, including Mike Masaoka, a young Nisei who was becoming the spokesman of the Japanese American Citizens League. He was accompanied at the San Francisco hearings by two other community leaders, Henry Tani, a Christian who had graduated from Stanford University, and Dave Tatsuno, a Christian businessman who was president of the San Francisco JACL chapter.[22]

The Tolan Committee hearings gave the JACL a chance to emerge from obscurity by voicing the opinions of at least one segment of the Nisei.[23] Still a small organization, in 1941 it had, for example, only 650 members in Los Angeles, a city with a population of some 24,000 Nisei. The JACL was overshadowed by the Issei, who as elders in an ethnic group accustomed to deferring to age were the natural spokesmen for the community.[24] The JACL represented the younger generation, and its leadership emphasized that the Nisei were loyal American citizens and should be exempt from the discrimination inherent in exclusion. The Tolan Committee hearings presented the JACL its first opportunity for a forum.

Mike Masaoka had moved with his father from California to Salt Lake City in 1918, at the age of three. The young Mike became a member of the Church of Jesus Christ of Latter-Day Saints. After graduating from high school in Salt Lake City, he attended the University of Utah and in 1941 was teaching in its Speech Department. He had also joined the local chapter of the JACL and had risen to be chairman of the Intermountain District Council. In August 1941 he was hired as the JACL's first full-time employee, and he spoke for the organization in this capacity.[25] In his testimony he stated that the JACL had no quarrel with evacuation *if* there were a military necessity, but he urged that the citizen Nisei not be made the victims of purely racial discrimination, political opportunism, or economic greed.[26]

Masaoka spoke for the JACL and for those Nisei who were willing to concede the Issei to the military as security risks, but his statement did not appease the people who wanted all Japanese removed from the West Coast. The case for evacuation was made by segregationists who claimed that all Japanese looked alike and the guilty could not be separated from the innocent. The few friends of the Nikkei attempted to counter this. In addition to Galen Fisher, who had worked for the YMCA in Japan, and Seattle resident Floyd Schmoe of the Quakers, they included a few university people, attorneys, and others who had gotten to know and like the Nikkei. Their words fell on deaf ears. The Tolan Committee hearings concluded on March 19 that there was no alternative to evacuating the entire community, but it advised against internment. Although the fate of the Japanese Americans was still in doubt at this time, the hearings were largely a sham, a forum for the expression of hatred against the Nikkei. The executive order paving the way for evacuation had already been issued. On March 11 the Wartime Civil Control Administration was established under Colonel Bendetsen's direction. On March 17 the new organization opened sixty-six offices on the West Coast and made preparations for the actual evacuation. On March 24 a curfew was ordered for all Nisei.[27]

From this point on the JACL, in an act that cost it dearly later, supported evacuation as an opportunity to prove the patriotism of the Nisei community, and its members became openly hostile to anyone who opposed it. Given the relatively small size of the Japanese American community, it had no choice but to give in, but the JACL went into camp willingly, almost with enthusiasm, leading the Nisei like "Judas goats," as Masaoka put it years later. It was this attitude, as much as anything, that enraged those who objected to the blatant unconstitutionality of the government action.[28] The dispute between the JACL and its opponents continued in the assembly centers and the camps, in some instances provoking outright violence, and it lasted far beyond the war years. Its repercussions extended into the 1980s and even affected the drive for redress. Topaz was largely free of such fury, but it too felt the vibrations of the controversy.

❧

Weeks of confusion, anxiety, and frantic activity followed the issuing of Executive Order 9066. Blackouts and states of emergency were declared in both San Francisco and Oakland. The Kibei and Issei who had grown up in Japan believed that their homeland was invincible, and they were encouraged by news of Japanese victories. Some rumors circulated that the war was almost over, that General Douglas MacArthur was dead, and that Japanese planes had bombed Alaska. Others thought the evacuation had been ordered because an invasion of California was imminent; some even refused to plan to leave because they thought Japan would win the war before they had to. The Nisei laughed at the outrageousness of such rumors.[29]

Whatever they believed about the true military situation, the 110,000 Japanese Americans on the West Coast—70,000 of them U.S. citizens—were quickly affected both by the army's orders and by their economic effects. On January 29 Attorney General Francis Biddle designated twenty-nine areas on the West Coast as vital to the nation's security and announced that enemy aliens would have to leave them; they included the San Francisco waterfront, but few Japanese Americans were affected. More orders followed: first, curfew and travel restrictions and then, the proclamation of two military zones. Congress debated a bill to deprive the Nisei of their citizenship, and the few Nisei Californians who worked in the civil service lost their jobs. Although evacuation was clearly only a matter of time, the army gave the Nikkei no particular guidelines about disposing of their household possessions and real property. On March 12 the Federal Reserve Board, whose twelfth district was headquartered in San Francisco, was authorized to offer help to anyone who requested it. It provided minimal assistance to the Nikkei who came to its field offices, some 26,000 of the 110,000 people affected by the evacuation orders. However, its advice was generally to use the resources of the white community—its real estate agencies and banks—and the lack of time made the resolution of complex problems virtually impossible. The bank's program was "hastily-devised, ill-conceived, and procedurally sloppy"; its agents could only "prevent the grossest abuses, and then only for a few of the thousands uprooted." Many were simply victimized by whites eager to take advantage of their distress.[30]

Most San Francisco and Bay Area Japanese Americans, like their counterparts elsewhere along the coast, did their best to dispose of their assets by themselves or with the help of Caucasian friends. The last thing they wanted was help from the federal government, which seemed to be their avowed enemy, although many did accept the Wartime Civil Control Commission's offer to store their goods in federally owned warehouses. Some panicked and sold at giveaway prices the possessions and land for which they had worked so hard. Others, like Kenji Fujii's family, were fortunate; they were able to entrust their Hayward nursery to the care of a sympathetic second-generation German family. Tomoye Takahashi's family rented their San Francisco home and put their personal possessions in a locked room—only to return after the internment and find the room broken into and their valuables gone.[31] Grace Fujimoto Oshita's family ran a miso factory in the city, producing the soybean paste so important in Japanese cooking; they stored their most valued possessions with professional companies and put the rest in federal warehouses or in the Buddhist church. Their losses were small.[32] People who rented their living quarters had no choice but to dispose of their belongings, storing what they could in churches, with Caucasian friends, privately, or with the government. The real property and goods the San Francisco community held in China-town had ready buyers. Automobiles also were easy to sell, but the prices obtained were a fraction of their value. Shopkeepers whose merchandise was Japanese had an extremely difficult time liquidating it.

The situation was much more difficult for families whose heads had been arrested by the FBI—especially men who were active in the Japanese Associations, language instructors, and religious or business community leaders. Other Issei considered dangerous were those employed by Japanese businesses, such as the large Mitsui and Mitsubishi import-export firms, and by Japanese banks. Don Nakahata's father, Shiro Yasuchika Nakahata, who was picked up by the FBI on December 8, worked for both the newspaper *Shin Sekai* and the local Japanese Association in San Francisco.[33] Grace Fujimoto's father was taken in February. Masako

Tsuzuki's father, an insurance agent, was arrested very quickly, leaving her, at the age of sixteen, the effective head of the household.[34] Yoshiko Uchida, a college student in Berkeley, also lost her father, Dwight Takashi, the assistant manager of Mitsui; he was sent to Montana by the FBI. She, her mother Iku, and her sister Keiko packed frantically to meet the ten-day deadline for departure, but as she realized later, the women "sold things we should have kept and packed away foolish trifles we should have discarded." They realized how much they missed the "practical judgment" of her father. Particularly painful was having to look for a new home for the family dog.[35] Their pet found a kind owner and did not end up at the pound as many others did. But the new owner did not have the heart to tell the Uchidas their dog died a few weeks after they left.

⚜

In addition to the problems the Nikkei faced in disposing of property and possessions, they were emotionally distraught by uncertainty about their future. There were many rumors about where they would go, and when. Some people were in such a hurry to sell their goods that they ended up sleeping on the floor while they awaited orders to leave. Governmental arbitrariness and vacillation made the Nisei bitter and the Issei stoic. Tamotsu Shibutani, who studied rumors in the community before and after the evacuation, said that "vagueness and indefiniteness" were the worst conditions to deal with, and that when the actual evacuation orders came it was a relief.[36]

⚜

The actual business losses of the San Francisco and Bay Area communities were the subject of much debate in later years. The entire economic loss of the evacuated Japanese Americans has not been precisely determined and probably never can be. Some observations on the San Francisco situation were noted in 1945 in the dispassionate reports made by Oscar Hoffman, the Topaz

Community Analyst. Hoffman was concerned with how well the community would be able to reconstitute itself after the war. As the result of interviews with people at Topaz, he reported that the economy of Japanese San Francisco was struck differentially by the evacuation. The fishing fleet, for example, was speedily liquidated for fear the federal government would confiscate the boats, as it had at other ports, notably Los Angeles. The inability to find suitable buyers on short notice meant that the owners obtained very low prices.[37] The laundry operators leased their businesses, so their losses were in equipment and the trade they had developed. One laundryman who planned to return noted in 1945 that his equipment had been idle for three years; it was not in good condition, but it was usable. He still had several years left on the lease to his shop and he had kept up the rent, so he was in a good position to return. Most other laundry operators were not so fortunate.[38] The dry cleaners and dyers in the city had little to lose, since they rented or leased their shops. At first they anticipated many problems with the outbreak of war, but after a few days their customers returned; by the time of the evacuation they had regained three quarters of their original business. They lost their press equipment in the evacuation, but its used value was small anyway. Since they utilized their private cars for both business and pleasure, their main loss was in clientele and good will. Most of them believed they could regain their business easily if they returned.[39]

Some Nikkei in the arts goods business suffered heavily. One respondent noted that when his partner, who owned more than 80 percent of the stock, departed for Japan before the outbreak of the war, the government seized the entire stock. Another respondent described how his father sold his stock at a good price but could not get more than 30 percent of the value for his furniture and fixtures. However, the Japanese Grant Avenue merchants did not own their stores; they all rented or leased instead.[40]

At the time of the evacuation Nikkei operated sixteen hotels and nineteen apartment houses in Japanese town and five hotels in Chinatown. Some Issei hotel owners were quickly seized by the FBI. One woman's story was typical: after her husband's removal, she and her young children tried to continue running the hotel, but they lacked experience. The bank could not take over the business without a manager to run it. Ultimately the owner, who was Chinese, assumed it for nonpayment of rents. The bank said it could not sell the furniture because of its dilapidated condition. The Issei who had operated the hotel successfully for twenty-five years could not understand how he could have lost a stake he considered to be worth at least $2,000. He and his wife were not alone. Many hotel operators lost everything when they were unable to liquidate fast enough. Some of the people who were evacuated returned to San Francisco before they left the assembly center in San Bruno for Topaz and discovered their personal possessions had been looted from locked rooms as well.[41] Hoffman's account may not have captured the immediacy of the anguish felt by these victimized evacuees, but two years did not diminish their feelings of devastation because of the upheaval.

In San Mateo businesses catering to a Japanese clientele did not immediately feel the effects of the war and those serving Caucasians were only temporarily depressed by the immediate shock after Pearl Harbor. Owners rented their homes at too low a price, and renters had to dispose of personal possessions at rock-bottom prices. Local churches aided the departing, providing storage for possessions. Close ties between the Nikkei and the Caucasian community cushioned the shock there.[42] Masako Tsuzuki, sixteen years old and female, made what preparations she could for herself, her siblings, and her mother, who did not speak English; since they did not own real property, their losses amounted to their personal possessions.

The Issei in the Richmond–El Cerrito area were ordered to evacuate in February 1942 because they were supposedly a threat to the Standard Oil refinery in Richmond. Their Nisei children remained behind to tend the nurseries, recalled Heizo Oshima, but they were untrained and lacked the knowledge to manage the financial details of the family businesses.[43] Their losses were substantial.

Oakland's community also suffered. One family that owned an art and dry goods store could not sell its merchandise because of its Japanese origins, so it stored an inventory worth more than $50,000 in a Japanese Methodist Church that had been converted into a warehouse.[44] Hiro Katayama recalled that his mother stored their goods in a home being purchased by his brother-in-law where his own family also resided. They placed everything in the attic, but when they returned after the war they found it had been broken into and ransacked, and their goods strewn all about. Like so many others, they suffered not only physical loss but the trauma of having their personal possessions vandalized.[45]

Farmers in the Mount Eden–Washington township areas, like so many others, could not believe in the imminence of the evacuation. It was beyond their comprehension that they would have to leave their strawberry crops just as the fruit ripened and would have to dispose of their farm equipment, so painfully and laboriously acquired. People without attorneys were aided in their departure preparations by the Farm Security Administration, because the federal government did not want to lose their food crops either, as the nation entered a war and mobilization brought labor shortages. But, as in the cities, most Nikkei sold in a hurry and at great losses. One Issei who held eleven acres of prime strawberries plus a house, a truck, and cars received only $2,000 for all his possessions. The new owner realized over $10,000, according to a report the former owner received later.[46]

The town of Alameda was located on an island with airports at each end, near a shipyard. Since the army considered it a strategic military area, its Nikkei residents were among the first to be evacuated. The departure began on February 15, a second group left February 24, and the remainder went in May. Only the third group went directly to the assembly center at Tanforan; many of the others moved first to other parts of California and had to relocate twice.[47]

The floral industry of the East Bay suffered substantial losses. More than a thousand Japanese were employed in this trade, and about 75 percent of the growers owned their own property, worth millions of dollars. They specialized in roses, carnations, gardenias, poinsettias, shrubs, and bedding plants. Chrysanthemum growers leased rather than owned land because that plant exhausts the soil's fertility, but they had a heavy stake in buildings and equipment. They all lost a great deal and received inadequate governmental advice on the disposition of their property. Many Caucasians took advantage of the situation to buy land and greenhouses at extremely low prices. One carnation grower suffered tremendous losses. His family had been in business for more than forty years; he owned a large home, 1,500 linear feet of greenhouse, a boiler and boiler house, and all the other necessary equipment. He made an "eleventh hour contract" after much haggling and rented his property for $60 a month, including house, goods, greenhouses, and carnations. After a year the contract expired, but on investigation the War Relocation Authority found the renter had departed and five unknown families had moved into the house. They were evicted and the nursery was then rented to a Chinese who operated it but was four months in arrears on his rent. The Issei owner received no word on his missing stove, refrigerator, washing machine, or piano, nor was there information on his personal goods, stored in two rooms of the house.[48] The floral industry also suffered in Menlo Park and the East Bay, but some residents reported that they incurred smaller losses because of the consideration of the Caucasians in the area.[49] If so, they were more fortunate than most other Nikkei.

The total losses for the Bay Area can only be estimated. The traditional figure estimated for Nikkei losses throughout the West Coast and Hawaii was for many years assumed to be $400 million, a total supposedly derived by the Federal Reserve Bank, but not documented in any of its studies. The 1946 report of the War Relocation Authority concluded that evacuee property was poorly managed, especially during the period between the issuance of Executive Order 9066 on February 19, 1942, and the granting of authority to the Federal Reserve Bank on March 6.[50] The report of the Commission on Wartime Relocation and Internment of Civilians, published in 1982, concluded that "economic losses from the evacuation were substantial, and they touched every group of Nikkei." The commission referred to possessions, liberty, and livelihood, but it also cited "the loss of so much one had worked for, the accumulated substance of a lifetime—gone just when the future seemed most bleak and threatening."[51]

❧

The actual evacuation was delayed because no specific plans for the relocation of the Nikkei to the interior accompanied Executive Order 9066. Efforts to find cooperative governors willing to take the Nikkei failed, and facilities to hold that many people simply did not exist.[52] It was one thing for the FBI to arrest a few thousand community leaders, who could be—and were—treated like common criminals and housed in prison facilities. It was quite another for the military to contain over 110,000 men, women, and children. The military's indecision and the lack of specific information to the Nikkei reflected this uncertainty. On March 2, 1942, Lieutenant General John L. DeWitt issued Public Proclamation No. 1, which divided the West Coast and Arizona into two large military areas and a number of smaller prohibited areas, and an accompanying press release made clear that persons of "Japanese ancestry" would be excluded from them.

Voluntary evacuation was first encouraged; since the goal was to clear the West Coast of these potentially dangerous people, their voluntary resettlement could solve the problem. Yoshiko Uchida and her family considered such a move, for they feared what would happen to three women alone in a government assembly center, but they learned of "arrests, violence, and vigilantism encountered by some who had fled 'voluntarily'" and hesitated. The loss of husband and father made it especially difficult to come to a decision, but in the end the Uchidas decided to wait and go to an assembly center.[53] Rumors of rejection kept many others in place, while most simply lacked the resources to move and had no destination in any case. When a few thousand Nikkei did try to relocate voluntarily, most were unsuccessful, for the rumors of ill-treatment were correct: no one else wanted them either. Many who tried to drive east found it difficult even to purchase gasoline, let alone to buy food or find lodging.

There were a few success stories. About 1,500 West Coast Nikkei moved to Utah during the period of voluntary migration, despite the unhappiness of Governor Herbert B. Maw and his administration, who believed that if they were dangerous on the West Coast, they would also be a threat in Utah. The new arrivals were a source of some consternation to the resident Japanese American population, who feared that discrimination would become more pronounced if Japanese faces were more noticeable. Most were able to fit in, with assistance from the local community. Oakland businessman Fred Wada led a group of Japanese Americans from the Oakland area to Utah during the voluntary phase. The tiny community of Keetley, west of Park City in the Wasatch Mountains, welcomed the group. Wada had carefully arranged with local authorities and rancher George Fisher in advance for his people to move and settle on Fisher's ranch. The group took advantage of the growing labor shortage to farm Fisher's ranch on a cooperative basis and sharecrop or work for other farmers in the more fertile Spanish Fork area. Despite one episode of violence, they were well received and soon won the respect of their formerly cautious neighbors.[54]

The family of Nobu Miyoshi also went to Utah and settled south of Salt Lake City. They moved from Sacramento, abandoning her father's shoe store in order to leave quickly, and traveled to Salt Lake City. Nobu remembered the haste with which they left California and the uncomfortable housing they were able to obtain in Murray, south of Salt Lake City: a shut-down Japanese schoolhouse with an outhouse. The only available work was in agriculture, and they all labored in the fields for a time. Nobu finally found a position interviewing and translating for Issei from Topaz who, having left the camp and unwilling to burden their children, had to apply for welfare when their jobs ran out. When her two sisters and father also found other work, they were able to move to better housing in Salt Lake City. Nobu remained in Utah long enough to graduate as a social worker from the University of Utah.[55] Lacking the support system the Keetley settlers had, theirs was a less successful venture. They suffered discrimination in obtaining housing, and work was hard to find. They did not even receive much support

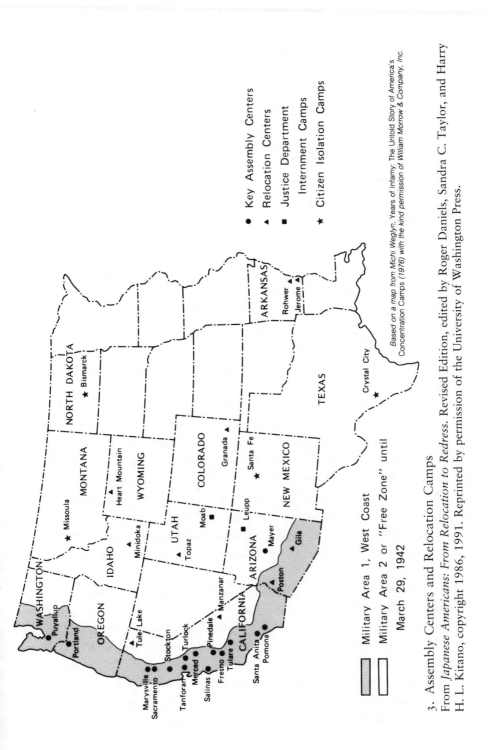

3. Assembly Centers and Relocation Camps

From *Japanese Americans: From Relocation to Redress*. Revised Edition, edited by Roger Daniels, Sandra C. Taylor, and Harry H. L. Kitano, copyright 1986, 1991. Reprinted by permission of the University of Washington Press.

Legend:

● Key Assembly Centers
▲ Relocation Centers
■ Justice Department Internment Camps
★ Citizen Isolation Camps

▨ Military Area 1, West Coast

▢ Military Area 2 or "Free Zone" until March 29, 1942

Based on a map from Michi Weglyn, *Years of Infamy: The Untold Story of America's Concentration Camps (1976) with the kind permission of William Morrow & Company, Inc.*

Map locations:

WASHINGTON — Puyallup, Portland
OREGON
CALIFORNIA — Marysville, Sacramento, Tanforan, Stockton, Turlock, Merced, Salinas, Pinedale, Fresno, Tulare, Santa Anita, Pomona, Manzanar, Tule Lake
IDAHO — Minidoka
MONTANA — Missoula
NORTH DAKOTA — Bismarck
UTAH — Topaz, Moab
WYOMING — Heart Mountain
COLORADO — Granada
ARIZONA — Leupp, Mayer, Poston, Gila
NEW MEXICO — Santa Fe
TEXAS — Crystal City
ARKANSAS — Rohwer, Jerome

from Salt Lake City's beleaguered Japanese American community, which had its own problems in trying to be inconspicuous and avoid hostility from local whites. At least the Miyoshis had left California on their own, and their residence in Utah, like that of the Keetley settlers, was not behind the barbed wire fences of Topaz.[56]

Of the 5,000 or so who attempted voluntary evacuation, San Francisco and the Bay Area contributed its share. But most preferred to wait for whatever the army had in store. In mid-March the army established 4 more military areas, as well as 933 prohibited zones. A third proclamation established a curfew for Japanese in the first military area and prohibited them from voluntarily attempting to relocate; they were now required to await orders to be evacuated. The population displacement officially began with Civilian Exclusion Order No. 1, which dislocated several hundred residents of Bainbridge Island, in Puget Sound. But the navy had actually ousted the Nikkei residents of Terminal Island, San Pedro, on February 27, 1942, with only two days' notice.[57] The people of San Francisco had to wait longer to learn what would become of them, and this was a period of great anxiety.

The problem of what to do with the population the army had so arbitrarily designated as a security risk plagued the military. As a temporary expedient, the Wartime Civil Control Administration (WCCA), established by DeWitt to carry out the army's part in the evacuation, decided to use assembly centers as holding camps for the Nikkei while more permanent facilities were constructed. It took over large facilities that could be easily adapted, such as fairgrounds, livestock exhibition centers and racetracks. The unsuitability of these places for housing human beings was of little concern to the army.

The pattern of distributing the Japanese American population among the sixteen assembly centers was not totally random, and most people from one area went to the center and camp together. On April 1 San Francisco received its first evacuation order, with departure set for April 7. The first 660 Nikkei went to the Santa Anita Racetrack, an arbitrary decision based on the area of the city in which they resided—hence Morgan and Al Yamanaka, whose family lived in Pacific Heights, moved to Santa Anita, where Morgan found a wonderful job working for the volunteer fire department (there were no fires). The remainder of the San Francisco community and most of the Japanese from the Bay Area north of San Jose and Palo Alto were moved between April 19 and May 20;[58] they were assigned to Tanforan, a racetrack located in San Bruno, just south of San Francisco. A few went to Gila River Relocation Center and some to Poston. The elimination of the Bay Area Japanese community had begun.

Chapter Three

Life in a Racetrack

The departure for Tanforan was an event that San Francisco and Bay Area Nikkei would never forget. Colonel Karl R. Bendetsen, director of the WCCA, and his staff had divided the West Coast into 108 areas, each containing about a thousand Japanese, or 250 families. Orders were posted in each area telling the residents what they should do, what they could take with them, and when they should report to be transported.[1] First the residents of an area were registered; Nikkei family heads and single people went to WCCA control stations to fill out forms and obtain a family number and tags for identification and baggage. The actual move took place about a week later.[2] Everyone gathered at the designated location at the appointed time, each family member labeled with the "family number" and holding the few bags that were permitted. As befitted such a formal community, most Japanese Americans were very dressed up, for they did not know their ultimate destination. Some encountered sympathetic Caucasians or African Americans who drove them to the assembly point and gave them tea or coffee and sandwiches, but many, like Fumi Manabe and her Berkeley family, saw nothing friendly about the departure, only the armed guards. Yoshiko Uchida was terrified when she and her family gathered at the First Congregational Church in Berkeley and saw the guards with mounted bayonets.[3]

The departing Nikkei of San Francisco and the Bay Area communities were escorted onto buses that took them down the Bayshore Highway to Tanforan. Faith Terasawa recalled that the buses all had brown paper on the windows, but she lifted the paper to see where they were; her twelve-year-old nephew Don Nakahata was alarmed by her action, fearing she was doing something illegal that would get them into trouble.[4] (Some evacuees drove their own cars, which were then confiscated by the army and sold by the Federal Reserve Board for whatever price it could obtain.) Leaving their comfortable homes was agonizing, but the sight of their new, temporary home was even worse. The shock of Tanforan was profound for the Uchidas and the other arrivals; its high fence made them feel at once that they were prisoners. Throughout April and into May, the exodus continued.

⚜

Tanforan Assembly Center, which at its maximum held 7,796 people, very quickly became not only a Nikkei holding pen but a small city.[5] Charles Kikuchi, one of the residents, noted in his diary that it was the site of sixty-four births, twenty-two deaths, and fifty-nine arrests. He was not the only resident to chronicle its 169 days of existence, for the very proximity of the camp to Stanford University and the University of California made it a more likely site for complete documentation than the other assembly centers.[6] Sociologists at the University of California, whose faculty members tended to be more liberal than other Californians, were shocked by the evacuation and, unable to prevent it, decided at least to record it completely. The resulting participant-observer study, the Japanese Evacuation Research Study (JERS) headed by Dorothy Swaine Thomas, faced a multitude of problems. Thomas had no training in minority group studies and no previous interest in Japanese Americans, and the Nisei she recruited may well have been "contaminated" by their involvement in both relocation and the project, but the data they kept have been invaluable, if controversial, to later scholars, providing a very useful counterpoint to the voluminous records kept by the War Relocation Authority.[7]

Many of the evacuees stated later that their experiences at Tanforan were the most disturbing of the whole relocation period. It is easy, in retrospect, to see why they felt this way. The dislocation caused by the evacuation was profound. By 1941 the San Francisco Bay community had achieved a modest middle-class existence. Its residents were not as segregated as the Seattle community was, since their occupations as domestics, fishermen, and flower growers led to a diffused residential pattern rather similar to that in Los Angeles.[8] Many Nisei, including Tomoye Takahashi, Morgan Yamanaka, and Michiko Okamoto, recalled that they intermingled with Caucasians in high school and had friends among them. Although they experienced discrimination, it did not profoundly traumatize them. Yoshiko Uchida remembered that she mixed with Caucasians when she was growing up and even lived in a "white" neighborhood, but she was always reluctant to join the white children for fear she would be excluded, and in high school she and her sister did not participate in any white activities.[9] The evacuation ended the comfortable existence of these young people and their parents. The loss of their possessions and homes was abrupt, and being deposited into a space enclosed by barbed wire was frightening. The loss of their freedom was most disturbing of all.

The Tanforan Assembly Center was not ready for them. It was raining heavily on April 30 when many arrived, and the baggage was soaked. The new residents were searched for contraband and the men checked for venereal disease, then taken to filthy barracks rooms or horse stalls where they spent a sleepless night on straw-filled ticks. In the morning they lined up at the mess hall to discover the food was virtually inedible; for the first ten days they were served lima beans, cold tea, canned food, stale bread, and sometimes Jell-O. Other meals consisted of boiled potatoes, canned Vienna sausages, and a few slices of bread. There was barely enough even of that unpleasant fare, and no provision was made for special diets. Grace Fujimoto's six-month-old cousin was allergic to condensed milk. He developed eczema all over his body and nearly died. The weather was windy and dusty, but the internees had no complaints about that, as they did later at Topaz, for at least it was familiar. The atmosphere, according to three student recorders from the University of California, resembled a prison.[10] The fact that each family was just a number to the administrators underlined the prison atmosphere and intensified the gravity of the situation.

❧

The overall appearance of Tanforan was decidedly institutional. There were 180 buildings, of which 26 were converted horse stalls. In the middle was the former racetrack, with a grandstand next to it. The latrines (since the army ran it, military terminology applied) were hastily constructed and in short supply; there were only 24 for the entire population. Each had holes cut out of a board, one next to the other, unseparated by any kind of partition. The lack of privacy was deeply embarrassing to the modest Issei women, who tried to shield themselves and their daughters with towels or sheets, or even by standing in front of one another. Privacy, they soon learned, was unavailable for almost every function.

The inhabitants were housed in barracks or horse stalls. At first the stalls did not have closed ceilings but merely walls that extended upward toward the external roof, and these did not close off one room from the next. Yoshiko Uchida wrote that even visual privacy was relative, since many of the wallboards contained open knotholes.[11] Even the quietest conversation could be heard by one's neighbors. Often the linoleum floors had been laid right over manure, and the odor permeated everything.[12] Miné Okubo, an art student at the University of California who came from Riverside, had an even more abrupt introduction to life in an internment camp. From a poor family of seven children, she had worked hard to attend UC, recommended to her because of her talent. In 1938 she won a traveling fellowship to continue her art studies abroad. Despite the imminence of war in Europe, she visited most of western Europe, sketching people and scenes that she intended for a book. She returned in 1940 on the last American ship leaving Bordeaux, thinking that she was escaping the horrors of the war that had engulfed Europe. The irony of her choice still haunted her in 1988. Her family underwent personal hardship with the death of her mother in 1941, and the FBI picked up her father and a brother and sent them to a prison camp in Missoula,

Montana. Miné returned to Berkeley, and there she learned that the family home in Riverside, vacant since the arrests, had been ransacked and her sketches destroyed. Her family scattered: her sisters and their families were sent to the Heart Mountain internment camp, where her father later joined them; another brother went to Poston. She and a younger brother, also a UC student, were evacuated to Tanforan as a "family group" of two. There she began the project of recording camp life that became *Citizen 13660*.[13]

Miné kept careful notes to accompany her illustrations. She described the stall she and her brother shared as having walls where "spider webs, horse hair, and hay had been whitewashed with the walls."[14] Each resident was given a tick to fill with straw or, in the case of some horse stall residents, a cotton mattress as partial compensation for their disgusting lodging.[15] Most attempted to sweep the floor, but the dirt just came back in. Okubo drily noted that the first month was the hardest because "adjustments had to be made to the new mode of life."[16] The JERS observers agreed, noting that "accommodations were atrocious for those used to city living, but paradise for those from rural areas,"[17] but actually few rural residents had lived in such squalor. The Issei bachelors and single Nisei males were housed together in the grandstand; according to Okubo's colorful description, "they slept and snored, dressed and undressed, in one continuous public performance."[18] They were later moved to the barracks since the presence of so many single males in their midst frightened some of the mothers, who worried about their daughters' safety.

The newly constructed barracks were scarcely an improvement over the horse stalls. Located in the center field, they were built of green wood, which shrank as it dried, allowing grass to grow between the boards and the wind to sweep through. More than three thousand people still remained in the stalls after the barracks were built; the more fortunate residents tried to avoid the smell (which often meant just avoiding the inhabitants). Midori Shimanouchi recalled that she was courted for many months by a "man who smelled like a horse." She and her mother tried to ignore the odor, but it really was unpleasant.[19]

For both the stall and the barrack dwellers, hot water for the showers and laundry (located in separate buildings) was in short supply. The shower rooms presented problems to the elderly, accustomed to traditional Japanese baths. The younger residents found it amusing that the old folks carried in tubs late at night to construct makeshift baths in the showers. Construction continued through much of the time the Japanese Americans were in residence. "I wondered how much the nation's security would have been threatened had the army permitted us to remain in our homes a few more days until the camps were adequately prepared for occupancy by families," wrote Yoshiko Uchida.[20]

It seems surprising that a community would arise in such a setting. This was a prison city, different from a jail in that the keepers promised self-government, allowed education and recreation, and provided entertainment. They talked about how the incarceration was for the inhabitants' own protection, but the lack of civilized accoutrements dramatized the difference between the keepers and the kept. Nevertheless, even though Tanforan was no ordinary community, the Nikkei interned there retained many of the elements of their previous community life. Because they were not locked in individual cells, they could interact with one another. They attempted to fill the time with creative activities, especially ones that would keep the young people busy. Since the white administrators had to rely on the Japanese to keep order and perform such basic functions as feeding the people, in a sense community life went on. Yet a gulf lay between the administrators and the jailed. Japanese were not perceived as the equals of whites, a difference that was dramatized by their incarceration while German Americans and Italian Americans went free. This discriminatory treatment based on race and color made the concept of community tenuous, because it meant that the Nikkei, whether in assembly centers or relocation camps, were in fact in concentration camps guarded and directed by Caucasians. Their situation differed from enemy prisoners of war held in the United States in that they were, for the most part, with their family members, but the POWs were better housed and fed. Even prisons were an improvement over the facilities the Nikkei inhabited, especially at Tanforan.

⚜

The center was run by the Wartime Civil Control Authority, a civilian branch of the army that, unused to this type of assignment, had little idea how to carry it out. The WCCA divided camp control into five sections: administration, works and maintenance, finance and records, mess and lodging, and service. Caucasians were hired to run things; they were mainly men too old for military service who were willing to take a short-term job. Most shared the prevailing view of the Nikkei as "Japs," yet they had to keep their prejudices in bounds enough to work with them. Some, a rare few, sympathized with the interned and tried their best to help them. Most jobs at Tanforan changed hands several times, either because a worker was incompetent or because he acquired a better position. It was widely known, for example, that the first manager in charge of food service was so incompetent that he was fired after a few weeks, but he had already ordered insufficient food for May and June so that the inmates did not get enough to eat for nearly four months.[21]

Feeding the community was a real problem, which the initial administrators addressed poorly. The Nikkei were supposed to be provided with food worth 50 cents a day, but they probably received less. Miné Okubo remembered it well: before mess tickets were issued, "most of us were hungry after one meal, so we would dash to another mess hall for a second meal. Some managed to get three meals this way."[22] John Yoshino, a Nisei JERS participant-observer who worked for the public relations office in the center, wrote his superior that in three successive meals rice and beans alone were served, and people got sick. According to a rumor that spread like wildfire in the camp environment, the kitchen staff was eating the meat.[23] Complaints of constant chili con carne and sauerkraut were testimony to the ignorance of the Caucasian food workers about Japanese preferences.[24]

The food situation improved when the first food manager was replaced; inmates then began to receive meat and fresh vegetables once or twice a week. Additional mess halls were opened, two of which disobeyed the rules and served meals family style, and people got more food. The administration finally adopted a ticket system so that people could no longer eat more than once. Uchida complained that the new mess halls prepared food just as badly as the main one did, but by the end of the Tanforan stay people were finally getting fried chicken and ice cream for Sunday dinner.[25] Persistent diarrhea also began to abate after the first few months.

Many things about Tanforan reminded its inhabitants that they were incarcerated. The camp was surrounded by barbed wire atop a fence, and armed military police stood on guard. The residents were warned to stay away from the fence. They could receive visitors in the grandstand for two hours in the morning and three hours in the afternoon, but their guests could not enter the grounds, living quarters, or mess; all outsiders had to have a pass and their parcels were inspected.[26] It was the responsibility of the internee to inform the visitor of the rules. Miné Okubo decided it was simply easier to discourage friends—especially after one man waited three hours to give her a special Chinese meal, and the egg flower soup leaked through the carton and onto his pants.[27]

All administrative units consisted of Caucasian supervisors and Japanese workers. Since the Nikkei were normally law-abiding people and the JACL ethos was accommodationist, the use of Japanese labor worked well at Tanforan and the other assembly centers, as it did at most of the relocation camps. The desire to prove themselves model citizens precluded rebellion for most, as did the lack of leadership. Few of the Caucasian administrators were outrightly hostile to their charges, so cooperation between white and Japanese was usually possible. The mentality, particularly at first, was not that of prisoner-guard. Many people were anxious to work, finding any occupations preferable to boredom.

One of the first areas of cooperation was policing. The head of internal security appointed a Nisei, Frank Tsukamoto, as his assistant in charge of the Japanese police force. By May 13 there were seventy-three men on the force, which worked twenty-four hours a day. The first Caucasian supervisor was unpopular with the Nikkei for both his policies and his rudeness to visitors, but there was also grumbling when he was replaced by another white without consulting the Japanese policemen. In fact, there were six heads of internal security in Tanforan's brief existence. The Nikkei force did its job, which consisted primarily of patrolling inside the grounds. When the administration subsequently determined that Caucasians should have this task, there were complaints, especially by Issei who did not want whites talking to Nikkei women.[28]

The criminal element in camp was negligible. The main problem was petty theft from the rooms or stealing lumber from construction sites to build shelves and furniture for the spartan quarters. Everyone quickly put locks on their doors. Items also were taken from laundry lines, usually by poor people who lacked a particular article of clothing.[29] But the most common item stolen was toilet paper, since the latrines were usually out of it and the canteen, established in the early days to supply the residents with basic commodities and candy and cigarettes, had almost none for sale. The snatching of toilet paper went on until everyone had a roll. Those who had access stole food from the kitchen, especially during the food shortage. There was some rowdyism.[30] Hardly serious crime, but as Yoshiko Uchida noted, "there was little inclination for anyone to feel responsible for anyone else. In the early days, at least, it was everyone for himself or herself."[31]

The crimes reported give an insight into the nature of the Tanforan community. There were two known cases of prostitution and two sex offenses in the first month. Voyeurism was a persistent problem, especially with the large number of single men housed together in the grandstand and the lack of privacy in living quarters. The departure of the single men for the barracks brought large sighs of relief from the women. A search for "contraband" netted sewing scissors, saws, cooking knives, screwdrivers, and Japanese-language Bibles, some of which were confiscated and some not, since a lack of consistency marked Tanforan's history and of course none of the guards read Japanese. The goods taken were, in any case, hardly dangerous objects. One of the JERS reporters, Earle Yusa, noted that Tanforan was the most orderly center, because of the "high type people there."[32] This comment may have reflected a bit of local pride, since he and many of the residents were educated city dwellers who were law-abiding and the JERS staff seemed to have a bias against rural people, but there was, in fact, little disorderly conduct. Even so, Yoshiko Uchida was horrified to discover women emptying bed pans into the troughs where they washed their faces, and her mother quickly wrote signs in Japanese urging people not to do this.[33] Not everyone was a "high-type person."

The biggest problem for the camp authorities was gambling, a clear case of conflict between Japanese American ideas of entertainment and Caucasian morality. Since there were few jobs and little else to do, the numerous single men, especially Issei and Kibei, began to gamble. The administration, abiding by local laws, cracked down and lodged repeat offenders in the San Mateo County jail. But the reasons for the "crime's" prevalence—boredom—insured that the problem would recur. As the community settled into a routine, gambling was just one way to pass the time.

☙

A host of regulations surrounded the incarcerated Nikkei, constant reminders of Caucasian authority. Religious services, for example, had to be held in English unless the congregation could not understand that language. Religious freedom was to exist, but it did not extend to Shinto, which the authorities interpreted as emperor worship. However, they often confused Shinto with Buddhism, since they were familiar with neither. The center manager was to make sure that religious services were not used to propagandize or incite the congregation; all written materials were to be cleared by the camp authorities. Caucasian religious leaders could assist in services if necessary, but they could not live in the center.[34] Caucasian pastors from the surrounding communities who had worked with Japanese Americans did sometimes visit their communicants.

In addition, there were elaborate regulations to prevent fires, a great fear of the administration. This task was made more difficult by the residents' use of hot plates, irons, and heaters to improve the circumstances of their lives and to provide special food and comfort for the elderly, the ill, and the very young. Roll calls took place in the mess halls each morning at breakfast time, and those who missed breakfast had to stay in their rooms until they were counted. At night there was a curfew and a physical count by name. Some regulations also pertained to the residents' continuing their obligations or benefits as (free) residents of the United States: citizens were urged to vote by absentee ballot, and the elderly could obtain old age and survivor's benefits from Social Security. The residents had a post office and could receive packages after they were searched; they could purchase items from mail order catalogs, irritating the administrators who then had to examine the incoming goods; and they could receive banking services through the San Bruno branch of Bank of America, which sent a teller to camp to handle financial matters, including the purchase of traveler's checks and war bonds. They had to observe blackout regulations, and they were constantly reminded to stay away from the fence.[35]

There was entertainment. For example, the administration provided movies weekly in the grandstand; Miné Okubo recalled how people brought blankets and pillows and folding chairs and waited several hours for the films to begin, playing cards, knitting, and gossiping to pass the time. Residents held talent shows. The Nisei organized educational activities not only to keep the younger children occupied but also to raise the elders' morale. The Nikkei valued education too highly to ignore it, whether it was in a basic subject or a hobby or skill. Volunteer evacuee teachers taught classes from the preschool to the adult level, in everything from Americanization and history to sewing, art, and music. Grace Fujimoto took piano lessons in the recreation hall, and Miné Okubo taught elementary and college art classes. A library was created, with gifts of books from the outside to occupy idle minds.[36]

In two administrative areas the Nikkei played particularly important roles. They were block managers, the all-important functionaries who made the day-to-day rules by which people lived, and they participated in the brief and illusory self-government. The latter reminded people for a while that they still lived in democratic America, where government rested on the consent of the governed.

Block managers were appointed for each block to serve as a liaison between the residents and the Caucasian supervisor of housing. Originally they were selected randomly, but the position became self-selecting as the original group found their own successors. Their tasks were so multitudinous that holders of the position almost inevitably had to be single and male, or at least without children. There were forty-five managers by the end of the first month, two of whom were women and most of whom were bilingual. They took care of bedding, supervised the cleanliness of the surrounding grounds, were responsible for tools, advised people of the regulations, and cooperated with the internal police. They had to make sure that residents did not use irons, heating stoves, or cooking utensils, unless they were tending the elderly, the sick, or young children.[37] Some of the tasks were more onerous: the house managers had to arrange the cleaning of the latrines, a job for which no one volunteered. The managers solved the problem by rotating the job among those who were not working full-time.[38] One Shinto woman cleaned the grounds daily, since that was a virtuous custom in her faith.[39]

Tad Fujita, the Berkeley Nisei whose father's arrival in America opened this book, was in his early thirties in 1942; in later years he remembered well the thankless tasks he did as a block manager. He and his wife had a child, and he also cared for his elderly parents in the adjoining stall. He recalled, "I had my own problems, yet I had to take care of the problems of all the other horse stalls. . . . I had to tend to [people's] needs, the ailing and the old people." The requests people made were varied. "Medication. Not enough. 'I didn't bring this, I didn't bring that. Can you get hold of that nurse and get it for me?'" Quickly he and the other managers organized a council, elected a chairman and secretary, and began to meet every morning at 8:30 A.M. to discuss common problems, meet people's needs, and report to the administration. Fujita said that the managers were well-respected by the people: they were the altruistic and the pragmatic members of the camp community, who had been businessmen, teachers, and officials in the YMCA or churches before the war.[40] They represented all religious groups and political factions and were both Nisei and Issei.

Not only were the block managers frequently unappreciated; some were labeled as stool pigeons, agitators, and even FBI agents. John Yoshino appealed to his Caucasian boss, George Greene, the head of public relations, to express his support for the managers and his appreciation for what they were doing. As the mood of the center deteriorated over time, they were the natural scapegoats when people's needs could not be met.[41] Yet without them the center could not have functioned, and the administrators knew well that the jerry-built system would break down entirely if they did not use the incarcerated to help run it.

The politics of the Japanese American community quickly adapted to the new conditions, with one dramatic change. Since most Issei leaders had been arrested by the FBI after Pearl Harbor, the new leadership was Nisei. Among the Nisei the most prominent were the members of the JACL, but they were controversial because of the organization's stand on the evacuation. The three writers for the JERS project described the JACL in words that captured some of the hostility many felt toward its members: "super patriotic, defensive, and subordinate to the Caucasians."[42] But JACL members were considered friendlier than other Nisei toward the Issei. Many Nisei used the following logic to blame the older generation for the incarceration: they should have known that language schools and a pro-Japan stance would irritate the Caucasians; therefore their actions brought shame and punishment on the entire community. The attitude of the anti-JACL factions toward the JACL is summed up in a note in the JERS files: "It is well known that they have left or rather placed key men in each of the camps in order to maintain their power and control. In Tanforan there is a small group of trusted men who had been leaders in the bay region. They meet secretly among themselves and what is planned at their meetings is not known to outsiders." The JACL members were between twenty-five and thirty-five years old, mostly Christian, and speakers of English interspersed with Japanese. They stuck to the "party line" of voluntary cooperation with the administration at all costs. Their JERS opponents acknowledged that they had not actually resorted to "red baiting"—taunting or ostracizing the more liberal elements as pro-communist—but they conveyed the possibility that they would.[43]

Was the hostility toward the JACL justified? Clearly, the young opponents of the JACL had their own biases, too. What the angry young Nisei wanted—opposition to internment—put them at odds with the JACL, which was undeniably accommodationist. However, the alternatives to its strategy must be weighed before judging the JACL too harshly. An unarmed, disliked ethnic minority with few friends in the majority community stood little chance against the U.S. Army, particularly when the legislative and judicial branches of the federal government as well as the states had for years ignored or rejected their case.

The JACL had strange bedfellows in the Nikkei members of the Communist Party. The CP supported the war against the fascists and advocated cooperation with the JACL; this was no time to fight one another, its members said, even though they decried the slowness of the JACL to respond to Pearl Harbor. Karl Yoneda, a member of the party and a writer for the *Doho* newspaper in San Francisco, recalled that the CP had earlier expelled its Issei members; his own union, the Longshoremen, was strongly opposed to militarist Japan. However, the party also dropped its Nisei members after Pearl Harbor, in order to prevent infiltration by fifth columnists. Yoneda considered this action an example of Earl Browder's own racism.[44]

The radical Nisei Oakland Young Democrats and their followers also opposed fascism. Ernest Iiyama and Anne and Michio Kunitani had announced after Pearl Harbor that they would participate in the evacuation if the military determined it was necessary. Only a few of the Young Democrats had actually been Communist Party members, and they were inactive because the Party had expelled them for their ethnicity. Kenji Fujii—like many of his friends, a radical when he was in camp—shared their sentiments; the evacuation was wrong, but for the time being opposition to it had to be subordinated to the defeat of the Axis.[45] Yoneda said that he and party sympathizers believed the "evacuation order" violated their constitutional and basic human rights, but opposing it would have been counterproductive, since an Axis victory would have cost them, as leftists, all their rights.[46] All radicals, whether party members or not, were violently antifascist and hence, during this period, pro–United Front; consequently, they were hostile to Japan and suspicious of Issei and the more militant Kibei. Older Kibei, like Karl Ichiro Akiya, who had left Japan in opposition to militarism, were leftists and some—notably Akiya—had been active in the party. (But Akiya did work for the Sumitomo Bank in San Francisco.) The leftist faction was scattered throughout Tanforan, meeting in the laundry room at night to "cook things up," as their opponents charged, or more likely, just to talk. Most had been white-collar or skilled workers before the war. Their favorite text was the magazine *The New Republic,* although a few preferred *The New Masses* or the San Francisco progressive newspaper *People's World.*[47] Since the Young Democrats thought the Issei were pro-Japan, they hated and in turn were hated by the Issei, who considered them all Communists—including their Kibei members.

The recognized leader of the Young Democrats at Tanforan was Ernest Iiyama, a Kibei from the East Bay. Iiyama was born in the United States but educated during the 1920s and early 1930s in Japan, where he absorbed radical political ideas. Like Akiya, he was strikingly different from Kibei educated later in Japan, who had absorbed militarism. Reflecting on this period, Iiyama recalled that the Young Democrats organized first in Los Angeles and San Francisco, but the northern group persisted after the southern group died out. At least half the members in the prewar years were from the University of California at Berkeley. The radicals faced the problem of attracting a following while competing with the stronger and larger JACL. Almost all the Young Democrats were evacuated to Tanforan. Iiyama, who was unable to afford college, had worked in a white-collar job before the war. Because he was older than the students and was bilingual, and also because he was a Kibei, he was able to win Issei support despite his political views.

The Young Democrats were, as Iiyama said, "idealist and all that. We had a feeling that we were doing something for the future . . . even though it was kind of scary at times."[48] He added that the Young Democrats were not numerous, probably no more than fifteen at most, but they had an influence far beyond their numbers.

⚜

The issue of self-government brought politics to the fore. The administration temporized, wanting leaders whom they could coopt and fearing a real opposition. Since the premise of relocation was couched in terms of "teaching democracy" to this alien people, some self-governing experience was deemed necessary, yet the army and the WCCA did not want to lose control of the camp. And many Nisei were in fact eager to participate, for this was the first time they had been permitted to compete for positions of prestige. At the outset the Issei were not allowed to take part, on the grounds that they were aliens, but this regulation soon changed. The administration also felt that participation by the inmates would make running the camps easier by enabling it to work more closely with the Nikkei. The issue demonstrates the inconsistencies of internment: the Nikkei were not criminals or ordinary prisoners; as American residents they were entitled to self-government but not too much because, after all, they were incarcerated. They could be trusted to exercise some forms of democracy but not, of course, the right of self-determination, because they were not free. The Nikkei who most appreciated this anomaly probably were the least inclined to participate, since by doing so they would have allowed themselves to be coopted, yet for many it was an opportunity to enjoy one of the benefits of democracy, running for and holding office. The result, at Tanforan, was a huge wrangle.

The first stage in the process of self-government was the election of a temporary council by a vote of the block managers; the council consisted of five men representing different areas of the center. Among those elected were the well-known Tad Fujita and the later arrival Kenji Fujii. The internees objected to the arrangement, however, because the temporary councilmen had not been directly elected by the entire population, and they raised questions about the candidates' qualifications and competence. General elections were called for, set, and then postponed when the first center director, William R. Lawson, was replaced. The JACL and a group around the Young Democrats, including Iiyama, pushed for early elections. Of the original councilmen, only Fujii supported the demands. Finally, rules were adopted that allowed all Nisei over the age of twenty-five to vote by precinct. The Young Democrats nominated Iiyama to run, thinking that, as a Kibei, he could attract the votes of the Kibei, who were unhappy over the administration's crackdown on gambling and would not support anyone who agreed with it.[49] The Issei, bitter and alienated because they were disfranchised, formed an underground council to serve as their pressure group. They were also angry that the single men (most of whom were Issei) had been summarily moved to barracks just because families had objected to their presence in the grandstand.[50] The election, held in June, was very emotional. The bilingual Iiyama capitalized on his strengths, despite red baiting by his opponents that marred the campaign. When he won, his Kibei supporters were jubilant and wanted to hold a victory parade, but Iiyama, recognizing the need for prudence, counseled against it. Although he was not a Marxist, some of the Kibei were, and he saw no point in antagonizing the conservative Issei and Nisei.[51]

The newly elected council drafted a constitution, swearing to uphold the U.S. Constitution, allowing voting by everyone (including Issei) over the age of twenty, selecting an executive council, and voting for members of an assembly. The council was given to understand it would function much as a city council, in effect administering the day-to-day concerns of Tanforan, but that it would not be able to sit in the meetings of the administration.[52]

This was probably the high point of Tanforan's sense of community, but even then the atmosphere was becoming turbulent. Problems between Nikkei and the Caucasian administrators began to reach beyond issues of food quality and housing. Censorship of the newspaper, the *Tanforan Totalizer*—another inconsistency inherent in the incarceration of a free people—also angered them. The administrators intended that, as elsewhere, center newspapers in Tanforan would be little more than bulletins where WCCA pronouncements could be published, but the staff members tried for more. They hoped to create an organ that would play the role of a real newspaper in a real community and to provide an authentic voice for the people. White opinion, of course, won out, and Japanese Americans were incensed. The election further increased tensions, and the center manager warned that "agitators" would be sent to a prison camp if tempers did not calm down. The resignation of the center director did not help, for his replacement was perceived by the Nikkei as even more anti-Japanese than he had been. The administration proceeded to blacklist the Nikkei it considered troublemakers, and ill will became rampant.[53]

The Nisei involved in center politics had placed great faith in self-government, only to see it shattered. The elections were no sooner held than they were voided, as the WCCA determined that no self-government would be allowed. On May 31, 1942, the chief of the reception center division, R. L. Nicholson, sent a memo to the manager of each assembly center marked "personal and confidential," in which he expressed "grave concern" that councils were attempting to develop real self-government. He stated, "It has never been my intention that these representatives should function in any way other than strictly advisory." He warned administrators to guard against attempts by councils to take over administrative or directorate responsibility.[54] In their advisory capacity, the councils could only offer opinions on innocuous topics: recreation, education, health, sanitation, lodging, food, work, personnel, religion, welfare, internal security, and discipline.[55] In other words, the center was a company shop, halfway between a company union and a prison. Accustomed to life in a democracy, the Caucasian administration was unwilling to rule totally without the consent of the governed, but the prison aspects of the situation predominated, as they did later in the ten relocation centers (i.e., concentration camps). True self-government was an interference with the basic intent of the internment.

❦

Over the remaining few months of Tanforan's existence the residents attempted to improve, however minimally, the quality of their lives. Maintaining their health, educating their children, learning new skills, working at various jobs, and participating in recreational opportunities gave some meaning to their lives. Meanwhile, the administration endeavored to make them tractable without being too overtly punitive. This boiled down to small matters of adjustment in the behavior of both prisoners and guards.

Health was one of the most pressing problems, especially given the haste with which the population had been moved and the congested and unsanitary conditions in which they were housed. One example suggests how terrible the situation was. Grace Fujimoto's grandmother had just been operated on for stomach cancer when the news came to evacuate their section of San Francisco. Despite her fragile condition, she was moved to a hospital in San Mateo, where Mrs. Fujimoto, her daughter, was unable to visit her. After a week she was removed from the hospital to join her family in the horse stalls at Tanforan, with their lack of heat, clean surroundings, and nearby sanitary facilities. One month later she was dead.[56]

One of the first public health concerns was to vaccinate the residents against typhoid and smallpox, and this was done before they entered Tanforan. The inoculations were not pleasant. Miné Okubo recalled, "For nights we heard groans in the stable. Almost everyone was sick from the typhoid shots."[57] The first occupants of Tanforan also suffered from a large outbreak of diarrhea, the result of unsanitary cooking utensils and strange food. Drawing as it did on the urban San Francisco population, Tanforan probably had a "better staff of doctors, dentists, optometrists and nurses, but the facilities were inadequate."[58] There was a chronic shortage of medicines; the clinics lacked equipment and were understaffed. There was no hospital in the center, so emergencies had to be sent to San Mateo. Childbirths took place at Tanforan, where infants were placed in wooden boxes that served as cribs, while their mothers lay in cots in empty barracks with no privacy. A premature infant died before the staff could clear up the red tape to transfer him to the county hospital, adding to the wrath the population bore toward their incarcerators.[59]

Eventually a number of clinics were established, with a Nikkei physician directing other health professionals, all of whom were supervised by the U.S. Public Health Service. The dental clinic functioned with an improvised chair and could only provide emergency service and fill teeth, even after six months of existence. The WRA reported in September that the staff had worked with "unusual skill and efficiency and under trying conditions" to achieve whatever facilities it had.[60] Even for a prison, health services were inadequate, and for a normal community, they ranked as downright primitive.

As Thomas James noted, attempts to set up schools at Tanforan paralleled the effort to establish self-government: "The schools taught democracy in the idealistic images of the educated Nisei, while camp residents tried to organize a community government and create a leadership."[61] Although the attempt at self-government was crushed by the WCCA, education met a happier fate. Everyone favored the establishment of schools, even though the evacuation had occurred in late spring, for no one relished the idea of thousands of children with nothing to do. Established in early June, the elementary, junior high, and high schools met in the mornings, five days a week, with teachers' meetings and training in the afternoons. The schools were entirely voluntary and were staffed by Nisei college graduates from the San Francisco Bay Area, not one of whom was a certified teacher. At first the students showed little respect for their teachers, but as high school principal Henry Tani noted, their disrespect stemmed less from Nisei inadequacies than from unfamiliarity with Nisei teachers in the classroom.[62] By the end of June, 40 percent of the Tanforan population was either going to school or teaching, with adults in classes learning Americanization as well as crafts and skills.[63] Art classes were especially popular since the Bay Area had a number of gifted painters, and soon Miné Okubo, Chiura Obata, and George and Hisako Hibi, among others, began to teach. By the time the population moved to Topaz, more than forty-five classes were underway. The students rejoiced, as Charles Kikuchi recorded, that they no longer had to attend Japanese-language schools. When high school students cleverly chose red and white as their school colors, an FBI agent promptly stopped them; the colors of Japan were too provocative for an American school to use.[64]

An elementary and a nursery school were also created, the latter established by Keiko Uchida, a graduate of Mills College. The facility was a filthy shack that Keiko and her sister Yoshiko had to clean, and on the first day they had only ten students, who braved a heavy rain to attend. At first both sisters taught there, but later Yoshiko moved to the elementary school. The purpose of the nursery school was not only to educate but also to give the children something to do and some place to play, aside from their horse stalls or barracks.[65]

One additional opportunity for higher education was presented by the National Student Relocation Committee Council, the outgrowth of efforts by liberal West Coast educators such as University of California president Robert G. Sproul and YWCA and YMCA leaders to help students pursue their educations. The council was formed in May by a group of whites from Berkeley and another from the American Friends Service Committee. It worked throughout the summer to place students in institutions willing to accept them. Once Nikkei were moved to Tanforan, it used a questionnaire to solicit college students for willing educational institutions in the East or Midwest. But the administration would not admit interviewers into the center to talk with people who wanted to participate, and few students were able to leave. Not many applicants had the funds to attend distant universities or colleges on their own, nor could they prove that the community where the college was located would accept them.[66]

The library also received help from friendly Caucasians, as well as from Japanese Americans. Starting with sixty-five volumes, with donations its holdings increased to more than six thousand books. More than four thousand people visited it every week. As Miné

Okubo wrote, the schools and library were "an effective counter-influence to the bad atmosphere of the camp."[67]

Adult education was also important, and many volunteered to teach others. Tomoye Takahashi started with a few adults who wanted letters written. Out of her small effort grew a program of Americanization, where a group of teachers taught folk songs, social skills, and other useful things to adults. Bilingual teachers were preferred; they were usually college educated, and most were experienced, having taught English to Kibei before the evacuation. Once the program was underway, they hoped to have about five hundred students and to be able to continue the classes in camp. Takahashi was not alone in noting that adult education built morale.[68] Although the classes taught Americanization, at the same time they intensified the "Japaneseness" of the residents by helping them to practice traditional skills like flower arranging (ikebana) and paper folding (origami). The association of so many Nikkei with only one another also served to reinforce their ethnicity. Although some took the opportunity to learn ways of surviving in white America and assumed that they would stay there, other Nikkei deliberately used only the Japanese language and began to think of going to Japan, where they felt they would be more welcome. The residents were soon offered the opportunity to do just that: a number—surprisingly large to the Caucasians—evinced an interest and a few hundred actually left on the same ship as a group of Japanese diplomats who were being returned to Japan in exchange for Americans caught there by the war.

❧

Recreation was another pressing need. As a JERS study pointed out, "the need of a well organized recreation program was greater in the assembly center than in a more permanent or normal community." Occupying leisure time was a major problem for people unused to sitting idly. The many who did not work in the few available positions had little to do all day, and those who were employed lacked a means of relaxing once the workday ended. Children quickly grew restless and disruptive. In a pattern that became common at Tanforan, the Nisei took the lead and the center management followed in solving this problem. Five young Nisei suggested developing a sports program, and the administration approved (although it first appointed a white director.) Three weeks later a program materialized, with basketball, baseball, boxing, tennis, board games, and the like. Sumo wrestling and the board games of go and *shōgi* also drew a good following; the administration preferred the Kibei and Issei to play them than to gamble. A talent show attracted more than three thousand spectators by its third week. To stress Americanization, a flag-raising ceremony was held May 24, with the pledge of allegiance and the national anthem followed by an invocation, greetings, and a history of the flag. The six thousand in attendance closed by singing "God Bless America."[69]

Dances were another popular form of recreation, but they created certain social problems. Mothers complained that their daughters were out too late, and the events had to be strictly "couples only" to prevent too much "mixing and matching" outside the parents' scrutiny. There were few other social problems, aside from gambling, but in every community the activities of some disturb others, and in Tanforan the presence of so many single males worried mothers, even after the men were removed from their first quarters in the grandstand. One unidentified mother wrote her caseworker that her daughter was pregnant and would not reveal who the father was. She asked that the Salvation Army take care of the baby since she did not wish to be associated with it. She claimed other mothers were also worried about their daughters: the administration could catch a lot of people out after curfew if it would only try, "and the mothers would be grateful." She concluded, "This camp is too easy going." If they could not have a strictly enforced curfew, she suggested, the males and females should be "separated by a high fence."[70] But hers was surely a minority opinion. Young people complained that there was no place to go for privacy and nowhere they could court.

Social relationships reflected the difficult conditions in a variety of ways. Few couples married at the center; most who were going together wed before the evacuation to avoid separation. Romances occurred, but most young Nisei women wanted to wait until after the war for a real church wedding, and the situation was hardly congenial to starting a married life. Yoshiko Uchida recalled the marriage of a teacher she knew, who dressed in a traditional white gown and was wed in the Protestant church at Tanforan. The couple was showered with rice and then "climbed into a borrowed car decorated with 'just married' signs and a string of tin cans." They drove around the racetrack a few times, held a reception, and began married life in a horse stall.[71] There were some divorces, but they tended to be hushed up. Parent-child conflicts were exacerbated by the close surroundings and the lack of privacy, and the parents often had to accept a child's rebellion or risk having him or her leave the family quarters, with the resultant loss of face.

There were other problems stemming from too much togetherness. One newlywed complained bitterly when her mother-in-law wanted to live in the same room with the bride and groom; the administrators favored keeping families together but this was too much. However, the worst complaints were usually over the daughter's late hours or the son's choice of friends.[72]

Far more taxing were the problems facing members of mixed marriages. Few Nikkei married out, since both legal and social pressures mitigated against it.[73] According to a JERS report, couples with a Japanese American husband and a Caucasian wife could leave the center if they then left the Western Defense Command. If they stayed there, both went to camp. If the husband were Caucasian and the wife Nikkei, both could stay in the WDC provided they had lived in a "white" environment. Adults of mixed blood who were American citizens could remain in the WDC if their environment was Caucasian, but couples where the husband was non-Japanese but not an American citizen had to leave. These rules did little to clarify the decisions made by the actual couples involved or to ameliorate the hardships endured by the children of such marriages, who belonged totally to neither culture. Nor did it express the unhappiness faced by families whose non-Japanese spouse remained outside the camp to work, who could visit the interned family but was unable to talk outside the prisonlike visitor's arrangements. The JERS reporters noted that Caucasian and Filipino spouses were ostracized by the Japanese.[74]

The closing of Tanforan in September 1942 brought the termination of its peculiar community. Rumors had circulated for weeks about where the residents would go, with the relocation centers rated in terms of the desirability of their climates. The residents were given no clues by the administrators, who probably had little information from Washington themselves. Topaz, with its desert climate, rated fairly low. Again the powerlessness of the inhabitants was emphasized by their lack of knowledge as well as their lack of choice in the matter. Families that had been separated by the assembly centers or prison camps remained separated in relocation camps, although some were reunited later. The anxiety of the internees as they faced another move was considerable.

In one of the many ironies of evacuation life, some of the Tanforan residents were able to make a last visit to their prewar homes to check on businesses or possessions. Miné Okubo related her feelings: "That one day of liberty was wonderful. I was like a child. I wanted to buy everything."[75] But for many the trip home was not so pleasant. Dave Tatsuno recalled years later that the couple to whom he had rented his small store had broken into the locked back room and basement and had taken the family car to Los Angeles. Tatsuno had to stay behind for a few extra days in order to make new arrangements for the family's possessions. His misfortunes were shared by many.[76]

There was no announcement of the impending move to Utah until just before the departure. Faith Terasawa recalled that she only learned they were going to Utah when they arrived at the train station.[77] But since her family was not among the first to depart, in fact everyone probably knew the destination by then. Several serious inspections signaled the inhabitants that a move was near, and they packed their possessions, more carefully this time, since their goods would be shipped by train. Crating the larger items the community had acquired, like the five thousand donated books in the library and the borrowed pianos and organs, was more difficult than packing personal possessions. All government property had to be returned. Each traveler was to wear his or her identification tag bearing the family number.[78] Again, they moved as prisoners and were carefully guarded.

❦

The train trip to Utah was a new experience for many Nikkei, who had never been on a train or traveled outside the Bay Area. The ubiquitous block managers served as many of the train managers and car captains needed for the trip. The evacuees moved east over a period of weeks as transportation became available. The trains were old, with velvet seats, antimacassars, and gas lamps; they often appeared to have been reactivated from some distant train graveyard for their unique journey. Many of the passengers later recalled the antiquated fixtures, which did not add to the comfort of the trip. The windows were closed with the shades drawn both for wartime security and to hide the movement of the imprisoned population. An Issei woman, Fumino Adachi, commented, "We were not allowed to raise the shades. It was reassuring to know that this was to foil an attack from the outside, but the thought of such an attack made us uneasy."[79] The Nikkei's last views of California were hidden by the night. The journey, which took two nights and a day, provided a nightmare conclusion to the first prison community at Tanforan and an introduction to the second at Topaz.

Many of the procedures and problems defined at Tanforan were amplified at Topaz, but there were many changes, too. Tanforan was temporary at the outset, an unfinished, prisonlike holding pen to contain the residents for a brief but indefinite period until the relocation centers were constructed. The residents were bound together there by ethnicity and the conditions of internment, and the frustrations surrounding the attempt at self-government and the alienation from the white administrators, who were themselves a very transient lot, doomed any attempt to create a community. Topaz, also unfinished when the occupants arrived, was built as a permanent camp that would last for the duration of the war. Yet its permanence was transitory in a way Tanforan's never was, for the resettlement program, which encouraged the evacuees to leave for new "free" locations, was introduced almost at the outset of this phase of relocation. Topaz was both more physically permanent than Tanforan and yet more ephemeral in the lives of some of its residents. Nevertheless, the Bay Area Japanese American community would be permanently transformed by its move there, to what was—in every sense of the phrase—a concentration camp.

Chapter Four

Welcome to Utah

The long trip to Utah in antiquated trains was an ordeal for young and old alike. Much about the journey reminded the Nikkei that they were prisoners. The trains, which took various routes over the Sierra Nevada, stopped once to let the travelers stretch their legs as they crossed the desert. Armed guards were posted every fifteen feet to keep them away from a narrow barbed wire barrier, hastily constructed next to the train. When they were underway, the curious peered out the windows despite the drawn shades, ordered closed from dusk to dawn, and the bleak vistas depressed them. Many became ill from the bumping and swaying. The journey took two nights and a day, time that passed slowly and uncomfortably despite the novelty of the experience. One traveler remembered being able to sleep only in "fits," about an hour at a time. In addition to the brief stop, they were allowed to move from car to car twice a day.[1] Sixteen trains ultimately moved the population of Tanforan to Topaz.[2]

Some Japanese Americans had vivid recollections of their journey. Kenji Fujii, appointed a monitor, remembered his train was called the "diarrhea train" for the illness that swept the inhabitants; one man was so sick he had to be removed in Sacramento.[3] Yoshiko Uchida recalled how the restrooms soon became intolerable. Artist Miné Okubo had more pleasant memories of the trip, such as the fresh citrus fruit provided by the WRA to keep them healthy, a generous touch to offset the discomfort of the journey. Eating in the dining car and being waited on by black waiters were novel experiences for her and her brother.[4] Tad Fujita was appointed a car captain by the Tanforan administration since he had been a block manager. His job was to watch over the occupants of his car, to help them get seated in an orderly manner, and to provide for their needs. While Fujii found his task involved few duties (he was to compile a master list of passengers; seat them in the order of their numbers; warn them to go to the latrine before leaving; provide them with ashtrays, blankets, and pillows; and bring books and magazines for himself),[5] Fujita remembered running from his car to others to take care of people's requests. Years later a man thanked him for bringing a blanket to his sick wife and arranging for her to sleep in a berth, but for the most part his efforts were soon forgotten.[6]

The advance contingent from Tanforan arrived in Utah on September 11, 1942. The first real group of evacuees reached Topaz September 17, and the last of the original residents came from the Santa Anita Assembly Center, arriving October 11. People filled the camp at the rate of five hundred new arrivals a day. The total population of Topaz in December 1942 included 550 from Santa Anita and 7,673 from Tanforan.[7] Those traveling from Tanforan crossed the salt flats and passed the Great Salt Lake, turned south at Ogden, and eventually reached the town of Delta, a settlement of more than 1,500 people in Millard County and a railhead of the Union Pacific line. From there they were bused to the prosaically named Central Utah Relocation Center, located fifteen miles away from Delta, near the tiny settlement of Abraham. Most came to call the relocation center Topaz, after Topaz Mountain, a local landmark at whose base the semiprecious gemstones could be found. From the name "Topaz" it was an easy step to the sarcastic label "the jewel of the desert," a slogan proudly printed at the top of the camp newspaper. The camp was surrounded by mountains: to the northwest, the Drum Mountains, from which strange noises emanated at night; to the west, the House Range; and to the east across the valley, the Fishlake Plateau. Topaz Mountain was nine miles northwest of the camp's center.

To people whose homes had been in the moist, green Bay Area, central Utah was a shock. The first disturbing feature was the desert, which seemed barren, with no water or greenery. Mormon pioneers had founded nearby Hinckley and Deseret in the 1880s, but the larger town of Delta had been settled by the railroad. It was a small farming community, created in 1907 under the Carey Land Act. Although it was a center of alfalfa seed production, the San Franciscans found it hard to believe that the drab surroundings could produce much of anything. Greasewood, a wiry gray shrub common to alkaline soils, was the dominant native vegetation that they saw, interspersed with carefully tended alfalfa fields. Then there was the weather. The evacuees arrived in the early fall, a dry time in Utah, and aridity coupled with wind produced dust storms. Morgan Yamanaka, a former student at San Francisco's Lowell High School who had come to Topaz from the Santa Anita Assembly Center, remembered, "There seemed to be a wall way out there; to see the blue sky and then the more you look at it, the wall seems to be moving. It was a dust storm rolling in, and it just engulfed you, and before you knew it, you could not see anything."[8]

Many of the later arrivals were greeted by a brass band, former Boy Scouts from Berkeley; this anomalous entertainment must have intensified their sense of estrangement from their new surroundings.[9] The band churned up irrepressible feelings of homesickness for Berkeley in Toyo Suyemoto Kawakami, who was one of the last of the Tanforan residents to arrive, entering camp on October 3.[10]

Although Miné Okubo also remembered the band, she was more amazed by the dust, which made an indelible impression on all the inhabitants. She wrote that it was "impossible to see anything through the dust. . . . When we finally battled our way into the safety of the building we looked as if we had fallen into a flour barrel."[11] Dave Tatsuno, whose father had owned a store in San Francisco's Nihonmachi, recalled it was like talcum powder, a white, fine film that was everywhere.[12] Faith Terasawa remembered that the alkali in the dust made her skin itch as though she had been burned.[13] The first task of the new residents was to clean their rooms, but the dust made this an almost endless occupation. Each barrack had only three brooms, and one layer of dust was quickly replaced by another.[14]

The desert climate was one of extremes, and temperature fluctuations of as much as 50 degrees in a day were common. The temperature ranged from 106 degrees in the summer to 20 below zero in the winter. The first residents to arrive saw frost only days after they left the trains, and the first snow fell on October 28. Yoshiko Uchida was shocked to find ice on the water they had left in their room overnight. Faith Terasawa, who had to care for her eighty-five-year-old father and eighty-two-year-old aunt, worried about the cold; they went to bed with their clothes on, but sleep was difficult. Winter snow kept the dust down until the paths between the barracks could be graveled, but it soon melted into a gooey muck. The cold in the uninsulated barracks was extreme and the wind blew unceasingly, summer and winter, working its way through the poorly constructed walls and depositing layers of dust. The rainfall averaged only seven to eight inches a year, making the area a true desert. Since the soil was nonabsorbent, any moisture just turned the ground into sticky mud.[15]

Even more important to the new arrivals were the facilities that awaited them at Topaz. The camp was constructed hastily between June 1942 and January 1943 by the San Francisco firm of Daley Brothers. The work was contracted by the Salt Lake District of the Mountain Division of the U.S. Corps of Engineers, and laborers came from the surrounding communities. The cost was $3,929,000; the WRA spent an estimated $1 million more for additional structures.[16] George Gentoku Shimamoto supervised an advance party of three hundred Japanese Americans from Tanforan that arrived in early September to complete the project. The group first finished the barrack where hospital cases were to be housed, to protect the patients from the severe chill of winter. Then they began to complete and winterize other essential buildings and partition areas for privacy.[17] But the camp was still incomplete when the evacuees from Tanforan began to arrive, and some barracks even lacked roofs.

Although the Japanese Americans were depressed by what they saw, Topaz was in many ways an improvement over Tanforan. There were no horse stalls, and thus no manure. The camp consisted of tar paper barracks, twelve to a block; there were thirty-four

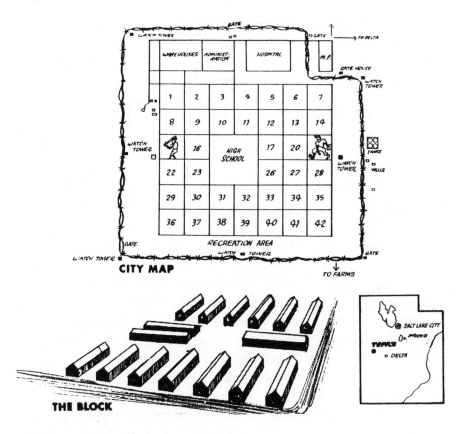

4. The Central Utah Relocation Camp
Reprinted by permission of the artist, Miné Okubo.

blocks for housing and the remainder for administration. At its high point there was a total of 408 buildings at Topaz. The construction was pine board sheeting covered with tar paper. Even the Deltans noticed the shoddiness. "The sheeting had cracks at least a quarter of an inch between each board. . . . No insulation whatsoever. . . . There were bare [light] bulbs, eight to every hundred and twenty feet [in length], and that's all the wiring was. Just one wire down the length and a switch over by the door . . . one per apartment. . . . There were no concrete foundations under the barracks," recalled Roger Walker, a former serviceman who worked at the camp during its final year. He wondered at the minds of the people who had built such structures in the desert, where the wind would blow under them all the time. "It is really difficult to see how they survived."[18] Fujii remembered putting a sheet on the floor to stop the wind from blowing through the cracks and seeing it puff up like a balloon when anyone opened the door.

Each barrack was divided into very small rooms, each intended for a family or four or five unrelated individuals. The rooms had no inner walls, although later, in December, they were finished with gypsum board.[19] Although the area was frequently plagued by mosquitoes, there were no screens.[20] There also were few window panes. During the construction phase, the first six weeks or so, two families or as many as eight bachelors were crowded into a single room. Ultimately each barrack was divided into six rooms, which ranged in size from 16 by 20 feet to 20 by 25 feet. The new arrivals found that their quarters were furnished only with cots. At a central location they obtained tick bags (which were soon exchanged for cotton mattresses) and two blankets apiece, insufficient for the winter's cold, and even in early October the nights were chilly. To obtain a little privacy the residents fashioned partitions from sheets or blankets. They were provided with pot-bellied stoves for the rooms, which were unloaded from trucks in front of the barracks and had to be hauled inside. Everyone had to grab what coal they could from a pile occasionally deposited outside on the road. The latrines and the bathing and washing facilities were located in a separate central building in each block, but they too were unfinished; the toilets lacked seats and often doors. There were to be four bathtubs for the women and four showers for the men in each block, but these were not immediately available. For older residents, learning to use a shower was an unpleasant experience. The first residents nonetheless fared far better than the later arrivals, who found no rooms remaining and had to sleep on cots in empty mess halls, laundries, and the corridors of the hospital until the work on the barracks was completed. Yoshiko Uchida recalled that "one unfortunate woman received second degree burns on her face when boiling tar seeped through the roof onto the bed where she was asleep."[21]

Creating individual living space was an immediate necessity for the newly arrived residents, at least a third of whom received unfinished quarters. Dave Tatsuno recalled having to help complete the installation of the gypsum board. Roscoe Bell, chief of the agricultural division, described work parties held by the residents, but even after the plasterboard was in place there were still many air leaks.[22] Mel Roper, a teacher from Delta who watched the construction of the camp, thought it shoddy and "very inappropriate for the type of weather that these people were to live in."[23] The temperature dropped below zero on several occasions that first winter, and the barracks were not insulated. The pot-bellied stoves provided some heat, but much of the warmth escaped up the crude chimneys. Ill health was a constant companion to all residents, Nikkei and Caucasian alike, recalled Eleanor Gerard Sekerak, one of the teachers at Topaz High, who, like many of her students, had come from Berkeley. One early arrival commented on October 3 that "everyone seems to have diarrhea, heat exhaustion, or colds."[24]

Residents had to build chests or shelves for their possessions from scrap lumber, some of which the administration provided; the inhabitants pilfered the rest of what they needed as internal security looked the other way. This became a veritable sport for the men and boys. Tom Kawaguchi recalled how he and his brother would "sneak out at night and steal scrap lumber. . . . Everybody was doing it," a proposition seconded by Ken Fujii and others. The director of internal security, Ted Lewis, told his future bride that he allowed the residents to take boxes and lumber to divide their rooms because "the sexes and ages were all mixed inside."[25] Obtaining nails was more difficult; they had to be saved from any boxes that came into camp.[26] Toyo Suyemoto Kawakami remembered that her father "made a table and stools of varying heights from scrap lumber."[27] Maya Nagata Aikawa, whose father had died before the evacuation, never forgot how difficult it was for her, her mother, and her sisters to obtain such amenities. She recalled, "We didn't have any [shelves]. We used the two-by-fours which were a part of the framework of one room." Boxes became their tables until friends built them some furniture.[28]

Obtaining lumber for furniture was not without its perils. Lee Suyemoto, who was a teenager in Topaz, remembered that when he and a friend went out to find wood, a guard pointed his rifle at them and shouted, "Stop!" Lee continued the story, "And we stopped and he clicked his rifle at us and said 'Get the hell out of here.'" The guard, probably a civilian since the boys were inside the fence, sounded drunk to Lee, but whatever his condition, the two frightened youths ran away. Many later asked just what kind of people the guards were.[29]

All meals were in a central dining hall, one for each block. (The camp director told the residents that they were no longer to refer to it as a "mess.") In time, the camp also included a community auditorium, a gymnasium, canteens, schools, libraries, churches, a post office, and a fire station. There were athletic fields near the schools and south of Topaz City and a fifteen-acre community garden plot. The cemetery was never used; instead the 144 people who died at Topaz were cremated and their ashes ultimately returned to the Bay Area after the war.[30]

The food was sufficient for the adults, even if it hardly qualified as either typical Japanese or good American cuisine. The first meal for many was cauliflower, mashed potatoes, rice, stewed meat, bread, cabbage salad, milk, and an apple. Yoshiko Uchida reported that, because of a lack of refrigeration, many residents got diarrhea from eating spoiled food, but in her area meals were skimpy and the hungry residents were not too choosy.[31] The WRA food allowance was 45 cents a day per evacuee, lower by a nickel than the military allowance, but it was reportedly cut down to 31 cents a day at Topaz, partly because of the cattle and hog raising at the center. Typically, food is a major source of complaints in an institutional setting, and at Topaz many were unhappy over the frequency with which liver, tripe, or other organ meat was served. These were considered inedible in Japanese culture. The residents sought to meet their own food needs by obtaining permission to open a plant to manufacture tofu; it was in operation by the end of February

1943. Some 1,500 pounds of tofu were produced each week, supplying all the dining halls.[32] Water was obtained from three wells, which produced an almost undrinkable alkaline beverage. The new residents were warned to eat a lot of salt with their food as a protection against heat exhaustion.[33] There were the usual digestive problems associated with strange food and water: Kenji Fujii described the resulting complaint as the "Topaz trots."[34] A local doctor made a concoction to counteract the affliction; it was sold at the drugstore in Delta until 1984 and called the "TT mix"—with the first T standing for Tokyo.[35]

❧

The camp was constructed to house 9,000 people, but its top population was only 8,232, still enough to make it the fifth largest city in Utah. A total of 11,212 people were admitted over its three-year history. There were 4,434 males and 3,798 females.[36] Many things set the camp apart from the normal small town, but most noticeable was the surrounding barbed wire fence interspersed with guard towers. It was under construction when the first internees arrived. Residents were repeatedly reminded not to approach the fence, which was also patrolled. An enclosed area in one corner of the compound housed the military police. For most of Topaz's history there were 3 to 5 officers and 85 to 150 men stationed there. The guards checked the credentials of every person entering or leaving the camp. Every quarter of a mile, searchlights were set in the guard towers, where squads or detachments of armed men were positioned.[37]

The administration ultimately occupied eight blocks located some distance away from Topaz town, where the internees were held. The administrators resided in barracks in this compound: the senior officials on one side of a barrack; the more junior people, such as teachers, on the other. The main administration building initially contained offices for the mail service, files, transportation, personnel, food service management, the carrier service, Western Union, the switchboard, and the deputy and the assistant director. Another building housed the project director and his assistant, the attorney, and offices for community services, project reports, community welfare, education, and statistics. The relocation and employment officer was in an annex that joined these two buildings. There were separate buildings for the post office and the fire department, the fiscal offices, and relocation and placement. Approximately two hundred Caucasians supervised and staffed the various divisions; about half came from nearby towns, while the remainder lived at the relocation center. Some sent their children to school in Delta, and others educated them with the Nisei. Many attended religious services at the camp's Protestant facilities.

Roscoe and Gladys Bell came to Topaz from Berkeley, California, where he had worked for the State Agricultural Board. At first they lived in Delta, since they had four children and could not be accommodated at Topaz. The Bells' eldest son, Paul, attended Delta High School for a year before the family moved to Topaz. Roscoe Bell described their Topaz housing in a memoir he wrote years later. Since they were a large family, they were assigned a suite of three rooms, with a stove, a picnic-style table, and beds. In 1944 staff apartments were completed on the grounds, and they then had a suite of very small rooms composed of a kitchenette, a furnace room, a living-dining room, and a small bedroom, plus a "passageway" bedroom and a bath. The two older boys had to room in the bachelor's quarters nearby. Paul attended Topaz High School, his brother Earnest the junior high, and Gordon and Winifred the elementary schools. The Bells, who had known and liked Japanese Americans when they were in California, had been horrified as they watched the evacuation and felt they could best help by taking employment in the relocation camp.[38] They became friends with many of the internees, in part because they were involved in religious activities in camp. Bell described the services as "very meaningful to us because of the enthusiasm and meaningful Christianity that was practiced by the church members."[39] One of the best-liked administrators, he directed agricultural activities and later became assistant director, and his wife Gladys taught music and helped found a USO group at Topaz.

Eleanor Gerard also came to Topaz from California. She recalled that she had been forewarned by Lorne Bell (no relation to Roscoe) not to expect much of the physical arrangements at Topaz, for it was after all an internment camp. She did not complain about her quarters, but she never did get used to the "dust storms and the sticky, slippery mud that followed rain." She soon met Emil Sekerak, who was a conscientious objector from Ohio and—unlike her and the Bells—had never seen a Japanese American before. As single people (they married after the war), they shared housing with roommates. Emil, who organized the camp cooperative and later headed the relocation office, had the singular distinction of being the lowest-paid employee at camp. As a CO, he earned $5 a month.[40]

There were twenty-nine Caucasians in place as of October 1, 1942.[41] Unlike the transients who directed Tanforan, many of the white staff members remained throughout most of the camp's life although the teaching staff did have a high turnover. There were two directors, first Charles Ernst and then Luther T. Hoffman, who replaced Ernst in 1944. The War Relocation Authority, which administered the camps, noted that selecting key personnel was "something like the paneling of a jury." The agency sought to find men who had not formed opinions on the major issues of the program, who did not have "marked antipathies against all persons of Japanese descent" but were not what they termed "overly emotional" about the "plight of the evacuated people." The WRA historians noted the difficulty of that task; many of the administrators had never known Japanese Americans before, and those from the West Coast who did had already formed opinions about them.[42] Everyone remembered Pearl Harbor. It was easy to confuse Japanese Americans with the Japanese enemy, but it was also hard not to learn to like the people with whom one worked. The WRA's success in picking the right people for this unparalleled task was at best mixed. Some administrators who began as dispassionate bureaucrats came to sympathize with the plight of the evacuees. Others found it difficult to overcome their racial attitudes, and still others found the harsh desert environment itself hard to accept. Paul Bell described the administrators as running the "full spectrum" from very racist to extremely empathic, but he remarked that the real racists did not last long. Many of the Cau-

casians debated heatedly with one another whether the evacuation
was an unchallengeable "military necessity"; to Roscoe Bell it was
just the result of economic greed on the part of the Californians.
Working at Topaz was for such people "doing their part" in the
war effort.[43]

Many Utahns at Topaz had not known Japanese Americans
before the war, and they approached their jobs with apprehension
about working with this apparently dangerous minority group.
Claud Pratt, head counselor of the welfare section and later assistant director of relocation services, was one Utahn sensitized by
the camp experience. He described how he and his wife "had
somewhat ambivalent feelings about the work. We tried to feel
comfortable about the decision of our government to remove these
people from their homes on the West Coast. But we could not help
feeling a great sympathy and empathy for them." He became
friends with the people with whom he worked, attending their
weddings and, like the Bells and the Sekeraks, keeping in touch
with them for years after the war. Although the Pratts did not
believe there had been any military necessity for the evacuation,
they differed sharply from most Utahns, including Governor Herbert Maw.[44]

❧

One Nisei student described the first group of administrative arrivals for the JERS records. Foremost in the Topaz administration
was Director Charles F. Ernst, a Harvard graduate from Boston
who had begun his career in settlement house work. He had worked
in unemployment relief in Seattle, a center of the West Coast
Japanese American population, then had gone to Chicago, and
finally to Washington, where he was employed by the American
Red Cross. Ernst joined the War Relocation Authority in August
1942, when he was in his mid-forties; he was assigned to Topaz.
The director impressed the JERS informant with his "sincerity and
caring attitude" and seemed to have been well-liked by the residents, at least at the outset.[45] Yoshiko Uchida described him as a
"kind and understanding man of considerable warmth," who wel-

comed the evacuees (whom he insisted on calling "residents") to
Topaz.[46] The Nikkei appreciated it when Ernst ordered the staff to
drive the thirty-mile round trip daily from Delta instead of pre-
empting the limited housing.[47] Eleanor Sekerak remembered him
and his wife as "typical Bostonians, very dignified." His wife always
wore a hat and gloves, and he was a "perfect gentleman," who
roundly criticized any Caucasian who called the residents "Japs."[48]

Not all of the staff members shared this admiration for the
director. Roscoe and Gladys Bell remembered that he kept a garden
in front of his residence filled with cacti to keep the children and
Japanese Americans out. He was, they recalled, very status-
conscious and preserved a distance even from the whites who
reported to him. Ernst resigned in 1944 to take a position with the
United Nations Relief and Administration. Oscar Hoffman, the
community analyst, believed that Ernst's arrogance and aloof attitude had created a "caste system . . . between the administration
and the residents." Hoffman, a native of Kansas, had studied for
the ministry before switching fields and earning a Ph.D. in sociology
from the University of North Carolina at Chapel Hill. He was too
old for the draft and took the position of community analyst in
1943 because he needed a job and that one sounded interesting. He
moved his family to Topaz, replacing Weston LaBarre, an anthropologist who was drafted after a few months of work at the camp.
Hoffman's dislike for Ernst began virtually the day he arrived. The
director had seen no need for an inquisitive social scientist on his
staff and did not want LaBarre's position to be filled. According to
Hoffman, Ernst feared that the analyst's reports to WRA headquarters in Washington would challenge his own interpretation of
his administration. Hoffman also felt that the proper Bostonian did
not have sufficient empathy with the plight of the internees; years
later he still found Ernst "weak . . . in his sensitivity to a sorely
wounded people." Whereas Eleanor Sekerak thought Ernst even-
handed and cordial toward residents and staff alike and caring
toward the Japanese Americans who worked for him, Hoffman and
Bell considered him cold and standoffish. The residents who did not
have personal contact with the man seemed to have been simply
indifferent to him.[49] Ernst's successor, Luther T. Hoffman, was a

career bureaucrat who had worked in the Bureau of Indian Affairs before the war. He had been the assistant chief of the WRA relocation division in Washington before coming to Topaz.[50] Oscar Hoffman recalled him as an administrator who had "pets" among the staff and gave great power to those few he liked. Eleanor Sekerak typified him as a bureaucrat who saw Topaz as just another Indian reservation to be pacified. The residents were indifferent to him as well, especially since his tenure coincided with their final year in camp, when they were overwhelmed with concerns about their future in the outside world.[51]

The other administrators received mixed approval ratings. James F. Hughes, the first assistant director, opposed Ernst's decree that some whites should commute from Delta until the housing shortage abated, implying that he placed the needs of Caucasians first. Lorne Bell (no relation to Roscoe) was from Los Angeles and had worked for the YMCA before coming to Topaz. He supervised welfare, camp self-government, religious activities, education, the library, and recreation. He impressed the residents with his competence and piety; one of the JERS recorders noted that Bell, like the Roscoe Bells and the Sekeraks, attended Protestant services with the Japanese Americans. Lorne Bell returned to YMCA work after a few years at Topaz. Eleanor Sekerak recalled that Ernst, Roscoe Bell, and Lorne Bell made a "great team." Another whose kindness prompted fond memories from some of the evacuees forty years later was George LaFabreque, a former resident of Sacramento who directed welfare. He was described as "full of energy; he [had] a fair and unselfish attitude with a tolerant understanding of his job."[52] Claud Pratt also worked closely with the families of Topaz and was sympathetic to them.[53]

Several of the initial appointees could not tolerate the circumstances at Topaz and soon left; the draft took others. Another Berkeleyan, Arthur Eaton, was a University of California graduate and had known many of the evacuees in college. He headed housing, a sensitive position and already a problem area when the first residents arrived. The JERS reporter noted he was "likeable, but a little young for his job." His arrival a week late "accounted for all the trouble at housing," the observer added. The draft ended

Eaton's brief tenure. The chief steward, Brandon Watson, also started off badly. He did not take suggestions well, and in the first few days a strike occurred in food service "because people did not like him."[54] He also did not last long.

Oscar Hoffman occupied an ambiguous position. His job description required him to report to Washington on the nature of the Nikkei and their reactions to internment, and this necessitated his getting to know them as individuals. He prepared detailed reports that he sent weekly to Dillon Myer's office, as well as special studies on topics of concern to the camp administration. Although his academic background qualified him to be an objective and dispassionate observer, his religious training sensitized him to the tribulations of the people around him. Fumi Hayashi remembered him as one who always watched them, as indeed he did. However, Michiko Okamoto, who briefly worked for him, felt he was a considerate and well-meaning man, and she never forgot how he urged her to relocate and leave the camp, an action that helped her to break a cycle of depression. As he recalled at the age of ninety-two, "I was convinced beyond any doubt that evacuation and internment were uncalled for. There was no military necessity. I have never thought there was." He held a difficult and controversial position and tried only to do his best, and his reports on camp life are a valuable and perceptive source for the scholar, whatever their original purpose.[55]

As the months passed the relationship between administrators and evacuees became established. The Caucasians made friends or kept their distance, as they saw fit. The Japanese Americans for their part rated each new administrator according to his or her degree of "Jap-hating" or friendliness. The ideal was a Caucasian who was empathic, humanistically inclined, aware of but not identified with any particular clique, yet attuned to the differences between the governors and the governed.

⚜

The handbook *Welcome to Topaz,* prepared by the early evacuees for incoming residents, informed them that the residents were mainly urbanites from the cities of the Bay Area, San Francisco and Oakland, and the small communities of the East Bay and the peninsula as far south as Menlo Park. Only 248 were farmers; the rest were professionals, semiprofessionals, managerial and office workers, nursery workers, fishermen, and forestry and unskilled workers.[56] This community of city dwellers from the lush Bay Area was now to attempt to create a farming community in the desert.

The parameters of the town of Topaz were already being defined, and Oscar Hoffman attempted to describe them. He noted that the Japanese Americans were incarcerated in Topaz, but it was a unique form of captivity and they were anything but typical prisoners. The Nikkei were not people who would submit passively to the whims of a white administration, even if they had accepted relocation itself with minimal objections. They were well educated, mostly successful businesspeople who had done well by asserting themselves. They would "bitterly resent what they called being 'pushed around,'" Hoffman told Myer, and he noted with unconscious irony that the Topaz Nikkei would demand "more of relocation than [would] most other elements of the population." (Since he only worked at the one camp, he really was not in a position to compare its residents with those of other camps.) The Nikkei had identified and obtained rights at Tanforan that they did not intend to lose. They would not work at tasks that were "subject to the will and whims of an employer," for they were used to being independent entrepreneurs. No matter how much such people wanted to start again outside camp, wartime conditions (not to mention discrimination) posed so many obstacles that they "often despaired of resettlement." Such "proud and confident" individuals would insist on more competent administrators than would Japanese Americans "less experienced in the ways of urban America" or not as well educated. They would, consequently, demand a good school system, for they valued education highly.[57]

One can deduce from Hoffman's notes that the community of Topaz differed from the other nine relocation centers in some specific ways. Dave Tatsuno commented, "They said that we were put into camp for our own protection, but the machine guns and army rifles were turned not out, but inward."[58] This description was true of all the camps; nevertheless, the great majority of Topaz's inhabitants did not at the outset resist their incarceration but resolved to make the best of it. The Reverend Joe Tsukamoto told a group that they could either accept internment as part of the experiences of wartime, or they could turn Topaz into an Indian reservation and just sit around. There was never any question of their choosing the second option.[59] But neither would they respond passively to arbitrary actions on the part of the administration.

The Topaz manner of resistance was rarely violent, as its history was to show, but it did include opposition to what was perceived as unwarranted authority. The community forged by the Japanese Americans at Topaz was a peculiar blend of self-government and individual initiative coupled with submission to a Caucasian authority that was, if ultimately absolute, rarely dictatorial or coercive. The morale was never high and it declined with time, but most never gave in to total apathy. The rulers ruled with the cooperation of the ruled except in one matter—the insistence of the administration that they should leave camp for the outside world. Topaz became such a secure environment that it was, for many, home.

Japanese Americans had lived in Utah long before the establishment of Topaz, a small minority in a predominantly Caucasian and Mormon society. The first Japanese were temporary residents, prostitutes brought in during the early 1880s to serve Chinese and Caucasian railroad workers. Men came later in the decade to work on railroad gangs. One of the first permanent arrivals was Y. Hashimoto, a labor agent sent to recruit railroad workers; he brought along his nephew, Edward Daigoro Hashimoto. The younger Hashimoto founded a company to supply section gang workers for the railroads, and he also provided them with Japanese food and helped them with their other needs. By 1904 the Salt Lakers were calling him the city's Mikado.[60]

Most Japanese who lived outside Salt Lake City worked either in farming or as railroad section hands and laborers. By 1909 the

Report of the Bureau of Immigration, Labor, and Statistics determined that there were 1,025 Japanese farm workers in Utah, mostly
laborers who had turned to that occupation in preference to railroad work; the majority of the Japanese immigrants still remained
in railroading. Hashimoto, in addition to his activities as a railroad
labor agent, owned several farms where he employed other Issei to
raise sugar beets. Issei farmers produced celery and strawberries as
well.[61]

Utah's Nikkei were urban as well as rural; a Nihonmachi was
established in Salt Lake City in the late 1880s, with shops, boarding
houses, and restaurants. The community had its own newspapers,
the *Rocky Mountain Times* (founded in 1907) and the *Utah Nippo*
(founded in 1914). The Issei and their children lived in a close-knit
Japantown with their own places of worship, groceries, Japanese-
language schools, and a tofu factory. There were 2,936 Japanese
American residents in 1920.[62] However, the community lost 1,059
people during the interwar years; many returned to Japan, while
others went back to California.[63] Utah offered limited agricultural
opportunities, and its small Nikkei community had fewer employment possibilities than the larger Japanese settlements in Los Angeles, San Francisco, or Seattle could provide.

The Salt Lake Nikkei did not mingle with the surrounding Caucasian community except for business dealings, and they apparently
met with far less harassment than other immigrant groups did.
Hashimoto, by 1920 an established businessman with many interests, was well known. Another Issei leader, Henry Y. Kasai,
worked to abolish discrimination in Salt Lake's restaurants and
swimming pools. Although most Nikkei residents were Buddhist,
a Japanese Church of Christ was established in 1918, and some
Japanese Americans converted to the relatively tolerant Mormon
faith, like the man who became the community's most well-known
product, Mike Masaru Masaoka. Masaoka's work with the JACL
helped bring other members of the Salt Lake Nisei community into
the fledgling organization.[64] (After World War II there were two
branches in Salt Lake City, one Mormon, one not.)

Delta, the future site of Topaz, also had some limited experience
with Japanese Americans before the war. Daigoro Hashimoto

briefly owned a sugar beet farm there. The Imai family resided in Delta at the time of the evacuation; daughter Masi and her siblings attended the local schools while their father worked for the railroad (they were, of course, not interned).[65] Other small towns where Japanese Americans lived included Price, where many worked as coal miners, and Ogden.

The outbreak of World War II brought fear to Utah's small Japanese American community as it did the West Coast; they did not know what to expect of their Caucasian neighbors. Dr. Edward I. Hashimoto, son of the Issei businessman Daigoro, told the students of his anatomy class at the University of Utah on the day after Pearl Harbor not to stare at him; wearing a tam o'shanter, he joked that "I'm Irish. I was home in Dublin at the time!" The popular professor encountered no problems.[66] But few had as much courage as he did, and most kept a low profile. The Caucasian population's reaction was mixed; there were incidents of kindness on a personal level as well as discrimination in the economy at large. Railroads and mines were classified war industries, and Japanese American laborers lost their jobs. Henry Kasai was termed a "dangerous" community leader and interned with other prominent Issei, first in Montana and then in New Mexico; he left his wife Alice and six children to fend for themselves, a task made even more difficult by the freezing of their funds in a Japanese-owned bank.[67]

Fred Wada's Keetley colony was a unique success story. In addition, many families, like Nobu Miyoshi's, made the trek individually. Both the Miyoshis and the Wada group found the Mormon people courteous and friendly once the initial barriers had been broken. The state government began to relax its hostility toward the voluntary migrants as they gained a reputation as good workers.

Governor Maw initially hesitated to let Japanese Americans move to Utah. In January 1942, when the "Japanese problem" was being widely debated in the nation, he convened a meeting of county representatives to discuss the matter of voluntary evacuees. He found that all but two of the officials opposed Japanese settlement; they passed resolutions expressing the fear that white-owned land might be confiscated by the federal government for labor camps and the worry that the Japanese Americans might commit sabotage. The American Legion, the Veterans of Foreign Wars, and other groups passed similar resolutions. Lacking any direct contact with the Nikkei, the white community feared that Utah would become a dumping ground for people the West Coast feared and disliked. Positive experiences gradually changed their minds.

Most citizens of Delta were too far removed from the problem to share the Salt Lakers' strong sentiments, but some found the establishment of a camp at Topaz suspicious or even frightening. LaVell Johnson, historian of Millard County, commented that "we were afraid of the Japanese in the camp. I don't know why. It seems strange now that we were." She was speaking more than thirty years later, when the Topaz site had been nominated for the State Register of Historic Sites.[68] Others were not afraid to profit from the government's decision. Homer U. Petersen had been working with George S. Ingraham's agricultural interests in the Delta area since 1939. The two operated or sold 110-15 farms taken over from farmers who failed during the Depression. Petersen told Jane Beckwith, a Delta high school teacher whose father and grandfather ran the local paper, that the WRA had investigated sites in the Delta area in January or February 1942, looking for locations for possible relocation camps, but had rejected the area for fear the water supply was inadequate. The *Millard County Chronicle* reported the search in its May 28 issue, noting that the WRA had investigated the potential location and mapped it without even informing the owners. Petersen and his father, who held seven to eight thousand shares of water in the area,[69] went to San Francisco to convince the WRA that they could deliver the amount necessary to plant a town. The Petersens had purchased most of the water around Abraham, Utah, for $7.50 a share, but the appraiser set the price at $20.00 a share and after much negotiation the government accepted that figure. The WRA ultimately acquired 20,000 shares of water; three deep wells were dug, producing water that was considered drinkable, and reservoir water was available to irrigate crops.[70]

The land around Abraham consisted of some 1,400 acres that were in the public domain and federally owned, 8,840 acres of county property, and 9,760 acres that were in private hands. Some had reverted to the county during the 1930s for nonpayment of taxes; several privately owned parcels had been acquired by a New York syndicate during the Depression for failure to pay interest on loans. The Central Utah site was selected in late June 1942. On June 25 the residents of Delta learned that a "Japanese Center of 10,000 people" was to be built on 19,000 acres in nearby Abraham. The government paid a dollar an acre for the land that it condemned for the camp.[71] Some of the owners were pleased with what was a relatively good price for land that might, in good years, grow alfalfa or sugar beets, but one owner, Sherman Tolbert, complained that he had been "forced" to sell recently acquired farmland at a price so low that it was virtually being "confiscated" by the federal government. Tolbert remained embittered by the experience and believed ever after that the federal government "coddled" the people they incarcerated on his land.[72]

Most residents of Delta were advised that even during construction the camp would be patrolled by jeep "to keep check on the people therein" and subsequently the army would provide armed guards for the internees, who would have little contact with the local people. All precautions would be taken so that no one could escape, although the Japanese would have maximum freedom inside the camp. Many jobs would be provided for Millard County residents during the construction of the camp, and the WRA would also rent necessary equipment locally. The WRA expected it would need 1,200 men to work twelve hours a day, six days a week, to complete the six hundred buildings deemed necessary. Although the cost was expected to be about $3 million, the money would not simply be wasted on the Japanese, because the government planned to use the camp after the war as a rehabilitation facility for returned soldiers and as a showplace to demonstrate the latest in agricultural methods. Topaz was expected to be ready for occupancy in sixty days. It was to be self-sustaining, with an economy based on agriculture and whatever industry could be done by hand. Since workers had been allowed out of some relocation camps and assembly centers to relieve the shortage of agricultural labor, the Delta residents were advised that this labor might be available in Utah as well. In any case, the WCCA added, "The community has nothing to fear from the camp."[73] Construction began in early July.

&

Although most Japanese Americans from the San Francisco Bay Area were moved first to Tanforan and then to Topaz, the army did not relocate all its charges so smoothly or simply. Some Bay Area Nikkei, like Charles Kikuchi, were sent elsewhere: Kikuchi went from Tanforan to Gila River, Arizona, a move he requested because of his work recording events for JERS. Others, such as the Kitano and Yamanaka families, went to Santa Anita. The Tanforan and the Santa Anita groups did not merge well at the outset, testimony to the strong sense of community identity each group developed during the six-month assembly center period. When the Santa Anitans arrived at Topaz, they too received unfinished housing. Their belongings were soaked in the rain while completed barracks designated as the high school lay vacant. This situation did not sit well with the Santa Anitans, some of whom "took crowbars and sticks and went after Art Eaton, the head of housing, for not providing them with finished rooms and necessities."[74] Violence was averted, and a mass meeting was quickly convened to discuss the problem. Its tone gradually changed from anger to community spirit when the Reverend Taro Goto, the leader of the Japanese Methodist Mission Conference in America before the evacuation, rose to lead the group in song.[75] Then the camp administrators were introduced and entertainment followed. The protest rally had by chance coincided with another meeting already scheduled to welcome the new arrivals.[76]

Yet despite this appearance of unity, the two groups tended to remain separate communities. But they were closer to each other than they were to the group of a thousand Hawaiian Japanese that arrived at Topaz the next year, complete with ukuleles. The Hawaiians spoke their own pidgin dialect and appeared very "Japanesy" to the Americanized Nisei. Roscoe Bell recalled that the largely Kibei group had been interned at Sand Island, near Honolulu, as "Japan sympathizers" before being moved to the mainland. (Only a very small portion of Hawaii's Japanese were interned.) Bell said, "They were viewed with suspicion by the others and were considered potential troublemakers."[77] The treatment of the Hawaiian Japanese at Sand Island gave ample reason for those people to be depressed and angered; imprisonment there had been intended to break their spirits, and only the most resistant were shipped to mainland internment camps. Their treatment at Sand Island was far worse than the Nikkei had experienced at Tanforan, and their reaction to life in Topaz differed markedly as well.[78]

The evacuees who were moved from Tule Lake to Topaz during the segregation crisis there fit in better than the Hawaiians: they were Nikkei who had decided to stay in the United States, and their attitudes were much more "American" than those of the islanders. The Hawaiians remained apart, and most of them eventually went to Tule Lake and from there to Japan after the war.

The divisions between Issei and Nisei created a larger schism than the minor tensions between populations from differing assembly centers or Hawaii; the generation gap affected everything from food preference, language, and custom to attitudes about the war. These points of contention added to the difficulties of camp life, with its lack of privacy, social amenities, and relative poverty, and produced a community that was "a goldfish bowl with lots of stress and tension." Roscoe Bell recalled that many residents were admitted to the hospital with hypertension each time changes in policy occurred.[79] A small number actually broke down under the stress of camp life. Faith Terasawa, who worked as an interpreter with the social worker in the hospital, remembered that "quite a few people went haywire." She and the social worker made home calls, and Faith recalled that occasionally they had to send people to the state mental hospital.

❦

The administrators who arrived to direct the new community had high hopes for Topaz. They ordered 10,000 seedlings, 7,500 small trees, and 75 large ones, thinking that the foliage would eliminate the dust clouds. Delta merchants also donated trees to the project. The dust eliminated the trees instead of the other way around, and almost none of them survived.[80] They planned a skating rink for the winter, as well as a hardball diamond, softball grounds, and a football field, and they discussed landscaping for a miniature park.[81] Many of the Caucasians viewed the camp as an experiment in applied democracy, a project that would teach the Nikkei about democracy by creating it around them. In October 1942 a high school and two elementary schools opened, signs of the ideal community they hoped Topaz would become. Yet at the same time placards were posted warning residents that they would be arrested if they crawled through or under the fence that surrounded the camp, and no one could ignore the presence of the armed guards, soldiers whose hatred of the "Japs" was all too evident. This was a barbed-wire democracy, a community under guard.[82]

Compounding the fundamental ambiguity in the nature and function of the Topaz concentration camp was its purpose as the WRA defined it. The agency did not intend Topaz or the other relocation centers to be permanent prisons, and indeed many of the officials concerned with what they called the "Japanese question" saw the evacuation as an opportunity for a diaspora, a dissolution of the ghettos that would scatter the Japanese American population around the country.

The first resettling began even before the evacuees arrived in Topaz. The need for college students to continue their education produced the first opportunities for some Nisei to shorten their time of confinement. Leaders of the YMCA and YWCA and a few California educators, including University of California president Robert G. Sproul, did not want college students' education to be disrupted by the evacuation. Sproul contacted Representative John Tolan about the problem, and ultimately President Roosevelt allowed Nisei to move to willing institutions away from the West Coast. On May 29, 1942, the National Japanese Student Relocation Council was formed in Chicago by Clarence Pickett of the American Friends Service Committee and college and university educators from around the country.[83] Relatively few students at Tanforan benefited from this program, since not many could meet the educational requirements, acquire a sponsor, raise the funds for tuition and residence, and locate a college in a friendly community. About seventy-five students did resettle in the spring of 1942, under the auspices of the council and its West Coast predecessor, the Student Relocation Council.[84]

More were able to leave from Topaz. The first brave souls left Delta on October 7, 1942, headed for the University of Nebraska, Union College in New York City, Huron College in South Dakota, and the University of Utah (the president of Utah State University, Elmer G. Peterson, refused them admittance).[85] By June 1943 the council had sufficient contributions to provide financial aid to students with "reasonably good grades but no money." More than four hundred colleges and universities had been cleared by the army and navy to take eligible Nisei.[86]

During the first week of October 1942, another group returned to the outside world. These young men and women were recruited for the sugar beet fields of Utah to help alleviate the war-induced labor shortage, and the Utah farmers welcomed their hands. Since few were actually from farms, the primitive conditions of rural Utah—no mattresses to sleep on and no showers—shocked them.[87] Their exodus as seasonal labor was as important as the students', for both groups exemplified the goals of the WRA's resettlement policy: to move the Nikkei population away from the West Coast. The War Relocation Authority determined almost from the outset that resettlement, or relocation as the WRA termed it (the designation was confusing since the original movement from the coast to the camps was also termed relocation), would be its goal, but its method of implementation was devised slowly over several months. In July 1942 WRA director Dillon Myer announced that incarcerating the evacuees for the war's duration was neither "necessary, desirable, or wise,"[88] and many Caucasians who needed workers agreed. Some Utahns would have preferred the Japanese American workers to be bound to them by some form of indenture for the war's duration, but they were willing to take them on any terms they could get. The WRA's first director, Milton Eisenhower, was apprised of the need for farm labor; when he resigned June 18, 1942, after only three months on the job, it was passed on to Myer.

On September 26 Myer announced regulations for the screening of people who wanted seasonal or permanent leave from the camps.[89]

The regulations provided for loyalty investigations, hearings that "supposedly could not have taken place on the West Coast [before the evacuation] because of lack of time and because those rounded up all looked alike."[90] In fact, loyalty checks conducted on the West Coast would have left most Nikkei there, something those responsible for the relocation wanted to prevent. Myer's plan accomplished two ends. It provided a relatively quick way out of camp for evacuees who wanted freedom whatever the risk. Nisei could move to virtually any location except their former homes. Ultimately more than three thousand people left Topaz under this program.[91] It allowed the white population to utilize Nikkei labor, usually at very low wages, to take up the slack created by the draft, and it kept the Japanese Americans away from the West Coast until the final months of the war.

As the resettlement began, Bay Area Japanese Americans followed two paths, one that moved toward freedom outside and another that remained inside as long as possible—which for some meant until Topaz closed. Since this history is primarily concerned with the people who remained incarcerated, the story of those who departed can be told relatively briefly.

Myer wanted to resettle loyal Nikkei to other parts of the United States, permanently removing them from the Pacific coast. Despite some initial confusion over leave clearance regulations, which were complicated and slow to process, eligible Nisei who wanted to could soon depart on seasonal leaves. As a replacement for farm labor drained off by the mobilization and the lure of higher-paying war industries, Nisei labor quickly became essential to the war effort. Initially, the predominantly urban Topazeans were reluctant to take such jobs, but their desire to escape confinement and earn more money changed their minds. (Wages paid inside the internment camps ranged from $16 to $21 a month, depending on the level of skill required, plus camp lodging and board. The low wages were to ensure that the Japanese Americans did not earn more than an army private.) People wishing to resettle had to fill out forms to establish their loyalty, which was then checked by the FBI, a process that took about a month. The first to depart were adult Nisei, since Issei were originally ineligible. Most Issei did not want to leave the safety of the camps anyway, but gradually the policy changed and some ventured forth. Many Nisei also feared a hostile reception outside and adopted a "wait and see" attitude toward the program.[92]

Resettlement was a two-way street. Many employers were eager to meet their labor needs with the industrious internees and actively sought them out. Prospective employers were supposed to pay prevailing wages, maintain adequate living quarters at no expense to the evacuee, provide transportation from the center to the job site and back, and assure that employment of the Nikkei would not cause the displacement of local labor. State and local officials had to show that law and order would be maintained. All these stipulations were honored to a greater or lesser degree, but enforcement provisions were sorely lacking. The seasonal workers were valued; it has been estimated that they harvested enough beets to make nearly 300 million pounds of sugar.[93] The more sugar, the more money for the growers and the more food for the army and the civilian population. The Topaz literary magazine, *Trek*, noted in June 1943 that three out of four internees going on seasonal leave were citizens; among those leaving "indefinitely," the percentage was slightly larger. The majority were young men between twenty-one and twenty-seven years of age, educated in the United States.[94]

During the remaining months of 1942, a steadily increasing number of Japanese Americans left Topaz for northern and southern Utah, other nearby states, or even Delta. As early as September 22, 1942, Topaz's construction agent hired a Nisei as his payroll clerk. Soon others were being hired by the same construction firm, by Delta farmers, businessmen, and by individuals who needed domestic help. Frank Beckwith, the publisher of the *Millard County Chronicle*, hired Harry Yasuda to operate an intertype machine. (Beckwith explained to his readers that it would be "decidedly unpatriotic to hire a man from defense work when there is plenty of suitable help at the relocation center to fill our needs.")[95] Yasuda was paid a wage by Beckwith but then had to pay rent at the camp.[96] Considerable animosity was aroused by the wage differential between those privately employed but living in camp and those working for the WRA. One JERS recorder commented that he and his brothers were "classic examples." Two of his brothers were employed in Delta for $20.00 a day, and he earned $1.25 an hour working for a private construction firm in camp; they all resided in Topaz. The contrast between this income and that of an older Nikkei physician at Topaz was striking: this young laborer earned $300.00 in a month. The recorder was not troubled by the resentment this difference caused, as he planned to leave for college in Massachusetts soon.[97] On September 24 the U.S. Employment Service established itself in camp to coordinate hiring, and representatives of three sugar beet companies and several turkey-processing plants came in to recruit. Seasonal labor peaked in October and declined as the weather grew bad in December. The local farmers were pleased and expressed regrets only that more workers had not volunteered.[98]

The first seasonal laborers were people who had the courage to face the unknown, to take jobs for which they had no training or experience. They were generally young, with few dependents. Their reception in the towns and rural areas of the Intermountain West varied greatly. People who went to Provo, where a farm labor tent camp was set up to house four hundred laborers, found a populace generally hostile to Japanese Americans. Some Nisei reported that the local Woolworth and Penney stores would not sell to them, and others complained about segregation in the movie theater and the refusal of local restaurants to serve them. Small groups were mistreated and verbally abused on the streets, others were stoned while riding to and from work, and worst of all, the camp itself was fired on. Five youths were later arrested for terrorism, and the subsequent investigation determined that two buildings had been hit by fifteen to eighteen rounds of rifle fire. The residents hugged the floors and the camp manager, H. W. Bartlett, testified that the shots were aimed directly at them. The Japanese Americans refused to work the next day, a Sunday (October 3, 1943), but returned on

Monday. The *Salt Lake Tribune* admonished its readers to put aside their prejudices because the farm labor the Nikkei provided was necessary to the war effort. A group of local citizens adopted a resolution condemning the violence and pledging future law enforcement and "tolerant participation in the democratic spirit."[99]

The Nisei surveyed by JERS representative George Sugihara blamed most of the violence against them on "hoodlums and drunks," and most rated their treatment while on seasonal leave as "fair." Some who remembered the experience, like Harry Kitano, a teenager at the time, were not so generous in their appraisal; to him the experience was very frightening.[100] Sugihara found that seasonal workers considered Delta "fair" and Salt Lake "fair to good." He noted that large groups of Japanese together tended to make a "poor impression" and commented that their "moral standards have proven very low," a judgment that probably reflected more on his own values than on those of the group he surveyed. Most Nisei who went out blamed the hostility of the locals and cautioned others against resettling in Provo. An additional factor was the presence of large numbers of defense workers at the Geneva Steel Mill in nearby Orem, whose work made them exceptionally hostile to Japan. They "made it impossible to mingle with the local people."[101]

⚜

By the end of 1942 the first Nikkei had begun to depart on permanent or indefinite resettlement. Like the seasonal workers, they had to satisfy the complex bureaucratic procedures of the WRA, which included an FBI security check and the approval of the camp director, who had to be satisfied that the area they intended to resettle in offered good work prospects and favorable community sentiment. Once they were out of the camps, the Japanese Americans were supposed to check back with WRA field offices located around the country to assure that all was going well, although few actually did.[102] They took jobs in the Midwest, where Chicago, with its history of diverse ethnic groups, was the favored destination. Nikkei were well-treated there because local residents felt that at least they were not African Americans. The Intermountain West was also popular. Salt Lake City was the most attractive nearby destination until it was closed to Japanese Americans because the local population claimed it had "too many." The East Coast also attracted a venturesome few. Many communities in the East and Midwest were eager to have them because of labor shortages; in areas where few Asian Americans lived, racial prejudice was minimal. Many Nikkei found permanent homes and employment there and never returned to the West Coast. Lee Suyemoto's family, for example, settled in Cincinnati, located jobs and schools, and encountered little prejudice; they had no desire to return to Berkeley. For most, however, San Francisco and the Bay Area were still home, and they owned property or possessions there that they hoped to reclaim when the war ended.

The pace of permanent resettlement increased by mid-1943 but declined in 1944, and it never achieved the popularity the WRA desired. Seasonal work leaves were a far easier alternative for those seeking extra money. People for whom resettlement was easy departed early, and those who remained had many reasons to keep them in camp, as succeeding chapters make clear. By early 1944 most people were no longer interested in resettling, partly because of the poor conditions Nikkei lived in outside. Some reported back they were put in "poor shacks [to] do the dirtiest jobs." As one man who refused to leave camp commented, "Here, there is little freedom; but we are not stared at. We do not get what we want here, but we live anyway and do not feel lonely."[103] Many Issei believed that since the government had deprived them of home and livelihood, it was now the government's responsibility to care for them. There was a certain logic to their thoughts.

Chapter Five

The Jewel of the Desert

As the first few months passed, life at Topaz settled into a routine. Warren Watanabe described it in the first annual report for JERS: "People settled in; it was a quiet center with no serious outbreaks of trouble, no apparent resentment at the regimented life. Bitterness and anger were natural but lay dormant."[1] The apparent tranquillity was due in part to the establishment of the institutions of community life—schools, self-government, a newspaper, public health services, churches, and an opportunity for work, self-improvement, and recreation. In part it stemmed from the nature of the residents and their backgrounds. But before long the Caucasian administration precipitated events that came close to tearing the camp apart: the killing of James Hatsuaki Wakasa and the registration and segregation controversies. One must first consider the positive to appreciate properly the effects of the negative.

❧

Creating schools for the children of Topaz was even more important than it had been at Tanforan. Schools would keep the nearly two thousand children occupied and provide instruction in at least the basic skills.[2] Historian of education Thomas James wrote that the schools could also be "used to explore the nature of democracy and to prepare students as citizens. For educators, the connection between democracy and education was an article of faith." But the question arises of how well camp educators could keep that faith,

119

given the conditions of internment.[3] The director of the WRA's western regional office called a conference in July to discuss guidelines for the curriculum, and everyone there agreed that the interned students had to learn how to be participating citizens in a democracy.[4] The assumption seemed to be either that nothing in their prior educational experience had taught them this, or that if it had, life behind barbed wire would quickly eradicate the effects.

Instruction based on planning by the education school at Stanford University had already begun at Tanforan, and the WRA intended to open schools as quickly as possible at Topaz—at least by October 19, in order to meet Utah's requirement of a nine-month school year.[5] But these good intentions were delayed by unfinished construction and the lack of supplies.

Yoshiko Uchida recalled with some bitterness the beginnings of school at Topaz. Superintendent of Schools John C. Carlisle and the assistant director of the WRA's education division attended the first meeting of the teaching staff. Uchida was pleased that they seemed sensitive to the situation and were willing to use a curriculum that was not only flexible but omitted such ironies as saluting the flag. But the facilities appalled her. When she looked into the barracks in Block 8, where one of the two elementary schools was to be located, she saw a barren room devoid of stove, light bulbs, and equipment. That was actually the better of the two barracks, since Caucasian teachers were to be assigned there. The schoolroom in Block 41, for the Nisei teachers, had "large holes in the roof where the stove pipes were to fit in, inner sheetrock walls had not been installed, floors were covered with dust and dirt, and again there were no supplies or equipment for teaching." Nevertheless, the "insensitive and ineffectual white man" in charge ordered registration to begin. Classes started on October 20, but because it was too cold for the children to remain in the unheated barracks, they moved outside. A monstrous dust storm brought matters to a head. Uchida and some of her pupils tried to carry on, then gave up. When the principal of the elementary schools chastised the teachers for threatening to resign rather than teach in such appalling conditions, Carlisle stepped in. Uchida recalled, "Because he was wise enough to respect our dignity and accord us some genuine understanding, the mass resignation of the resident teaching staff was averted." Classes finally resumed later, after a new supervisor had been appointed.[6]

By December 1942 classes were underway again. The same residents who had spearheaded the educational effort at Tanforan took the lead at Topaz. Yoshiko Uchida earned $19 a month as an elementary school teacher, and so did her sister Keiko and her classmate, Mills College graduate Grace Fujii, who set up a nursery school as they had at Tanforan. Three preschools were functioning, with 182 students, fewer than half the eligible children. Caucasian supporters supplied them with materials from schools in the Bay Area. Nursery school was not only a babysitting function: it helped the young students learn or practice English and to adjust to the strange and often disturbing environment in which they now lived.

The elementary schools enrolled 675 by the year's end, and the high school had 1,037 students. The Stanford-based curriculum was progressive, in line with current thinking; in addition to vocational education, it followed a "core" program combining English and social studies. The high school offered a limited college preparatory program, including mathematics, journalism, music, Latin, modern languages, physics, and speech, in addition to the "core." Laboratory facilities were virtually nonexistent, and the quality of instruction at the outset was an unknown and variable commodity.[7]

Certified Caucasian teachers were scarce but the deficiency was made up by resident Japanese Americans. They lacked training in pedagogy (since few Nikkei had been allowed to teach in prewar America) but they generally had college educations. The white administrative staff was quickly assembled; salaries were generally higher than in their previous positions, especially for administrators in Utah. Carlisle came to Topaz from Logan, where he had been a dean at Utah State University (then Utah Agricultural and Mechanical College). LeGrand Noble, a former superintendent of schools from Uintah County, was the first high school principal and succeeded Carlisle as superintendent in February 1943 when the latter returned to Utah A & M. Laverne C. Bane of the University of Utah and Reese Maughan, an educator from northern

Utah, accompanied Carlisle to Topaz. Wanda Robertson, who
had supervised teacher training at the University of Utah, later
became principal of the elementary schools.[8] By December 1942,
the preschools had two supervisors and twenty-six assistants, all
camp residents. The elementary schools had thirty-five teachers—
seven Caucasians and twenty-eight Nisei—and there were two
Caucasian librarians. Topaz had the "finest public library of all the
centers, drawing an average weekly patronage of 2,500."[9] The
high school staff included four counselors and directors and one
librarian, all Caucasian, and forty-five teachers—twenty-five Japanese Americans and twenty whites. The schools still lacked an
additional nine or ten Caucasian elementary teachers and four or
five secondary teachers.[10] By November 1943 there were forty
high school teachers, thirty-six elementary teachers, and twenty-
one preschool teachers.[11]

Many problems remained. A heavy snow shut down the schools
completely in November. The facilities reopened in mid-December
after they had been completely winterized.[12] At best the schools
were crowded, with student-teacher ratios of 48:1 in the elementary
schools and 35:1 in the secondary, compared to an average of 28:1
outside.[13] The classrooms were bleak, with insufficient equipment
and makeshift supplies, but energetic teachers and willing students
tried to overcome the drabness with their artistic endeavors. The
totally Japanese faces presented a vista that was unlike both the
teachers' and the students' prewar experience. Many of the Caucasian teachers were returning older women, young college graduates, missionaries, or conscientious objectors, and their qualifications varied greatly.[14] They tended to stay only a short time,
because there were teacher shortages everywhere and for some the
camp environment was just too harsh. Topaz administrator James
F. Hughes commented that "our judgement in the selection of
personnel was tempered all too freely by the urgency of obtaining
the needed employees,"[15] and this judgment certainly applied to the
teaching staff.

Nonetheless, the schools did their best with what they had. The
high school students published the *Rambler*, which was printed in
the *Millard County Chronicle* pressroom in Delta. They studied art,

performed plays, formed a choir, organized chapters of the American Association for the Advancement of Science, the American Red Cross, and the Future Farmers of America, and set up a language club. On-site teacher training was undertaken to improve the resident staff, and a scholarship fund was created to help the abler students to go on to college. In March 1943 a chapter of the Parent-Teacher Association was established. The tendency for gang behavior that developed at Tanforan seemed to have disappeared, at least for the moment.[16]

Eleanor Gerard Sekerak had vivid memories of her experiences teaching at Topaz. She had just graduated from the University of California and her first job choice, a prestigious California school district, hired a man in preference to her. She was then recruited for Topaz by Lorne Bell, who met her at the train when she arrived in Delta. Students welcomed the young teacher, for a few had known her in Oakland during her student teaching days. Their "Miss Gerard" was determined to fit in with her charges and began to attend the internees' Protestant church (a combined effort of some fourteen denominations). The resourceful teacher acquired surplus textbooks from her old high school in Berkeley and devised lessons that would emphasize democracy and local government, using Topaz as a model. Her students also participated in the economic life of the community by growing their own vegetables, and later they studied towns in which they wished to resettle. These students, she wrote later, "arrived at class on time, with homework completed, worked diligently, took their exams, and otherwise observed normal classroom standards." They participated in "all the normal life of a typical high school," including a "student chorus, student newspaper, yearbook, student government, drama, athletics, dances, and the usual senior week activities." She even borrowed caps and gowns from the University of Utah for the high school graduation. She accompanied her teenaged girls on a seasonal job near Ogden and brought them home again when she discovered they had been assigned to unsanitary lodgings. When she was moved to larger quarters, she made her room a center for visitors and student meetings and parties. Topaz was an injustice for the Japanese Americans, as Eleanor Gerard well knew, but she tried her best to make its high school a worthwhile learning experience for her students.[17] The favorable impression she made on her students is still apparent five decades later.

Paul Bell and his siblings were some of the few Caucasian students in the Topaz schools. The four children of Roscoe and Gladys Bell attended schools briefly in Delta, but then moved with their parents when housing became available. Since the Bells were from the Bay Area, they knew that Japanese American students were very hardworking, and they wanted that kind of educational stimulation for their children. Paul spent his junior and senior years as a student in the Class of 1945, and those were years he never forgot. The Class of 1945 had a special identity, since it was the only class to spend all its years in camp at Topaz High, and Paul spoke at a class reunion in 1980 about his experiences as a resident of Block 2 and a classmate of the Nisei. Initially he had been intimidated by them, he confessed, for in the Berkeley schools he remembered that they were—as he put it—"brains." Even though he was much taller than his classmates, he learned judo and participated in sports with the other students; he also joined student clubs, worked on the newspaper and yearbook, served on student committees, became involved in fundraising and service projects, and went to dances. And as a teenager he enjoyed the surreptitious drinks of homemade sake or bootlegged booze his classmates acquired. The administration segregated the races in peculiar ways, he found. He could not invite his Nisei friends to his Caucasian block recreation room, but if he were ill, he would share the same hospital. Forty years later he recalled Topaz as a "rich, rich and special experience for me during which time a very high respect grew within me for Japanese culture and tradition." But he confessed that he did not realize the pain the experience had caused his classmates.[18] He was, as he later termed himself, an "inside-outsider."

⚜

What was Topaz High like for Paul Bell, Maya Nagata, Ryozo "Rosie" Kumekawa, Fumi Manabe, and the other students in the Class of 1945? What sort of nursery school did Keiko Uchida establish? What kind of elementary school did Dave Tatsuno's son attend? Interviews with Nisei who attended camp schools and Caucasians who were involved with them produced a very mixed picture, for what to some was an intolerable situation was quite acceptable to others. Some students learned despite inadequacies in equipment and poorly trained teachers and went on to successful college careers or jobs. Some had teachers who cared for them and provided a good learning environment despite the obstacles. Others felt cheated out of the education they might have if they had remained in San Francisco. Many eventually attended college, but only after they returned to their former homes or resettled elsewhere, since without a scholarship it was "close to impossible to go to school" directly from Topaz High, as Fumi Manabe Hayashi recalled.[19] To some who were not interested in higher education, camp schools were fun precisely because they were not as rigorous as elsewhere, and parents could not enforce good study habits in the cramped living quarters. Others found the highly competitive Japanese Americans around them more challenging than the Caucasian students in the schools they had attended back home. An analysis of the educational system thus presents a varied picture, one in which the elements do not all mesh.

The first impression of the Topaz school system was of its makeshift character. Although the administrators set aside buildings within the blocks to be used for education, nothing was ready in October 1942. Harry Kitano of the Class of 1944 wrote that at Topaz High state standards of education were established, but "some courses were taught by local evacuees who were not yet college graduates, and others were taught by Caucasian Ph.D.'s" (among them conscientious objectors.) His education was very uneven in quality.[20] The teacher shortage intensified as time passed. Caucasian teachers earned far more than the Nisei, $150-$200 a month with room and board, compared to $19 a month for residents, as stipulated by the WRA, and of course the Caucasians lived better. They also occupied all positions of authority, reflecting the general administrative policy of the camp. Topaz had more than eight hundred residents with college degrees, but because few had been trained as teachers, they learned on the job, sometimes from less well educated Caucasian colleagues. The experience of Henry Tani, the high school principal, who had established the educational system at Tanforan, counted for naught. The Nisei were under no illusions that teaching experience at Topaz would accredit them in the outside world after camp. Many of the first resident teachers resettled as soon as they could because they could earn more outside, and they were replaced by younger, less experienced evacuees. Those who remained often took easier jobs, since the compensation was the same and teaching, with its endless round of papers to grade and students to inspire, was hard work.[21]

Each crisis in camp life affected the children. According to James, whenever the community was racked by a disturbing event the younger children became disoriented, the adolescents tense and unable to concentrate. High school students felt the trauma of events that could significantly alter their own lives—the draft or segregation to Tule Lake or the possibility of accompanying their parents to Japan. Because they followed a progressive curriculum, they were encouraged to write about their feelings in class. A common subject was the ambivalent meaning of democracy, with its record of intolerance toward minorities, and the students had much to say.

Japanese Americans had traditionally been very well behaved students, since they came from homes that stressed obedience and hard work. As Frank Miyamoto observed about Seattle, because many Issei had received little education in Japan, they were all the more determined that their children would be well educated; they insisted that they "strive to their utmost in their school work, and thus pay their filial obligations."[22] At first the children responded similarly to the camp educators, but as time passed their behavior changed. Youth gangs appeared; they were called "juvenile delinquents" by shocked staff members and parents alike, and they behaved in ways all but unknown to the Issei before the war— talking back, cheating, abusing the furniture, committing vandalism, bullying younger children, and gate crashing at parties.[23] Grace Fujimoto said they were just "being American," and she recalled that before the war there had been groups the other teenagers called *yogure,* or dirty, who emulated the "zoot-suit" culture of delinquents elsewhere.[24] The administrators decided that the problem stemmed from the adult orientation of the Topaz community, which at first offered little for children to do. They worried that gangster movies and comic books might contribute to delinquency, but the WRA concluded that children's behavior was still the parents' problem.[25]

Part of the "delinquency" was a result of the breakdown of family life in camp. Parents whose roles were undercut by the internment were unable to control their children, who left the small rooms early in the morning and returned only to sleep. Almost everyone ate at long tables in the mess halls, and teenagers often sat with their friends; even the semblance of normal family life disappeared. The lack of privacy also made disciplining difficult.[26] As school-aged children grew older, the peer group became increasingly important in determining their behavior. Particularly devastating was the loss of self-esteem and prestige in the family group suffered by the father as a result of internment.

The Parent-Teacher Association was a traditional adjunct to school life, but its agenda was different from the normal one in the American school system. In 1943 more than seven hundred parents attended a mass meeting to call for a more conservative approach to education. They disliked the experimental "core" curriculum. So did many of the students, who wanted more emphasis on basics and feared the inclusion of vocational education would route them away from college, which they saw as the best way to success in postwar America. Their concerns were mirrored in the fate of the students who graduated from high school in June 1943. They seemed to have lost their ambition: of 219 seniors, only 20 went to college in the fall. Fumi Hayashi and Grace Oshita both recall that the first class had an especially difficult time obtaining scholarships, which were essential because of the drop in family income.[27] Many students believed that the high school curriculum and inadequate teachers had ill-prepared them for higher education. George Sugihara, who worked in the Topaz reports office, conducted a survey of the Class of 1942 that purported to show that two-thirds of the girls and three-fourths of the boys felt they could not meet the challenge of college.[28] Some of the students never intended to go on to college; Grace Fujimoto (who married Ben Oshita in Salt Lake City after the war) had trained in high school in San Francisco for a secretarial career, and after graduating in 1943 she became the secretary to elementary school principal Wanda Robertson, a position she was very pleased to obtain. Others just feared leaving their parents and the security of camp life.

The graduating class of 1943 expressed many of the sentiments of Nisei in Topaz in general. One student wrote that the future still lay within themselves, and that if their minds ceased to be free, so would their world. Many decried the paralysis of spirit caused by the internment—the creation of an "evacuation mind." Some also feared that along with mental laziness would come a dependency mentality, a willingness to be content as wards of the government. Above all, these students knew they had to work for tolerance.[29] But they were much less assured that higher education held the answers for their own lives.

⁂

Adult education presented fewer problems. Laverne Bane directed this program, which included basic English, divided into four levels of difficulty, a creative writing class, personal and commercial sewing, music, art, math, nurses' aid, first aid, flower making, and phonetics, as well as geography, Americanization, and carpentry. Most adults were eager for activities to occupy their time, especially women whose traditional homemaking tasks had been preempted by camp institutions and who had previously enjoyed little access to instruction in English. Ultimately, adult education offered 150 classes to more than three thousand residents. It also sponsored frequent lectures and hobby and art shows. The shows were particularly important events in a camp with a number of distinguished artists. Chiura Obata had taught at the University of California before the war, Miné Okubo had traveled in Europe on an art scholarship, Hisako and George Matsusaburo Hibi had exhibited widely in California in the 1930s, and Byron Takashi Tsuzuki had already established himself as an artist. They founded an art school in Tanforan for the residents, and instruction continued at Topaz.

The camp had the largest number of professional artists, including Suiko Mikomi, Masao Mori, and Yonekichi Hosoi. There was also a music school.[30] Many of the residents learned to paint, play the piano, grow bonsai trees, or create beautiful and delicate jewelry from the shells of the old Sevier lake bed. Even the Boy Scouts were organized under the adult education division.[31]

The young people's reaction to their education experience varied and changed over time, for the schools, like every other camp institution, were not static but suffered with the loss of trained personnel in the last year. For many the time passed quickly. In later years, people who were children or adolescents at Topaz remembered only scattered events. Abu Keikoan, for example, looked back on junior high school as a featureless blur, of which she remembered little. Athletics, the endless opportunity to play—these memories she recalled fondly—and of course lunch; "I really don't remember much about the school. Maybe that says something."[32] Maya Nagata Aikawa was bitter: "We knew we really didn't have to study, because it was a camp school. I don't remember anything I learned in camp." She had to spend an extra year in Los Angeles after the war completing her high school education.[33] Michiko Okamoto said that Topaz High School did not provide her with the kind of education she wanted. No physics was taught, nor was there advanced French. Instead of college prep courses, she took drama from teacher Eugene Lewis, who encouraged her to explore the field that later became her career. Although after further study in New York she did become an actress, she always regretted the college education she believed the camp high school had denied her.[34]

Shigeki Sugiyama also studied drama at Topaz High School, but his experiences at the school and the camp were much briefer than Michiko's, and internment marked him in quite different ways. Sugiyama was originally from Alameda, where Nikkei were uprooted with little notice in late February 1942; the county was deemed a restricted area because it had two airports, a harbor, and a naval shipyard. The family, which at that time consisted of the parents and seven children, settled in French Camp, where Shig's father worked as a farmer. Shig, then fourteen, did not return to school but worked to supplement the family income, which was shattered by the suddenness of the upheaval. In May they were moved a second time when French Camp became part of the general evacuation of Military Districts One and Two. Their new home was Manzanar, both an assembly center and a camp, and from the outset a turbulent community where hostilities between the accommodationist JACL members and their opponents led to violence. After a riot in which two people were killed and twelve injured, Shig—although just a bystander—was deemed "pro-American," and he became persona non grata to people who opposed the administration. He tried to stay away from trouble, even eating at a different barracks from his neutral parents, and he began working at the hospital after school to keep out of sight. Despite his youth, he did the tasks of an orderly and even a nurse's aide as more experienced personnel relocated. The Sugiyamas decided to move out of Manzanar to the more tranquil Topaz in November 1943.[35]

Sugiyama found many aspects of Topaz tolerable. He affiliated with the Buddhist church, as he had at Manzanar, and taught Sunday school. He worked at the hospital as soon as a position became available. While an eleventh grader, he did advanced tasks such as surgical preparations when the professional staff relocated. School was a pleasure for him. Quite accidentally he was recruited into dramatics, and he enjoyed not only the plays but also his teachers, as well as the opportunity that performing provided for him to travel outside camp. He found several teachers especially inspiring, and he still corresponded with one, Jack Gooding, in 1988. As first he was conscientious about his studies, for his work in the camp hospitals had stimulated an interest in attending medical school, but then he, like many others, got lazy. He recalled slacking off in history class by moving from the front of the room (where he usually sat so he could see the board) to the back, nearer the stove. He found he could look up the answers to the teacher's questions before she called on him, and this amused him until she surprised him by making him take three examinations (made up for three different classes) one after another. His "A" grades showed that he had learned despite himself.

In his senior year, after eight months at Topaz, Sugiyama and a friend applied to relocate to Ann Arbor, Michigan, to work cleaning dormitories at the University of Michigan. Although his father was at first angered by Shig's temerity, he soon agreed that it was a good idea for his eldest son to leave camp. The boys had not completed high school. When they reached Ann Arbor, they found that one school, University High school, was affiliated with the university, which Shig aspired to enter because of its famous medical school. He won a scholarship and was one of four Nisei in a class of fifty. He entered the university, but a year later his medical dreams were deferred by the draft. He made the military his career and later joked that it took him "twenty years to get a B.A." He returned to school at the University of California in 1966 and earned a master's degree in Public Administration. He retired in 1988 in the office of the special counsel of the Civil Service Commission.[36]

Shig Sugiyama's experience with camp education was exceptional. Like many gifted students, he learned in spite of himself, and his parents' emphasis on the importance of education led him to strike out on his own. Robert Utsumi's reaction was probably more typical. He did not respond well to Topaz High school. Like Maya Aikawa and Michiko Okamoto, he rated the teachers in his junior and senior year of high school as terrible, especially after all the college graduates among the resident teachers had resettled. He responded with disruptive behavior, as did many of his friends. He recalled one occasion where his chemistry teacher, whom he described as "dangerous" because of his lack of knowledge, was attempting to show what happened when sodium reacted with water. Egged on by Utsumi and his classmates, the teacher added more and more sodium. Finally the tub blew up, sending water all over the ceiling and the first few rows of the classroom. "This is why I say it was dangerous, but it was so hilarious at the time," Utsumi laughed. He mentioned several more times when the students got out of control. These occasions were very funny to the participants, but the result was not humorous: "I really don't think I learned anything. If I did it wasn't very much, and I just felt that I didn't get a high school education." Utsumi certainly did not acquire the study habits necessary for success in college, and he soon dropped out of the University of California to join the armed forces, which he made his career.[37]

Lee Suyemoto also recalled disrupting the educational process. He led his classmates out of the classroom in rebellion when a Caucasian teacher made a racist remark. The boycott was a tactic in which Topaz students specialized. Suyemoto's class remained out for two or three days, demonstrating the students' power in that classroom. The same pattern appeared in family life: parental control weakened as peer pressure grew. Lee related only to the members of his block gang and spent as little time at home as possible. He learned to smoke when he was thirteen, to his parents' great dismay. Despite his youthful rebellion, Lee continued his education after the family relocated, and he earned a Ph.D. in mathematics at the University of Cincinnati. As he demonstrated, for many teenagers rebellion was a temporary reaction to the extraordinary situation of internment. Harry Kitano, himself a rebellious Topaz youth, has shown that juvenile delinquency was not intrinsic to Japanese American culture.[38]

The school system operated with several liabilities: a nationwide teacher shortage; differential treatment of Caucasian and Nisei teachers, which made the students contemptuous of their own people; a high student-teacher ratio; poor facilities; and an inadequate number of books and other supplies. Probably the most devastating feature was the harm incarceration brought to family life. A culture that esteemed education was enough support for some students; they made the most of their schooling and continued on to college outside, especially with the help of the National Japanese Student Relocation Council. Some did poorly in camp schools but, like Kitano and Suyemoto, compensated in universities after the war for the inadequate secondary education they had received. Others, like Fumi Hayashi and Grace Oshita, felt that the schools were adequate for their needs. Still others found that their schooling stifled all interest in higher education and handicapped them for the rest of their lives.

The first year of the Topaz school system was its best. Many of the problems it faced then could be overcome by the sheer determination of those involved, by acquiring materials and adjusting to the internment situation. Other problems reached a crisis point later, triggered by the collapse in morale that beset Topaz in its final months.

Harry Kitano analyzed the camp experience as a sociologist more than a decade after his student days at Topaz High. He emphasized the positive aspects of community life of Topaz as well as the negative. He noted that it was, for many people, their first exposure to "an American model of a small community. Block votes, community services, community decisions, and the like, provided a taste of 'ideal' American community democracy, the likes of which few Americans have actually ever seen."[39] In its first few months this community began to develop the features that distinguished it from a prison camp. Not only was education inaugurated; self-government became a permanent feature. This development was, as Roger Daniels wrote, a "matter of convenience for each side" and not exactly participatory democracy. Having "some evacuees govern, regulate, and manipulate their fellow Japanese Americans . . . was simpler and certainly cheaper than having large staffs." He compared the Nikkei participants to "trustees in a prison system, monitors in a crowded school."[40]

In many camps such involvement led to charges of collaboration, especially since some who took part were members of the already-suspect Japanese American Citizens League. The JACL was a source of contention at Topaz, too, but opposition to it did not break out into the open, as it did at Manzanar. Topaz had its share of acrimony, which sometimes led to fights between cliques as well as individuals, but neither self-government nor the JACL was usually the cause. The problem there was how to sustain any kind of continuing leadership that could present Nikkei demands and concerns to the administration, when the most active and responsible residents left camp quickly, abandoning government and block management to the more intractable Issei.[41]

The WRA realized the advantages of having the Nikkei govern themselves, "not only as a matter of human decency but as the most practical way of insuring cooperation and mutual understanding between administrators and administered."[42] But implementation was left vague. Since prewar Japanese American communities had been led by Issei who were imprisoned by the FBI after Pearl Harbor, creating new leadership was a real challenge. The WRA hesitated between forcing a plan on the residents and waiting until they devised something themselves. The administration finally sent out a memo on June 5, 1942, announcing that all center residents eligible for membership in the work corps—that is, over sixteen years of age—were eligible to vote but restricting officeholding to citizens over the age of twenty-one. The WRA called for the election of a temporary community council made up of one representative from every block, plus an executive committee to advise the project director and a judicial committee to aid in maintaining law and order. At a WRA conference held in San Francisco on August 24, the voting age was set at eighteen. Again the Issei were excluded from holding elective office but were eligible for appointive positions. This exclusion was rescinded on April 19, 1943, when it became clear that most of the people remaining in the camps who were capable of governing were Issei. As Leonard Arrington noted, the new regulation helped to lessen the gap between the Issei and the Nisei.[43]

From the WRA's perspective, self-government at Topaz was not a great success. Since the Issei were generally unsympathetic to the WRA's overall goal of resettlement, their officeholding made the councils into obstructionist forces. Issei leadership also negated the councils' roles as liaisons between the evacuees and the administration, for many of the members became adversaries rather than collaborators. Continuity in office perpetuated the disagreements; members served six-month terms but were frequently re-elected. Unable to manipulate the councils, the WRA then curtailed their authority to enforce ordinances, so that the residents saw them as powerless. The WRA's attitude was obviously highly paternalistic. Washington believed that it was magnaminous to allow as much self-government as it did, but the evacuees considered the limitations evidence that they were not trusted. By early 1944 the two sides had reached a standoff.[44] The councils had become increasingly dominated by intransigent Issei, sometimes rubber stamps for the camp director, but at other times sources of opposition and acrimony as well. They ensured that rules and regulations were obeyed but had no real governing function. By the end of the year, councils in many camps had ceased to operate. The dilemma only underlined the paradox that lay at the heart of internment: how could people held without cause by a supposedly democratic system possibly govern themselves in any meaningful way when internment itself denied them their freedom?

In addition to the community council, each block had a block manager, appointed by the administration and paid at the rate of $16 a month. This official looked after the needs of the block community of 250 to 300 people, providing brooms, soap, light bulbs, and the like, and made sure that the area was well maintained. The block managers were initially the men (and occasionally women) who had held this position at Tanforan, but as the Nisei relocated Issei and Kibei took their places. The managers helped alleviate food shortages and problems in coal distribution, and they oversaw the winterizing of the barracks and the dining halls. As liaisons between the population and the administration, they also informed residents of official announcements and regulations. The block managers' group was not intended as a governing body, although the administration frequently used it as a sounding board.[45] Michi Weglyn has written that the Issei consolidated their power behind the block managers, who played key roles in attending to the needs and wishes of the people and hence wielded considerable influence. By 1944 they overshadowed the community councils in importance.[46]

Roger Daniels has been harshly critical of camp self-government, seeing it not in terms of community but rather of collaboration. He compared the councils and block managers to the *Judenräte* in Nazi concentration camps; the latter went far beyond the camp block managers and actually selected their fellow inmates for death.[47] Perhaps the two groups were comparable in that both contributed to oppression simply by helping the camp to function, but otherwise the comparison seems disproportionate. At Topaz the first few councils seemed genuinely interested in improving life for the incarcerated residents and thus helped to build a sense of real community; the last three were ineffectual, motivated by self-interest and personal agendas. The block managers did work to help people in their daily lives, and this service became increasingly important for the people who were determined to remain in Topaz for the duration of the war.

⚜

Topaz's self-government was inaugurated by a provisional council chosen in October 1942, which served three months; it helped ameliorate the housing shortage and drafted a constitution for the camp as well.[48] The first regular council, elected by all residents over the age of eighteen, was headed by Tsune Baba. This council received a baptism of fire in the period after James Wakasa was killed; it mediated the crisis and helped to prevent further violence. In the second council, elected six months later, Issei were allowed to hold office, although those who had opted for repatriation to Japan or answered "no-no" on the loyalty questionnaire (see below) were ineligible. Before the election several prominent residents were assaulted for being too "pro-administration," an indication of growing tensions between the Caucasians and the Nikkei and among the camp residents themselves. The victims included a Christian minister and art professor Chiura Obata. Director Ernst announced that the administration would maintain "law and order" and protect the officeholders.[49]

⚜

The first council had to contend with the most difficult events in the camp's history, the segregation controversy and the killing of James Hatsuaki Wakasa. Both took place in the first half of 1943; although the segregation issue surfaced first, it continued long after the crisis surrounding the Wakasa's death had subsided.

James Wakasa was a sixty-three-year-old Issei bachelor who had graduated from Keio College in Tokyo in 1900. He immigrated to the United States soon afterward. He studied at Hyde Park High

School in Chicago for three years and completed a two-year post-graduate course at the University of Wisconsin in 1916. Wakasa worked in San Francisco as a chef and served in the U.S. Army as a civilian cooking instructor during World War I, for which he had received American citizenship (which was rescinded in the *Ozawa* decision). When he was killed, he had been in the United States for forty years.[50] Because of the Exclusion Act, he was never able to marry. He worked primarily as a cook and was in California almost by chance in 1941.

Wakasa's death was outrageous and unexpected, and the circumstances surrounding it were the subject of considerable investigation. No one actually saw the incident, but these facts are generally agreed on: Wakasa was shot by a military police sentry just before sunset, at about 7:30 P.M. on Sunday, April 11, 1943, near the west fence but inside the camp, about three hundred yards north of Sentry Tower No. 8 in the southwest corner. Immediately after the shooting his body was taken by Director of Internal Security Ted Lewis to the hospital and then removed by the military police to their compound.[51] At 8:16 P.M. Lieutenant Henry H. Miller, commander of the military police, notified a member of the WRA staff that a Japanese resident had been shot forty-five minutes earlier and that his body was now in the military area. The MP said that Wakasa had approached the west fence; despite four warnings he had continued walking as if to escape, and finally the sentry in the No. 8 post had shot him. Although the MP originally said Wakasa was attempting to crawl through the fence, that story was quickly amended and the military admitted that he was from forty to sixty-five inches inside the fence when he was shot. Wakasa, who was facing his killer, was hit in the chest at the third rib; his spine was shattered, and he died instantly. The report by the WRA stated that the body had been removed and measurements made from the bloodstains.[52]

The camp administration contacted the sheriff and the attorney of Millard County, who quickly arrived, but military staff members would not talk to them. The deputy coroner was only allowed to examine the body and report the cause of death. There was some delay since the internal security officials in camp did not know that the acting director, James Hughes, was in Salt Lake City and Charles Ernst was in Washington. Finally Lorne Bell, chief of community services and acting director in the absence of Hughes, was located, and he took charge. About 10:00 P.M. the administrators contacted the chair of the community council, Tsune Baba, who brought several other councilmen into a discussion of the incident. It was not until 2:30 A.M. that they learned the identity of the deceased; he was identified by his glasses, since the military police would not let anyone see the body, which had no identification on it. Then the councilmen were allowed to confirm the identification by viewing Wakasa's remains. Unsure how the Topaz residents would react to Wakasa's death, Lieutenant Henry H. Miller called a general alert, complete with machine guns, gas masks, and tear gas, which further terrified the distressed population. The alert was canceled two days later.[53]

The camp's residents were shocked and outraged when they learned what had happened; they feared that this act of violence was a precursor to others. They immediately demanded an open investigation of the killing. Chairman Baba first attempted to determine the facts and then called a meeting of the council, to be held Monday night.[54]

A special edition of the *Topaz Times* carried the story in both English and Japanese on Monday, April 12, and the news was then released to the local media.[55] The story was carefully worded, intended to inform but also to calm the residents, but it only raised more questions: why had the residents of Block 36, where Wakasa lived, not been notified immediately; and why had all the councilmen not been invited to the first council meeting? Baba and Lorne Bell thought that the announcement in the *Times* would control the public reaction, but they quickly recognized their error. The council then decided to select a campwide Committee of Ten to investigate the death. In addition, a special committee of the council (the Committee of Five) was appointed to work with the first committee. The council committee agreed to cooperate with the administration, although the members were rightly concerned about being labeled "stooges." Most council members believed that the WRA administration, like the members themselves, wanted only to find out what had happened and to prevent a recurrence.[56] After all, the military, not the WRA, had done the killing.

The funeral preparations raised other issues. The council decided on Monday that Block 36 should make the arrangements, since Wakasa had no family. But Hughes informed the council on the next day that the funeral had already been set for the following Monday and that workers and students would be excused from their normal tasks to attend. There was disagreement as to where the funeral should be held: the residents wanted it to take place on the spot where Wakasa had died, claiming this was Japanese custom. The administration feared that a ceremony there would cause a riot but conceded the point rather than have the dispute itself bring on demonstrations. Preparations for the funeral proceeded amid growing tension between the two groups, which nonetheless did not cease their dialogue.[57]

The press coverage of the story indicates the unimportance it had for white America. The *Millard County Chronicle* noted the story briefly, and the *Millard County Progress,* printed in Fillmore, Utah, picked it up. Its brief article in the weekly issue of April 16 told of the death, stressing that Wakasa had been warned four times before he was shot and that the WRA felt a careful investigation would be necessary. The paper printed the statement issued by Bell, which read in part: "The administration joins with the community in the feeling of genuine sadness as the result of this tragic incident." While making clear his hope that such an event would not be repeated, Bell urged "every resident to familiarize himself with the rules and regulations." Clearly Wakasa had erred in choosing to walk so near—if not under—the fence. The Salt Lake City newspapers carried equally brief stories on the day after Wakasa's death and nothing of the aftermath. The only paper to give daily space to the story was the *Topaz Times,* which ran brief articles from April 12 to April 20, the day of the funeral. Its stories, clearly censored, stated that Wakasa had been shot "while attempting to crawl through the west fence." The sentry fired after warning him four times.[58] That initial error was never corrected. Readers then learned that the anonymous sentry would be court-martialed at Fort Douglas, near Salt Lake City. Representatives of the Spanish embassy and the Spanish consulate in San Francisco would investigate, because Wakasa was a Japanese citizen and Spain had undertaken to act in Japan's behalf in the United States. Someone from the State Department would also participate. The residents protested the killing, but only nonviolently, through their representatives on the council. Succeeding stories in the *Times* dealt with the way the military police was to be restrained in the future and gave an account of the elaborate two-and-a-half-hour funeral.[59] The *Times* never printed any opinions about the event, its causes, or its resolution.

The community council met daily to review the case. A few days after the killing, the Spanish consul and the State Department representative arrived; Mr. Young, from the State Department, came solely to learn what the Issei were telling the consul, who would, presumably, inform the government of Japan. Chairman Baba again raised the question of the location of the funeral with Acting Director Hughes, who had returned to Topaz. Baba and the other councilmen reiterated that it should be held where Wakasa had died and cited Japanese precedents. Hughes was equally insistent that such a location would only stir up the populace and might give the military police further occasion for violence. A compromise was reached, perhaps through the intercession of the Spanish consul: the funeral was held later than originally scheduled, on April 20, near where Wakasa died but away from the fence.[60]

The Caucasians did not present a united front. A military sentry had shot Wakasa, and the military closed the WRA staff out of the investigation as quickly as it had the Delta officials and the community council. Expecting trouble, the military grew defensive. MPs harassed a group of evacuees who came to the site later to investigate, warning them that if they did not stay away, they would "get what the other guy had gotten." Army officers from Fort Douglas arrived with the consul and the State Department representative.[61] The military was alert and hostile toward the Japanese Americans but it was also uncooperative with the camp administration. Lieutenant Miller refused to hold an inquest, although he did open a board of inquiry.

When James Hughes returned from Salt Lake City, he took charge of the investigation inside the camp. He learned that the soldier who fired the shot, one Gerald B. Philpott (whose name was never released to the camp residents or the press), was to be arrested, taken to Fort Douglas, and tried at a general court martial.[62] (He was exonerated.) This was scarcely the open trial the Topaz residents wanted, but when Charles Ernst returned to camp he obtained only a few further concessions. In a letter Miller promised that henceforth his men would be less heavily armed. (The *Topaz Times* noted that sentries were ordered not to carry extra weapons such as tommy guns and tear gas bombs, but that sidearms were an indispensable part of their regular uniforms.) The soldiers would not enter the camp without clearance from the WRA, and they would not harm or carry out "unusual" surveillance of the residents of Topaz. On April 20 Ernst announced that day guards inside the camp would be eliminated, and only one soldier would be present at the main gate to check entering people and baggage.[63]

Wakasa's death alarmed Topaz residents in part because it came from an initial shot, with no warning round, fired by a sentry at someone he presumably thought intended to crawl under the fence. Whether this was the first such incident is a matter of dispute. According to one source soldiers had fired warning shots at Topaz residents some eight times in the months previous to Wakasa's death.[64] The matter of the fence had been, from Topaz's beginning, very ambiguous; it was not completed when the first residents arrived, and on occasion people had been able to obtain passes to walk or hike in the areas around the camp. One man even got lost on such a hike and was missing for several days. However, when the military took control of security, it assigned combat veterans and less capable men who were clearly trigger-happy to the Topaz duty. The Wakasa case made the guards more careful, but not necessarily less determined to prevent "escapes" of the people they identified as the enemy. On May 22 a sentry in the southeast watch tower fired a warning shot into the ground to prevent a couple from strolling too near the fence. The sentry subsequently reported the incident to headquarters, and there was an investigation. Rumors of another Wakasa case flew around camp, but no one had been injured. Once again the administration warned people to stay away from the fence, particularly in the early evening and at night.[65]

The Topaz Nikkei conducted two nonviolent responses to the shooting. They planned and held a large funeral, which was preceded by spontaneous work stoppages around camp. After Wakasa's death absenteeism increased among residents seeking a safe way to demonstrate their outrage. The administration was remarkably unsympathetic to this tactic. Russell Bankston, the WRA reports officer, recorded that it gradually became clear that no one would return to work until after the funeral—even after the Japanese Americans were informed they would not be paid for work missed. He was surprised that they would accept punishment for these actions and even continue them. Soon virtually none of the Nikkei were working. The council won its battle with the administration over the funeral's location. All work stopped while the religious leaders of the camp held a moving open air funeral. The women had made huge wreaths of paper flowers, Miné Okubo recalled, and the administration estimated that between 1,500 and 1,700 people attended. The *Topaz Times* raised the number to 2,000. The Protestant service included hymns, special music, prayers, and a sermon, with words of condolence offered by the Reverend Z. Okayama of the Interfaith Group, Council Chair Baba, and Assistant Director Hughes. The Reverend Barnabas Hisayoshi Terasawa pronounced the benediction.[66] The funeral seemed to defuse tensions in the camp and everyone returned to work.

After the ceremony the administration, the council, and the military put together a compromise to prevent another such shooting. The special council committee achieved little in its meeting with the Spanish consul and the administration, but the problem was really with the military, not the WRA. In fact, the army was ready to back off a bit; in addition to restricting the use of arms and the presence of MPs in camp, the officer in command announced that soldiers who had seen war service in the Pacific would be withdrawn and no more would be assigned to Topaz.[67] Not everyone was pacified, as Okubo noted; "the anti-administration leaders . . . started to howl."[68] Some of the innocence and presumed good will that had existed between the interned and the incarcerators died with Wakasa and was not reborn. Philpott, the sentry whose name the military so carefully guarded, was found not guilty of violating military law and reassigned. The residents were never told of the disposition of the case. In June a member of the landscape crew erected an illegal monument to Wakasa, but it quickly disappeared.[69]

⚜

Two Issei remember the Wakasa incident very well, but from different perspectives. Karl Akiya was a Kibei friend of Wakasa's who had dinner with him on the fateful day. Akiya was born in the United States and educated in Japan, but his opposition to Japanese militarism led him to return to America in 1932. The evening of Wakasa's death Akiya talked with him, as he had many times; they liked to speak Japanese together and reminisce about Japan. Wakasa was from the East Coast, said Akiya, and had been interned only because the war had caught him on the West Coast, where he had come on business. Akiya and Wakasa usually left the dining hall together, but that night his friend left early to take a walk after dinner. Most accounts say that Wakasa went to walk his dog; the WRA report on the incident stated that he was "known to walk his dog in the area." Camp residents were allowed to keep dogs or cats; however, Akiya did not think Wakasa owned a dog, but rather that he was playing with a stray.[70] A half hour after they parted, Akiya recalled, he learned that his friend had been shot by a sentry. After the shooting he went to the scene of his death and found an unusual flower just outside the fence. Akiya believed Wakasa might have been reaching for the flower when he was shot. He said there were scuff marks on the ground indicating the body might have been pulled outside the fence after the shooting. He also emphasized that the sentry had just returned from the war in the Pacific and thus had an exceptionally strong hatred of "Japs." Akiya insisted that Wakasa would not have tried to escape; after all, where would he have gone?[71] Ted Lewis, who worked for internal security, knew Wakasa and remembered that he complained a good deal about the internment of U.S. citizens, but he agreed with Akiya that Wakasa had no reason or incentive to escape.[72]

George Gentoku Shimamoto related a different story. An Issei from San Francisco, Shimamoto had supervised Nikkei construction workers in camp and was prominent in camp politics. He was selected to serve on the general residents' committee investigating Wakasa's death. In contrast to most other residents, he concluded that Wakasa had probably been trying to escape and was crawling under the barbed wire fence when he was shot. Shimamoto was not as concerned about Wakasa's being punished for disobeying the rules as he was bothered by the excessive use of military force and the lack of a warning. He too reflected that there was no place for Wakasa to run.[73]

Shimamoto was not the only one concerned about the use of lethal force. Many residents were terrified that they would become targets for the armed, "Jap-hating" sentries. Richard Drinnon noted sarcastically that any movement "endangered their lives, from beginning to end. Technically, the inmates were free to walk to the barbed wire and be killed, as happened to James Hatsuaki Wakasa."[74] Michi Weglyn commented that death, rather than thirty days' imprisonment as the regulations stated, seemed to be the penalty for attempted escape from the camps.[75] It certainly was in Wakasa's case. Since there was no recurrence, however, one might conclude—without in any way excusing this reprehensible action—that it was an exception. Nevertheless, after this event, no one tried to escape, either inadvertently or on purpose. The point had been made: Topaz was an armed concentration camp.

Former internees also stressed the shock of the incident in their published memoirs. Yoshiko Uchida thought, like Karl Akiya, that Wakasa had been looking for something and was distracted. She recalled that people often walked with their heads down, looking for the occasional trilobite or arrowhead. Everyone was outraged that the guard had not at least fired a warning shot before killing the man; after all, how far could Wakasa have gone even if he had crawled under the fence? If this happened once, it could happen again, and parents worried especially for the safety of their children.[76] Uchida and Miné Okubo both were troubled because "particulars and facts of the matter were never satisfactorily disclosed to the residents."[77] And indeed, the WRA did disclose its bias against the Japanese American internees by depriving them of significant information that affected their lives. Once again it demonstrated the powerlessness of the Nikkei.

Former administrator Roscoe Bell and his wife Gladys remembered the event clearly, forty years later. They recalled that Wakasa was hard of hearing, and Gladys Bell noted that the wind was blowing especially hard that day, so that he might not have heard the sentry. Roscoe Bell knew that many of the sentries were "misfits, wounded, or disabled and were not fit for other active duty." He thought that Philpott was a disabled veteran of the Aleutian campaign, which had probably made him a "Jap-hater." He reflected that everyone was uneasy about the guards; he himself was because they were so arbitrary in their actions. Sometimes they would stop farm trucks he was sending to the fields, while on other occasions they would wave everyone through. Sometimes they carried handguns, and at other times rifles. Many former camp residents agreed that the guards were misfits. Roscoe Bell feared that Japan would retaliate and use the incident to mistreat American prisoners of war, but it did not.[78] Probably the event was never known in Tokyo, since the Spanish consulate took its duties in such matters very lightly.

Whatever the truth of the Wakasa killing, it was a profoundly disturbing event, especially to camp residents who knew or lived near the man. Michiko Okamoto was traumatized by the event, and it was one of her most prominent memories of camp life forty-five years later: "We were totally vulnerable. We were helpless. There was no way of defending ourselves from anybody who just got trigger-happy and wanted to shoot us."[79] It suggested the ultimate nightmare, that concentration camps could turn into death camps for everyone as they had for one unfortunate man. Although Hughes, Ernst, and Roscoe Bell took pains to make sure that there would be no repetition at Topaz, the very presence of armed guards made violence against the residents a permanent possibility.

❧

Although the initial outrage at Topaz over Wakasa's killing was considerable, it was relatively mild; at Manzanar or Tule Lake the residents would have rioted. Both the military personnel and the camp administration at Topaz expected that the Nikkei would riot there, too. Maintaining order and conducting business as usual were of greater concern than expressing solicitude over the residents' fears. The MPs planned riot control measures, and the administration tried to keep the residents at work. The reasons for the relative calm of the Nikkei can be traced to the lack of aggressive leadership and the desire of their elected representatives to avoid confrontation. The council cooperated with the administration to defuse the crisis and deflected the residents' anger. It might be said that it was acting as a "tool" of the WRA, but it was also realistic and fearful. The administration, although not openly sympathetic to the residents' fears, gave in on the location of the funeral and separated itself from the military. It obtained restrictions on military activities within camp, which significantly reassured the inhabitants. The historian Richard Drinnon charged that some members of the WRA really had little sympathy for the victim, and he cited a letter from Luther T. Hoffman (who succeeded Charles Ernst as Topaz's director) to WRA Director Dillon Myer written in July 1944. In the letter Hoffman, who was not at Topaz at the time of the Wakasa killing, wrote that the camp newspaper had frequently warned people not to go near the fences, and "the WRA could hardly have been in a position to specify the action the military would take in case persons approached the fence or attempted to go through or over it."[80] It is doubtful that many Caucasian staff members were as cold-blooded about the killing as Luther Hoffman seems to have been. Eleanor Sekerak's depiction of him as the consummate bureaucrat helps make his comment understandable, if still reprehensible. According to Jane Beckwith, the Delta residents who recalled the Wakasa incident years later considered it murder, since they knew by this time that the internees posed no threat to them. They explained Wakasa's behavior as an inability to hear or understand the sentry's orders because of the wind or his poor English.[81] The *Topaz Times* had warned people to stay away from the fence, but no one had told them what the consequences might be.[82]

❦

The whole subject of self-government in the camps is highly controversial. One analyst, Norman R. Jackman, called the relocation centers "at best, a benevolent authoritarianism." Drinnon put it more harshly: "From WRA social scientists the word *community* had much the Orwellian ring of the word *truth* from the lips of a minister of misinformation."[83] In such circumstances self-government was an oxymoron. Community councils did not function completely effectively at any center. The members were either regarded as pawns of the administration and were therefore disdained, ignored, or physically attacked by the other residents, or they sided with the activist elements in camp and were disregarded by the administration. The councils in Topaz went through both phases.

The registration-segregation crisis, which overwhelmed the second community council, demonstrates the two aspects of camp self-government. George A. Ochikubo, a Nisei dentist from Berkeley, was elected the chair, with George Gentoku Shimamoto as assistant. Shimamoto favored adjusting to the circumstances of camp life as tranquilly as possible, in order to co-exist peacefully with the Caucasians. The council was one-third Nisei, two-thirds Issei, demonstrating the changed balance of power in camp as Nisei began to resettle. But even though Ochikubo was a Nisei, he was much more obstructionist than the Issei toward both the administration and his fellow council members. Frequently threatening to resign if he did not get his way, he was difficult to work with, yet his continuing popularity with the residents suggests that his belligerency was quite acceptable to them.

In the winter of 1942–43, before Wakasa's death, the administration announced a new policy that affected the residents even more directly than the killing. The crisis began innocuously. Eager to determine once and for all the "loyalty" of male citizens of military age in order to draft those who were eligible, the army decided to circulate a questionnaire. The WRA thought such a device might be useful for clearing "loyal" residents for resettlement. The Justice Department had similar sentiments: Edward Ennis of Justice reflected much later that he thought the questionnaire would be a simple device that would separate the "very small" number of disloyal from the loyal, enabling the administration to remove the former and process the latter to leave.[84] The army saw its needs as paramount, and it believed that loyal camp inhabitants could better serve their country by fighting for it than by picking sugar beets. Its goal was the formation of a special all-Nisei combat team. The WRA told the evacuees that they would regain "status" by signing up with the army. The plan began to take shape in January 1943 and was modified as its purpose expanded. First intended just for male Nisei, the questionnaire was ultimately expanded to apply to all Nikkei seventeen or older, so the older people could be identified for resettlement. The questionnaire, ambiguously entitled "Application for Leave Clearance," was announced on February 10, 1943.

A special edition of the *Topaz Times* informed the residents of the new procedure and a series of mass meetings, chaired by Council Chairman Tsune Baba, explained the purpose of the questionnaires. Problems cropped up immediately. To begin with, the form was poorly titled, since most Issei had no desire to leave camp and were too old for the army.[85] With superb bureaucratic obfuscation, the WRA allowed no questions at the mass meetings, which quickly turned into gripe sessions, the "scratching of old wounds," as Bankston characterized them in his report. To many Nikkei the purpose was more devious than the government admitted; they believed they would continue to be segregated and then formed into a suicide battalion. The poorly worded questionnaire quickly became controversial, as the sharp-eyed residents read into it more than the bureaucrats intended. The discussion centered on two key questions: Number 27, which asked draft-age males if they were willing to serve on combat duty in the armed forces of the United

States, and Number 28, which requested the Nikkei to swear allegiance to the United States and forswear allegiance or obedience to the Japanese emperor. For the noncitizen Issei the latter was unacceptable, since their action would turn them into stateless persons. After considerable agitation Ernst called Washington and Number 28 was reworded, but the damage had already been done.[86] Some Issei, however, made the opposite response: they signed a petition renouncing their Japanese citizenship and asking to volunteer for the army. They were not accepted, since there was no procedure for them to enlist, but they filled out the forms anyway. Many Nisei considered the question a trap: by giving up allegiance to Japan they would be admitting that they had in fact held it. As Michi Weglyn pointed out, "to the once starry-eyed Nisei, highly sensitive to their citizenship obligations, registration was the ultimate insult."[87] Question 27 provoked almost as strong a response. Many felt it was not only an insult but unanswerable. Given that they were in concentration camps with their civil rights suspended, how could they be asked to take up arms and defend the country that had incarcerated them? They felt only a conditional answer of "yes ... if" was possible.[88]

The response of Topaz residents to Question 27 was similar to that of people in the other camps: over all, some 4,600—22 percent of the 21,000 Nisei males eligible to register for the draft—answered "no," gave a qualified answer, or made no response, but many were protesting internment rather than expressing disloyalty by their answers.[89] The response at Topaz was not violent, as it was at Manzanar, nor did it take the form found at Heart Mountain, where draft resistance led many to civil disobedience and jail. Like the residents of the other camps, the people of Topaz accepted the question but showed by their responses how disturbing they felt the issue was. The controversy aroused strong emotions on both sides, forcing men who had never thought of questioning their American citizenship suddenly to do so, and putting those who supported volunteering in a precarious and sometimes dangerous position. A committee called the Resident Council for Japanese American Civil Rights was formed, which encouraged registration but only if Nisei civil rights were restored.[90] In many of the meetings the Nisei remained silent, fearing violent attacks by strongly opposed Kibei if they spoke in favor of volunteering. One block manager proposed a resolution calling for the free movement of volunteers back to the West Coast as well as the elimination of segregation in the armed forces, but its passage assured nothing, since the WRA was in no position to grant either. Most Nisei eventually registered, although there was much "confusion," as the WRA put it: some thought registering and volunteering were interchangeable, while others felt that registering would mean one would have to be resettled. There were originally 5,364 yeses and 790 noes to Question 28, but subsequently 30 percent of the noes changed to yes and seven yeses changed to no. Ultimately, 113 men volunteered, of whom 59 were accepted into the military. At the same time, the controversy sparked a large number of requests for repatriation and expatriation: 447, with 201 coming from draft-age citizen males (159 Kibei and 42 Nisei). By September these requests had almost doubled. Only 36 people, however, actually left Topaz to sail for Japan.[91]

The repatriation requests came as a shock to Washington, for the originators of the questionnaire had not anticipated that kind of response. Oscar Hoffman attempted to explain to Director Myer why such requests had occurred. He concluded that the Issei—especially those whose English was poor or nonexistent—felt America promised no future for them. The children of the renunciants were simply demonstrating traditional patterns of obedience by following their parents' lead. Some were embittered by the evacuation, while others had money and property in Japan that they did not wish to lose. Some wanted to move to Tule Lake, believing that changing camps would help them to avoid the draft.[92] Ernst, too, was disturbed by the many requests for repatriation and expatriation, which he could not reconcile with his image of the "loyal" Japanese Americans in Topaz. But even Hoffman, whose job it was to "understand" the Nikkei, did not realize that the renunciants who answered "no-no" might have reasons unconnected to loyalty. Japanese Americans' anger, frustration, and fears were deeper than many sympathetic whites could comprehend.

One of the Kibei who signed "no-no" was Morgan Yamanaka. Reflecting on the episode forty-five years later, he recalled his confusion. He and his brother were well aware that the questionnaire was connected to the recruiting efforts of the U.S. Army, but they felt their civil rights should be restored before they were asked to serve. These teenagers had no comprehension of the consequences if they did not give affirmative answers to the pertinent questions: "There was no discussion of the consequences. It came only after." Were they disloyal? Certainly not. Even though Morgan Yamanaka was technically a Kibei, he had been a young child when he was living in Japan and had not acquired any militaristic sentiments. It was simply his family home, where he had many relatives and his family had property. Regarding the fateful questions, Yamanaka said, "I don't think we were particularly bitter. I don't think we were particularly angry, but we were 'pissed off,' in the jargon of the 1980s." It was insulting to be asked such questions at such a time in such a place. Why should he have to demonstrate his loyalty or serve in a segregated army while the rest of his family remained behind barbed wire? The registration crisis caused Morgan Yamanaka to renounce his American citizenship and request expatriation to Japan. (He quickly withdrew the request later.) His actions, supported by his family, resulted in their being transported to Tule Lake, where Morgan ended up in the infamous stockade.[93]

The registration controversy certainly intensified opposition to the army's volunteer Japanese American combat team. Even people who were interested disliked the idea of a segregated force made up of men whose civil liberties had been terminated, and they worried about the care of their families in their absence. Those who did volunteer found themselves and their families threatened by Nikkei who had become violently anti-American as a result of the controversy. Volunteering went slowly; finally, one group was recruited, from Block 5. At first only 58 volunteered, but when the camp administration took over the effort from the military, letting the Nisei themselves encourage others to join, the number gradually increased to 113. The induction of several hundred young women into the Women's Auxiliary Army Corps (which later became the WAC) stimulated the men to volunteer, since they did not want to appear less patriotic.[94] The young women also held parties for the male volunteers, and suddenly enlisting became exciting and fun.

One of the volunteers was Bill Kochiyama, a Nisei from New York City, who was raised in an orphanage after his mother died. Kochiyama was an accidental Californian; he had come to Berkeley to try to attend the University of California, but his hopes were dashed when he learned he would have to pay out-of-state tuition. Unable to afford that, he was just knocking about San Francisco trying to find a job when the war stranded him. Kochiyama felt very alien in the San Francisco–Japanese American culture; he did not speak Japanese and his English had a strong New York accent. He also had a sense of outrage and a willingness to express it that contrasted strongly with his peers in California. He went into camp protesting every inch of the way, determined to get out as soon as he could. Movie actor Lee Tracy came to Topaz to promote volunteering, and Kochiyama listened to him speak. He told Tracy that if he could be taken out of camp the very next day, he would enlist. Tracy assured him this could be done, and Kochiyama signed up. He was indeed on his way to war the next day.[95]

The registration controversy culminated in the segregation of the "disloyal," as the army had intended. The WRA concluded that all who had signed "no-no," along with their families, should be separated from the loyal and placed in one particular camp. In fact, registration was not a War Department order and failure to register was not a violation of Selective Service regulations, but few found out that it was not before they reached Tule Lake, the camp designated for recalcitrants.[96] The Topaz administration, fearing a repeat of the turmoil that had greeted the questionnaire, prepared for the departure of the "no-nos" (as they came to be called) long in advance. The council set up community cooperation committees, and the administration created an information consultant's committee. A transfer office was established to handle logistics, and a board of review was created for those who might change their minds—but only before July 15, when decisions became irrevocable. (In fact, the movement was in the other direction; more and more decided to leave.) A manual was even prepared to guide staff members working with the departing ones. Evelyn Hodges, a social worker from Logan who later married Ted Lewis of internal security, was hired to interview people who were considering going to Tule Lake. She found that there were many issues on their minds. One man wanted to know if there was any sand there: Topaz's infamous dust aggravated his asthma. A young woman wanted to stay with her boyfriend at Topaz but her family wanted to go to Tule; the couple finally resolved their problems by marrying, since the girl's parents would not let her remain in Topaz without their supervision. The counselors were not supposed to tell people what to do, just help them come to some conclusion.[97] The administrators made special provisions so people could move their pets (there were five departing dogs and three birds).

Ultimately 1,447 decided to depart, 1,062 Nisei and 385 Issei. The camp prepared a festive sendoff. At the same time, 1,489 Tuleans arrived, "loyal" Tule Lake residents who were being moved away from the "disloyal." Some of the latter were actually "old Tuleans" who just did not want to move again. Because of a mixup the Nikkei from Tule Lake arrived a day early, so there was one night of real overcrowding, but they all managed and the departure went smoothly. The aim of segregation was to create more homogeneous camp populations, but this was not entirely achieved. Some "yes-yeses" remained at Tule Lake, and as people at Topaz became more disillusioned, an increasing portion of the population there was considering moving to Japan at the end of the war but could not be accommodated in the overcrowded Tule Lake camp.[98]

The mood at the time of the departure for Tule Lake was, despite all precautions, "abnormally tense," as Oscar Hoffman reported. Clashes broke out between employers and employees, and even an abortive general strike. Hoffman noted that a few evenings before the transfer many residents "sought relief in drink," something that was ordinarily illegal at Topaz.[99] Apparently, many of the tipplers were Hawaiians, whose transfer was augmenting their resentment for the way they had been treated at Sand Island in Hawaii. Since most of them were bachelors, their rowdiness was somewhat expected. Decked out in leis, they shouted "three banzais" as their bus pulled away. The others left solemnly, and some of the women and girls cried. The camp was in the habit of making a festival out of every possible event, as a morale-building device, and this was no exception. The arriving Tuleans were greeted warmly, and pretty girls were met with whistles. The newcomers submitted without protest to the inevitable baggage search. With many friends and relatives among them, Hoffman thought their assimilation would be rapid, especially since the facilities at Topaz were better than those at Tule Lake. The only sour note was the lack of jobs at Topaz, since the WRA had recently been ordered to cut back. The Tuleans immediately complained.[100]

Roscoe Bell was assigned to accompany the departing Topaz residents to Tule Lake. As their train approached the segregation camp, everyone became tense, he recalled. Someone played a recording of "You're in the Army Now" over the public address system—black humor, for the travelers were entering a facility under military control, not the relatively benevolent jurisdiction of the WRA. The return trip had a much different atmosphere, for compared to Tule Lake, Topaz was almost free, and the Tule "yes-yeses" were happy to be leaving one camp for another, even if it was still internment.[101]

Abu Keikoan remembered that move from Tule Lake to Topaz. A native of Sacramento, she and her family had been interned in the nearby Walerga Assembly Center and then sent to the northern California camp. She found Tule Lake "like a horse barn," and she was very impressed with the "nice white bathrooms" at Topaz. A junior high school student, Abu hated to leave her cousins, who remained at Tule Lake when their father opted with the other "old Tuleans" and refused to move again. Since the Keikoans were "yes-yeses," they moved to Topaz. Abu's older sister soon resettled in New York and her brother joined the armed forces.[102]

With the end of the segregation conflict, Topaz completed the first phase of its brief life as a community. The camp's population was complete, although it was slowly being drained by resettlement, transfers, and the occasional in-migration of family members from other camps or prisons. Self-government in the form of community councils had been established, complete with a constitution and elections, and other major institutions were also in place. It had all the external trappings of democracy—except freedom.

One important institution in camp was the newspaper, the *Topaz Times,* which printed all the news the administration wanted printed. (The WRA had mandated a newspaper for each camp to keep the residents advised of its policies and to maintain morale in the centers.) The paper was published in English and Japanese three times a week at the *Millard County Chronicle* offices in Delta. It cheerfully recorded vital statistics including the latest number of new arrivals, either by train or by birth, along with the scores of recent baseball games, news for women in a special column, and accounts of other camp activities. Although the administration almost never resorted to overt censorship (except in the Wakasa case), Russell Bankston, who supervised the *Times,* indirectly controlled what the paper printed by the type of people he appointed as journalists. On one occasion, the administration "learned the Japanese language section of the *Topaz Times* was being subverted; that the translators were calling on citizens to resist registration." The offenders were asked to resign, Bankston noted, adding that they were both "no-nos."[103] He found someone more reliable to make sure the Japanese version of the text corresponded to the English version.[104]

Topaz also was the home of *Trek,* a literary magazine that featured creative writing and the marvelous illustrations of Miné Okubo. It only lasted for three issues, because its staff opted for resettlement.

Religion was another important aspect of camp life. Approximately 40 percent of the residents were Protestant and 40 percent Buddhist. The other 20 percent were Catholic, and there were twenty-six Seventh-Day Adventist families, plus a small number with no religion. There were also members of several smaller faiths. Several hundred people belonged to "Seichō no Iye," described by the community analyst as resembling Christian Science. (In fact, this was one of the "new religions" of Japan, a syncretistic belief that had cooperated with the militarists in prewar Japan.) Some were affiliated with the Kagawa Christians in Japan, nondenominational believers who followed the leadership of Kagawa Toyohiko. Some also observed the "Nishi System of Health Engineering," which Fumi Hayashi described as a practice involving a half hour of exercises in the morning to help the practitioners, of whom her father was one, deal with pain.[105] There were several other faith-healing groups, which Hoffman described as "cults."[106]

Among the Protestants were a number of ministers from the Bay Area. All denominations met as one group. They chose a common creed, and various ministers in camp shared the leadership. Before the evacuation the Reverend Taro Goto served as pastor of the Pine Methodist Church in San Francisco and the Reverend Lester Suzuki presided over the Berkeley Methodist United Church; they were leaders in the Protestant community in camp. Suzuki described Yoshio Isokawa as the "most active lay person in the center." Dave Tatsuno and Tad Fujita were also very involved in church activities. Devout Caucasians, such as Roscoe Bell and his family and Eleanor Gerard and Emil Sekerak, joined them. An Interfaith Church Council was created under the direction of Lorne Bell; it elected the Reverend Goto as its chair and the Reverend Kenryu Kumata as secretary, who was later succeeded by the Reverend Howard Toriumi. The Reverend Carl Nugent, the former pastor of the Japanese Evangelical Reformed Church in San Francisco, joined the ministerial staff in spring 1943; he and his family resided in Delta. His primary function was to assist with resettlement, but his concern for the Christian flock was remembered warmly years later. Publication of the activities of the various religious groups was assigned to several of the faithful: Tad Hirota for the Buddhists, the Reverend M. Nishimura for the Protestants, and H. Honnami for the Catholics. The two largest groups, the Protestants and the Buddhists, met in an old CCC camp building moved from Callao, Utah, and the Catholics and Seventh-Day Adventists shared another building. Services were held in both English and Japanese. The Protestant ministers rotated their preaching, and they were aided by Caucasians from outside: Nugent, the Reverend Frank

Herron Smith, and others, including the well-known missionary to Japan, the Reverend E. Stanley Jones. The Protestants were concentrated in Block 28.[107]

The first Christmas in camp was inevitably a sad and trying time, as Miné Okubo's drawings depicted.[108] The Christians helped to organize an all-camp program, and Quakers and a few other generous people around the nation cooperated by sending small gifts for the children. Among those who were touched by this generosity was Tad Fujita, whose son David received a little pocketknife. When Fujita found the name of the donor—Barbara Crocker of Fitchburg, Massachusetts—inside the package, he immediately wrote her a letter of thanks. This began a friendship that lasted until her death more than thirty years later.[109] This episode was the more touching because it was so rare; most Americans were unaware of the camps.

The Buddhists also organized, a task made difficult since so many priests were imprisoned after Pearl Harbor because of their supposed loyalties to Japan. The headquarters of the Buddhist Church in America were transferred from San Francisco to Topaz. There were ultimately five priests at Topaz serving some 40 percent of the camp's population. Buddhists were most numerous in blocks 36 and 37. The priests served congregations of 400–500, meeting on Sunday with an overflow service on Wednesday.[110] Like the Christian services, the Buddhist services were in English and Japanese. Buddhists and Christians cooperated at Topaz, forming an interfaith group; this was apparently unusual among the relocation camps. In 1944 Easter and Buddha's birthday fell on the same day, so both congregations held Easter services in the morning and Buddhist services in the afternoon.[111]

⚜

The residents devised a number of activities to keep themselves busy. Many worked in the camp. By June 1943 some 75 percent of the able-bodied residents were employed, working for the administration, in the dining halls, on farms, the cooperative, or the hospital. Most earned $16 a month for a forty-four-hour week, at a time when other Americans made $150–$200 a month. This discrepancy brought much resentment and encouraged resettlement, as it was in part designed to do. Unemployment compensation was also paid: $3.25 to an adult male, who also received $2.75 for his wife and $1.50 for each of his children—per month. This practice was helpful when the WRA decided in late 1943, in the interests of governmental economy, to reduce the number of employees allowed at each camp. The cuts hurt people whose financial resources were already meager, and it also created serious morale problems. Since many workers could not afford to resettle away from the camp, it seems to have been a bit of additional stupidity on Washington's part. Unskilled workers were paid $12 a month. Soldiers, with whom the evacuees were compared, made $21 a month and also got board and "room," of a sort, but their pay was later raised to $50 a month while relocation camp wages remained unchanged.[112]

In order to help purchase needed clothing and other items, the residents organized a consumers' cooperative; they charged a membership fee and borrowed from their numbers to capitalize the enterprise. They selected a general manager and division heads and also established a credit union. The WRA co-op supervisor, Walter Honderick, soon earned the respect and friendship of Dave Tatsuno, manager of the dry goods section. Tatsuno and his assistant, Tad Fujita, were able to leave the camp on buying trips, traveling as far away as Saint Louis. They kept the residents supplied with goods and necessities.[113] The managerial positions gave them both experience that they used later in the outside world. In addition, the trips made it possible for Tatsuno to smuggle film into camp for his movie camera. He had loaned the camera to a friend, but Honderick voluntarily requested it to be sent to Topaz. Tatsuno was thus the only Nikkei in camp to document its story on film. The film was processed outside and mailed to Tatsuno's brother at the University of Utah; it ultimately came back to Tatsuno at Topaz. Many years later it returned to the University of Utah to be used in a documentary about camp life made by the resident public television station, KUED. (The original film was donated to the Japanese American National Museum in Los Angeles in early 1992.)[114]

Relations between the Nikkei workers and their Caucasian superiors could be very cordial. Chiyoko Yoshii Yano was asked to

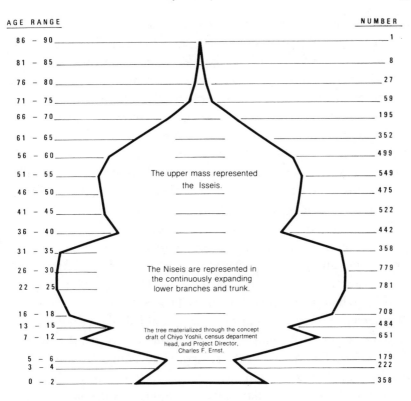

The Tree of Topaz
Reprinted by permission of Chiyoko Yoshii Yano.

set up the central statistics department, which reported to Charles
Ernst, the project director. She and her staff collected vital statistics, and she produced the demographic "tree of Topaz" that became the camp's symbol. Forty-five years later she was still very
proud of her work. Kazu Iijima, one of the few Nisei who held civil
service jobs in prewar Oakland, worked in the social welfare department with George LaFabreque, whom she described as a
"wonderful man . . . a warm person with a marvelous sense of
humor." What was even better, LaFabreque "really liked us a lot."
Iijima recalled that Charles Ernst and his staff members would
meet over coffee and they would tell him their grievances; he was
even sympathetic at 2:00 A.M. After her fiancé, Tad Iijima, volun-

teered for the military, they married in Salt Lake City, where he was sent for a physical exam. Kazu stayed at Topaz only until she was able to join him in Mississippi.[115] LaFabreque also left camp for the army in April 1943.[116] Some of the Caucasians made many lasting friendships at camp; several teachers kept in touch with their students, and the annual Christmas card exchange was mentioned by many. Gladys Bell did volunteer work among the residents, teaching English and music, and she helped organize a USO group for servicemen and women and their families. The Bells, like the Sekeraks and the Pratts, had close friends among the internees.

Recreational activities were another positive experience for the residents. They ranged from adult education to physical activities. There were picnics in good weather, dances every week, and entertainment and parties for everything from departing draftees and WACs to arriving Hawaiians and Tuleans. The singer Goro Suzuki, who later had a television career as Jack Soo, was a favorite. In summer 1943 a recreational camp was established on the site of an old CCC camp at Antelope Springs, at the foot of nearby Swasey Peak. Grace Fujimoto Oshita remembered going on a picnic to nearby Oak Creek canyon, where local residents provided fried chicken dinners for a dollar apiece.[117] Since it was some distance from Topaz, trucks transported campers there to swim and hike. Adults were allowed outside the residential compound to hike that fall, to roam the entire 19,000 acres of the project. Occasionally someone got lost, but no one tried to run away. The Nikkei also had a community New Year's Eve party with the Caucasians in camp, and there were several occasions when they invited people from Delta. They were entertained in turn by the Delta High School Concert Band. In November 1942 they even had turkey for Thanksgiving dinner. (The following year they would not be so fortunate; there was a turkey shortage in the WRA, so only administrators got to eat the bird, even in Topaz where they raised turkeys.)[118]

But even apart from actions precipitated by Caucasian violence, Topaz was far from a harmonious community. A number of problems came from its Kibei population, some of whom were not comfortable with Nisei customs and values. The WRA files mention episodes when "troublemakers," often Kibei, were arrested for beating up residents whom they considered too pro-administration. Tom Kawaguchi recalled with some bitterness how his parents and those of other volunteers were harassed by Kibei "no-no" youths.[119] Kazu Iijima stated that her husband went with a group to Salt Lake City for their preinduction physicals to avoid attacks in camp. On one occasion Kibei were sent to an old Indian school in Leupp, Arizona, that had been made into a prison for citizen "agitators": The "Topaz Eleven" were arrested in July 1943; although not charged with anything, they transferred to Leupp after FBI agents interviewed them. Even the prison's director was later convinced that they were guilty of nothing and had been bullied by the FBI agents.[120] WRA reports filed at the time indicate that the young men, apparently Nisei, sent to Leupp had announced they were disloyal and would commit sabotage if they could.[121] The Kibei, although a diverse group, were often pro-Japanese, and their "Japanesy" ways isolated them from the Americanized Nisei. There was also a language barrier, since they more often spoke Japanese than English. They were hard for the Caucasian administrators to understand as well, and their "foreignness" made it easy to identify them with the hated enemy.

Topaz experienced disturbances over registration and the Wakasa killing, but increasingly it suffered from what Hoffman termed "bad morale." He pointed out that "the aggressions of the very polite, threatened Japanese-American group [were] increasingly turned inward." He saw a number of social problems as evidence of "this hypochondriasis," or suppressed hostility, and suggested that it also led people to blow personality conflicts out of proportion.[122] There were also instances of severe stress, as conversations with retired social workers Faith Terasawa and Kazu Iijima revealed. Sometimes these resulted in hospitalization, but ordinarily the families took care of such problems at home.[123] At the time these problems were seen as morale issues, but clearly they were situational responses to incarceration. Internment just made people sick.

A problem arose at the hospital that demonstrated this stress and "hypochondriasis." As early as November 1942 the staff members presented a grievance petition stating that they had been promised a 175-bed facility but when they arrived it was just "a pile of lumber." A month later they still had only half the promised beds and lacked basic drugs and equipment. There were no facilities for infant dietary needs. An emergency appendectomy required permission from the chief medical officer to remove the patient to Delta, and a staff member had to go to his home three times to obtain it because the doctor was drunk. The petition found its way to a hospital committee chaired by Kenji Fujii, but a satisfactory response was slow in coming, probably because hospital needs were great everywhere in wartime.[124] When the shortages were filled, the staff members then began to quarrel over personnel. When Dr. James Goto arrived with his physician wife from Manzanar, the staff signed a petition refusing to work with him because of his abrasive personality. After much dissension, the administration agreed to transfer him, but Washington refused to concur. Goto worked for a while in public health, and after his wife gave birth the family moved to another camp. Meanwhile, the rest of the staff began to squabble over other issues. Some of the Caucasian personnel resigned and the Nikkei relocated, but the contentious situation continued to the end of Topaz's days.[125] The complaints of the hospital staff probably stemmed from differences in status between Caucasian and Nikkei personnel in the concentration camp setting. No physician was accustomed to being told what to do, and having to work for a pittance while their white counterparts made outside wages was an intolerable affront to many interned physicians. The staff's strong reaction to the turmoil in the hospital seems to reflect the general social malaise of Topaz.

There were, in addition, occasional episodes of social deviance. The reports contain vague references to illicit sexual relations and prostitution, but these are hard to document. An anonymous Nisei bragged to JERS interviewer Charles Kikuchi in Chicago after the war that he "had enjoyed sex with dozens of girls in the Topaz camp, and forced himself on several more when they were let out together to work in the fruit harvest."[126] This statement may just have been an example of male braggadocio. Paul Spickard concluded that since the Nisei had little to do in camp but socialize, a great many either became engaged or married before leaving. Given the lack of privacy and the generally high moral values of the Nikkei, illicit sexual liaisons were uncommon in the camp itself, but references to women operating out of the beds of trucks or in unoccupied barracks appear in the files and were mentioned by some of the people interviewed for this study. (These were reported as rumors, ordinarily not as something the respondent had direct knowledge of, and as Shibutani documented, rumors were the leaven of camp life.) Liquor was smuggled in or made from grain alcohol obtained from the hospital, and some residents even made sake, although surplus rice was hard to obtain. Gambling, the bane of Tanforan, appeared again; the third community council banned the playing of bingo on the grounds it had become a "racket," but the chairman admitted that the ordinance would be hard to enforce.[127]

Many expressed their disgust with camp life by resettling, joining the army, or requesting repatriation, which was a statement of disillusionment with America itself. Others remained and became morose, withdrawn, or bitter. Young people vented their frustrations in disobedience to parents and teachers, and some became vandals or thieves. There were cases of assault and the harassing of *inu*, or dogs, the term for people perceived as stooges of the administration. Nonetheless, Topaz was a remarkably peaceful and law-abiding community, which did not even have a detention center or jail. (The few lawbreakers were incarcerated in the town of Fillmore.)

Labor troubles were another area of conflict. Like the problems at the hospital, they reflected underlying tensions in the camp, conflicts between Caucasians and Japanese Americans, and specific precipitants such as segregation. There was a work stoppage in the garage repair shop on September 3, 1943. The director decided to put a guard at the truck gate when the military sentries were not on duty because he suspected liquor smuggling. By mistake, a military guard rather than a civilian watchman was placed there, and the Nisei truck drivers refused to pass. When the garage superintendent, Carl Rogers, ordered the crew back to work in a way they interpreted as an insult, they refused. Included in the group were some Kibei who were scheduled to leave soon for Tule Lake, and they turned on Rogers, insisting he be discharged for discriminatory behavior. The motor pool shut down. Agricultural crews joined the dispute, and farming stopped. Even the livestock were not fed (although Roscoe Bell recalled that his loyal workers came to him in great distress over the plight of the animals, and he sent his sons to do the job). The community council delegated the problem to its labor committee, which held discussions with workers and the administration. Rogers himself was investigated by the WRA on grounds he was anti-Japanese, and for a while it seemed all Topaz would join the strike. A compromise was worked out, in a settlement that was an important victory for the council: Rogers "took a vacation," and the workers returned to the fields and trucks. The charges against Rogers were dropped and the whole matter blew over when he received a draft notice and departed for the army. Everyone felt satisfied with the outcome.[128] Although the Nikkei residents of Topaz felt that conditions were barely tolerable, many Utahns believed otherwise. Governor Herbert B. Maw and some members of the state legislature were convinced that the evacuees were being "pampered" (a feeling still held by some in Delta in 1988). Maw and the senators came for a visit in March, were shown around the camp, and finally pronounced themselves satisfied with what they saw. The episode demonstrated the persistence of racism; it is hard to imagine that Caucasians could believe that a camp for interned Japanese Americans in the middle of the desert was somehow like a summer resort. Members of the Dies Committee of the U.S. Congress arrived in the fall to look for un-American activity on the part of inmates and administrators, but they too were disappointed.[129] Topaz was what it professed to be: a concentration camp in the desert holding people whose only crime was the fact that they had the faces—not the minds—of the enemy.

1. The Nisei Grill in San Francisco was closed when the Japanese American community prepared for evacuation to the assembly center at Tanforan in March 1942.

2. Registration, San Francisco. All Japanese Americans were required to register prior to their evacuation.

3. The Tanforan Assembly Center in San Bruno. Muddy streets and plank entryways added to the general unpleasantness of these former horse stalls.

4. In the summer of 1942, Tanforan residents attempted to supplement their army rations by growing fresh vegetables.

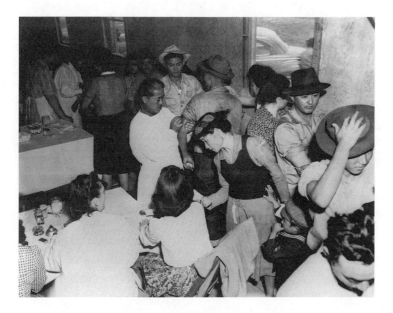

5. Evacuees arriving at the Tanforan Assembly Center were checked for infectious diseases and given vaccinations against smallpox and tuberculosis.

6. New arrivals at Tanforan were given cotton ticks to stuff with straw for mattresses, and these, along with their meager belongings, were dumped in front of the assigned stalls.

7. Children pledging their allegiance to the United States despite their internment. The child in the center, Mary Ann Yahiro, lost not only her home but also her mother, who was removed to another camp and died before being reunited with her family. Mary Ann Yahiro was living in Chicago in 1992 and still had bitter memories of camp (*San Francisco Chronicle*, February 1992).

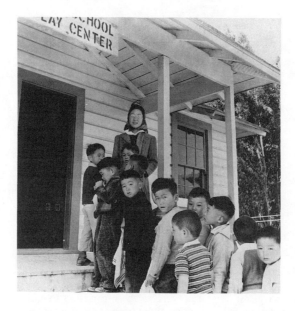

8. The nursery or "play center" at Tanforan established by Keiko Uchida in a small four-room cottage.

9. Memorial ceremony honoring the Nisei killed in the war, December 1944.

10. Buddhist church headquarters staff packing supplies for the return to San Francisco.

11. Kosaka Takaji's "mug shot" being taken when he was transferred from Topaz to Tule Lake Segregation Center for answering "no-no" on the loyalty questionnaire.

12. New Year's Eve, 1944, Topaz.

13. One of the last trains to leave Delta in the fall of 1945 brought fond farewells from the remaining administrative staff.

14. Nikkei property stored by the federal government for those who could not make other arrangements was not protected; vandalism was not uncommon.

Chapter Six

Dissension, Departure, and Grim Determination

By 1944 Topaz's existence could be summed up by the old adage, "The more things change, the more they stay the same." Registration and segregation brought some dislocation of the original population, but the community was transformed more slowly and persistently by the policy of resettlement, which caused nearly a third of the population to leave camp for new lives elsewhere. Most of the people who left eventually saw their lives improve, but at the cost of wrenching farewells to the friends and relatives—often aging parents—they left behind. The process of resettlement was fraught with uncertainties, beginning with the decision to leave. Would the new community accept the Nikkei without too much overt prejudice? Would the job work out? Was freedom worth the loss of security? For some the outside world was too harsh and they returned to camp, whose administrators had, reluctantly, to readmit them. These people bore powerful testimony to those who remained inside that the outside world was a more difficult place to live in than the WRA depicted. Communications from those who remained outside echoed their fears: racism was still alive in America, even in places that had not known Japanese Americans before the war.

The departures also affected those who remained, for the tasks of maintaining the community and its physical plant had to be performed by fewer people. Since it was usually the young and resilient who left, the capabilities of the remainder were often strained. Issei leaders were far less willing to cooperate with the

Caucasian WRA in policies that seemed to threaten their interests. As the ongoing war affected all sectors of civilian life, hiring whites for administrative positions was more difficult, and teachers in particular became harder to recruit. Obtaining laborers from among the resident community was also challenging, particularly since the jobs were of uncertain but presumably brief duration. There was increasing resentment over the miserably low wages that the WRA paid and some residents decided that they would rather not work, especially when the jobs available were laborious and tedious. The WRA did not consider increasing the compensation for Nikkei labor in the camps.

❧

Oscar Hoffman, the community analyst, detailed social problems at Topaz with insight as well as certain biases. Unlike his predecessor, Weston LaBarre, who held the position for only six months and had little time to become acquainted with the newly created community, Hoffman came to know the residents well and to become friends with many of them. The position was always controversial: administrators like Charles Ernst did not think they needed a social scientist to tell them how to do their jobs, and scholars of the internment, as well as many of the residents, tended to view the analysts as "stool pigeons" who befriended the Japanese Americans in order to report on them to Washington. The community analyst lived among the Nikkei and liked them, but he was not one of them.

Asael Hansen, who worked at Heart Mountain, wrote that his role was to observe what he saw, establish rapport with the residents, and learn enough about them to improve their lot. He was not to be involved in security or police matters, he was to keep his sources anonymous, and he was to have no administrative responsibility. Roger Daniels, who was critical of this supposed impartiality, noted in an introduction to Hansen's reflections that "the perceptions of the analyst and his circle of informants are not universally shared."[1] Hansen viewed his role benevolently and considered himself above the fray, but even presumed impartiality can amount to taking sides, as it did in Hansen's case. Hoffman was involved in nothing as traumatic as the draft resistance movement at Heart Mountain, which enveloped Hansen and many of the Nisei there, and his reports were usually straight reporting rather than advocacy journalism. They presented a weekly narrative of events at camp as well as occasional detailed analyses of specific topics or problems. Peter T. Suzuki studied the work of the analysts, arguing that they had their own agendas as well as specific instructions about relocation, registration, and segregation. (He especially criticized LaBarre's work.)[2]

Hoffman had his own point of view, which was sometimes favorable to the camp administration and sometimes not. A sociologist with a doctorate from the University of North Carolina, he seemed at the outset to be very sympathetic to the internees. He grew up in Kansas and studied in Michigan before going to Chapel Hill, and probably had never known or even met a Japanese American before he arrived in Topaz. Like many others, Hoffman wished to serve his country during the war but not through combat, and the position at Topaz seemed to meet his educational background. Although Hoffman did not get along with Ernst, he agreed with Luther Hoffman that resettlement was a wise and correct policy and that the Nikkei should be encouraged to leave Topaz. This was official policy and the analysts had all been instructed to promote it. Hoffman's reports reflect his agreement with that dictum, but they also offer useful insights into education, the hospital situation, labor, and morale in camp, especially during the last year as conditions deteriorated. Hoffman's was a Caucasian perspective; although his job brought him into closer relations with the Nikkei population of Topaz than most administrators, he usually supported the interners rather than the internees. The oral histories reveal how different his perspective was from the Japanese Americans'.[3]

❧

Over the years there were certain constants in the Topaz community, and even some improvements. Relations between the top administrators and the evacuees continued to be cool, since Director Ernst discouraged fraternization. Hoffman termed this attitude "formal aloofness"; he and Roscoe Bell agreed that Ernst believed close relationships with the internees were "not in good taste" and that he cared only about the few Nisei who worked closely with him. Hoffman said that the block managers referred to Ernst as "the fox," since they never could be sure how he really felt about anything. The director used the community councils to give the appearance of democracy, but in reality he intended his administration to be the ruling force, and it was. This gap between appearance and reality was soon discerned by the residents, who discounted the council as a result. The second director, Luther Hoffman, was more informal in style, establishing "close and intimate" relations with the council chairmen, thereby causing them problems when the residents wanted policies changed over which the council had no control. The end was the same: the council chairman was stigmatized as the "stooge of the Administration" for working closely with the director, yet he was unable to give the residents what they wanted. Because of Luther Hoffman's focus on the council, the block managers had more power during the first director's tenure and less during the second.[4]

Other aspects of community life appeared tranquil. The camp's Protestant and Buddhist religious organizations flourished and served as a bulwark for the faithful, convincing them that there was some greater purpose for which they were being called to suffer. Hoffman reflected that "in times of dislocation, anxiety and distress, people . . . [seek] psychological security in all sorts of ways,"[5] and religion has always been a source of solace. The residents and the military worked out an uneasy coexistence after the settlement of the Wakasa case, and by spring 1944 only nine military policemen remained at Topaz. Student relocation increased, and by the end of 1944 high school graduates could aspire to attend colleges and universities not only in the interior and the East but also on the West Coast. The consumers' cooperative provided an increasing amount of goods for the residents. In addition, the camp provided a beauty parlor, a photo service, a barbershop, and several large rooms in the barracks where movies were shown. Residents had their own post office, libraries, and fire station.[6]

Relations between the Nikkei, the residents of Delta, and the population of Utah generally continued to improve, as each group accepted the other for what it was. Topaz residents could, by obtaining a pass, shop in Delta for themselves and others in their block, and their business stimulated the town's economy. Many Topaz residents worked for the townspeople as housekeepers and farm laborers. Topaz young people exchanged games with Delta football and basketball teams, and both boys and girls traveled to other small towns around the state to play. Members of the girls' basketball team asked the girls from Wasatch Academy to spend a weekend as their guests at Topaz, where they entertained them and showed them around; the guests were lodged in Block 2. This prompted a reciprocal visit by the Topaz girls to the town of Mount Pleasant, in central Utah, about a hundred miles east of Topaz.[7] Although Topaz was an internment camp with barbed wire and armed guards, the residents had surprising opportunities to come and go, provided they went under the proper auspices. Since official policy encouraged young adults to resettle, exposing teenagers to life outside helped to promote that goal.

Civic clubs throughout Utah were also invited to visit the center. In April 1944, Director Ernst guided a group through the hospital, the farms, the tofu factory, and the high school. Afterward there was entertainment in the auditorium, and the visitors announced that whatever prejudices they had held against the camp's inhabitants had vanished. One man said that before the visit he had thought of the Japanese Americans as prisoners, but now he was "sorry for citizens so held." All admitted to being "enlightened" and promised they would inform others about the true nature of the camp.[8] Such a conversion to the evils of racial prejudice seems highly unlikely since values change slowly, but it was a beginning. At least most residents of Delta, who had more sustained contact with the residents of Topaz than such infrequent guests did, seemed to realize that the Japanese internment camp was a temporary intrusion and its residents were helping, not harming, the war effort; they were certainly no danger.

The mellowness of spring and summer changed in the fall. Tranquillity gave way to apathy and boredom, especially among the young. Oscar Hoffman, always sensitive to problems of social deviance at Topaz, reported in October that two small boys had been seen entering the football team's locker room, where they apparently robbed the players who were out on the field. Hoffman blamed the crime on the usual underlying causes: the lack of privacy, which made disciplining children difficult, and the parents' diminished authority. He also pointed to a new source: children were receiving smaller allowances as their parents' cash resources diminished, so these normally law-abiding youngsters were stealing for money.[9] The breakdown of discipline in the schools as well as the homes was also a contributing factor; some youths had little respect for any authority.

Hoffman was not alone in his concerns. Parents complained to the churches that their children were "playing cards all day long in some of the wash rooms, latrines, and recreation halls,"[10] and they feared the children were becoming "addicted" to bingo games.[11] Youth gangs in the camp harassed younger children and committed occasional acts of vandalism. These were small matters individually, especially as the overall crime rate remained well below that of communities outside, but they pointed to a problem that was deeply troubling and united the older generation and the administrators. Unhappy young people were bored, restless, and less cooperative; as a result, they were harder to teach and potentially less productive citizens in the outside world. As educational historian Thomas James pointed out, the environment intensified the solidarity and disaffection of the youths in every camp; they would obey no authority figures and resisted "official coercion and traditional authority" alike.[12]

❧

Part of the disaffection among older teenagers stemmed from the military's decision to implement selective service among the interned Japanese American population. Topaz had already experienced difficulties in meeting the military's goals. The attempt to secure volunteers for the all-Nisei combat battalion had not enticed many. Like the other camps, Topaz had failed to meet its WRA-assigned quota. The search for volunteers had produced a history of turbulence: registration, the schism of the "no-nos" and the "yes-yeses," and segregation at Tule Lake.[13] On January 20, 1944, Secretary of War Henry Stimson announced that "because of the fine record of Nisei volunteers normal selective service procedures would again be applied to Japanese Americans, both inside and outside the camps." This was a bit of sophistry: Stimson implied that such outstanding soldiers as the Nisei should be better-represented in the army, but in reality the army just needed more men as the brutal conflict drained its forces.[14] The secretary's solution was to draft the Nisei. The Topaz administration announced that Stimson's call "indicated national approval of Nisei soldiers," but this statement was either wishful thinking or inept propaganda designed to increase the enlistment rate. Perhaps, as many Nisei suspected, they just made good cannon fodder.

The Nisei in Topaz reacted to selective service with a combination of eagerness, reluctance, and in a few instances, rejection. Some joined willingly, anxious to demonstrate their patriotism; others sought to bargain with the army, to exchange their service for a restoration of their civil rights. A few tried to avoid service altogether, particularly when they realized that the draftees would be used as replacements for the 100th and the 442d, the segregated and by now decimated Nisei battalions. At first 121 names were called by the Millard County draft board, but since the Caucasians were unfamiliar with Japanese names the initial list included some women and a few Issei, while others who were eligible were omitted. A refined list of 166 potential draftees was then circulated by the administration, including men as young as eighteen. High school students could be deferred until graduation. By March 1, when the first contingent left Topaz, 216 had been called up, and the army had accepted 163.[15]

An extensive report on selective service was prepared for Dillon Myer by Oscar Hoffman's assistant Hiro Katayama, a Nisei from Berkeley who was himself ineligible for the draft. Katayama characterized the attitude of those who were eligible as cooperative at the outset; most people agreed that selective service was a logical extension of the volunteer program and believed it presaged the restoration of their civil rights. This thinking was encouraged by the JACL, which believed that joining the military would prove the Nikkei's unequivocal loyalty to their country. Their optimism was soon crushed by the announcement that the new draftees would replace casualties in the all-Japanese battalions.

The Topaz Nisei were not deterred, but instead organized to press their demands. Some were openly opposed at the outset, since they were considered noncitizens and incarcerated in a concentration camp. They discussed contacting groups at other camps that were protesting the draft, but rejected this approach because they believed that they could accomplish more by working alone for the restoration of their civil rights. They did not involve the Issei; those who were parents generally opposed their sons' being drafted. The Nisei considered it a Nisei issue.

An all-male citizens' committee was formed to work for the restoration of civil rights. It soon gained an unusual ally when a separate mothers' committee was formed in an extremely unusual action for normally reticent Issei women. This committee met and drew up a petition urging the restoration of civil rights and liberties for their sons. While the women utilized male help in wording the petition, the impetus was theirs alone. When there was disagreement with the wording, a second meeting was held to resolve the differences. Although this was a women's meeting, two Issei men entered it, demanding to speak for two blocks that thought the wording of the original petition was too weak. The women deferred to the men, who then drafted a stronger statement (even though most of the women felt the original statement was strong enough). Some mothers rejected the petition approach altogether, preferring to request the Spanish consul to act on their behalf. Despite these differences in strategy, the women were optimistic that their moderate approach would achieve more than a confrontational one. The mothers and their sons were greatly disappointed when the strategy failed.[16] The army was not interested in redressing the grievances of draftees or their mothers, especially if they were Japanese Americans. It also refused to consider Nisei objections to serving in a segregated battalion. In the words of the day, there was a war going on, and all the army wanted was more soldiers. By late March 1944, Hoffman reported that most young men had "reconciled themselves to the inevitable."[17]

Some Nisei did not lose hope, believing that WRA director Dillon Myer might at least clarify various aspects of selective service. Myer visited Topaz and delivered an address, but he adroitly sidestepped the civil rights issue, saying that only the War Department could speak on it. As Hoffman observed, Myer's visit made Topaz feel more a part of the war effort, but the result was an anomalous situation where uniformed Nisei soldiers on their way to the front visited parents who were interned behind barbed wire.[18]

Despite Myer's exhortations and the optimistic response of some Nisei, the imposition of selective service further lowered the camp's sagging spirits. Katayama reported that it even demoralized high school students, who "took the draft as an excuse to pursue their lazy ways." The camp idioms "waste time" (waste of time) and "lose fight" (give up) became catchall phrases to reject any exhortations to study, since the teenagers felt they were just marking time until the army called them.[19] Work habits among laborers also became sloppy, for many young men became convinced that their fate was to die in a segregated suicide squadron in some forlorn and distant battlefield.[20] This was hardly conducive to applying oneself with diligence to the mundane task at hand.

Although some young people viewed the draft with apathy, anger, or depression, others reacted with vigor and even eagerness. A few used it as an opportunity to resettle, to see some of the country before they went into the service, while others considered it an excuse to stay where they were. The WRA made clear that Nisei males of draft age who filed for repatriation after January 20, 1944, would be guilty of draft evasion, effectively closing that way of escape. The U.S. government informed the Spanish consul that American citizens were not permitted to use his office as an avenue of protest. The question of the legality of drafting men behind barbed wire aroused considerable interest, and some Nikkei wanted a test case to resolve the issue. The majority believed that course of action would be unwise, since it might cause an even more unfavorable public response to them in wartime.[21] The American Civil Liberties Union informed the Nisei citizens' committee that it would not handle a test case on the legality of the draft in a WRA center, thus closing off this option.[22] Again the Japanese Americans were on their own.

Once legal resistance to selective service was out of the question, Nisei males began to register without protest. Administrative files from Topaz featured many cheery stories of enlistments, followed by farewell banquets and parties given for the departing soldiers. The *Millard County Chronicle* also noted the departures and later listed the casualties. In spite of the controversial nature of selective service in other camps, it was relatively uneventful at Topaz, where the population was basically conservative. But it was not without pain. People who welcomed enlistment were opposed by those who did not, and even within families there was disagreement over the proper course of action. Tom Kawaguchi recalled that his parents let him and his brother make their own choices and supported their decision to sign up. Other families, he reported, were split when brothers chose a course different from their parents' wishes, or when siblings took opposite sides. He noted that there were situations where "brothers don't talk to each other [even] today."[23] Once again a government action had fractured the fragile sense of community in Topaz.

The tensions regarding the issue of military service came to the surface in mid-1944 when a number of individuals and groups asked the community council to hold a memorial service for Nisei soldiers who had fallen in battle (seven volunteers and three draftees at that point). The council was dominated at this time by Issei who were determined to be neutral about service in the war. They believed that was the only way they could avoid harming their children's position as American citizens while protecting their own Japanese nationality. They took seriously Japan's strictures against aiding the American "enemy" war effort and knew they had no other citizenship to protect them. The councilmen believed that the proposed memorial service would only be acceptably neutral if it honored all who had died since the center opened, not just military casualties. Their stance put them in opposition to Issei who were parents of American soldiers and strongly favored such a service. The controversy lasted several months. Only when the block managers' organization, the Interfaith Group, the USO, and others who wanted the memorial lent their support to the idea was it resolved. Those in favor argued that such memorials had been held in other centers and Issei had accepted them; why should Topaz be different?[24] The opposition had no rebuttal, and the ceremony was held in mid-December 1944.

The memorial was simple and solemn, a combination of Christian and Buddhist services with sermons by the leaders of both faiths. The audience was primarily Issei.[25] The Delta chapter of the American Legion offered to conduct a flag service; the idea was debated at length because of the Legion's well-known hostility to Japanese Americans, but it was ultimately accepted.[26]

The duration of the dispute was testimony to the depth of the rancor; clearly the divisions in the community that had been provoked by the registration controversy were still present despite the departure of the segregants. An unwillingness to honor men who had died in service to America showed that there were many theoretical "no-nos" still resident in Topaz, and many others were becoming convinced that their future lay with Japan.

❧

Although the Issei agonized over the implications of the draft, for many of the men who served the issue was clear. Tom Kawaguchi thought, "What have we got to lose? Nothing besides our lives. . . . Well, why don't we at least demonstrate that we are patriotic and see what happens and take our chances that way?" He later recalled that the decision he and his brother made brought opprobrium on his parents from the opponents of the draft, and there were some bad moments he would never forgive. But the "rabble-rousers" in Topaz were loyal, he said. Even though the camp "had its moments," it was never violent like some others, but it had its share of searing rifts.[27]

For others, being drafted while they were denied civil rights was more problematic. Kenji Fujii did not push his opposition to the point of becoming a "no-no"; he was an only son and the main support of his mother and four sisters, and his departure would have worked considerable hardship on them. His reluctant "yes-yes" stance alienated him from his friends in the Young Democrats, who eagerly supported the draft. Fujii soon left camp to resettle and somehow, in the moving about, was not called up until after the war. President Harry S Truman ended selective service just as Fujii's number came up. Although his loyalty to the United States was unquestionable, Fujii never regretted missing military service. To him the period from December 1941 to September 1945 meant internment, not soldiering; the first ruled out the second.[28]

Some Japanese Americans were asked to serve in military intelligence. Bilingual Americans who resembled the enemy were invaluable as translators and interpreters in the Pacific war and during the occupation of Japan. The army, which assumed that recruiting volunteers to teach Japanese would be easy, was surprised to learn that most Nisei were not fluent in the language, especially in its written form. Tad Hayashi was one Nisei who was proficient in Japanese. He had finished his formal education before he was relocated, and after a few months in Topaz he decided to resettle in Detroit, hoping to make some money in the factories. When his draft classification was changed from 4C (enemy alien) to 1A in January 1944, he received a draft notice. He returned to Topaz to await his orders; they came two months later. Hayashi was a "yes-yes," so he expected military service. He was sent to language school in Fort Snelling, Minnesota, where his language skills were honed, and then he served in Japan with the occupation forces.[29]

Tomoye Takahashi had majored in Oriental languages at the University of California before the war, so her skills were especially good. She took the test to qualify as a language instructor at Fort Snelling and was pleased to hear she had done well, but since she was pregnant she could not serve the required two years. Three of the four men recruited from Topaz for Fort Snelling worked as Japanese-language editors on the *Topaz Times,* and Tomoye Takahashi, who wrote community news for the paper, recalled that their departure depleted the staff.[30]

Arguments over enlistment worried the Topaz administration. With the departure of the "no-nos" to Tule Lake, the people remaining at Topaz were certifiably "loyal" but not necessarily eager to fight. In May 1944 the WRA arranged a visit to Topaz by Sergeant Ben Kuroki, a genuine Nisei war hero, in an attempt to build patriotism and support for joining the armed forces. Kuroki spent four days in the area, where he addressed a large crowd, relating his experiences as a member of a bomber crew in Europe and Africa and his participation in the famous raid on Ploesti. He appeared before other Topaz audiences, including the high school student body and the USO, and he spoke at a banquet. He signed autographs until his hand gave out. Civic groups in Delta and Hinckley also heard him. The irony of Kuroki's appearance only emerged as his visit drew to a close. He confided to a few people that the order to speak at Topaz had made him very bitter. After he returned to the States he had made three requests for a furlough to return to Minidoka to see his ill father, and he had spent exactly one day with him when he was ordered on the publicity tour to Topaz. Ever the good soldier, Kuroki concluded that the respect and kindness shown him at Topaz had erased his bitterness. Kuroki's successful visit was followed by one by Private Thomas Higa, a Kibei, who was so "Japanesy" the Nisei could not understand him; despite his background he exuded loyalty to the United States and gushed over how well he was treated to the point where his audience completely discounted his remarks.[31]

Two interrelated themes marked the last year and a half of the Topaz relocation center: the first was the administration's increased efforts to resettle the population throughout the country before the war ended; the second was a growing sense of pessimism and even desperation on the part of a population afraid or reluctant to leave. The partial success of the administration's efforts meant that every institution of camp life, from the hospital and the schools to the mess halls and the farms, suffered since the remaining population was smaller but generally less cooperative. Camp self-government deteriorated, and school life was more disruptive; even the community analyst changed from an impartial observer to an advocate. Hoffman delightedly used his social science expertise in an attempt to explain to Washington what was "going wrong" and why. He and most other administrators assumed that the "right" way for the Nikkei to behave at this juncture was to make plans to leave camp as soon as possible, since their eligibility had been certified by the loyalty questionnaire. The Nikkei perceived life differently. Although camp had never been pleasant for most of them, it had become more comfortable—if one can use that word—for at least the situation was familiar and nonthreatening. But even if they were determined to stay or rather, reluctant to leave, this point of agreement was insufficient to bind them in harmony. The institutions of community life trembled as each issue, however small, became a bone of contention.

The hospital, for example, was even more turbulent than before, for several reasons. Hoffman explained the tension of the medical staff in terms of "hypochondriasis": the doctors literally made themselves sick. A more plausible explanation is rooted in the loss of status suffered by the Japanese American doctors who served there. Before the war they had belonged to the small group of Nikkei professionals, the elite in the Japanese American community. Now they earned a mere $21 a month, only $7 more than the lowliest ditch digger. Further, they had to serve under Caucasian doctors who earned considerably more and whose prestige was infinitely greater, but who worked no harder—if as hard—to meet the medical needs of the community.

The medical situation at Topaz was beset by situational problems as well as personality issues, both of which grew worse over time. The early hostility to Dr. James Goto and his wife was apparently a reaction to his abrasive personality. After that difficulty was resolved a shortage of physicians—at one point there were only three—created hardships for the staff and the patients. Topaz seemed to have a lot of illness, for many people reacted to the strains in community life by becoming physically or even mentally ill. The administration offered to loan the hospital a doctor from the military police, but because of the Wakasa incident that solution was deemed unacceptable. In addition, staff members complained that there were insufficient medical supplies; they also lacked a diet kitchen, and the elderly needed a separate residence.[32]

By the middle of 1944, there were additional sources of trouble in the dentistry division. In July it was announced that the resident members of the dental staff would be reduced from seven to three and the pharmacists from four to one. The entire medical community protested the pointlessness of requiring four dentists to remain idle when dental service was already six months behind demand. Since the dentists were almost all Issei unwilling to resettle, the action made even less sense.[33] At least one dentist, George A. Ochikubo, worked in the clinic voluntarily for a while, and the work load was eased somewhat by having dentures made or repaired elsewhere.[34] The residents' resentment at being denied the medical services they wanted or needed adversely affected morale.

The dentists' situation was just part of a larger problem of medical staffing. To function properly, the hospital required sixty nurse's aides, but by 1944 only thirty-six were reporting for duty. The reasons for the shortage ranged from simple absenteeism to an unwillingness to work at night or with people who had communicable diseases. Hoffman reported that the "rank and file residents generally evince an abnormal concern about matters affecting their health,"[35] which was understandable given the demography of camp. Topaz's population was becoming predominantly middle-aged or elderly, and many residents were depressed by their internment and frightened by the prospect of returning to life in a hostile white America. Poor health was a natural reaction to stress.

The WRA administration addressed the hospital situation first through personnel changes, in mid-September 1944 adding a new chief medical officer, a head nurse, a hospital dietician, and other personnel, all Caucasian. But the death of two newborn infants touched off another crisis when the resident Issei doctor serving at one birth, a Caesarean section, accused the Caucasian attending nurse of criminal negligence. While this charge was being investigated, an argument broke out over whether the hospital should offer elective medical procedures since it was so understaffed. The underlying issue in both cases was who would run the hospital, the resident staff members or the Caucasians.[36] Within two weeks the community council had brought charges against the Caucasian chief medical officer and demanded his transfer to another center. A meeting was held with the key members of the administration, the council, the block managers, and a physician from the surrounding community. The latter tried to persuade the residents to withdraw their demand that the medical officer leave, pointing out that because Topaz already had a reputation as a very difficult place to work, their action would further impede the recruitment of nurses.[37] When the residents refused to back down, a stalemate developed.

The chief physician chose this moment to announce the creation of a rest home in Block 3. This facility was something both residents and staff had desired, but the manner in which their wishes were met spoiled the outcome. Resident doctors charged that they had not been consulted about the site, and patients complained because they thought the block was to be remodeled with inside toilets—a luxury they could not have. (The administration flatly denied ever having suggested their availability.) Oscar Hoffman's reports reveal his irritation with a population that seemed to be increasingly unreasonable, a sentiment the other administrators may have shared.[38]

By the middle of October, the residents and the administration reached a compromise that allowed the chief medical officer to stay. Nikkei who knew him apparently did not dislike him, and others, evincing an apathy that was becoming more and more widespread, no longer cared to fight. The officer then tried to solve the shortage of nurse's aides by inducing older women to take the positions, even part-time,[39] but when that attempt failed the task was turned over to the block managers, the providers of last resort for community services. They ultimately were given responsibility for recruiting ambulance drivers as well.[40] If the block managers could not persuade people to work for the wages offered, they had to coerce the residents of their own blocks. Somehow the task was done, but not without rancor.

❧

Like the hospital, the community council faced problems that suggest the tensions just beneath the surface of camp life. Balanced precariously between its duties to the residents and the authority allowed it by the administration, the council had less to offer the community than the block managers, who could improve the quality of life in small ways. The first council leadership was Nisei: Tsune Baba, an accountant from San Francisco, played an important role in the peaceful resolution of the Wakasa case. Baba succeeded Carl Hirota, a dentist from San Francisco, who chaired the provisional council. Baba was followed by Masato Maruyama from Alameda. None of these men created any difficulty for the administration, but George Ochikubo, the chair of the fourth council, did. A dentist from Oakland who had been educated at the University of California, Ochikubo had just established his dental practice before the evacuation. The loss of all he had worked for and his family's experiences with discrimination had, according to Hoffman, "conditioned his thinking in the direction of accepting the Issei viewpoint in matters affecting center life." Ochikubo was very popular, especially with the Issei, but his rigorous independence made him a thorn in the administration's side. He played an adversarial role in a dispute over the use of Topaz workers as strikebreakers in a Tule Lake labor dispute, and this action signaled to Hoffman that Ochikubo was a "troublemaker" about whom Dillon Myer should be informed.[41]

The problem began at the Tule Lake Segregation Center in late October 1943. A truck carrying farm hands overturned, seriously injuring five of the twenty-eight passengers and killing a man from Topaz. It became apparent that the driver was very inexperienced. Camp director Raymond R. Best mishandled the incident by punishing the residents, who blamed the WRA for the death. Best cut off the public address system to prevent a large crowd from gath-

ering at the funeral, and he then gave the widow a pension the
Nikkei considered inadequate. The residents responded by stop-
ping all farm work. Many of the strikers were, like the accident
victim, former residents of Topaz. Since Tule Lake produced a
half-million-dollar food crop that supplied the army and navy as
well as other camps, it was essential to the WRA that the crop be
harvested quickly. The Tule residents immediately demanded a
number of improvements in camp life, but negotiations quickly
broke down. Best decided to import workers from Topaz as the
strike entered its second week.[42] News of the Tule situation was
well known at Topaz, since many friends and former neighbors
were among the 1,400 internees who had been moved there.
Ochikubo vigorously protested when Ernst decided to cooperate
with Best. The residents of Topaz also refused to allow people from
the Topaz labor force to be used as strikebreakers. As far as they
were concerned, the army could just harvest the crops themselves.
Ernst blamed Ochikubo for their resistance, and he was subsequently investigated by the FBI, presumably for "disloyal" behavior. Hoffman, who had only been at Topaz a few months, learned
from informants that the administration had specifically targeted
Ochikubo for investigation, even though other members of the
council shared his sentiments.[43] The council chose to resign en
masse rather than confront Ernst on the issue, and dissent went
underground. As punishment, the FBI announced that Ochikubo
was excluded from the restrictive zone of the West Coast. (The ban
was unusual: at this time all Japanese Americans were excluded
from the West Coast, but the implied threat was that he would be
prohibited from returning after the war's end as well.)

Ochikubo resigned from the council but remained involved in
community government as well as his dentistry practice until July
1, 1944, when he decided to devote all his time to fighting the
administrative ban. He went to Los Angeles in September to appear
before what he termed a political clearance board to challenge the
conclusion that there was sufficient evidence to exclude him permanently from the West Coast. His legal activities temporarily
ended his political career in camp, but he told Hoffman that the
council was too large and elected for too short a term to be effective

anyway. When the West Coast was reopened to all Japanese Americans in January 1945, even though in theory Ochikubo could have left Topaz, he chose to remain with the Issei holdouts. On March 30, 1945, he was elected co-op representative from his block. As feisty as ever, he led a movement to oppose the fiscal policy of the co-op's board of directors. The board was finally forced to resign and Ochikubo became chairman of the new board.[44] He ran again for the council in July and missed becoming chairman by only one vote. His final statement was yet to come. He gave a rousing speech in July 1945 against closing the center, much to the consternation of the director, who wondered why the council let him speak, since closure had long since ceased to be a debatable issue.[45]

Generally, the council and the administration endeavored to get along, and there were even times when administration, council, and residents saw eye to eye. The director occasionally wanted the council to initiate certain measures of social control that might be unpopular if they came from the WRA alone. Gambling, an issue that Nikkei and Caucasians had disagreed about since Tanforan days, was a good example. It was common at Topaz to hold lotto or bingo games to raise money for parties or gifts for children at Thanksgiving or Christmas. No one objected at first, but as the residents came to have less money both they and the administration sought to curb this practice. The council finally adopted a resolution prohibiting such games, but it was furiously opposed by blocks that already had received permission to conduct them. In this case, the council's action was something the administration wanted, and the policy was sustained by the general population.[46]

When the council members felt frustrated by the administration, the Issei—who dominated the council by now—appealed directly to Washington or asked the Spanish consul to intercede. These efforts were generally fruitless, for the consul's interest was sporadic and he had only as much power as Washington allowed, which was not much.[47]

Oscar Hoffman thought many racial conflicts might be avoided if the administration were "educated" in what he termed "Issei patterns of thought."[48] His records suggest, however, that he was unsuccessful in his educational efforts. If he supported the Issei too vigorously, he compromised his own position, since the administration had difficulty understanding the place of a social scientist in a concentration camp anyway. But if he appeared too impartial, the evacuees distrusted him. He was, after all, a Caucasian and an employee of the federal government. Had he been an ombudsman he might have actually helped the camp inmates, but all he really did was observe or—as it seemed to them—spy.

⚘

The final Issei-dominated councils had little power or authority. Elections continued to be hotly contested, but primarily over the degree to which the chairman would cooperate with the administration. By this time, the residents had very little interest in what the council actually did, and fewer and fewer people were willing to hold office. The previous council had been ineffective, and it was unlikely that the new one would be different. George Gentoku Shimamoto, the Issei who had just served as vice-chairman, considered running for chairman, but just before the election he learned that an architectural firm in New York City was seeking an experienced draftsman. He withdrew his name and resettled.[49]

A final observation on the council's activities is in order. One of its chief functions was to draw up ordinances to govern the camp's daily life. They included measures regulating solicitations from room to room in the blocks, traffic laws, boundaries for school districts, the owning and keeping of pets, and gambling as well as social problems such as disorderly conduct, petty theft, and returning books to the library. The administration often amended the council's work by substituting one word for another. One cannot read the measures without being struck with their trivial nature (for example, residents were prohibited from washing pet dogs in the laundry tubs). And the administration's interventions often sounded insulting in their pettiness. It seems unnecessary for people being trained for democracy to receive instructions about the specific wording of regulations such as the following: "Take out the reference to Section, Township and Range, as this is too technical for general use. . . . Use Center instead."[50]

❧

Although the population decline impeded the camp's functioning, staff members were instructed to continue to push the reluctant residents out into the world, and they did. At first there were quotas for resettlement, which were quickly filled by enthusiastic Nisei striking out for freedom, following the students and those departing for military service. By early January 1945 most of the remainder were Issei, some of whom were too old, poor, scared, or tired to leave. Others had a more belligerent attitude. They acted as if they considered it their duty to "sit tight," to remain in camp deliberately as a burden on the government that had callously incarcerated them. Some took this stand in the service of what they considered the interests of the Japanese government, and others tried to block resettlement in order to force the federal government to support them after the camp closed.[51] A few Nisei also had reasons for not leaving: ill parents, large families, small infants, or simple hostility to U.S. policies. An increasing number of Nikkei could not afford to leave, for the $25 given them by the WRA as a resettlement grant ($50 for a family) was inadequate. Many people had exhausted their meager savings on living expenses in camp, since their earned income was insufficient to provide minimal amenities. Around camp the collective wisdom was that obstinacy would force a change in federal policy, so many stayed who could have afforded to leave. They also knew that state or local social services would never be so charitable as Washington, for all its cheapness. Topaz was poor, resentful, and distressed as it awaited the end of the war and an uncertain future.

Given these attitudes, it was somewhat ironic that the landmark case of Mitsue Endo, which resulted in the closing of the camps, was tied to Topaz. Endo, a California civil servant from Sacramento, had protested when she and other Japanese Americans lost their jobs after Pearl Harbor, but she was reluctant to take her case to court. A suit was filed in her name only after she was transported to the Tanforan assembly center. Endo, like other Nikkei employees of the state of California, had been dismissed for being of Japanese descent (she was a Nisei). Her lawyer, James Purcell, had solicited her case. Working pro bono for the American Civil Liberties Union, he argued that the federal government had no right to detain her when no charges had been made against her. The ACLU held that it was unconstitutional to segregate the Nikkei solely on the basis of race; Endo should therefore be released from Topaz, where she had been removed, without having to go through the process of leave clearance. The young woman never appeared in court during the proceedings and dropped from public view after the war, but her case was a landmark. The decision in *Ex Parte Endo* was handed down on December 18, 1944. It stated that citizens could not be detained without due process of law. Announcement of the decision was delayed long enough for Roosevelt to make a polit-ically expedient announcement the preceding day that the camps would be closed.[52]

In mid-December 1944, after the *Endo* case and Roosevelt's announcement, the War Department took over the leave program from the WRA. It promptly termed the Nikkei "guests of the government" who stayed only at its pleasure. Troublemakers could be ejected. Three lists were drawn up: the first—or "white"—list consisted of people who could depart for any location; the "black" list contained names of those still prohibited from the West Coast; and the "gray" list enumerated those about whom there was some question.[53] The vast majority of the residents were placed on the white list, but the problem lay in persuading them to leave.

From December 1944 until the closing of the Central Utah Project in late October 1945, the issue of resettlement acquired a different twist. Persuading the Nikkei to depart—convincing them that the camps were going to close and federal policy would not change—was a slow process. When Director Luther Hoffman dis-covered that many single people were moving into larger vacated quarters instead of resettling, he asked the community analyst to study the problem. Both men agreed that if the singles would not leave it would be even more difficult to eject families.[54] In early February Oscar Hoffman attempted to analyze the residents' baffling resistance to leaving camp. Most people he surveyed said they did not object to resettlement in principle, but the money provided was insufficient, the jobs were menial, and the wages were poor. Most of their resettled relatives and friends reported they were happy and successful despite a difficulty in finding housing, but this reassurance did not convince them. They knew it was culturally unacceptable for the resettlers to complain. Although discrimination was rarely mentioned, everyone knew it existed, and the stories told by returning seasonal workers verified it. Young adult males doubted they could earn enough to provide for their families, and the elderly worried that no one would care for them if they fell ill. Parents did not want to be a burden on their children, while their offspring feared they would not have sufficient resources to help them. Issei bachelors doubted they would find community acceptance or good jobs, especially given their inadequate language skills. When asked what they wanted of the WRA, the residents usually answered, "Assurance of protection and better public relations, . . . more substantial subsidization" and "better job opportunities."[55]

Hoffman concluded that "without meaning to become facetious, it must be admitted that Topaz has its advantages over the outside." In fact, he and the camp director could not comprehend how the security Topaz offered compensated for its drabness and boredom; how the guaranteed housing, food, medical services, wages, clothing allowance, and care for the aged made up for internment itself. Camp provided all the ingredients for a condition of dependency. In view of the trauma that the Japanese Americans had endured during the evacuation and their fears of mistreatment by whites in the future, staying where they were had a certain logic to it. After all, the government could hardly abandon them, could it? There were other considerations too, especially given the uncertainty about the draft. Young men feared that if they were called up, their families, living in strange towns without a supporting community, would be stranded with no means of subsistence.[56] Many people simply did not want to move again, at least not until the war was over and they were assured that they could return to their former homes and live in safety and dignity.

Hoffman recognized that financial security was a legitimate issue. He knew from his studies that the Nikkei had suffered tremendous monetary losses during the evacuation, but Washington either did not remember or did not care. By 1945 the residents of Topaz watched their assets diminish even further. One person, described in Hoffman's anonymous interviews as a "leader," explained that before the war Japanese Americans had enjoyed a higher standard of living than the average American, since people owned their own homes, "had good jobs, beautiful gardens, well kept, and money in the bank. We like to live in neat and clean surroundings. Feeling that way, we do not like to move out of the centers and get into dirty homes—homes we could not buy and fix up." He stated that "the average person goes in the hole here $25 per month—getting poorer and poorer." Nikkei who resettled might be free, but they were not happy: "Here, there is little freedom; but we are not stared at. We do not get what we want here, but we live anyway and do not feel lonely."[57] It was inconceivable to the Caucasians that the holdouts really intended to spend the rest of their lives living at government expense in tar paper barracks in the desert, yet by the end of January 1945 only 3,599 people had left Topaz. This meant that 5,839 remained, out of a high population of 9,438.[58]

Powerful arguments were made against resettling, and they were amplified in the months ahead by those holding out against the WRA's wishes. Sure that the WRA would not cast them adrift, they became more and more intransigent. Their determination did not make their lives any easier; instead, out of frustration and fear they bickered and quarreled among themselves over almost every issue that arose. One man slashed another on the arm with a pocketknife during an argument at a block meeting over raising funds for the Supreme Court cases. The victim was, according to the administration, a "known troublemaker," while the assailant was a "man of good character." Because of his reputation and the council's intercession, the knife-wielder was given only a thirty-day jail sentence.[59] According to his many advocates, the assailant was angry because he believed the seasonal leave program helped the U.S. war effort, and when the fund-raising issue came up he lost control of himself. Staff members recognized that fund drives had come too often and annoyed some of the residents, but they did not expect so much agitation. As a result of the fight, both the councilman and the block manager from the attacker's unit resigned because they were unable to prevent the outburst.[60] It was a very traditional thing to do.

Even though residents continued to resist permanent resettlement, many did seek seasonal agricultural work, which enabled them to replenish their cash reserves yet return to the security of camp. This option especially appealed to family heads, who could leave their dependents in the safe confines of Topaz while they ventured out. By May many Nisei and Issei were accepting farm work who never had before. The increasing tensions, inadequacies, and irritability of camp life also drove people out. As one man commented, "What I need is a tall glass of cold beer and I'm going out to get it."[61]

⁂

The situation at the consumers' cooperative illustrates the divisiveness of the camp population during this last year. One of the co-op's leaders traced its acrimonious history for Hoffman. The organization was formed by some 5,300 members, who each paid a dollar to become a member. The institution was supervised by Walter Honderick, a white staff member in charge of Nikkei enterprises, who was popular with all his employees. A temporary board of directors was elected in October 1942 to advise him. The members were almost entirely from among San Francisco's Grant Avenue merchants. The popular Methodist leader the Reverend Taro Goto was excluded from the board, although he had been influential in organizing the co-op. The anger of Goto and his supporters started the venture on a discordant note. Next the board of directors disagreed about merchandising policies, and then the members argued over dividends and the payment of a cash rebate of the original membership fee. The group split into two factions, led by D. T. Uchida, the chairman, and S. Yamate. The majority believed that the co-op was too undercapitalized to supply goods for a population of around 8,300, but the minority believed that even so, they should keep their original promise to return the fee after a certain time. The proper method of raising additional capital for the enterprise and the return of the rebate were the points of contention in the election of the first permanent board in 1943. Among the fifteen members elected to the board of directors were Yamate, H. Honnami, S. Matsumoto, and Mas Narahara. They decided to raise additional capital by a $20,000 loan from the camp residents, and the original membership fee was returned.[62]

The co-op became a very successful venture and factionalism died down, only to be reborn over the issue of a credit union. The co-op already had a banking department, which seemed to function satisfactorily, but a newly elected board decided in March 1944 to create a separate credit union, to be headed by S. Matsumoto. The co-op now had a credit union, a banking department, and a treasury. At one point the same man headed all three. After it was determined that they should be individual entities, arguments developed over which operation should do the camp's banking. At this point the community council intervened and created a conciliation committee composed of members from the "elder statesmen" of the camp, in the hope that this group could reach a settlement.[63] By early 1945 the co-op's financial problems had intensified the tensions in camp and divided the community.[64]

Another nasty quarrel developed over the repair of the water and sewer pipes serving Topaz. The original pipes were cheap and thin, and the alkaline soil often caused them to corrode and leak.[65] Work on the pipeline had always been unpopular. It was hot and dirty in the summer and cold and miserable in the winter, and residents felt the compensation scarcely justified the discomfort involved. In 1943 the need for laborers was solved by drafting new arrivals from Tule Lake, who had little choice because there were no other jobs available when they came. Since the Tuleans were primarily farmers and the Topazeans were urbanites, giving the job to the former was

not totally arbitrary, at least from the perspective of the latter. As
the pipeline job neared completion, the WRA cut the pay from $19
to $16 a month and the former Tuleans decided they might as well
quit working on it.[66] The situation was exacerbated when a Caucasian foreman accused a crew of laziness and summarily fired the
workers; the two remaining crews then quit in sympathy. Just then,
when there were no crews available to fix it, a major pipe broke.
The WRA immediately restored the $19 wage but most of the former
laborers declined to return to work, not trusting the administration
to abide by that figure. During the summer high school students were
hired to make emergency repairs, but their labor ended once school
started in the fall.[67] By late 1944 the pipeline renovation was a
matter of urgency that concerned all residents alike.

Recruiting for the pipeline dragged despite the best efforts of the
block managers, on whom the task of obtaining workers fell. Every
time they managed to assemble a new crew, seasonal or permanent
relocation decimated it. The permanent residents would have done
the job had the money been there, but at this point only considerably more pay would have been acceptable.[68] As long as seasonal
agricultural work was available, those who needed employment
preferred this more lucrative occupation. Hoffman noted that the
Buddhists in camp had done an excellent job laying water pipes
to their new building, suggesting that motivation, not ability, was
the problem.[69] The standoff continued until mid-December, when
Hoffman informed Washington that the pipeline work was finally
underway. He commented that "if resident foreman and appointive
staff supervisors will use the necessary tact in keeping this crew, the
job can be completed." The workers felt "their efforts should be
appreciated," which seemed reasonable to Hoffman, too.[70]

⁂

Education was an even more troublesome issue. In spring 1944
many of the Nisei teachers indicated they planned to quit. They
liked teaching, but they thought their experience would be useless
to them when they resettled since, as members of an ethnic minority
without college degrees, they would be unable to teach outside.

Teaching was not a pleasant experience for the young Nisei because the classrooms had become very disorderly. The senior boys, waiting to be drafted, were uninterested and uncooperative, and they were particularly rowdy, unruly, and disrespectful toward the Japanese American teachers who were barely older than they were. Teachers complained that during the home room period, supposedly a study hall, students sat on the tables, visited with their friends, and wasted time; students noted that teachers often left the room during this period to get away from them. Staff turnover had affected morale and student productivity dropped. Many students complained that they had no tables and chairs at home on which to do their homework, but for some this lack was only an excuse to avoid something they did not intend to do anyway.[71]

Relations between the Nisei and some Caucasian teachers had also deteriorated. The Nisei told Hoffman that there was a "definite line [of] demarcation" between the races. One of the Caucasians addressed a Japanese American educator as "my child," a term they felt was patronizing.[72] Students, too, were on guard against racist remarks and some led walkouts in protest. The students boycotted class for two or three days until, as Lee Suyemoto recalled, "we finally got rid of the teacher and somebody else came in to teach the course."[73] Others led walkouts for less specific reasons. Oscar Hoffman learned from an anonymous informant, the Reverend T., that the mass walkout tactic was one the "kids [got] a lot of fun using. . . . I hear the kids talk about this method and they discuss what teacher it will work with and what teacher it will not! They know if they used it with some, they would not get back into the class."[74] Thomas James suggested that, in fact, most teachers were "neither saints nor villains, neither more nor less prone to prejudice than other Americans during the war. They were ordinary people who saw themselves serving their country, while trying to give Japanese American pupils an education."[75] Nevertheless, by 1944 everyone's patience was wearing thin.

Hoffman also interviewed some high school students and found that they considered the teachers "untidy and undignified" and incapable of teaching, and not even interested in the students. The teachers showed favoritism and did not even bother to learn names.

The constant turnover of instructors upset the teenagers; in the German class there were six teachers in one semester, some of whom did not even know the language. The common belief was that the more frequent the replacement of teachers was, the more unruly the students would be. Hoffman learned that the resident teachers had to assist with all student activities, but the Caucasians took the credit. There was almost no student advising and few close student-teacher relationships; no one was available to help with questions about student or job relocation.[76] A high school senior told Hoffman that when his favorite civics instructor, whom he described as strict but fair, was transferred to another class, she was replaced by a recent graduate whose best qualification was his athletic prowess. The students regarded him as one of themselves, joking around and trying to trip him up, and the class disintegrated. Clearly morale was low.[77] Whether it was as bad as this particular group indicated is unclear, however; many years later some former students in Topaz High gave their educational experience mixed evaluations, and a few were not critical at all.[78] Many praised Eleanor Gerard and a few other Caucasians who stayed through until the end. The protesting students may have exaggerated for Hoffman's benefit, but they were not isolated in reporting negative experiences with many teachers.

Matters were not helped when a popular Caucasian teacher was dismissed in April; the students could not understand why such a good instructor had been terminated. Rumors circulated that he had been let go because he was a conscientious objector, or that the administration did not like him, or that he had been picked up by the FBI.[79] The students never learned what happened to the man, and his case does not appear in camp files. The incident caused students and parents to have increased misgivings about the school system.

The student relocation counselor pointed out another concern, a marked decline in the number of applicants seeing her. She attributed the change in part to a declining interest in higher education because of the problems in the high school and the draft situation. It seems unlikely that, as she claimed, few of the teachers knew about the National Student Relocation Council and its work, but the students, like their parents, had fears about leaving camp.[80] Graduating seniors were advised to coordinate their plans for higher education with their family's resettlement intentions, but the reverse could also happen: some families that did not intend to leave kept their children in camp with them, especially if they were considering returning to Japan. Family solidarity overrode the traditional valuing of education, especially in those uncertain times.[81]

As the school year came to an end in May 1944, morale seemed to improve. Graduating seniors rented caps and gowns. They planned a prom and banquet, and the appearance of the school annual caused much excitement.[82] The rituals of the academic year brought their usual feelings of gain and loss, of excitement over taking one's place in the adult world. But just before commencement a teacher examining transcripts discovered that many students had obtained credit for repeated work. When the seniors' records were checked, it seemed that most were ineligible for graduation because they were either deficient in credits or had not fulfilled the requirements. Administrators began checking with the schools the students had attended in California to locate missing records. Apparently someone had misinformed the seniors regarding their eligibility for graduation. Students and parents were apprehensive, and one administrator blamed another for the mistake. The tempest subsided, however, when the administration adopted the policy of giving students credit for all work they were taking at the time of evacuation. The 127 members of the Class of 1944 received their high school diplomas.[83]

Following the ceremony a special PTA meeting was held to apprise parents of the school's ongoing troubles. The superintendent read an announcement that a teachers' training course would be held during the summer for high school graduates who wished to return and teach, but indignant Issei parents opposed the idea. Instead, they urged the community council to persuade the school administration to treat Nisei teachers more equitably so they would not resign. Oscar Hoffman reported that the parents had heard a rumor that some anonymous visiting Caucasian educator had pronounced Topaz High School one of the poorest of the WRA schools.[84]

Many Nisei teachers did indeed resign after graduation, and the superintendent announced that unless twenty-two replacements were hired immediately the schools would have to close. Hoffman found it symptomatic of the general malaise that even the serious teacher shortage did not prompt the PTA to meet again.[85] There was a flurry of suggestions, including one that potential teachers be recruited block by block, to be trained in the summer at $16 a month for the following fall. As summer passed, rumors raced through the community: the school day would be shortened and the students sent out to work; the number of classes would be reduced and the school week diminished. Some parents favored opening Delta High School to the Nisei students, and some students decided to resettle in order to obtain a good education during their senior year so they could enter a better college.[86] Seventeen-year-old Shigeki Sugiyama actually moved with his brother to Ann Arbor to complete high school so that he could enroll in the University of Michigan. Most parents would not allow their children to go out alone, but the situation did prompt some families to relocate.[87]

The teacher shortage sparked a general round of criticism among all parties, with parents in the fore. They agreed that recent graduates were unacceptable in the classroom and condemned the treatment of the resident teachers that had prompted them to resign. They singled out only four of the Caucasian teachers for praise.[88] And they criticized some white instructors for encouraging bad habits in their children; one man had distributed cigarettes so his pupils could learn to smoke. Some residents blamed the students' unruliness for the teachers' departure, muttering that their parents had not raised them properly.[89] Hoffman noted that children were becoming "rougher, ruder, and rowdier" and that the rate of juvenile delinquency and gang behavior was increasing. High school students, both males and females, had broken holes in the walls of the school building, boys had destroyed the high school bathroom, and there was vandalism all over the camp. He believed that many of these acts were due to family problems; he saw more quarreling, selfishness, and irritability at home. The parents were generally unaware of their children's behavior in school and had little means of disciplining them in any case. Hoffman suggested that parents be brought in closer touch with the schools to facilitate cooperation.[90]

Many Caucasian teachers drew their own conclusions about who was at fault. They blamed the parents for showing little interest in working with them, ignoring the fact that most were Issei and many spoke only Japanese or very poor English. They were angry with the administrators for moving them about, keeping poor records, and changing the pupils' advisors too frequently. Some teachers perceived the students' behavior as "gangster-like," especially when some of them passed a petition calling for one instructor's removal and threatened nonsigners with violence. They also complained about the boycotting of classes.[91]

In the midst of the teacher shortage Charles Ernst, the camp director, resigned. Oscar Hoffman was strongly critical of Ernst, and others who remember him have differing opinions. He seems to have merited some of Hoffman's criticisms: he believed in keeping his distance from the evacuees, and clearly he, like any good bureaucrat, believed in the program he was administering. Whether he had the respect and confidence of the residents we cannot judge; Hoffman remarked that the announcement of Ernst's resignation was greeted by "a high degree of indifference."[92] Perhaps his assessment was accurate, but by this time the Nikkei were apathetic toward most things that did not directly concern their well-being. None of the Nisei interviewed for this study had strong feelings about Ernst, if they recalled him at all.

School opened again in the fall; courses were taught, somehow, and the last pupils to file into the tar paper classrooms received a measure of instruction. But the reprieve was only temporary, for by December the camp was again awash in rumors that the schools would have to close in late January because of continuing difficulties in staffing them. Caucasians left for new positions, and others would not apply because of the impending closure of the camps (which was announced in December). Nisei who were skilled teachers were resettling. The last months in the Topaz schools must have been bleak.[93]

The mood of the camp deeply concerned the administration, and on November 1 community analyst Hoffman began a new feature in his weekly newsletter to Washington entitled "Trend of Resident Thought." The trend, naturally, was ever-downward, demonstrated by the issues that preoccupied residents contemplating resettlement. Some new factors emerged, which played an increasingly important role in the months ahead. Hoffman interviewed a Reverend S. and learned that people's moods were "ugly," that there was a "rising tide of bad feeling." By this time most of the respected leaders had resettled, and according to the minister, the remainder were uneducated and mercenary, unfit for leadership positions. Most of the residents were Issei who were very pro-Japan in their outlook. A new attitude toward seasonal leave began to emerge: Hoffman reported that many now refused it because they believed that agricultural work helped the American war effort, and they rejected resettlement out of hand.[94] These holdouts, the "stand-pats," were very suspicious of the Issei who did relocate, occasionally threatening them, and as a result people had became secretive about their plans. The realization that Japan was losing the war also began affect those who believed the reports (many refused to), for they could see that the camps would not last forever. Hoffman cited no figures to back up his "trends," so the reader is only able to speculate how widely these views were held. It seemed to him that the change of mood indicated a downward shift in the longstanding malaise of the residents.[95]

These changes affected Hoffman's own position. He complained to Myer that the residents either would not talk to him or would dissemble, telling him that they had no plans to relocate and then leaving the next week. They acted out of fear of antagonizing the rigid Issei and perhaps out of a growing perception that Hoffman was, after all, a Caucasian bureaucrat and a staunch advocate of resettlement. Perhaps they truly were uncertain, making up their minds at the last minute. Whatever detachment Hoffman once possessed had disappeared as he joined forces with the other administrators in attempting to resettle the Nikkei, whether they wanted to leave or not.

The residents seemed to be in what Hoffman called an "escapist" mood, anxious to find a mental release from the camp's drab surroundings, and indifferent rather than angry. Everyone flocked to the movies, especially the free ones, and Japanese films and athletic events were very popular with the Issei. When the auditorium's motion picture screen was damaged by an act of vandalism, everyone was angry and the adults immediately assumed the culprit must be a "juvenile delinquent." But the poorly attended council meeting could not even find anyone to investigate the matter.[96]

By late fall 1944 interest in resettlement was at a standstill. The only region that residents manifested any interest in was the Bay Area, their former home.[97] In the November newsletter Hoffman told Myer that the only way to combat the "creeping lethargy" in camp was to "push" the residents to action, but no one could be forced out as long as the camps remained open. Unusual job offers to groups of families from, for example, the Sioux Ordnance Depot and Seabrook Farms in New Jersey prompted some to discuss relocating. The experiment at Seabrook, a frozen-food operation where trial groups had been sent, sounded encouraging. Isao James Yano translated the literature on Seabrook into Japanese, and many Issei left camp to work there. But the remaining residents soon learned that the wages were poor, and the location seemed isolated to the few lonely Issei there. Family housing in Seabrook was no improvement over camp; the work was hard, and the hours long—fifty-six hours a week at times.[98] Residents who went to the Sioux Depot in Nebraska also found little to recommend it. They did not face discrimination, but the work was arduous. Attempts to portray life at Seabrook or the Ordnance Depot as preferable to the possibly unfavorable conditions on the West Coast failed. When these job offers did not live up to their advance promise, the residents dropped the subject of resettlement once again. The federal elections attracted little interest: the few Nisei eligible to vote supported Roosevelt just because he was a "known evil" as opposed to an unknown, but few bothered even to obtain absentee ballots.[99]

The community of Topaz was becoming increasingly atomized. The residents, Hoffman said, thought "less and less in terms of the total population of the Center and of community welfare and apparently more and more in terms of their own individual interests and plans." He complained that "homogeneity is breaking down," as demonstrated by the struggle for control of the co-op and the factionalism of the council. Even the Buddhist church was divided over the question of who should control the organization once the members returned to San Francisco. The wrangling made people unwilling to cooperate with the WRA over matters concerning the general welfare. No one wanted to take care of problems outside his or her own block. One woman, Hoffman noted, refused to work in the hospital even when her own husband was a patient there: its labor shortage was the WRA's problem; the care of her husband was his right and not her duty. Camp elections attracted few voters, and people began to ignore the needs of their own blocks. Families exercised little control over their children, who were even "noisier and more arrogant" than before. Hoffman found many elements to blame for the situation, in fact almost everything except the most obvious: that internment had so worn people down that they had ceased to cooperate in their own incarceration. Many had lost the initiative to help themselves, even to leave. Hoffman concluded that the growth of factionalism showed that the "wounds of evacuation . . . [had] begun to heal." Instead of sticking together against the Caucasian WRA, the Nikkei were demonstrating a "more normal state of mind" by their individualistic responses to events.[100] More likely, the reverse was true; the directors had never presented the WRA as a common enemy but had attempted to divide the residents by using groups against each other. Individual initiative, already blunted by the effects of institutionalization, was now being destroyed completely by the uncertainty of the impending camp closure, coupled with fear of the outside world.

⚜

Oscar Hoffman found some cause for optimism when the new director, Luther Hoffman, tried to clarify the separate roles of the community council and the judicial commission by prohibiting the council from insisting on the removal of the chief medical officer. Unfortunately, his action only made the residents more aware of the council's lack of power. The new director also attempted to solve problems quickly, unlike his predecessor, and he was more accessible to the residents. By this point it hardly mattered.

In mid-November Oscar Hoffman described the remaining 5,800 residents of Topaz. He predicted that approximately 1,500 would relocate in the Midwest or East in the next eight to ten months, following their children's lead. Many of these Issei would eventually return to the West Coast. Another 1,800 would resettle only on the West Coast; they included many infirm elderly people whose children had remained in camp to care for them. They intended to stay until the camp closed. There were about 500 who felt they had no future in America. They remained at Topaz only because Tule Lake was full and intended to leave for Japan once the war had ended. About 2,000 were "unrelocatable," including many Issei who were over sixty years old, had no families, and were virtually penniless. This category also included the chronically ill and the physically and mentally handicapped.[101] Hoffman's analysis scarcely gave cause for optimism, but neither the camp administration nor the WRA gave serious concern to the problems posed by those who could not be relocated.

Thanksgiving was observed quietly, but the presence of many servicemen and women on leave enlivened the occasion somewhat. As Christmas neared, the residents took comfort in the news that *omochi,* rice cakes, would be available, and there were many plans for parties, films, and other entertainment.[102] Yet another disappointment came when the *omochi* did not arrive on time, but nonetheless Christmas marked the end of the period of apathy, indifference, and "stand-pat-ism." As the residents of Topaz accepted the fact that the camp would be closed during the summer, they began to either make plans to depart or "accept the consequences of being left stranded in the Utah desert with some doubt as to whether they would be transferred to another center or to another government agency."[103]

Chapter Seven

An End and a Beginning

The closure of the relocation camps actually began when the Jerome Relocation Center in Arkansas shut down on June 30, 1944, and its remaining occupants were transferred to other camps. On December 17, 1944, Major General Henry C. Pratt, acting commander, Western Defense Command, issued a public proclamation restoring the right of the evacuees to return to their West Coast homes, effective January 1, 1945. Roosevelt announced the termination of relocation just before the *Endo* decision on December 18, 1944.

The announcement of the termination of exclusion from the West Coast included a statement that the camps would close within six months to a year. It initially brought more gloom, for the wording of the proclamation led some Nikkei to believe that the West Coast would not welcome them until after the war had ended. (The announcement in the *New York Times* stated that "the common sense and good citizenship of the people of the Coast is such that the inauguration of this program will not be marred by serious incidents or disorders," hardly a reassuring statement.) Many concluded that they had no choice but to stay in camp until the war was over.[1]

Yet for many other Japanese Americans, the opening of the West Coast meant the end of the most important excuse to procrastinate about resettling. Even those who were awaiting the end of the war had to reconsider their options, because time was running out for Topaz. A series of specific announcements about the impending

closure of the camp came in mid-July. All Japanese Americans who
had been deemed loyal to the United States were free to return to
the West Coast; only those identified as Japanese nationalists were
to be excluded, on an individual basis.[2] (These exclusions were
lifted on September 4.)

After Pratt's announcement, the administration of Topaz informed the remaining Nikkei that they were "now [to] be considered guests of the government . . . [and] that the centers were being
kept open [just] to help the residents make a satisfactory transition
to normal life." The internment camps had become nothing more
than very temporary shelters for them until they resettled.[3] People
were stunned by the speed of events. They next learned that Topaz
was scheduled to close on November 1, 1945. Hoffman reported
to Dillon Myer that the residents, who learned this date in mid-July,
showed no "outward signs of bewilderment, exuberance or anger.
The residents were utterly calm and showed absolute lack of interest in the entire matter." He described how the official teletype
had been distributed by the block managers. The residents were
"sitting in the cool of the evening breeze" at the time, gossiping,
playing go or *shōgi*, or discussing the events of the day, and they
continued in those activities. He concluded that their response
resulted from their prior assumption that the camp would close by
December 1. Those who already had made plans to leave were
unaffected, while those who had no such plans were waiting for the
government to make the next move.[4]

These events set the stage for the rapid transition that followed.
What Hoffman termed "bad morale" still affected the residents,
but it ceased to be of much significance. Despite what anyone
wanted, the remaining residents of the Central Utah Relocation
Center had to find new homes. Many of the "stand-pat" Issei
could not believe that the government would just "dump them out
into the desert." Surely one or two camps—at least Gila or Poston—would remain open to house those who had nowhere else to
go.[5] They could not imagine that the American government, which
prided itself on its humaneness, would just abandon them. They
still thought that passive resistance would work, and they trotted

out the old arguments in a last effort to convince others to join them. Many hoped that by holding out they could get a larger resettlement allowance, receive more assistance in finding homes and work, and perhaps even persuade the WRA to keep a few camps open for a longer period of time. But as the months passed, even the most dependent began to realize that the WRA itself was going out of existence; they would soon have to fend for themselves, either in America or in Japan.

Relocation thus took on a new urgency. Throughout the late summer and early fall of 1945 the residents made plans, considered offers, and made "scouting expeditions" to the West Coast, while the administration gave them all manner of verbal encouragement and exerted subtle pressure to get them to leave. Their continued reluctance led Oscar Hoffman to undertake a new assignment, to understand and explain to Washington why the intransigent residents moved so slowly. He then devised ways of persuading them to change their minds, whether or not their fears had been allayed. All pretense of scholarly dispassion was abandoned, for the administrators themselves had to plan for a future after the WRA (it was terminated June 30, 1946).

The functioning of the Topaz community slowly wound down. The schools, the hospital, some dining halls, and the co-op continued to function, but each had to construct a timetable for closing and devise a way to implement it. Certain services had to be provided as long as people lived at Topaz, and this meant retaining an adequate staff and filling a certain number of vacancies as residents departed. There was little incentive to labor for the community at the same time that the residents were being encouraged to leave. Jobs that were unpopular during the best of times became doubly so. Beset by uncertainties on all sides, residents who had worked in specific mess halls were angry and unwilling to shift to other locations as the administration tried to consolidate operations. The community council, dominated by "stand-patters," virtually ceased to function, and even the block managers no longer cared for their flocks with their previous efficiency. The Caucasians, too, began to depart as they found jobs elsewhere, and the sympathy some of them had felt for the Japanese Americans' plight began to be over-ridden by concern for their own families. Topaz was operating under a sentence of death.

☙❧

The administration's overriding concern was to persuade the residents to resettle as soon as possible. The opening of the West Coast offered an incentive for many who had previously been unwilling to leave, but everyone was cautious, especially as reports of violence against returnees reached them. Most waited to hear reports from those who had undertaken scouting expeditions, for they feared discrimination, hostility, and bodily harm. The WRA either underestimated or discounted the possibility of attacks on returning Nikkei and the difficulty of their finding housing and work. Hoffman told Washington to expect that people who had an economic base on the coast, who owned homes and businesses, would be the first to leave, while others would await the end of the war. The security of the center, with its provision of food, shelter, and safety, made them reluctant to leave. They knew housing was scarce in California. It would be hard for tradespeople to obtain equipment, and finding jobs in competition with returning soldiers might prove impossible.[6]

Those few residents who had been black- or gray-listed by the army were interviewed by officers who arrived at Topaz on December 17, 1944. Operating with speed and discretion, the army soon cleared most people. Few residents other than those involved even learned of the proceedings.[7] But residents were reminded that they still remained under surveillance. On March 27, 1945, Frank Shizuo Sasaki was ordered transported to the Santa Fe Detention Center when it was discovered that he had made a shortwave radio. Various groups called on Director Luther Hoffman in Sasaki's behalf; the council held a midnight meeting, and prominent community members who were deemed pro-administration received threats. Sasaki denied being a "troublemaker" or agitator and claimed he had been framed; he said he wanted to stay in the United States. George Ochikubo and others made speeches demanding a reconsideration of the case, but Director Hoffman was adamant. Sasaki was not pardoned. The camp director wrote Myer that his incarceration and removal had taken place quietly and "all [was now] quiet on this western front."[8]

Nisei students preparing for college had a special interest in returning to the coast, for as California residents they could attend the University of California without paying the tuition they would be assessed elsewhere (although they would be assessed modest fees). The young people and their parents were given a presentation about attending UC or the College of the Pacific by a student team from those institutions. They learned that the two schools would welcome them, but local residents and many of their fellow students probably would not; they should expect discrimination. The Nisei were even advised that going to midwestern and eastern institutions might be wiser. Of course, if they did, they would lose their California residency.[9] This type of mixed message was hardly reassuring.

While some residents were ambivalent, making cautious plans or awaiting the proper time to leave, others actively opposed resettlement. Resistance was centered in a group called the Committee of Sixty-eight, named for its composition of two "stand-pat" residents from every block. The size of its membership was due to the community council's desire to have each block represented, but the committee was too large to be effective and was dominated by a small and very negative group. Hoffman assured Washington that this group probably did not represent a majority of the residents, but its members were certainly the most vocal and the most determined to resist. They thought if they waited long enough, they could force Washington to give them better benefits and assistance and perhaps even convince the WRA to leave some camps open. A few committee members were also considering repatriation or expatriation to Japan. It seemed prudent to them to await the end of the war at the least before making a decision. (No one expected the war to end as quickly as it did.)

Instances of outright propagandizing also occurred. In January a one-page mimeographed sheet was distributed to residents; written in Japanese, it urged them not to leave the center, reminding them that it was their duty to Japan to stay where they were. The broadside made people even more anxious to postpone any decision.[10] Council chair Mas Narahara suspected Frank Sasaki had written it, but Sasaki denied the authorship.[11]

Most of the Issei, however, were tied to the interests of their children, and their resettlement plans depended on them. These people ultimately received help in resettling from children in the army or working outside camp. In the meantime they waited quietly and were cautious about what they said around their neighbors, fearing pressure and reprisals from the "negatives."[12] People made plans and departed without any prior announcement, leaving Hoffman and the administrators ignorant of what was really going on.[13]

The WRA was feverish with activity. Some of its actions were described by the residents as "squeeze plays," pressure tactics designed to force people out. One such device was the announcement that the schools would close permanently in June, offering an incentive to families to relocate before the new school year began. When two teachers resigned at the end of the first semester, parents thought this move was another squeeze and that classes might be suspended even earlier than June, but the system limped on to the announced closing date. Two mess halls were also shut down. Some employees were transferred to less desirable jobs when theirs were terminated, while others were just laid off. Seasonal and trial indefinite leaves were ended, and short-term leaves were cut from sixty to thirty days. Residents could no longer return to camp if their resettlement plans did not work out.[14] Director Hoffman wrote letters to WRA field offices all over the country, requesting follow-ups on dependency or welfare cases to insure they were cared for.[15] The WRA also advised state and local assistance agencies on the West Coast to look after people.[16] Once the WRA went out of business, its former charges would be on their own. The records are mute as to how much follow-up actually took place.

❧

The final word on the closing date of Topaz came from WRA director Dillon Myer. The attitude of the Nikkei at Topaz toward

Myer was at best mixed. When he visited Utah in 1943, he was greeted with a large sign, "Welcome Dillon S. Myer, the Great White Father."[17] Myer was apparently amused rather than embarrassed, but the head of the engineering section, whose unit was responsible for the placard, was mortified and apologetic. Myer, a career bureaucrat from the Department of Agriculture whose final posting was at the Bureau of Indian Affairs, may even have taken the sign as a compliment. He visited Topaz again in February 1945 to assure residents that the camp would indeed close by January 1, 1946, which he said would be beneficial for everyone. The director reminded parents that their children needed to be "integrated" into new schools. He assured residents that welfare agencies in their new localities could care for them if necessary, and he cautioned them that keeping the camps open would play into the hands of the exclusionists. He also advised that they could get a "jump on returning servicemen" in the search for jobs by leaving before the end of the war.[18]

Most Caucasians were pleased to learn that the center would close on time, for they were ready to move on even if the Nikkei were not. Myer himself moved in August 1946 to a new position as head of the Federal Public Housing Authority, after receiving the Medal for Merit for his services with the WRA. In 1947 he became head of the Bureau of Indian Affairs.[19] Although he was not greatly concerned about the future of Japanese Americans, on December 30, 1944, the WRA did open regional offices in San Francisco, Los Angeles, and Seattle to aid the returning Nikkei.

For those still at Topaz the little "squeezes" involved in closing down hurt more people than simply the intended victims. For example, the administration began to charge people a fare to travel to Delta to go shopping. The new policy drastically reduced the number of passengers, which in turn upset local businesspeople. A compromise between their needs and the WRA's desire to cut even the smallest costs was reached through the good auspices of the block managers' organization: the merchants agreed to pay half the shoppers' fare.[20]

The Topaz administration usually preferred to entice, rather than coerce, residents to move out. It failed to move people to Nebraska or Seabrook Farms, but it touted a government facility west of Salt

Lake City. Some Nikkei did resettle at the Tooele Ordnance Depot in the western Utah desert; they hoped there would be no discrimination there.[21] Finding work and good living conditions was not easy, whether one stayed in the Intermountain West or went east.

Since many of those who hesitated to leave Topaz lacked job skills, in February 1945 the WRA instituted a program in vocational training. Instructors taught tailoring, electrical work, and tractor repair to willing adult learners. Teachers also offered English courses to prepare elderly Issei for life outside. As the date for closing neared, some residents requested even more "practical" classes, such as one in American cooking; that skill, they hoped, would qualify them as fry cooks in short-order kitchens.[22] At last the administration had begun to address some of the concerns Hoffman had identified that bound the Issei to camp. The question was whether it was too little, too late.

The WRA also helped the Nikkei regain access to their California homes. The evacuee property section reported in February that property owners were "inquiring about the procedure they must follow to oust their tenants." They were advised to "go on record with the tenants" and inform them when they wished to reoccupy their dwellings.[23] Moving back into their own homes did a lot to bolster the courage of those returning to the West Coast.

***

In mid-February 1945, the WRA, supported by the Japanese American Citizens' League, decided to convene an all-center conference of evacuee leaders in Salt Lake City. Every camp except Manzanar was represented. The Nikkei attending the conference voiced the most extreme demands of the "stand-pats": to keep all the centers open for the duration of the war, to raise the cash assistance grants to something "more substantial" than the $50 allotted per family, and to make sure that aid would be provided for people who wished to reestablish themselves in business or agriculture. The Nikkei leaders at the meeting recommended that the WRA operate indefinitely and be prepared to accept back into custody "those of the evacuated people who could not, for reasons of age, infirmity, or demoralization, make some kind of successful readjustment to life outside the camps."[24] Such a wish list probably had more public relations than substantive value. Only a few residents of Topaz were optimistic about achieving the goals of the conference, but most were willing to see how the WRA would respond. Others thought there was no point in even having a conference at all. Their pessimism was quite justified. Myer called the conference "very constructive," but he told the delegates that "WRA policy determinations had been made on a sound basis and [would] not be changed."[25]

The WRA continued to concentrate on going out of business as fast as it could. When it recommended that the Nikkei be eligible only for programs of general assistance open to all citizens, the Issei were left with no recourse. Even the Spanish consul abandoned them, saying in effect that all the Japanese government had asked of him was to protect the lives of its citizens in the United States, not to intervene in resettlement, which was up to the individual.[26] Spain broke off diplomatic relations with Japan at the end of March, ceasing all efforts to intercede with the American government, which most residents felt had been futile anyway. No nation was willing to replace Spain as liaison.[27]

⁂

The mounting tension over resettlement affected people's health. Hoffman reported an increase in cases of high blood pressure and gastric ulcers. The imminent closure of camp prompted some people to take care of longstanding medical afflictions rather than pay for medical care outside, but the anxieties of daily life were also aggravating existing conditions.[28]

The WRA's exodus campaign made slow progress. During February most residents awaited the outcome of the all-center conference, but when they learned of the WRA's inflexibility they continued to delay, looking for the return of those who had left on scouting expeditions. The trips, however, never proved anything definitely; some people were welcomed back to their former homes and others were frightened or made cautious by their experiences.

Rural areas were more hostile than the cities, but in urban areas the lack of housing was most acute. There were reports from other parts of the country as well: Medford, Oregon, was hostile; New Orleans was friendly but had no lodging. The report that the American Friends Service Committee was reconditioning a large Buddhist church in San Francisco into a hostel was good news. The AFSC was looking for furniture and requested that the 250 families who had stored their possessions in the building remove them. But some Buddhists, still loyal to Japan and opposed to resettlement, protested the conversion.[29] A former Japanese-language school building was also being considered for temporary housing.[30]

Attempts to put people in the Salvation Army building were unsuccessful. The story of that building illustrates again the persistence of discrimination. It had been constructed in 1937 through the efforts of Major Masasuke Kobayashi, founder of the Japanese Salvation Army, who had raised a large amount of money from the community and from Japan. The Salvation Army refused to let the returning Nikkei use the building as a hostel, nor would it let them purchase it. Finally the building was sold to the Chinese government of Taiwan for use as a consulate. The Japanese Americans received $75,000 of the $2.5 million purchase price, and the money was used in 1952 to help construct the community center in Japantown.[31]

In the last week of February, Denver and Salt Lake City were reopened to Japanese Americans. Grace Fujimoto rejoined her parents in Salt Lake City soon afterward; they had moved there after Mr. Fujimoto was released from prison camp in Bismarck, North Dakota. Many other camp residents considered living in one of these two cities, which had been hospitable before the war. Nikkei who planned to remain in the Intermountain West tended to prefer Salt Lake City, disturbing a few of those Caucasians who still harbored prejudice against them.[32] However, the majority of Topaz residents still wanted to return to California.

Throughout the spring, signs of interest in resettlement appeared everywhere, as Oscar Hoffman noted in his weekly reports to Washington. The welfare office received an increasing number of inquiries from families with dependent members, and more residents visited the relocation office seeking terminal leaves to California. The interest in vocational courses flourished, although the instructor was puzzled when many of those who completed the work asked to repeat or take additional classes rather than make preparations to leave. There were other indications that people were accepting departure as an eventual reality. Hoffman and the head of adult education were both pleased at a surge of interest in conversational English, so great that they considered offering it on a block basis. They interpreted this as a sign that people realized they would soon be living in primarily Caucasian communities.[33] Berkeley appeared to be the most propitious location for resettlement. A former resident who had returned from a scouting expedition reported a most cordial reception there, with the only negative factor the lack of housing, and a hospitality committee had been formed in Berkeley to help those who were returning. The good samaritans were the wealthy; the scout could not vouch for the lower-class whites.[34]

In early March the block managers began to request packing boxes for people preparing to leave. Their action was new; most managers were Issei and had not facilitated departures before. The Nikkei were still quiet about their plans, but at least they now confided in the block managers. Hoffman was pleased that some young women had obtained jobs with the Social Security Board in San Francisco. When Hood River, Oregon, reversed its decision after people around the country condemned it for erasing the names of Nisei veterans from the American Legion war honor role, Hoffman praised the residents' change of heart. He closed his report by noting the induction of the new community council, a ceremony attended by almost no one except the block managers. He recognized that people soon to leave might be expected not to have much interest; he failed to note that preoccupation with their uncertain futures—not indifference—kept the residents away.[35]

March was the beginning of the diaspora. Hoffman labeled March 22 the "biggest day for applications [for indefinite leave] in the history of the project." In part this increase was due to an improvement in the weather, but it also stemmed from the residents' growing restlessness. From the reports of people who had already resettled, Hoffman judged that there still was considerable prejudice in rural areas like Hayward, but a minister in San Francisco said that conditions there were generally favorable. (Just the opposite seemed to be true, according to Kenji Fujii of Hayward, and the hostility to the Nikkei at the Salvation Army in San Francisco does not sound like the city was completely hospitable.) At least, the Nikkei were beginning to talk as if they had finally accepted the closing of the center by the year's end.[36]

But the unstable postwar economy was impeding the relocation of Topaz residents. There was disturbing news of increased unemployment in the Bay Area following the layoff of 3,300 shipyard workers, as well as significant reductions in the number employed in durable goods and manufacturing.[37] Reports from the state of Washington told of farmers' being forced off their land, and this seemed likely to happen in California as well. Those who had worked for Japanese American businesses were also in limbo, since few of their previous employers had been able to reopen their establishments: San Francisco laundry owners were a case in point. Grant Avenue merchants, international trading houses, and dry cleaners were in similar situations, unwilling and afraid to resume their operations.[38] And those who had worked for Japanese firms had no prospects for reemployment at their previous jobs.

Instances of violence against Japanese Americans who had returned to the coast had a powerful effect on Topaz, especially the story of the Doi family. Two of the Doi family's sons were still in military service when the parents and the other children returned to Placer County, California. A packing shed on the family property was set afire by vandals on January 8. After the eldest son discovered and extinguished the blaze, shots were fired at the home and dynamite was placed in the shed.[39] Some AWOL soldiers and their women friends were later arrested for attempting to destroy the building. Although they confessed, the jury acquitted them, to the jubilation of their neighbors. The story sent shock waves through the Topaz community, and many Issei decided that it was not yet time to return to California. After the Doi incident, some ten dwellings on the West Coast were destroyed, and more than thirty incidents of harassment occurred over the next two years.[40] Tales of the deaths of two Issei in Chicago further scared people.

Accounts of discrimination that came from people who had left Topaz were especially frightening to the remaining residents. When a draft-deferred Nisei returned to his nursery in the East Bay, he was subjected to a "silent boycott" and no one would buy his flowers. Another couple who went back to their chicken ranch in the same area encountered such discrimination that they left and went to work as domestics in Berkeley.

There was other news, both good and bad. As early as January 1945, Director Luther T. Hoffman warned Nikkei returning to San Francisco that the "Little Tokyo" district of the city had been taken over by "Negroes" and "it would not be healthful for any evacuee to return there."[41] In contrast, a report arrived that the Pacific Coast Fair Play Committee had held a two-day conference in San Francisco in mid-January for representatives of federal, state, and private agencies. Spokespersons from African American, Filipino, and Korean organizations pledged that they would not attempt to profit from discrimination against the Japanese Americans.[42] It was hard to know whom to believe.

The residents were also influenced by rumors that concerned Topaz itself:[43] that the center would close July 31, or that the WRA was going to liberalize its departure policy to increase the relocation grants. Both were false, to people's great disappointment. The center would close December 31, they learned, and departure assistance was fixed at $25 a person, plus train fare.

In addition, the death of Franklin D. Roosevelt affected the mood of the camp population. Nikkei, like Americans everywhere, were shocked by the news. There was a memorial service at the high school and the elementary schools, and an interfaith, campwide service was held as well. All entertainment was canceled for the weekend. The Nikkei had no reason to like Roosevelt, who had, after all, paved the way for internment by issuing Executive Order 9066, but they knew even less about President Harry S Truman and were apprehensive about his attitude toward them. Many Issei were deeply moved by the president's death, especially those with sons in the military.[44]

Block managers began to take an active role in assisting resettlement, beyond just providing packing crates. They became informed about opportunities for jobs and kept their residents better advised. The community council still refused to take a stand, but it worked to get Nikkei bank accounts unfrozen and the council's welfare committee advised residents about relocation assistance. Since the residents were often hesitant to trust the information that the WRA provided, the facts they acquired from one another were very useful.[45]

By the end of April the Topaz residents had become, according to Oscar Hoffman, "relocation minded." Departure was on their minds, even if many had not yet done anything specific about it and still demanded more financial assistance. Issei with children in school planned to move when school ended. The administration planned to continue adult education throughout the summer, and there was a steady enrollment in skills-related courses. A speaker from the New Orleans field office held a "New Orleans Week" to convince the Nikkei to go south, and he even showed the film "Dixie," but despite a large attendance few were convinced. They complained that wages were too low.[46] The administration tried to encourage resettlement by trapping aid recipients into discussing the subject when they were applying for funds. The consolidation of the WRA welfare office with the relocation division confused the Nikkei. It also aroused considerable opposition from Caucasian staff members, especially those who had lost their jobs.[47] As the end of the school year approached, the WRA scheduled two special railroad coaches to leave on May 21 and June 4; within a week they were well reserved.[48] The camp population had in fact been declining steadily since the first of the year, as statistics in the director's reports to Myer indicate:

February 1, 1945	5,807
March 1, 1945	5,700
April 1, 1945	5,512

Oscar Hoffman estimated that the May 1 population would be 5,300.[49]

Despite the declining population, community leaders still resisted any attempts to consolidate services. When the WRA announced that three mess halls would close, there was strong opposition from the blocks where the residents would be sent to eat.[50] The curtailment was both a reaction to the manpower shortage and an example of the "squeeze" in operation, and people in the affected areas objected but, interestingly enough, residents in other blocks scheduled to receive them did not. Acting camp director Roscoe Bell met with representatives of the block managers, the council, and the chefs to devise a plan. It took a week to implement Washington's mandate to shut down the messes; by the time the event took place the angry residents were blaming not the WRA but their own leaders for giving in and not coming up with an alternate plan.[51] Clearly, people needed more specific information in order to make wise decisions about where they should resettle. During the first week of May, a group consisting of the chair of the community council and his brother, the chair of the block managers, the chief of the resident physicians, and a prewar businessman departed on a scouting expedition to Los Angeles and San Francisco. The residents awaited their reports with great anticipation. The chair of the block managers returned in early June and gave what Hoffman described as a "neutral" report. He described how Japanese were beginning businesses in Los Angeles, while those in Berkeley were buying houses at inflated prices. Despite his supposed neutrality, he admitted that he intended to resettle.[52] However, when one of Hoffman's research assistants returned from a scouting trip, his report convinced his boss, at any rate, that there were many problems yet to be overcome in the Bay Area. He said that a number of Caucasians had been indifferent to him, but only because they confused him with a Chinese; other whites called him a "Jap" or worse. White-collar jobs were scarce because opportunities to establish businesses in the former Japanese town were nonexistent. He could not borrow money to buy property because of an insurance clause regarding the likelihood of fire damage—insurers feared terrorism and arson against Japanese. Violence plus the lack of housing, especially for large families, made the WRA's determination to force the residents out of camp both incomprehensible and inhumane. The man solved his problems only by purchasing a home at a very inflated price,[53] a solution open to few.

Nevertheless, by early June the signs of increased departures were everywhere. A group of elderly carpenters asked for a refresher course in carpentry. More Issei were taking English classes. Several Protestant ministers were resettling, establishing hostels for others. Resettled Japanese Americans reported that Berkeley was increasingly willing to accept Nikkei and its schools were far superior to those in Topaz.[54] College students were beginning to enroll in West Coast universities, many of them at the University of California, where they paid only state residents' fees.[55] Students at Cal reported no prejudice, but some had difficulty because of their poor study skills.[56] A group of former residents of Placer County decided to brave its discrimination, reputedly the worst in California, by returning in a body. Interest in the community council or the block managers' organization was almost nil, and people served on them only if compelled, and then only until they themselves could leave. Only George Ochikubo held on, planning to stay until the end as he continued to fight the ban against his return to the coast.[57] (It was lifted on September 4, and he too prepared to leave.)

By this time the camp had divided into two groups: those who were making plans to resettle and those who refused to. Even the latter were worried about their future. They included large families with young children and no resources, the aged and the sick, and the few who were still pro-Japan.[58] Hoffman described them as "sitting tight." They realized that they were being squeezed out by the consolidation of services and the closure of facilities, yet they made no plans and no longer even bothered to argue with the WRA about it. Even the former leaders of the negative faction were leaving. Despite the housing shortage, the news that the Federal Housing Authority planned to construct some five hundred units in the Bay Area did not induce these people to apply; Hoffman concluded, probably correctly, that their refusal stemmed from the Nikkei's unwillingness to trust any government agency after their experience with the WRA. The Issei described applying for this housing with their camp slang phrase, "waste time."[59]

⚜

In early July the WRA announced that Topaz would close by November 1, 1945, rather than January 1 as had previously been announced. Hoffman reported that he saw no signs of the recalcitrants making plans to leave. The hard core appeared to be settling in for the final days, waiting to see what, if anything, the WRA would do to dislodge them. Although many believed that California's Japanophiles almost balanced the Japanophobes and they knew they would have friends nearby, the "stand-pats" were worried about two stories they had heard of Issei bachelors who had resettled in Seattle and Berkeley and had committed suicide out of loneliness. People who knew them said that both men had written that their greatest mistake was to leave camp.[60]

In mid-July the final community council was installed. The moribund institution came back to life with the reemergence of George Ochikubo. Ochikubo, deeply hostile toward the WRA and the army, had become involved in a joint legal test of the order to exclude certain Nikkei from the West Coast. The case, tried in California courts, was sponsored by the American Civil Liberties Union with the cooperation of the JACL. The army ultimately issued "certificates of exemption" to the other two defendants, Masaru Baba and Shizuko Shiramizu, but not to Ochikubo; the army continued to claim that his presence on the West Coast would "constitute a potential danger to military security."[61] The case was still pending when Ochikubo was elected chair of a conference held in Salt Lake City to discuss the liquidation of cooperative enterprises.[62]

In a speech at his installation ceremony, Ochikubo blasted the administration. He divided Caucasians into three groups: the "rubber stamps," who did everything Washington suggested; the "humane," who wanted better conditions for the residents; and the others, who desired only to earn an "E" from Washington for efficiency. He blamed the WRA for creating petty annoyances to "squeeze" the residents even as they planned to move them out. Such pressures to force relocation were even more painful when people were under great stress. He urged the administrators to behave humanely at this most sensitive of times. Ochikubo obviously felt he had nothing to lose by antagonizing them, and his speech accomplished that handily, to the point where some of them even suggested he be tossed out on his ear. He was not, but instead remained until early September. The speech suggests some of the divisions within the Japanese American community that resurfaced later, during the debates over redress. The quarreling among individual residents had now spread throughout the entire population. The acting director, Roscoe Bell, merely wondered why the other council members had ever selected Ochikubo to speak.[63] Perhaps they saw that he was willing to voice sentiments that others shared but did not dare to express.

An anonymous pamphlet was distributed one night, clearly the work of another angry resident, a pro-Japan holdout. The author claimed the federal government had "promised" to hold the Japanese Americans for the duration of the war, not to throw them out prematurely, and the Geneva Convention protected them against such inhumane treatment. Obviously unwilling to believe Japan was losing the war, the writer charged that those who resettled were breaking faith with the mother country. The faithful who remained when the camps closed should continue to be cared for by the WRA, and schools should be provided for their children. The residents were mostly embarrassed by the anonymous pamphleteer's pathetic appeal, but Hoffman reported it to Washington, fearing that some of the timid might postpone resettling as a result. Bell assured Myer that the pamphlet had only aroused indifference.[64]

The effects of Ochikubo's speech and the pamphlet quickly dissipated. Most who could resettle were now busily planning to leave, causing further frustrations. Community leader Mas Narahara left to become an assistant relocation officer in Los Angeles, and Bell recorded that his own secretary was taking a job in the San Francisco office. The Buddhist hostel was to open in San Francisco in mid-August, and Bishop Socho Matsukagi departed on a special train to the coast. The impending surrender of Japan spurred the departure of many who had been holding out.[65] The news came as a great shock to those who had refused to believe their mother country could possibly lose the war. But many who left failed to find new homes and jobs, and the departure rate was slower than Hoffman had expected.[66] They complained that the resettlement grants were inadequate to meet their living expenses while they located work. Some who had property in the Bay Area needed assistance in evicting tenants so they could return to their own homes. Others encountered trouble arranging to have their goods shipped from Topaz to a location near the WRA warehouse in San Francisco. Nikkei remaining in Utah complained that the state had refused to provide education for their children. Such irritants made it harder for the willing to depart and caused the holdouts to become more resistant.[67]

Oscar Hoffman himself began to caution the WRA to expect a residue to remain in the camps when they were officially closed, "unless some unusual factors were injected into the situation." It was not a question of whether, but rather of "what should be done [about] it." His staff members assumed that all families with children would have departed by September 1, but they found their projections were incorrect. Only 471 people left in July, instead of the thousand that had been anticipated. Hoffman's concerns were shared by others in the administration, who made plans to open the schools in September despite Washington's orders. By the middle of August they realized that Washington would close the center regardless of how many residents were left.[68] Dillon Myer was not to be budged. On August 29 the population was 3,400.[69]

Oscar Hoffman completed his final report in early September and departed for Oregon State University to take the academic position he had trained for. When his series of reports ended, information about the weekly or daily activities of Topaz became less readily available. The facilities in camp gradually closed down. Community activities continued throughout the summer to sustain the residents' morale, but their mood worsened as the population dwindled to the desperate and dependent few. The adult education and vocational training programs were terminated in midsummer;

the special housing for the aged closed on September 1. The San Francisco office of the WRA was informed that the hospital and dependency cases would be sent there regardless of their wishes. Seven or eight patients at the state mental hospital in Provo were transferred to California institutions. Another resident suffered a mental breakdown shortly thereafter, and Director Luther Hoffman warned Myer that several other residents seemed to be on the verge of breaking down as well. But the exodus continued. On October 1, with fewer than 2,000 people in Topaz, the dining halls began to close. The community council held a final meeting and a farewell banquet in Delta, an ironic note that underlined the end of the barbed wire fences. The Nikkei seemed to accept the closure of the camp, and Topaz experienced none of the die-hard resistance seen in other centers. The community had never been violent, and its ending was in keeping with its previous history. October 31 was the official closing day. On November 5 the remaining administrators and residents had a "combination Halloween and closing party." The director was gratified to note that the administration had received many letters of appreciation from the resettled Nikkei, thanking them for all that had been done for them and for the fine community they believed Topaz had been.[70]

⚜

The difficulties of moving the large population, shutting down the camp's facilities, and relocating the white personnel were enormous, and for residents and administrators alike personal concerns overshadowed the external events that were reshaping their world: the defeat of Germany, the dropping of the atomic bombs, and the surrender of Japan. To parents of the servicemen in the all-Nisei battalion and combat team, these events meant that their sons would soon come home. The few residents who were still hoping for a Japanese victory probably did not believe reports of the atomic bombs, since they did not accept any news that did not accord with their preconceptions. Some Issei refused to believe the news of Japan's defeat, convinced that their native land was invincible and would fight to the bitter end. Tamotsu Shibutani described how the interned population in many camps believed rumors that the emperor's peace rescript was forged, that General Tojo's suicide attempt was faked, and that the war was not over.[71] The effect on the Issei of Topaz was probably similar; at least, the news dismayed and confused residents who were considering repatriating to Japan. For many others, it only reemphasized the need to leave camp and find their places in the postwar world.

Beginning in May, the administration had begun to charter special trains to take the Japanese Americans back to the coast, and by early September the population began to move in earnest. The trains rolled steadily west through the end of October. Temporary housing was made available in San Francisco for veterans' families, and administrators hoped this action would lead to the opening of government housing for everyone dislocated by the war. In early October lodging became available at Camp Funston, Hunters Point, and Marin City, all former army facilities in the Bay Area. The block managers left on October 18. The penultimate train left on October 26 with 325 aboard; only 200 dependency cases still remained. After the WRA announced that those with no resettlement destinations would be returned to the places they had left in 1942, Director Hoffman sent letters to the twelve families who had not stated their intentions, calling them in for counseling; all remaining family heads quickly set departure dates and destinations.. The eleven hospital cases were perhaps the most difficult for the director to resolve, but he assured them that they would be transferred to hospitals in San Francisco and told the WRA field office in San Francisco to expect them. The last to leave were 32 persons, mostly evacuees from Hawaii who had to await a boat. The center closed October 31, on schedule. Local residents were hired to help the remaining Caucasian staff members close the facility. In December the last dining hall and staff dorms were shuttered, and plans were made to turn the center over to the federal government liquidating agency. All property was declared surplus and the barracks were sold. The barracks became chicken coops, residences, and businesses, and their former incarnations were soon apparent only to old timers. The auditorium was moved to Southern Utah State College (now University), where it served another forty years.

Delta residents complained to Jane Beckwith that typewriters, refrigerators, and other useful and very usable appliances were simply buried in the desert. The visible reminders of the town soon disappeared; the site rapidly returned to wasteland and has remained barren to this day. Only a few pottery shards and bricks are left for the sharp-eyed collector.

In his closing report Luther Hoffman, the director who presided over the camp's last year, congratulated himself: "We were a conservative community but steady and sound. People left with renewed confidence in themselves and faith in the outside community."[72] Maybe.

The administrative staff members of Topaz did not complete their assignments until they filed their final reports. Luther Hoffman summarized the history of the project and the importance of resettlement. Tight housing on the coast, he concluded, was the main impediment to the latter, but as temporary residences were made available the situation eased. He prided himself on closing the center on time, and he made no effort to count the human cost. The position of director was beset by problems on every side when he stepped in, but he had taken command, shown who was in charge, and improved relations with the council and the community. Hoffman considered that he had improved communication with the people of Delta, Salt Lake City, and Washington as well. He held open houses every Sunday afternoon to improve relations with the residents, and they had learned, through his stern yet wise counsel, to help themselves instead of relying on the administration for everything.[73] The residents, had he talked to them, might have disagreed, and the other staff members would have been amazed as well.

Statistics seem to bear out his favorable assessment. The town, now abandoned, had held 8,316 residents at its height, including 200 Caucasians, half of them from the surrounding communities. The grand total admitted to the center was 11,212.[74] In all, 451 people joined the U.S. Army; 80 of them were volunteers. Fifteen

were killed in action. Despite fears of gangs and juvenile delinquency, there was very little crime, less than in comparable communities outside. There were 131 deaths,[75] but the level of health
was above average. Some of those who died were infants, but
mainly they were people over sixty who succumbed to the diseases
of old age (with the exception of one gunshot victim, James
Wakasa).

The welfare section reported in a tone almost as smug as Luther
Hoffman's. Social services were in great demand when George
LaFabreque arrived in 1943 to set up the division. Soon eighty-
seven case workers were at work, providing unemployment assistance, personal counseling, and clothing. They helped families and
individuals cope with the stresses brought on by the registration and
segregation crises, especially those who made decisions that divided
their families. Resettlement counseling subsequently became their
primary function. The division merged with the relocation division
in November 1944.[76]

The division of evacuee property was in charge of transporting
and storing the residents' possessions. Its employees handled fraud,
past due accounts, rents, taxes, and the like. Their biggest concern,
not surprisingly, was encouraging people to trust them, a difficult
task after the Nikkei's experiences on the coast. They, too, considered their efforts largely successful.[77] The many evacuees who
lost everything might have disputed that evaluation. The division
went out of business before a final accounting could be made of
what had been lost in storage; such a final reckoning was in fact
never made.

The same self-congratulation was evident in the project reports.
Director Russell Bankston oversaw all public relations: he reviewed
the newspaper, issued press releases, and documented the history
of the center. The newspaper published until August 1945, despite
increasing staffing problems. Although according to Bankston the
paper was not censored, it was "checked carefully for accuracy" by
the administration on all stories concerning policy. Because of the
wind storms, the paper had to be hand-delivered. The reporters
strove to be strictly neutral. As people began to depart, Bankston's
office published resettlement news, first as a weekly, and then as a

semiweekly when the *Times* ceased publication. The division also took and publicized camp photographs, which it copied for the National Archives. It showed informational films, attempted to dispel rumors, and covered visits of outside dignitaries.[78] Bankston, who remained at Topaz from the beginning to the end of its existence, considered the efforts of his office successful.

The education division also provided a history of its concerns. The report acknowledged that the perpetually inadequate school staff caused unrest and discouragement among the pupils. The director explained the high staff turnover on the grounds that the WRA could not grant teachers tenure. The author of the report claimed that the resident teachers were more effective than the Caucasians anyway because of language and cultural problems. He concluded that the high school program was as effective as any outside camp, given wartime conditions, and noted proudly that the Dies Committee had announced that Topaz had the best library system in the camps. The schools closed June 1, 1945, and the reports were shipped to Washington.[79] (Eleanor Gerard and Emil Sekerak moved there too, and married. Eleanor continued to collect educational records so the Nisei could pursue their higher education.) Clearly, the director of the education division never read the reports of Oscar Hoffman.

The recreation division catalogued its many activities: supervising the golf course, playgrounds, and picnic grounds, as well as sports competitions and festivals and parties. The author listed all the other amusements and diversions of the Nikkei, from religion and photography to go and *shōgi*.[80] From this glowing report one would hardly suspect the author was describing a concentration camp.

Oscar Hoffman's closing report on the community analysis section also emphasized his positive role. He discussed his attempts to improve the educational system, he reviewed the administrators and staff, and he extensively analyzed the resettlement program. An outside observer might conclude from this report that Hoffman enjoyed his job too much, for it provided him with a "laboratory under glass" to study, but his pain and frustration over the anguish of the residents was visible as well. Hoffman was extremely eager for resettlement to succeed, not only because it was the WRA's policy but also because he thought it best that the residents return to society as soon as possible. He concluded that his work had been both necessary and a success, but questions could be raised on both scores.

The picture of Topaz in the records of the WRA and the separate records of the community analysis division was created by Caucasians. Few of the records of Topaz were written by Nisei, for those working for the JERS project were among the first to resettle. The administrators in the camp could be divided, as George Ochikubo suggested, into people who were "humane," those who wished only to be efficient, and the "rubber stamps" who did exactly what Washington wanted. Probably Paul Bell's characterization of them as covering the spectrum from excellent to disastrous was more apt. The few who were humane seem to have made a real difference in the lives of those they helped: Roscoe Bell, Eleanor Gerard Sekerak, Emil Sekerak, George LaFabreque, Claud Pratt, Joe Goodman, and others whose names I did not learn. Fumi Hayashi recalled Barbara Loomis, a victim of polio who taught music, Emily Light, Mary McMillan, and Muriel Matzkin with great fondness and mentioned men named Carlson, Johnson, and Victor Goertzel as good teachers. She, Dave Tatsuno, and Tad Fujita all remembered the dedication of the Reverend Carl Nugent, who moved to Delta in February 1944 to help with the Protestant church ministry.[81]

Although Charles Ernst seemed more to fit Ochikubo's "efficiency" category, Chiyoko Yano, who worked directly for Ernst compiling statistics on the camp, had nothing unfavorable to say about him. Oscar Hoffman must have been a model of efficiency and his position made him seem a company spy, yet Michiko Okamoto, who worked for him, remembered him with great respect and fondness. Many administrators came to Topaz with little knowledge of Japanese Americans as people. They had not known any Nikkei before the war, and Topaz, especially under Charles

Ernst, gave them little opportunity to become close. There was, as Hoffman noted, a caste system among administrators, with divisions based on rank, housing, and the like. Even when Caucasians and Nikkei worked together, the Caucasian was the superior and close fraternization was not encouraged. Yet at times friendships and mutual bonds were forged. Caucasian and Japanese Americans not only worked together; they attended the same church, went to the same entertainments, and endured some of the same physical hardships. Certainly, no one interned at Topaz was unaware that the whites were free to leave while they were not, except under certain conditions, but they realized that not all who administered Topaz agreed with government policy. It was a concentration camp with a human face. When Topaz closed, little was left behind—some concrete slabs where buildings had stood, some broken dishes, old pot-bellied stoves, artifacts for later generations to collect as the Topaz residents had collected arrowheads. There were no graves, for the ashes of the dead went back to California with the descendants, no buildings, no trees, no survivors on site. All that remained were the dust storms.

Chapter Eight

Nikkei Lives:
The Impact of Internment

The official records of Topaz were the product of Caucasian thinking, even if they were often written by Nisei hands. The camp administrators were charged with running the camps according to the mandate given by the WRA. They viewed the residents as their responsibilities, in much the same way that the Bureau of Indian Affairs saw its charges. Many of the administrators had, in fact, come from the Bureau of Indian Affairs, and WRA director Dillon S. Myer took over Indian Affairs shortly after the war. Their paternalism fostered a condition of dependency in many Japanese Americans very similar to that created in the native Americans.[1] Some administrators were sympathetic to the Nikkei's plight, and a few were overtly hostile; most were simply neutral. Their jobs were created and necessitated by the racism and politics of the war. The decision to intern the Japanese Americans was not theirs, but it never entered the minds of most officials to disagree with it. Everyone had to sacrifice in wartime, they believed, and they equated internment with food rationing and the draft. This attitude was held by some of the camp residents as well, who simply resigned themselves to the situation. Since the officials had ample opportunity to observe Nikkei who had come to hate the United States as a result of their confinement, they had no cause to doubt that some might be disloyal. The Caucasians sought to be efficient and to do their jobs as effectively as possible given the circumstances; George Ochikubo was quite perceptive in his observations about them. For most of the administrators efficiency was enough, and the war's end was the long-awaited solution to everybody's problems. With the passage of time many, like Governor Earl Warren, have come to see relocation as a mistake. Others probably agree with John J. McCloy, who maintained until his death in 1991 that it was necessary and right.

The perceptions of the people whom they governed, the Japanese Americans, have also changed over the years. By the time the former evacuees returned to free America, whether to the East, the Midwest, or the West Coast, most desired only to pick up the broken pieces of their lives and start again. Although they did not intend to become the vaunted "model minority" so esteemed in later literature and now so controversial, they did want to avoid notice, escape racism and discrimination, and become good citizens, thereby proving to the country how loyal they always had been.[2] Memories of Tanforan and Topaz were suppressed, packed away like old kimonos in the attics of their minds. Thus, many in the third generation, the Sansei, grew up unaware of what their parents and grandparents had endured. And when they learned the story of the concentration camps, they could not comprehend why their ancestors had gone so blindly and silently to their incarceration. Why had they not fought back?

⚘

Public statements about relocation and concentration camp life during the first decade following the war were rare. In 1946 Miné Okubo published *Citizen 13660,* an illustrated memoir of life in Tanforan and Topaz, but the reader discerns her attitude only through her sarcasm and the evocative sketches of her camp-mates. She concluded with a description of her departure in January 1944. Describing the final red tape, Okubo stated simply, "I was now free." Perhaps the most moving moment was the one that followed. She looked back at the crowd left at the gate, the very old and the very young: "Here I was, alone, with no family responsibilities, and yet fear had chained me to the camp. I thought, 'My God! How do they expect those poor people to leave the one place they can call home.'"[3]

Standing on the ellipse south of the White House on July 15, 1946, President Harry S Truman awarded the Nisei 442d Regimental Combat Team its seventh presidential unit citation. He pointed out that these soldiers had "fought not only the enemy, but [also] prejudice—and they had won." On February 2, 1948, Truman made three references to the Nikkei in a speech on civil rights. Point 8 called for Hawaiian and Alaskan statehood (Hawaii was 40 percent Japanese American) and the dropping of racial bars to naturalization. Point 10 called for the rapid settlement of Nikkei evacuation claims. Congress enacted the Japanese American Claims Act, which Truman signed on July 2, 1948; it appropriated $38 million to settle all property losses incurred by Japanese Americans as a result of the evacuation.[4] The total amount was pegged for years at $400 million,[5] a figure with no basis in fact. The Claims Act was an inadequate approach to the question of compensation; some 26,568 claims were filed totaling $148 million, but the amount distributed was about $37 million.[6] Congress also limited claims to real and personal property and the petitioner had to document his or her losses; many, if they ever had documentation, had lost it in moving or discovered that it had been destroyed when their stored property was vandalized. By the time the act was passed, the Internal Revenue Service had destroyed the income tax returns for the prewar years, which would have been the most authoritative records on which to base claims. The few actual settlements were agonizingly slow as well, dragging on until 1965.[7] Few people who were evacuated appeared before general hearings or testified about their losses. Many of the most needy Issei died before their claims were even heard.

❧

The way former evacuees remembered and reacted to the camps in interviews from 1987 to 1989 adds another dimension to the historical reconstruction of Japanese San Francisco, Tanforan, and

Topaz. By the late 1980s not only had most Japanese Americans rebuilt their lives, recovering a semblance of relative prosperity, but the civil rights movement of the 1960s had legitimized ethnic protest. The Sansei, who were not afraid or ashamed to speak out, championed the rights of their parents and grandparents. The Japanese American Citizens League, which had survived the war in considerable disrepute because of its support for and acquiescence in the military's demands for evacuating the West Coast, championed the cause of redress. Other groups, too, began to demand financial compensation of some kind—whether a "token" amount for all or the equivalent of actual losses on an individual basis—as well as an apology from the federal government, a statement that admitted Washington's mistake in interning the Japanese Americans. Remembering the past was not only legitimized; it became almost essential. Japanese Americans began to speak out, not only to protest what had been done to them but also to address a new audience of Americans, most of whom did not know their story at all. This new generation was prepared to accept relocation as a mistake, an unbelievable error that stemmed from racism. The shape that the apology should take, however, was much more controversial, even among Japanese Americans.

When camp survivors told me their stories, they were speaking in a time totally different from the war years. Both interviewer and interviewee operated from the presumption that what happened was wrong. Both accepted the necessity for some sort of redress, although Nikkei differed over what it should consist of. The survivors' memory was selective, and the passage of forty-five years affected what remained. Some things were magnified; many others were forgotten. The events of the years since the war also influenced recollections. For those whose subsequent lives were happy and successful, the camps were a brief unpleasantness that was perhaps not so very bad, even if unconstitutional. On the other hand, many who did not prosper traced all their troubles to the camp years. Of course, many who were in the camps have died. It was hard in 1990 to find an Issei who had remained in camp until October 31, 1945, for most of these people are no longer with us. And those who were young children remembered almost nothing of the pain that Tan-

foran and Topaz caused their parents. The effects on them during
their formative years are even harder to assess.

⚜

Nonetheless, talking with even a few of the residents of Topaz
added many dimensions to the written record. The Issei played an
important role in the history of Topaz. The most elderly did not
work; they had labored hard all their lives and most welcomed the
opportunity to rest. Since they had recognized the peril the war
created because of their lack of citizenship, many were grateful that
nothing worse than internment befell them. They were not surprised when, at first, they could not participate in camp government, but before long they were the predominant element. Some
chose to return to Japan at the earliest opportunity, believing that
America held no promise for them or their families, while others
recognized that it was the land of their children's hopes and remained. Many of them became American citizens in 1952, when the
McCarran-Walter Immigration Act was passed. Their postwar economic situation was bleak: most had lost all they had accumulated
in a half century in America, and they were too old to begin again.
They were the real tragedies of the internment, and redress came
too late to save them.

The younger Issei suffered too, but they could not sit back and
rest in camp, and they found many ways to survive. Many of the
women and some of the men provided care for others through
religion, social welfare, or official positions such as block manager.
George Gentoku Shimamoto was one who chose that path. Born
in Wakayama Prefecture, Shimamoto came to the United States in
1918 when he was thirteen, making him, in the parlance of the day,
a "young Issei." At Tanforan and Topaz he drew on his architectural
background and carpentry skills and became resident chief of construction and planning, enabling him to make the camp more
comfortable for the residents. He helped install plasterboard on the
inner walls of the barracks and constructed an auditorium so the
children and adults would have a place to congregate. Shimamoto
served on the committee investigating the Wakasa killing and also

was in charge of the pipeline repair project, a truly thankless task. He helped recruit volunteers for the army, an assignment he supported because, although born an Issei, he considered himself a law-abiding resident and hoped that one day the Japanese would be permitted to participate in naturalization. When Shimamoto left Topaz in July 1944, he was pleased that the camp was self-sustaining. He went to New York City and entered a prominent architectural firm, where he worked for thirty-two years, retiring as senior partner and general manager. He had brought the organization from a 6-man office in 1944 to a leading firm with a staff of 125.[8]

George Gentoku Shimamoto lived his life in the United States, loved his adopted land, and became a citizen when, in 1952, he was at last eligible to do so. But like many other Japanese Americans, he did not believe that citizenship ruled out redress. When the United States put him behind barbed wire, it committed a wrong that should be acknowledged. Although monetary compensation was not necessary for his personal well-being, he said, "in the United States to correct the wrong, . . . [one] always makes a settlement in a monetary way. It is the American way of thinking or American way of doing it." Twenty thousand dollars was, he thought, far less than the value of the damages people had suffered, and he recognized that the sum would probably be paid so slowly that those eligible would keep diminishing in number. Shimamoto was not a bitter man; he accepted each new situation and strove to improve things for himself and those around him. Trying to bridge the gap between Issei and Caucasians, he retained his Japanese heritage yet was American in attitude long before he could be one legally.

Shimamoto was fortunate, for he was educated and well employed. Many other Issei bachelors had worked in restaurants before the war. They returned to the kitchens or other unskilled jobs, and as they aged many lived in severe poverty. Some existed in 1989 on as little as twenty dollars a month, paying minimal rent for shabby hotel rooms. For them redress came too late.[9]

Two women, Faith Terasawa and Chitose Nishimura Manabe, exemplified the many women and men whose religious faith drew them to help others and gave them strength to endure the hardships of camp. Although both these women were Christian, many devout Buddhists also reacted in this way. Faith Terasawa was a "young Issei" of forty-five when she entered Topaz. Her father was a retired Episcopal priest, and she assisted him in ministering to others, then continued his work after he died in camp. In 1987, when she was ninety years old, there were many things about internment she would never forget: the smell of the people who lived in horse stalls at Tanforan; the sight of her first meal at Topaz, a bowl of rice with a prune on top. Her allergies made it impossible for her to sleep on a straw mattress. Employed by the welfare division, her particular specialty became working with the mentally ill. She remembered clearly one young woman unhinged by the stresses of evacuation whom she and her supervisor visited. The woman opened the door and came at them with a butcher knife; they subdued her and took her to the state mental hospital at Provo. Terasawa also worked in the hospital, treating the tubercular patients that the young nurse's aides feared to approach. Faith lived up to her name: she believed that Christianity gave her the strength to do such work and remain healthy, and she did. She dealt well with the perpetual adversity of camp life. After the war, she returned to San Francisco with her family, who cared for her as she grew old.[10]

Chitose Manabe's devotion was given to God and her family. She was born in Sendai, the daughter of a wealthy merchant who died when she was very young. She attended a boarding school for girls run by American missionaries, learned to teach, and went to Tokyo to work. She married a Salvation Army worker converted in the United States who had returned to Japan to help with rescue work after the Tokyo earthquake of 1923. Mr. Manabe took his bride to the Oakland-Berkeley area, where the couple continued their religious work and raised five children. Both she and her husband worked, she as a domestic, her husband as a gardener, but after their children the center of their lives was their involvement with the Christian Layman's Movement. Topaz provided some relief from the heavy labor she had done all her life, but she also worked for the welfare department, learned sewing, and studied English, something she had long wanted to do. Both Manabes continued their Christian work in camp, he teaching Bible study groups for the Kibei, and she singing in the choir, an activity she remembered with fondness in 1990, when she was eighty-seven. Her attitude was both stoic and full of faith. About the horse stalls at Tanforan, she said, "War time can't be helped—everybody have some troubles. . . . We have to overcome." Religion gave her the strength to do that. The Manabes returned home to Berkeley, to put their house back in order and resume their prewar lives. Again they worked hard, this time to put their children through higher education. The Manabes became citizens in 1952.[11]

⚜

For Japanese Americans the years of internment were a benchmark, the pivotal experience of their lives. Even today Nisei ask any new acquaintance, "Where were you in camp?" In 1989 Kenji Fujii carried this preoccupation one step further. He did not ever refer to World War II: instead, he spoke of "before camp . . . and after camp." Camp name, barracks number, and room replaced the names of universities and dates of graduation that were reference points for non-Japanese friends. The WRA administration frowned on using the term camp, and especially concentration camp. Instead, the correct word was "center," as in "relocation center." Caucasian scholars and some Nikkei too, like Harry H. L. Kitano, have pointed out that relocation had its good side, dispersing the Nikkei population throughout the country and providing more opportunities than continued concentration in urban ghettos or rural slums in California would have done. However, as Harry's sister Chizu Iiyama has noted, in 1942 most Nisei were of high school age. "What high school population (including whites) would 'disperse' themselves throughout the country?" She said, "The end result did not justify the means." Internment was such a trauma, such a break with the past, that few Nikkei can consciously attribute any overall beneficial effect to it. One of the few who did, the well-known writer, politician, and educator S. I. Hayakawa, was not interned.

The Nisei are the generation of Japanese Americans for whom memories of camp are the strongest. As the Issei can be divided into the "young" and the "old," so can the Nisei—although these are very fluid divisions with much overlap. The "old Nisei" were already out of school and beginning careers and families of their own when the war began; some were in their early thirties. They were the first leaders in camp, acting as block managers and council members until resettlement provided the impetus for many of them to return to the outside world, where some achieved a measure of success. The younger Nisei were the school-age generation. Many were high school students, but they included the very young.[12] Some small children and infants were Sansei. Some teenaged Nisei seemed to be completely traumatized by the camp experience, while others took it as an excuse to play. Many Nikkei suffered damage to their self-image since they had to accept the notion of an "inferiority" that put them behind barbed wire. As part of families with school-age children, many younger Nisei remained in camp for several years or the duration of the war. The older teenaged males were also caught up in the registration controversy, forced to decide first whether to volunteer and later whether to be drafted. Many young men escaped camp to go into the army, where they grew up in a hurry. Some made the army their home and their postwar career. Others had to readjust to postwar America, contending once again with prejudice as they struggled to find jobs, start families, and establish their identity on the West Coast, where the old Nihonmachis had disappeared but not the prejudice against them—at least not for a while. In short, any generalization produces many examples of the opposite. Camp had differing effects on different people. The experience scarred some people for life, while others, like the members of the Topaz High School Class of 1945, formed unbreakable bonds based on the good experiences so that now they can even laugh at the adversities. They have held a series of reunions as recently as 1990. An all-camp "last" Topaz reunion was held September 4–6, 1992, in Burlingame, California.

◈

Tomoye Nozawe was born in San Francisco into a middle-class family, educated in the public schools, and graduated from the

University of California. She married Henri Takahashi, a graduate of Pomona. The evacuation to Tanforan was rough; she never forgot the mother of a friend who became ill from eating contaminated food and died of food poisoning because the guards would not let the ambulance leave the camp quickly enough to get her to the hospital.[13] Thinking Topaz would be better, the Takahashis volunteered to be part of the advance party leaving for camp. Tomoye and her husband Henri made the best of their new existence, founding and working on the *Topaz Times;* they took especial pride in the ways they avoided censorship through clever words and phrases. She remembered with fondness the kind members of the administration who had fraternized with them and become their friends. Some, she recalled, were conscientious objectors to the war.[14] The Takahashis left camp on seasonal leave to work as laborers harvesting carrots. They had never done such work in their lives, but getting out of camp was both exciting and a brief escape from its routines. Tomoye's skills in Spanish helped her to communicate with their Mexican co-workers. She was shocked to see Indians, who worked alongside them, treated even worse than they were by the locals.[15] After the Takahashis had a baby, they remained in camp until the end of the war. Returning to San Francisco, Tomoye crossed the bay on a ferry and watched the skyline of the city she loved emerge from the fog; it was an image that she would treasure as much as she recalled the anger and pain of leaving. Perhaps for her the best revenge was to become economically successful, as she and her husband did, thus proving just how worthy of being San Franciscans they were.[16]

Nisei Dave Tatsuno voiced no outright condemnation of relocation, although he did oppose the discriminatory way that Japanese Americans were treated. Dave was a San Francisco small businessman, married with one child, when he and his family were evacuated in 1942. Fearing they faced immediate evacuation, the Tatsunos held an evacuation sale at the beginning of March and closed their store on April 7, but they waited another month before going to Tanforan. There his wife delivered a second child. As manager of the dry goods section of the cooperative he made three purchasing trips all over the nation. His story of smuggling a movie camera into Topaz was recounted earlier. His film has been an invaluable document for the Japanese American community in the Bay Area and the nation.[17]

Dave Tatsuno, like Faith Terasawa and Chitose Manabe, was a devout Christian, and his religion gave him strength to endure the internment. He taught Sunday school, helped start a YMCA, became chairman of its board, and assisted in establishing a "Y" camp in the desert for children; he remained associated with the "Y" the rest of his life. Tatsuno was a leader of the JACL. He found internment much harder on the young Nisei than it was on him; they were bitter and saw only a bleak future ahead. Although he had lost his San Francisco store in 1942, he decided to open a new one in 1946 with the very limited capital left from the earlier liquidation. (He found it interesting that the younger Nisei later romanticized their experiences at class reunions; they sentimentalized the friendships they had made while forgetting the heartaches. He felt this tendency was especially true of the Class of 1945.) In 1944 Dave left the co-op to farm near Springville, Utah, with his brother-in-law. The brother-in-law and some friends had farmed near Provo the previous year, making $5,000 even though they had no agricultural experience. However, Tatsuno returned to camp because his wife was expecting another child. After his daughter's birth he taught public speaking and English in the high school. He enjoyed farming in Utah and found the Mormons sympathetic, but he also liked teaching.[18]

When the West Coast was reopened, Dave Tatsuno made an exploratory trip to San Francisco. He experienced no racist episodes, so he and his wife decided to return home as soon as they could. He concluded that "the people in camp really made the best of a very unfortunate situation and . . . any other group of people under the same circumstance . . . wouldn't have taken it as well as the Japanese Americans." Tatsuno accepted the JACL position that any protest in 1942 would have been futile and that the best thing to do was to go, but he also supported redress.[19]

Dave Tatsuno's optimistic outlook was matched by his neighbor Kenji Fujii. Fujii's father moved to the East Bay after he arrived in America at the turn of the century. Kenji, the only son among five

children, went into the family nursery business as soon as he finished high school. He helped put his four sisters through college,
but feeling that someone should work in the nursery with his father,
he did not attend college himself. Fujii remembered himself as "kind
of a radical kid," involved with the Oakland Young Democrats and
especially Ernie Iiyama. He opposed war during the 1930s because
he had seen so much suffering around him during the Depression.
When the evacuation came, Kenji leased the nursery and went first
to Tanforan and then to Topaz, together with his mother and the
three sisters still at home. In both camps he was a block manager.
Kenji's father worked cleaning the washrooms (only because his
son, the block manager, could not get anyone else to do it and block
managers, as Hoffman noted, had to fill in when tasks went un-
done), and his mother labored in the kitchen. Selective service
caused him problems; during the war his records were confused
with someone of the same name who was in the ultranationalistic
Black Dragon Society, so he was not called. Although he expected
to be drafted after the war, again he was not. Fujii's opposition to
the draft alienated him from the Young Democrats, who supported
conscription. Kenji, a perfect candidate for resettlement, left Topaz
early to work in a nursery in Michigan. After the war ended, he
traveled around the country before returning to the family business
in Hayward, which had been cared for by Caucasian friends during
his absence.[20] Fujii concluded his reminiscences with the comment,
"I do not find too many unpleasant things about the evacuation. I
do not, because it is not in my character . . . basically I'm a positive
person." Evacuation was an anomalous event in his life, a period
of discord in what otherwise had been a good life and continued
to be after the war. He took over the nursery from his father,
married, and raised two sons who succeeded him in the business.
He knew many others who were very disturbed about their internment; his friends Michiko Okamoto and Maya Aikawa certainly
did not share his sentiments.[21]

✿

The Kibei's experiences were different. Most of them were very
hostile to the evacuation and internment, and many WRA admin-

istrators, especially Dillon Myer, considered them "trouble-makers and agitators" who caused "difficulty."[22] They had not been acculturated into the passivity and acquiescence of the Americanized Nisei, and they certainly did not accept the position of the JACL on internment. Since most had spent their formative years gaining an education in Japan, they seemed even more "Japanesy" than the Issei. Even though they had been born in the United States, many did not understand their native country, for they did not live there long before going to Japan and they did not have time to readjust upon their return. Many spoke English poorly, if at all, and they did not comprehend democracy. But it is a mistake to lump all Kibei together, for they too were diverse. Those who went to Japan in the 1930s and attended public schools when militarism was being taught were very different from those who went in the 1920s, when Japan's government was more democratic. Interviews with Karl Akiya and K. Morgan Yamanaka indicate that even this general division is insufficient to explain the Kibei phenomenon.

Akiya had received a militaristic education, which radicalized instead of converting him, so that he became anti-fascist, anti-war, and pro-democracy. Like many others, he left Japan because he opposed militarism. He made several trips back and forth but returned permanently to the United States in 1931 and renounced his Japanese citizenship after the Manchurian Incident in 1931. When his father's hotel went bankrupt, the bilingual Akiya went to work for the Sumitomo Bank.[23]

Karl Akiya then became a kind of missionary to the Nisei, warning them of the dangers of war between the United States and Japan and urging them to support America. He organized a Kibei association in San Francisco in 1940 and got the association integrated into the JACL; he was even trying to organize the Issei when Japan attacked the United States. Akiya became even more radical after Pearl Harbor; he protested both Japan's attack and America's actions against the Japanese Americans. He soon was offered a chance to aid the American cause: naval intelligence asked for his cooperation in finding subversives among the Issei. The navy asked him and his friend James Oki to remain on the West Coast during the war, but he refused. The idea of being the only two Japanese Americans not evacuated did not appeal to them. In his radical days

Akiya associated with Ernie Iiyama and the Young Democrats. He worked with the communist Karl Yoneda on the Japanese American newspaper *Doho*, where he was in charge of circulation. Yoneda and Akiya sent a telegram to President Roosevelt on behalf of their 150 readers and subscribers pledging cooperation in the war against the "vicious military fascists of Japan."[24] Akiya also helped Iiyama in the election for the council at Tanforan.

At Topaz Karl Akiya continued his efforts for democracy. He worked for adult education, pressuring the camp administration to allow courses to be taught in Japanese so that Issei and Kibei would not be excluded. He urged that the *Topaz Times* be bilingual. He also advocated and taught Americanization classes, which aroused controversy when people claimed that "communists" were teaching. But he wanted to serve his native land more directly, so when the army called for volunteers, he applied—not to fight, for he was over thirty years old, but to work in intelligence. Akiya went to Ann Arbor to the language school, where he became an instructor. This course of action, Akiya stated forty-five years later, was taken by many Issei who wanted to serve in the army but were too old for combat.[25]

Despite his patriotism, Karl Akiya was very conscious of his civil liberties and his rights as an American citizen, and he opposed their violation. He argued that it violated his right to free speech when his reading material was searched and he was denied the use of the Japanese language. Above all, he protested the evacuation because it was totally illegal as well as financially devastating. It had cost Japanese Americans as much as $2 billion, and he believed the U.S. government should compensate them for their loss. He went to New York after the war, where his family did not experience the racial discrimination they had found on the West Coast. Akiya testified before the Commission on Wartime Internment and Relocation; in 1987 he expressed his pleasure with the progress that the redress movement was making.[26]

Morgan Yamanaka was a very young child when his family sent him to Japan, and aside from teaching him to speak excellent Japanese, the militarist education had little effect. Born in San Francisco in 1925, he went to Japan when he was two, spent the next five years there, and then returned to California. Because Yamanaka was so young, he was only technically a Kibei, but his family was split by the war. His eldest brother went to Japan during the war, the family held property there, and their overseas ties were strong. Morgan had an older brother and a younger sister who still resided in Japan in 1988. His Japanese years made him perhaps "more aware of the Japanese culture than many of my Nisei colleagues," but he was quickly Americanized when he returned. His parents were in domestic service and lived in Pacific Heights, a very exclusive area of the city. He and his brothers and sisters were the only Japanese students at Lowell High School, but their social life was spent in Japan Town, where they attended Japanese school, studied martial arts, and participated in the life of the Buddhist community.[27]

The family was assigned to be evacuated to the Santa Anita Assembly Center, a quite arbitrary decision that was made because the Yamanakas lived in a section of San Francisco that was evacuated before Tanforan was prepared. They were housed in horse stalls at Santa Anita, which was a much larger camp than Tanforan, holding about 18,000 people. Since Morgan was a senior about to graduate, he decided not to attend high school but went to work in the housing unit and then made camouflage. In October 1942 the family was transported to Topaz, their first trip outside California. Like many others, they found the dust storms unforgettable. Their first task was to make the barracks room comfortable and then to find something to occupy their time. In Topaz, as in Santa Anita, Morgan worked in the fire department. He was more qualified for service than most of the residents: having lived across from a fire station in San Francisco, he knew something about hoses and couplings. He eventually became the captain. During the entire time in camp he never fought a fire, making it, he said, a very good job.[28]

When the loyalty questionnaire was circulated, the Yamanakas let Morgan and his brother Al make their own decisions about it. Many factors influenced them because they had siblings in Japan, and the family's ties to the homeland were strong. Their education at Lowell High had taught them about American government and civil rights, but questions 27 and 28 were difficult, and the teenagers were not clear about the implications of a negative answer. Morgan had turned eighteen the first week at Santa Anita and was classified 4C, and Al had volunteered and been rejected. Both answered "no-no." The act of rebellion cost them the right to remain in Topaz, and they compounded it by renouncing their American citizenship. This response meant expatriation to Japan—not what they had in mind at all. They did not think of themselves as anti-American when they replied as they did, but they were angered at what the United States had done to them.[29]

The result was segregation to Tule Lake for the entire family, for their parents opted to join them. Tule was far different from Topaz, much larger, much more turbulent, much more prisonlike because it was run by the army, not the WRA. Morgan was sent to the stockade when he joined a group protesting the death of an inmate. The contrast with Topaz could not have been greater, but despite the brutality of Tule, by 1945 Morgan and Al had decided they did not want to be sent to Japan. They asked that their renunciation and expatriation papers be voided. Ultimately, they were allowed to remain in the United States. Morgan looked upon the four years of evacuation and internment as a hiatus, "four years absence, essentially vegetation." Whatever else he might have done, at least his "mind probably would have been more active in those four years— which mine was not." All he had to read in the stockade was the Bible, which he read "forward and backward." Four years of vegetation and a pointless gap in his life, together with an anger he described as more like "being pissed off"—this was what he got from the internment. He resettled to Chicago and returned to San Francisco for his college education, which culminated in a master's degree in social work. He was first a practicing social worker and then a member of the faculty at San Francisco State University.[30]

❧

The lives of Nisei women who had finished high school and received no further education were almost as hard as those of their mothers. Tsuyako "Sox" Kitashima had three brothers; they lived with their mother on a farm in Centerville, now called Fremont. They were truck farmers, an occupation in which many Japanese Americans excelled precisely because they were willing to work long hours at stoop labor. The family all worked in the fields, planting and picking strawberries and vegetables. The announcement of the attack on Pearl Harbor caught them off guard, for unlike city dwellers they had not contemplated such a possibility. From that day on they lived in fear, not knowing what would happen to them. When announcements were posted telling of the evacuation, they had to dispose of the farm equipment at a pittance. Theirs included an old horse, and "Sox" remembered how sad it was to send the beast to its death; "no one wanted an old horse." They considered leaving during the voluntary evacuation period and traveling to Colorado, "but not knowing our future, my brother did not want to take that risk."[31]

Instead they went to Tanforan to endure the indignities of a horse stall with no privacy and the terrible smell of manure. "Sox" did all the family's laundry, and she remembered rising at 4 A.M. to make sure she got hot water and a tub. Her mother suffered from arthritis, which the dampness of the stall made worse. "Sox" remembered the kindness of a Caucasian family from whom her father had leased land; these people did many favors for them, bringing linoleum for the floor to spare her arthritic mother and providing them with breakfast the day they left for Utah.[32]

Topaz, with its dust, was just as bad as Tanforan. The family partitioned their one room to create some privacy for "Sox" and her mother, and the brothers made furniture from scrap lumber. The women made jewelry from the tiny shells they dug up around the camp and unraveled onion sacks to crochet carrying cases and purses. The loyalty questionnaire split the family; the sons and their mother went to Tule Lake, since the men refused to sign "yes-yes" and their mother feared she would lose her only citizenship if she signed. "Sox" stayed with a married sister and her husband, and in August 1945 she too married, returning with her husband to San Francisco on September 20. Claud Pratt, for whom she worked in camp, had been kind to her, and he offered to help her gain civil service status if she would stay to type the final report on the camp closing, but she decided to leave with her husband.[33]

"Sox" Kitashima participated in most facets of camp life. She took a seasonal leave to work in the fields in Ogden, but she was allergic to ragweed and had to return to Topaz. She then worked as an assistant block manager and heard a variety of complaints, many of them about food. A number of people told her that the Caucasian staff was engaged in black marketeering, selling meat outside camp and leaving the residents with organ meat. Work, "Sox" said, was necessary to keep one's sanity. She recalled that going to Delta to shop for her block was a great treat, just to get away, but by the time she made all the purchases her neighbors wanted there was no time to shop for herself. In addition, the shopper had to put up with being searched on the way into town. Pratt took her and her husband into town once to go to the movies, and "Sox" reflected that she "stuck out like a sore thumb" among all the Caucasians. Pratt's goodness to her was something she remembered forty years later.[34] She has exchanged Christmas cards with him every year since she left Topaz, she recalled in 1993.

Tsuyako Kitashima's strong resentment of the internment propelled her into the redress movement in the 1980s. She worked for the National Coalition for Redress/Reparation, a group separate from the JACL effort. Certain parts of her experiences stuck in her mind. She remembered Tanforan as the worst because it was such a rude and unexpected violation of her civil liberties. It galled her to have Caucasians say that the internment was "for our own protection." The barbed wire at Topaz kept them in, not others out, she noted, for the guards had "guns pointed toward us." The guards were not too bright, she reflected as she thought about the killing of James Wakasa. One day as she was traveling to Delta, a military policeman stopped her truck and took roll. When he got to the line that said, "And one Caucasian," he waited for an answer from this Mr. Caucasian and said he would not leave until the unknown person said "Here!"

The younger Nisei reacted to Topaz in a number of ways. There were the junior high and high school students: Kiyo Ito and Mari

Eijima, Class of 1943; Harry Kitano, Shigeko Sugiyama, Michiko Okamoto, and Fumi Manabe, Class of 1944; Maya Nagata and Ryozo (Glenn) Kumekawa, Class of 1945; Bob Utsumi and Abu Keikoan, Class of 1946; and Don Nakahata, Lee Suyemoto, and Masako Tsuzuki, Class of 1947.[35] There were some special cases, too, such as one mixed couple of Japanese and Portuguese ancestry. The Issei father was picked up by the FBI; the mother chose to go with her two daughters to camp, for she had identified with Japanese culture since her marriage and did not want to leave her children.[36] And there were a number of young Nisei—including Bill Kochiyama, Tom Kawaguchi, Tad Hayashi, and John Hada—who said "yes-yes"; they joined the military, either voluntarily or, later, through the draft. These men were not expressing their approval of relocation. They, too, were born of immigrant parents who had toiled to build a new life for their families in the Bay Area and had lost most of their possessions in the evacuation. Tanforan and Topaz were as unpleasant to them as to the "no-nos." Their response resulted in part from their families' insistence that their children were American citizens who had a duty to their government and whose future would be in the United States.

John Hada is representative of these men. He was the only child of a San Francisco family. Educated in city schools, he was fifteen or sixteen when the evacuation was announced. In Tanforan the Hadas lived in a horse stall. John remembered the way people helped each other there instead of emphasizing their miserable conditions. "It was just like perhaps going on a trip to the outback," he recalled, thinking of the response of teenagers like himself, but he knew the situation was very difficult for older people. Since their neighbors had agreed to take care of their property, visited them in Tanforan with baskets of fruit, and kept in touch later by mail, the Hadas did not feel too cut off from their former home. Kindness was perhaps what Hada remembered most from the internment, exemplified by Caucasian friends who stood by his family and by Nikkei who helped one another. His reflections on the schools also demonstrate his positive outlook: "The teachers did a remarkable job with the limited resources that they did have." When he was asked to complete the loyalty questionnaire, he asked his father's advice in answering questions 27 and 28. His father reminded him that he was an American, that he might have to die for his country, and that he could not afford to be bitter. Whatever problems the Hada family encountered John attributed to the death of his mother just before the internment and the death of his grandmother, who had raised him, in camp.[37] Hada remained in Topaz until the summer of 1945, when he resettled with an uncle in Cleveland and then joined the army, which became his career.

John Hada was a very patriotic man who valued the good experiences of camp, did not dwell on the bad, and was proud of his military career. He served in two Pacific wars. Nonetheless, he felt that the experience of internment was not one he would wish on anyone else: "Perhaps when I go to my eternal reward I would forgive those that did this to me. I would hope so." He did not consider this an attitude of bitterness, just of realism; despite it, he served his country well and had a full and productive life.[38]

Bob Utsumi also went to school in Topaz, was a graduate of the Class of 1945, briefly tried college, and entered the U.S. Air Force after his return to California. He too made the military his career and harbored no bitterness for the internment, even though he did not consider it just. He was more critical of the schools and the treatment of his family than John Hada, but he valued his service to his country and was not full of resentment over the camp experience.[39]

Utsumi's story differed from his classmate's in several respects. His grandparents on both sides were pioneers in the East Bay who had run nurseries, and he was one of the few Sansei in camp. Both his grandparents and his parents suffered considerable losses when they left their property. His paternal grandfather was a dentist. His maternal grandparents' nurseries were badly damaged, and his father, who was a professional photographer—an unusual occupation for a Nisei—had to surrender his cameras because they were considered contraband. Able to regain some of them in Topaz, he became the official camp photographer. Most of what Utsumi remembered of Topaz was the terrible education he felt he received there. He lost an entire year of high school because of the way camp schooling was organized. Bob enrolled in the University of California at Berkeley but dropped out and joined the U.S. Air Force Aviation Cadet program. Since the air force had not admitted many Japanese Americans during the war, Utsumi was particularly proud to have made his career as an officer and a pilot in that service. In 1988 he was the oldest surviving Japanese American jet pilot.[40]

Tom Kawaguchi came from San Francisco, where his parents managed an apartment house. He had attended junior college for several years but dropped out to work when his father had a stroke. When Pearl Harbor was bombed, he reacted in anger. "They can't win," he said of the Japanese; he had no particular liking for the country since the Japanese nationals at Mitsubishi, where he worked, discriminated against Nisei like him. Tom was employed by the JACL after Mitsubishi fired him. Despite his feelings about Japan, he was angered when the notices about the evacuation appeared, for he was, after all, an American citizen. Because Tom's father was an invalid, Tom, his mother, and his brother, along with his two sisters and their husbands, had to make the arrangements for evacuating the family.[41] Like many others, they sold most of their possessions at a loss and stored the rest within a private home; nearly everything was gone when they returned.

Life in Tanforan was terrible. Since the family was large, they were assigned a barracks room rather than a horse stall, but they were still cramped. The assembly center left Tom Kawaguchi with many memories—the inedible food, the allergies from sleeping on a straw mattress, the people who cried during the first few days.

The Kawaguchis were one of the first families to arrive at Topaz, which was even more depressing and harder on someone who suffered from allergies than Tanforan had been. They were assigned two rooms, which they partitioned further with blankets and sheets, but privacy was still nonexistent. Tom's mother told him not to forget what was happening, because he was an American citizen and should not suffer such indignities. He remembered well. Tom did improve the family's quarters; he made furniture for the rooms from scrap lumber he stole. He left camp for brief periods of seasonal work, but primarily he worked for the education department and later the cooperative as a cost accountant. Tom helped start a Boy Scout troop and other activities for the children, for he felt it very important to keep them busy.[42]

Although life at Topaz was bleak, everything was relatively harmonious until the loyalty questionnaire split the camp apart. Tom and his brother decided to volunteer, for they believed in America and felt that military service would clearly establish their loyalty; however, only Tom passed the physical. Feelings were so tense between the opponents and the supporters of registration that Tom left camp quietly, telling people he was relocating to New York, because he wanted to spare his family any trouble. Tom joined the 442d Regiment, an act that gave him great pride in later life. The close bonds forged by combat and the awareness of their tremendous military achievements not only gave these men a common identity but also reinforced their sense of patriotism. Tom Kawaguchi believed that the best way to fight injustice was to take positive action. Each person, he felt, paid a price: those who protested or refused the draft, those who were repatriated to Japan, and those who chose to go to war. There was no easy path. Tom served in the military for twenty years, first in the infantry and then as a finance and accounting officer. He retired as a major.[43]

Reflecting on his experiences, Tom Kawaguchi stressed that the government was wrong, that "all they did was take a bunch of innocent people and make prisoners of them," and that it had to apologize. Military service helped give many Nisei a positive image of themselves despite the damaging effects of relocation, and for that reason he felt it was good. After retiring from the military, Kawaguchi became involved in the JACL-sponsored redress movement, feeling that the story of relocation had to be told again and again so that it would never be repeated. He founded a historical society (Go for Broke, later the National Japanese American Historical Society) to preserve the history of the roles played by Japanese Americans during World War II. As a result, he became involved in the preparation of an exhibit on internment and the role of Japanese Americans in the military during World War II, which opened at the National Museum of American History (the Smithsonian Institution) in 1988 as part of the bicentennial celebration of the U.S. Constitution.[44]

Bill Kochiyama also believed the military was a positive experience in his life. He had been raised as a half-orphan in an orphanage in New York City after his mother's early death. He came to California for an education but instead was interned. Kochiyama was unfamiliar with prejudice, having come from New York, where he was only one of many minorities; in fact, growing up in a series of orphanages, he thought of himself as white like the other children. He had difficulty interacting with Japanese Americans; he did not speak Japanese and did not know the culture. He was surprised when he could not get a job in the Bay Area; the racism of the West Coast was alien to his experience. A Japanese American employment agency finally placed him in an all-Nikkei laundry in Oakland, but that establishment closed immediately after Pearl Harbor. Frantic, he then tried to enlist but was refused because of his race. Forced into an assembly center whose entryway was guarded by soldiers with bayonets, Kochiyama reacted violently, daring them to shoot him. His behavior was not typical for a Nisei. Cocky and aggressive, Bill talked and acted much as the average New Yorker, without the passiveness of a Japanese American. He just could not understand what was happening to him. Bill Kochiyama was not the only misfit in Tanforan, for he recalled seeing a white man there who was only one-sixteenth Japanese, but he certainly felt alone.[45]

Topaz intensified Kochiyama's sense of isolation. He was one of only six Nisei bachelors, who all lived together. He got a job working in Provo on a seasonal leave, picking and packing fruit, and there he became acquainted with a Mormon family, who treated him well. Back in camp he was employed in housing. By the time the loyalty questionnaire was issued, Kochiyama's anger had cooled off; he said later, "When the opportunity came to volunteer, I became a flag waver. I didn't know better."[46] He signed up, returned to New York, where he was reunited with his father, and was inducted there. Trained for almost a year at Camp Shelby, Mississippi, he visited the nearby internment center at Jerome, Arkansas, to meet other Japanese Americans. There he met and became engaged to his future wife, Mary. He served with the 442d Regimental Combat Team in Italy and France.[47]

Kochiyama was not angry in 1988, but he was highly critical of the internment. Tanforan was his first introduction to a concentration camp, and Topaz, he said sarcastically, was "really a mind blower . . . the jewel of the desert." Living conditions were probably not so hard on him as on others because he was used to institutional life, but he felt that there was no excuse for them. In his testimony before the Commission on Wartime Relocation and Internment of Civilians in 1981, Kochiyama spoke in favor of a redress of $50,000 for interned Japanese Americans as well as the Aleuts, whose civil rights were also violated, and he advocated establishing a community trust for the Nikkei. He called for the reversal of the Supreme Court decisions in the *Korematsu, Hirabayashi,* and *Yasui* cases and he urged that the American public be educated about the "flagrant injustices perpetrated by the government . . . that such crimes should *never, never* be permitted to happen again."[48]

⁂

The choices for young Nisei women were more limited, for it was not culturally sanctioned for them to go out on their own. Women left for the armed forces, too, although not in any such numbers as the men. Some entered higher education, like Chizu Kitano, or even left for secondary education, like Mari Eijima. Some left to work, like Miné Okubo or Fumi Manabe, who went to Saint Louis with her sister Grace (later, Grace Hattori) at the age of fourteen.[49] The Manabe girls cooked, cleaned, ironed, and babysat for three hours each day for room and board while they attended school. Some were imprisoned elsewhere en route to Japan, like Kiyo Ito. And some, like "Sox" Kitashima, Michiko Okamoto, Grace Fujimoto, and Maya Nagata, remained in Topaz nearly to the end.

Chizu Kitano came from a large family who lived in Chinatown, San Francisco. Her father immigrated to the United States around the turn of the century; her mother, a picture bride, came over somewhat later. The Kitanos were a close family that ultimately included five daughters and two sons. The parents were strong advocates of education, so Chizu, who earned good grades, went to the University of California, where she was a student when Pearl Harbor was attacked. Mr. Kitano was arrested by the FBI, which singled him out because he was a community leader and had helped found a Japanese-language school in San Francisco. Chizu and her sisters ran the hotel until they were evacuated. Since their mother was distraught over the arrest of her husband and the evacuation itself, the children had to prepare the family's possessions for departure. Although some of her relatives went to Tanforan, Chizu was sent to Santa Anita, where she was put in charge of recreation in the schools. Although she wanted a scholarship so she could continue her education in the Midwest or the East, her mother would not hear of her going so far away. The family was reunited at Topaz.

Ernest Iiyama was born in Oakland. His father and mother ran a store in North Oakland until 1921, when the whole family went to Japan. Ernie graduated from high school in Japan and returned to Oakland about the time of the Manchurian Incident. The Iiyamas were evacuated to Topaz, where Ernie met Chizu. He was employed in the housing division, she in social welfare, but they met through camp politics. He was also the executive secretary for the community council. The loyalty controversy put both of them at odds with many of their associates. Ernie, although a Kibei, favored answering "yes-yes" to the controversial questions, and he urged others to express their loyalty by doing the same. Chizu also reacted strongly to the controversial questions, speaking out in one of the meetings and urging people to make up their own minds and not be intimidated by others. Since young women were not encouraged to speak in public, such temerity brought her family much criticism and hostility. The episode convinced her that she should leave camp, and soon after she was accepted for student relocation in Chicago. Ernie left Topaz at the same time to work. When Chizu departed, she was told not to speak Japanese to people, not to gather in groups of more than three, and not to call attention to herself in any way—strictures that still rankled forty-five years later. Any misbehavior could jeopardize the whole student leave program, she was warned. She and Ernie married in Chicago.

Camp made a lasting impression on the Iiyamas. In 1988 Chizu still remembered the absence of privacy, the lack of places to talk or resolve differences. Her sister had a young baby, and there was no place for the infant to crawl because the floors were always dusty. When the baby cried, she would awaken everyone in the barrack, and the next day people would ask if the child were ill. Washing diapers with a washboard was very hard, and warming the baby's milk was also a problem. Chizu and Ernie recalled the bootlegging of liquor and the endless rumors that kept people upset. Ernie had tried to reform a camp prostitute by including her in discussion groups held by the Young Democrats. Chizu said, "He tried to bring her into our group and she could care less. She was having her own happy times somewhere else. . . . You all tried to rehabilitate her and you had to give up. It was her work." The Iiyamas found the administrators they worked for caring people who tried to make their lives better: George LaFabreque stood out especially. Nonetheless, they found the internment unforgivable; the loss of freedom, the confinement behind barbed wire fences, and the revocation of their constitutional rights marked their lives.[50] They returned to the Bay Area some five years after the end of the war.

Midori Shimanouchi told a somewhat different story. Her father came to California from Japan on what was to be the first leg of a trip around the world before running for political office, but he liked the area so well that he stayed and sent for his wife and their first child two years later. The Shimanouchis acquired farmland, and the family grew. After Midori was born, they moved to Pasadena, where her father edited a newspaper. In 1932 the Shimanouchis moved north to San Francisco, where her father worked on another Japanese-language newspaper until he was incapacitated by a stroke. Midori was eighteen when they were evacuated to Tanforan. She remembered how a young man came to visit her there in the barracks; he lived in the horse stalls and "he just smelled like a horse. It was awful, really terrible. . . . We tried to socialize and pretend that it wasn't bad, but it was quite bad." The FBI wanted to imprison her father as a community leader, but his physical infirmities were so disabling that the experience would have killed him. He died in camp in 1942.[51]

All the Shimanouchi children left camp on student relocation, one sister to Smith and the other to work for the American Friends Service Committee in Boston. Midori, who had attended the University of California for one semester before the evacuation, got a scholarship to Pace College in New York. Her brothers were in Japan. Her mother joined the daughters in the East, and they never returned to the West Coast. Midori married a man she met in Tanforan; they went to New Orleans, where neither she nor her husband associated with the few Japanese Americans who resided there. She recalled that it was almost as if they wanted to repress the ethnic chapter in their lives, the source of so much pain. They never talked about camp life, and when they divorced she lost one more link to the Nikkei community. It was only after she married again, outside the Japanese community, that she could begin to rediscover her heritage, and even then the process was slow. It was through her second marriage, to a man of Austrian descent, that Midori came to discover her own roots. After her return to New York she had worked for film magnate Michael Todd, and she stayed on with his organization after his death. She finally decided not to work since she did not need the money, but she was quickly at loose ends. Her husband advised her to look into community service, perhaps with Indochinese refugees, but when she learned of the many poor and aged Issei in the area, she decided to care for her own people instead. She founded JASSI, Japanese American Social Services, a New York service organization for the elderly, many of whom were single males who had been impoverished by the internment.[52] Her work has brought her much renown in the Nikkei community in New York.

Midori Shimanouchi Lederer discovered late in life how deeply she resented the internment. Her father had kept his family separate from the Japantowns wherever they lived because he felt his children were Americans and should be treated as such. Her friends were Caucasians, and when they visited her at Tanforan she felt like she was in prison. Midori considered herself a "survivor" who was strengthened by the camp experience, but she did not like what it did to her. She was angered by the incarceration and recalled feeling strongly that the young men in Topaz should not volunteer for military service. Midori even stood in the doorway to a room where the enlistment pitch was to be given, telling them, "Don't sign up. . . . How can you sign up with all of us in camp?" Out of rage she supported the class action movement for redress led by William Hohri of Chicago (the National Council for Japanese American Redress), an angrier, less conciliatory approach than the one taken by the JACL.[53] Her work with JASSI provided her with a way to reconnect to the past and, to some degree, work out her anger. But she will never forget.

The Nisei students at Topaz High responded to the relocation in many different ways. Some, like Bob Utsumi, John Hada, and Shig Sugiyama, went into military service and made it a career. Sugiyama spent twenty years in the military and completed his B.A. degree at the University of California after retiring from the army. He earned a master's degree at California State University at Hayward and eventually, as the associate special counsel and inspector general of the U.S. Merit Systems Protection Board, became one of the highest-ranking Japanese Americans in the civil service. Sugiyama was elected national president of the JACL in 1974, the year it adopted redress as a goal, but he personally never supported the concept. He also helped organize a Buddhist congregation in Washington, the Ekoji Buddhist Temple. His Buddhist faith, which became very strong as he organized the congregation in Washington, called on him to sacrifice, and redress and monetary compensation connoted a greed that made him uncomfortable. You could not put a price on the deprivation of a person's liberty, he thought, and the tendency of Americans to sue one another "at the drop of a hat" he found deplorable. Suing the federal government was even worse, he believed, for at the base of it all, the government was the people, all of them. Sugiyama thought that an educational program to teach the public about the evacuation and internment would help to prevent such an outrage from recurring. The apology of President Gerald Ford and his repudiation of Executive Order 9066 in 1976 were enough for Sugiyama; he felt honored when Ford shook his hand at the signing ceremony. That was his personal apology.[54]

Kiyo Ito was not bitter either, despite her camp experiences and life in postwar Japan. Her father, Ryuzaburo Ito of Oakland, was arrested before the evacuation because he had worked for an insurance company with a large Japanese clientele; he also was active in the Japanese Association and other Japanese groups. Because Ito had received a college education in the United States, traveled all over the nation, and was a leader in his community, he was marked for FBI attention. The Bureau agents called on him many times after Pearl Harbor, even searching the house and carrying off his treasured college records for no apparent reason. After his arrest Kiyo, at sixteen the oldest of the three children, had to become the head of the family because her mother spoke little English. Her father was imprisoned in Burbank City Jail with common criminals, then held at Santa Fe with other alien internees, and later moved to Bismarck, North Dakota. He was never charged with anything.[55]

Topaz was a sad experience for the family. Since her mother worked in the mess hall, she could not be with the children at mealtimes, but she insisted the children eat together to preserve a bit of family unity. Kiyo graduated from Topaz High, which she remembered as a rigorous school with fierce competition because the Japanese American students were used to striving for excellence and now competed only with each other. Her father communicated by mail every week, urging her to continue studying even after graduation, which she did, taking all the business courses the school offered.[56]

Because Ryuzaburo Ito felt that he would never again be able to care for his family in America, he asked for repatriation. The entire family left Topaz in January 1945 for a family internment camp at Crystal City, Texas. Ito was now classified as a "potentially dangerous enemy alien." There Kiyo went to a highly accelerated school taught by Buddhist priests from Hawaii; she polished her Japanese and studied math, literature, poetry, science, history, and calligraphy, all taught in Japanese. In early December 1945 the family traveled by train to Seattle and from there sailed to Japan on the SS *Matsonia*. Kiyo remembered the experience in Japan as "the most trying time of my life"; Japanese Americans were scarcely welcome in the devastated, poverty-stricken country, and the family first lived in a refugee camp. The Itos made their way to the Sendai region, where they had relatives. Kiyo and her father, both bilingual, eventually obtained jobs with the American occupation forces. Finally Kiyo made her way to Tokyo and took a position with IBM, for which she was well prepared by all the business courses she had taken at Topaz High. She soon returned to New York and was followed by her other siblings, but her parents remained in Japan, feeling that the relocation had destroyed their American lives. Kiyo was not bitter, but the disruptive moves, eight in all, created a sense of survivorship in her. Years later, as a mother, she was able to instill in her own children the ability to endure whatever came their way.[57]

Mari Eijima grew up in Berkeley, a liberal community where she had felt little overt discrimination, but within herself lay a strong inferiority complex. She was in high school there and thus entered Topaz High. After a year that included the registration controversy, she was anxious to leave camp. She got a unique opportunity to go east to school. One of her teachers, Joe Goodman, and his wife were Quakers with friends in Pennsylvania who wanted to support some interned Japanese American students and prepare them for college. They asked Mary McMillan, a teacher from Oakland who had taught in Japan before the war, whom she would recommend. The girls she suggested were Mari and another student, Lil Miyachi. Their parents agreed, so Mari and Lil went to school at Westtown, a Quaker institution in Pennsylvania. The Baileys, the family that sponsored them, encouraged Mari to go on to college. She tried the University of California briefly in 1945, but she did not like it and the Baileys were willing to take her back. She then attended nearby Guilford College, spending her vacations with the Bailey family. She recalled that college was a wonderful way to "shake" her Japanese identity, which at the time she found humiliating. But her inferiority complex persisted. She taught after college and then traveled in Europe with Caucasian friends, who persuaded her to try to recover her Japanese identity. She began by working for a Japanese company, and soon she got a position with the Permanent Observer of Japan to the United Nations. She learned to love her Japanese heritage. Subsequently, she took a job with the Japan Society, which in 1987 she had held for twenty-eight years. Reflecting on her life, Mari Eijima remarked that many of her friends from Japan considered her more "Japanese" than they were. She had to agree with them, partly because her parents had raised her according to Meiji traditions, partly because she traveled frequently in Japan and had many friends there. The old feeling of inferiority went away when she was able to realize that Topaz had intensified her insecurities by making her feel second-rate. "After all, why *was* I in camp?" Her new-found pride in her Japanese heritage and her successful career bridging the two cultures enabled her to put such feelings behind her.[58]

In contrast, Masako Tsuzuki and her parents were New Yorkers who, like Bill Kochiyama, were caught in California by the war. The Tsuzukis had moved west to San Mateo to tend a dying grandmother. Life in California before the evacuation and their experiences at Tanforan and Topaz convinced them that they did not want to live in the West after the war, so the Tsuzukis returned to New York City. Masako entered high school there and remembered with great clarity an event that occurred soon afterward. She asked a teacher if she could leave the room to go to the "latrine" and was told, "We do not use such language here. We call it the restroom." To use "soldier-talk" was to identify oneself as a "loose woman." The sensitive teenager was mortified. Soon after, when she had to give a speech in class, she was horrified to hear a jumbled, half-Japanese jargon come out of her mouth. Camp had marked her in emotional and spiritual ways she did not expect.

In 1974 Masako, now called Kitty, compiled and edited *The Japanese in America, 1842–1973*, and she was curator of an exhibit of art and artifacts from relocation camps for the gallery at Hastings-on-Hudson, New York, in the fall of 1989, both of which helped her put the experience in perspective.[59] The art she exhibited included paintings by her father, Byron Tsuzuki, brilliant expressions of beauty out of camp's bleakness. For Masako Tsuzuki, now

Nakagawa, the culmination of her search for roots came when she saw the Smithsonian exhibition "And Justice for All" and realized how her story and that of her people fit into the history of the Constitution and America itself. She was one of thousands of Nikkei who thronged to the exhibit, which opened September 1, 1987, at the Museum of American History in Washington, D.C. For many of them, the depiction of Japanese settlement and prewar life, the internment years, the exploits of the 442d, and the beginnings of the redress movement confirmed not only their ethnic heritage but their special role in American history.

Michiko Okamoto and Maya Nagata were both very scarred by the camp experience, and Okamoto eventually changed her name to Michi Kobi in an effort to create a new identity apart from her camp self. She was the first child of San Francisco radiologist Rikikazu Okamoto and his wife, born Ito Kobinata. When her father died in 1927, Michiko and her mother went to Japan for four years. When they returned to San Francisco Ito placed her daughter in an orphanage, studied English, and married a chef. She took Michiko from the orphanage when she was nine. When Ito lost her second husband, she worked as a hairdresser while Michiko went to school and participated in life in Nihonmachi. Pearl Harbor was a shock to them both, and so was the hostility with which Michiko was greeted by her Caucasian classmates and teachers. Suddenly it was not all right to be Japanese.[60]

The evacuation created more tensions between mother and daughter. During the voluntary phase Michiko was invited to move to Denver to live with a school friend, but her mother, hesitant and unsure, refused to make a decision until the day the program was canceled. The anger and shock of knowing they were going to the relocation center at Tanforan when freedom had been within their grasp made the traumatized Michiko temporarily blind, deaf, and partially paralyzed.[61] At Tanforan Michiko went to high school and also became a nurse's aide. Her anger against the government increased when she saw how it treated the ill and disabled, and her estrangement from her mother intensified in the close quarters they shared.[62]

The journey to Topaz was intimidating and exhausting, and settling into Block 36 was another shock. Forty-five years later, Michi Kobi still remembered the dust, the flat wasteland around the camp, and the guards. The people with whom they shared the block were hostile, too, seeing her mother as an "uppity Tokyo widow" with a fatherless child. Kobi described it as a "trap within a trap." Because she found even the Christian church in camp "aloof and lacking in conviction," she stayed away from what might have been a source of consolation and help. For her, Topaz High was an inferior school lacking the courses she needed for a medical career; the teachers were unqualified, and the facilities bleak. Even the camp newspaper annoyed her, for it seemed to avoid all controversy. Michiko and her mother became more estranged as time passed. She became friends with the older Nisei, the leftists in camp, a connection that later, during the McCarthy Era, hurt her dramatic career. However, their "yes-yes" posture antagonized her as it did her friend Kenji Fujii. When James Wakasa, who also lived in Block 36, was killed, Michiko was even more disturbed. Shortly afterward, her mother left camp for Chicago with a male friend, leaving her behind. She was, as she put it, "a fat, moody loner," who only was persuaded to put aside her fears and leave the security of Topaz by Oscar Hoffman, the community analyst.[63]

Having no desire to return to the West Coast with its deeply ingrained patterns of prejudice, Michiko made her way slowly across the country to New York, a deeply disturbed and angry young woman. It took seven years of psychotherapy to ease her self-destructive urges. She finally made her peace with Topaz by returning there alone in 1986, learning to appreciate the beauty of the desert, now a quiet and lonely place. She began slowly to recapture her memories in writing, as she relived the experience that changed her life.

Maya Nagata Aikawa also had harsh memories of Topaz. She grew up in East Oakland in a comfortable home with her parents and two sisters. Her father died of a massive heart attack in early 1941, a tragedy that left the family to fend for itself when the evacuation came. Maya was fifteen when she, her mother, and her

sisters moved to the assembly center at Tanforan and then, six
months later, to Topaz. She remembered the bleakness of the tar
paper barracks. The Nagata family's room was never insulated, so
the "winters were bitterly cold and the summers were ghastly hot."
Dysentery was common, and the dust storms were so fierce that
their legs bled. They all worked in the fields growing crops to feed
the camp. High school, with its lack of enough accredited teachers,
was a waste as far as she was concerned. As an example, she recalled
that her older sister taught typewriting, although she was not
certified. Maya left camp in her senior year, and when she entered
school in Los Angeles it took a full year of schooling to get caught
up enough to graduate. Of Topaz High, she said, "I don't remember
a thing that I learned there. Also, I don't even remember who my
teachers were."[64]

For Maya Nagata, Topaz was far worse than the family had
anticipated. Their comfortable middle-class existence was shattered, replaced by an inhospitable unfree environment far from
what they knew. The room they shared was crowded and uncomfortable. Her memories blurred the years together: the fields, the
chaos of school, the squabbling youth gangs, and the riots (actually
there were no outright riots at Topaz). For her the bickering between groups was real enough, "people picking on other people, . . . about to start trouble." It seemed especially threatening to
her family because they had no father or brother to stand up for
them. The root cause of the disharmony, she felt, was the lack of
privacy. "People would be fighting over very petty little things,
because the confinement got to you, [to] all of us." They even fought
over places in line in the washrooms and the latrine. Maya worked
part-time in the canteen and her mother had a trust fund, so they
were able to purchase some things to make life a little better, but
there was not much one could do to remedy the basic situation.[65]

Medical and dental care were particular problems. Maya was in
need of both. She had begun orthodontic care in Oakland, but there
was no one to adjust her braces in camp, where dental care was
restricted to toothaches. The shortage of dentists, which Oscar
Hoffman commented on, affected the residents. Maya remembered
standing in line from 4:00 A.M. on, because only twenty patients

could be treated in a day. Her teeth were filled by a dental assistant who left decay beneath the fillings; they all had to be extracted later. The medical situation was also difficult, again because the staff was too small. The physical plant was "very unsanitary and very understaffed." Because her mother suffered from what turned out to be an enlarged heart, they had to use the medical services often. Mrs. Nagata died after returning to California at the age of fifty-five, a victim of illness untreated in camp.[66]

The Nagata family left Topaz for Tule Lake when Maya's mother signed a petition requesting repatriation to Japan. Even before the war, her parents had intended to return to their homeland, because her father had become too ill to work. They were moved to Tule, but her mother then changed her mind about repatriating, so they returned, one at a time, to Los Angeles in early 1945. About a year later they resettled in their Oakland home.[67]

Relocation left Maya Nagata a bitter young woman, and this was still evident forty-five years later. The discrimination the family faced when they returned to California was doubly galling, given what they had been through. She blamed her mother's early death on camp and described the $20,000 compensation granted in the Congressional redress bill as "adding insult to injury." As a result of camp life she adopted many disturbing mannerisms; one of these was the need to push her way to the front of any line and demand immediate service. (Midori Lederer recalled that she too was unable to stand in lines.) Maya recognized that her behavior was "rude and obnoxious," especially embarrassing to her children, but she could not help herself; she had stood in too many lines where there was no option. Maya also felt that she was in some way "paying back this cook in Redding forty years later"; "this cook" had pulled out a sign saying "No Japs Allowed" just as she, hungry on the long trip back from Tule Lake, tried to enter his restaurant. In 1987 Maya wore her hair in a severe bun as a memorial to her mother and as a symbol of pride in her Japanese heritage. She claimed that she did not trust Caucasians, even though she grew up in a Caucasian area before the war and knew many white friends of her parents. What she believed the Japanese Americans needed most was the restoration of their dignity, the most basic concept that camp deprived them of—a very Japanese thing.[68]

❧

This narrative of the lives of some of Topaz's residents concludes with the story of Don Nakahata, a pre-teen in camp. In 1990 Nakahata was a dentist living in Mill Valley, California; when Pearl Harbor was bombed, he was twelve and living in San Francisco. His grandfather, an Episcopal minister, the Reverend Barnabas Hisa-yoshi Terasawa, was nearly eighty years old, and the nominal head of his family, which consisted of his mother Agnes, his father Shiro Yasuchika Nakahata, his aunt Faith Terasawa, a niece, his sister, and himself. His father was picked up by the FBI as a "dangerous alien" on December 8, 1941, because he worked part-time for the newspaper *Shin Sekai* (the predecessor to the *Hokubei Mainichi*) and also for the Japanese Association. Forty-five years later Na-kahata still remembered walking with his father down to the street-car to see his father leave for the office of the Japanese Association in San Jose. The FBI picked him up later that day, and Don never saw him alive again. Only from others did the family piece together where he had been sent and what had happened to him; at the time they only knew he had been arrested. Information Don obtained many years later under the Freedom of Information Act indicated that the Immigration and Naturalization Service had conducted a hearing to determine if his father should be released from impris-onment into the WRA system, but the family was never informed of it.[69]

When the evacuation was announced in February 1942, the fatherless family was still seeking the reason for his arrest. Their landlady sold their furniture for them and brought them the pro-ceeds at Tanforan. Nakahata recalled that they got literally "one cake," all she said she received for their goods, including a piano. Don could still recall the sense of insecurity he felt as their pos-sessions were liquidated and they went to camp without his father. After that his memories became very sporadic. He remembered that the family lived in the barracks at Tanforan and rode in a very old train to Utah.[70]

When they arrived at Topaz, many people helped them to get settled because his grandfather was an Episcopal clergyman from a very old Christian family in Japan. (His mother had been a Bible woman in Japan, reading the Bible to illiterate women to help convert them to Christianity.) People felt a great fondness for his grandfather since he had done so much for the Nikkei in San Francisco, and the Christian community helped the family throughout the years in camp. They moved into Block 26, at first into one room and then into two, with Don, his mother, and his sister by themselves. People built shelves and room dividers for them and a chest for Aunt Faith (which she still had in 1988). Don was assigned to bring in coal from the load dumped in the street out in front; he remembered people pushing each other aside to get some. Because he was small, people helped him to get his share, but in retrospect it seemed to be just another "dehumanizing experience" of camp.[71]

School was just another routine. The teachers came, he recalled, from among the internees, the surrounding towns, and the rest of the country. He remembered almost nothing of his classes, only that he "didn't make the cut" to get into a science class and so he took cooking. He did learn to make a lemon meringue pie, but he was behind academically when the family resettled. Nakahata worked on a poultry farm for a while, and then at the dental clinic (a result of his aunt's influence). He participated in the Protestant services, singing fundamentalist hymns that he as an Episcopalian had never heard before. He watched community movies, and he found arrowheads and trilobites in the soil.[72]

By the time the family resettled in Rochester, New York, they were fewer in number. Don's grandfather had died, and so—they learned—had his father. Aunt Faith and another aunt, Mrs. Nakamura, worked for the family that owned the Stromberg-Carlson radio company while Don went to high school in Rochester. The family returned to California because the university system there was inexpensive and Don could pursue his studies.[73]

What had happened to his father? On December 8, 1942, the "grapevine" brought news that he had been picked up and was at the immigration station. Don's mother and Aunt Faith gathered together some clothes and took a bundle down to him, but they were not allowed to give it to him personally. Before the war he had suffered a stroke, and they assumed he had a few more while in custody. They learned from other inmates who had been released from prison camps that he was in the hospital; his letters were censored and only a few actually reached them. They did not even know of his death until they received a telegram saying that they could claim his body; if they did not, it would be buried where he had died. Aunt Faith found someone to intercede and send them the body, which she and his mother claimed. The family never received a medical record, even though they filed a request under the Freedom of Information Act years later. The body was cremated in Delta. An uncle paid for an urn for the ashes, but when they received the box there was no urn, only some loose ashes in a wooden box.[74]

Chapter Nine

Coming Home, Wherever That Is

The people whose lives are chronicled in this book show a great diversity in their reactions to relocation and also in their decisions about leaving Topaz. Many left for the East or the Midwest, some for the rest of their lives, others for a few or more years. They decided as individuals, bringing many factors into play. It was clear that there would be no mass return to the Bay Area and that those who did go back would find their lives there markedly changed. Nonetheless, it is to the Bay Area we must turn, for that is where most chose to make their homes once again. They all knew the return would not be easy.

Permitting the Japanese Americans to reenter California did not ensure that they would be welcomed, particularly by the very people whose racist attitudes and hostile actions had forced them out in the first place. There had been considerable sentiment during the war among white Californians for "relocating" the Nikkei to Japan, and although the federal government did not adopt such a policy, there were many bigots who favored it. However, most ordinary citizens were cautious, conservative, and indifferent, rather than overtly hostile.

In April 1945, naval intelligence, whose curiosity about the returning Japanese Americans far outran any legitimate security interest, prepared an extensive "Counter-Intelligence Report" on what it termed the "Japanese Situation." This unusual document sheds some light on attitudes about the return of the Japanese Americans to San Francisco. The study was apparently prompted by fear that communists would use discrimination against the Nikkei to attract them and other susceptible minority groups to Marxism. It surveyed recent racial incidents, opposition to the return, and the role of the press, and it identified the groups that supported the Japanese. It also analyzed the role of the WRA on the West Coast, the actions of the Civil Affairs Division of the Western Defense Command, and the reaction of other minority groups to the Japanese Americans. The report reviewed events at three camps in the Twelfth Naval District—Topaz, Granada, and Manzanar—during the first three months of 1945. The author studied Japanese-language newspapers published in Salt Lake City and Denver and concluded that they were publishing pro-Japan news. He decried the number of Japanese Americans cleared to work in defense plants, of which the Tooele Army Depot was the most important. The tone of the report was distinctly anti-Nikkei, and its bias sheds some light on the opposition to the return of Japanese Americans.

Initially, the author discovered, not surprisingly, that several groups that had been hostile to Japanese Americans throughout the twentieth century still were. The Native Sons of the Golden West, headquartered in San Francisco, had worked for Japanese exclusion and the passage of the Alien Land Laws. Its members opposed any return to California, and they even favored depriving the Nisei of their citizenship. The Native Sons supported passage by the California legislature of a program that included prohibiting Japanese Americans from fishing in the state's waters, strengthening the alien land laws, and outlawing Japanese-language schools. Also strong in the Bay Area, the American Legion did not oppose the return of the Nikkei in theory after the war had been won, but the author of the report noted that local posts occasionally ignored the national program and presumably were free to discriminate if they liked. The Legion, the California State Federation of Labor, and the Native Sons all supported the California Joint Immigration Committee, the strongest advocate of discrimination in the state. The California State Grange and the State Farm Bureau had also been invited to join with the committee. The report added documentary evidence of anti-Japanese activities and organizations in the Central Valley and the Monterey coast, also part of the Twelfth Naval District.[1]

The naval intelligence report also tracked organizations that favored the return of the Japanese Americans, a position it portrayed as more ominous than the Japanophobes'. The author warned that the Caucasian group that the JACL relied on most was the Council for Civic Unity (not to be confused with the Mayor's Committee on Civic Unity, presumably a "safe" organization); he implied that the council was a communist front. The council was headed by Josephine Duveneck, a "well-known pacifist" and liaison with the JACL and an outstanding supporter of Nikkei rights since before the war. The most prominent pro-Japanese American organization was the Pacific Coast Committee on American Principles and Fair Play, whose honorary president was the president of the University of California, Robert Gordon Sproul. The Fair Play Committee had called a conference in San Francisco in early January 1945 to expedite the return of the Japanese, but the naval intelligence officer noted that it had not been active since then. Also involved in promoting the return of the Japanese were the Berkeley Inter-Racial Group and various churches, which took their lead from Gordon Chapman of the Protestant Church Commission and the Catholic Inter-Racial Group. These organizations had opened their facilities to Japanese Americans needing housing. Other suspect organizations included the American Friends Service Committee, the American Council on Race Relations of San Francisco, the International Institute of San Francisco, the Committee on Race Relations of the Northern California Council of Churches, the YMCA and the YWCA, and the San Francisco branch of the NAACP.[2] The writer also noted that other minority groups, especially the Chinese, had welcomed the Japanese back, fearing that discrimination against them might spill over into hostility against other Asians (since, of course, they all looked alike). Filipinos, however, were unpredictable because of Japan's atrocities against their homeland during the war. Taking no chances, many Koreans and Chinese were wearing identification buttons. Negroes had been friendly, despite the return of many Japanese Americans to the former Nihonmachi, now a part of the city where they lived.[3]

The report devoted considerable space to the activities of the JACL, which had recently reopened an office in San Francisco. A naval officer who visited its headquarters had learned of an incident in which a drunken white sailor bumped into a Nisei soldier and said he restrained himself from killing the man only because he wore a uniform. There were many Japanese American soldiers in the city (but no sailors, for the navy did not allow Nisei to enlist), and the naval officer said he was advising his superiors about such hostility in case further incidents occurred.[4]

The intelligence report also discussed the activities of the WRA on the West Coast. The WRA had field offices in Seattle, Los Angeles, and San Francisco, and it contemplated establishing six more in the Twelfth Naval District. Its staff was working to solve housing problems for the returnees, a greater problem than employment. The author concluded that there was no indication that the WRA was attempting to secure housing "other than on the open market," but many Caucasians suspected that it was. The WRA made several films that could be shown free of charge to community groups, including one on the 100th Battalion. Although a WRA spokesman came to answer questions, he did not present a talk; the agency found the response "most gratifying." The WRA employed Japanese Americans, but it did not give them preference over Caucasians and urged other governmental agencies to take the lead in hiring them,[5] presumably lest it appear prejudiced in their favor.

Since the opening of the West Coast on January 2, 1945, the Civil Affairs Division of the Western Defense Command had been authorized to list the names of Japanese Americans who were forbidden to return. The report noted that three individuals had challenged the right of the commanding general of the WDC to issue individual exclusion orders. (One of the three was George Ochikubo.) The report's author noted that it was unlikely the court would review anything beyond the due process questions involved.[6]

The writer reported that groups in each camp refused to leave, opposing the closing of the centers. The All-Camp Conference held in Salt Lake City in February 1945 had presented a list of recommendations to Washington on the problem. The author was more interested, however, in two incidents that occurred at Topaz in January and February. One concerned Frank Sasaki, his protests and distribution of the pro-Japan pamphlet; the report noted that he was under investigation. The second concerned a half-Japanese man named Saburo Henry Mittwer, who was picked up in February for possessing a home-made short-wave radio, which he used to pick up transmissions from Tokyo that he broadcast via loud-speakers all over his area of camp. He was to be sent to Tule Lake. The report noted also that the council at Topaz was dominated by Issei.[7]

As this report demonstrates, at least one officer in the Office of Naval Intelligence still did not differentiate between Japanese Americans and Japan itself; he was also attempting to link them to communism. The Cold War was in its nascent stages, and the tying of ethnic minorities to the supposed red conspiracy had begun. The author did not know his subjects well; most Nikkei had always been and remained politically conservative, and the camp experience had not shaken their political position any more than it had their fundamental loyalty to the United States. Racism was far from dead in the armed forces of the United States. Battalions remained seg-regated for another five years, but statements of blatant prejudice such as this became minority opinions as far as Japanese Americans were concerned.

⚓

The residents of Topaz were cautious about leaving camp for many reasons, including a fear of violence against them when they re-turned to California. The persecution of the Doi family in Placer County had attracted much attention in the press and alarmed the Topaz hold-outs. Then, on the night of March 6, vandals struck the ranch of Joe Takeda, who lived in Santa Clara County. This attack was even more alarming because it took place in the Bay Area. The assailants doused the Takeda home with gasoline and ignited it. When the family awakened and rushed outside to fight the fire, shots were fired at them from a moving vehicle. Deputy sheriffs arriving on the scene found empty gasoline containers and liquor bottles and discovered that the telephone lines to the house had been cut. Navy intelligence informed Washington that there had been "a total of twenty-five known acts of violence on the West

Coast against returning Japanese between 10 January 1945 and 7 March 1945," of which the Doi and Takeda cases were the best known. In Fresno County there were many smaller episodes like "rock throwing by children, anonymous telephone threats, isolated attempts to intimidate Japanese appearing on the street, and denial of business licenses."[8]

Since the press played up the dramatic acts of hostility, the Japanese Americans waiting to return to San Francisco had to rely on scouting expeditions for more encouraging news. These were made by determined and courageous people like Dave Tatsuno, whose reports that there was little or no discrimination emboldened others. But generally the news was mixed: people who returned reported violence in one locality, tolerance in another.

A variety of hate groups mounted campaigns to prevent the Japanese Americans from returning to California, and as before the war, the role of the press in publicizing their filth was critical. The California Joint Immigration Committee had long been the "primary force behind the anti-Japanese movement."[9] Groups and publications in the northern and central parts of the state promoted an anti-Japanese line. Vitriolic groups and publications were also found in the southern part of the state, where political rhetoric fanned the racist sentiments. For example, Los Angeles District Attorney Fred N. Howser called the expected return of the Japanese Americans a "second attack on Pearl Harbor."[10] San Francisco was not immune to such propaganda, but there were no acts of violence in the city.

Times, however, were changing. The naval intelligence report caught the drift: some of the most scurrilous hatemongers, particularly William Randolph Hearst's *San Francisco Examiner,* were slowly beginning to modify their attitude. In the first three months of 1945, "only" three significant anti-Japanese articles were published in the *Examiner.* Ray Richards, who had turned out a steady stream of anti-Japanese articles in the past, wrote one story warning that the returning West Coast Japanese would begin a nationwide produce price-cutting war to gain their revenge on California. Richards's alleged source was the Japanese-language *Utah Nippō,* which promptly denied the story. In another story he trumpeted that West Coast Japanese "have set up offices in Washington to prosecute $400,000,000 in damage claims caused by their removal from the West Coast."[11] The story was false, but the figure took on a life of its own, appearing in scholarly accounts as "the" amount of loss as late as 1983.[12]

But such stories as Richards's were becoming rare. The Hearst press no longer encouraged this kind of reporting, providing one example of a remarkable turnabout that emerged over the next year. Racism against the Nikkei was diminishing for many reasons. Fears were calmed by the return of far fewer Japanese Americans than anticipated. There was no reemergence of the large Nihon-machis of prewar years. Land holdings had been broken up and were often held and inhabited by others, and the returning exiles found residences in cities and towns throughout the state as well as rural areas. Responsible army and state government officials were also a factor; they now called for fair play. The war was over. There was no longer a reason to hate Japan or the Japanese, and political harmony was more important than catering to hate-mongering groups. Political leaders such as Los Angeles mayor Fletcher Bow-ron and California governor Earl Warren had favored evacuation and opposed the return of Japanese Americans to their state, but in January 1945 Bowron held a public ceremony to welcome them back. The Nikkei had always been productive members of society, law-abiding and industrious, and perhaps the mayor recognized that they could make a positive contribution (as, indeed, they had in the prewar years). Warren urged people to support the Supreme Court's decision in the *Endo* case. (It took him many years to acknowledge his own mistake, but at least he, unlike John McCloy and Karl Bendetsen, was able to.)[13]

Newspapers around the state began to reflect the new attitude. According to a story in the Hearst press, the attitude of University of California students toward Nisei returning to school was now one of welcome. The *San Francisco Chronicle* and the *San Francisco News* urged that full constitutional rights be given the returning Japanese Americans. The valley newspapers were not as hospitable and continued to print stories with a sensationalist, anti-Japanese flavor. The labor press, however, was extremely favorable to the return of the Nikkei, and on January 19, 1945, the *San Francisco Labor Herald,* a CIO paper, ran a story stating that the California CIO council welcomed their return. So did the *People's World,* a communist paper.[14] Karl Yoneda, who had served in military intelligence, did not receive such a welcome. For several months he was unable to find housing in San Francisco, and he had difficulty rejoining the Waterfront Employers Association. However, his union and political activities were working against him.[15]

The returning residents were but a fraction of California's prewar Japanese American population. Some 60 percent of the West Coast population had returned to their prewar places of residence by 1960, but others lived in Chicago, Cleveland, New York, or other midwestern or eastern locations. Some eventually made their way back to California—but others did not. Among the New York Nikkei community residents from Topaz were Miné Okubo, Michiko Okamoto, Mari Eijima, Karl Akiya, and eventually, Bill Kochiyama. Glenn Kumekawa and his sister Nobu Kumekawa Hibino both moved east, as did Lee Suyemoto, who received a Ph.D. from the University of Cincinnati. The San Francisco Nikkei community included many former Tuleans, including some who, like Morgan Yamanaka, had begun life as San Franciscans and had spent time in Topaz. Others from Topaz also came back to the Bay Area: Dave Tatsuno, Kenji Fujii, Tad Hayashi, and Fumi Manabe and her family. Tomoye and Henri Takahashi returned happily to San Francisco, where they set up an import-export business that thrived. Others, like Chizu and Ernest Iiyama, lived for a while in the Midwest and then returned. Maya Nagata settled in Los Angeles but eventually returned to Oakland. San Francisco's Nikkei population also included residents of other camps: Minidoka, Heart Mountain, Tule Lake, Poston, and Manzanar.

The economic costs of the internment have not been accurately measured, but in any case, the Japanese Americans returned to the Bay Area poorer than when they left. The $400 million estimate of their losses may well have appeared for the first time in Ray Richards's article in the *San Francisco Examiner* of February 20, 1945. It next appeared in testimony by the JACL's Mike Masaoka when he appeared before Congress to discuss the Redress Bill of 1948. The Federal Reserve Bank, usually given as Masaoka's source, did not in fact attach a dollar amount to the losses. The Commission on Wartime Internment and Relocation of Civilians estimated in 1983 that the total lay somewhere between $149 million and $370 million, but apparently that range of figures was not based on fact either, for the documentation of real property losses no longer exists and the costs of lost wages and denied freedom are incalculable.[16] Not only did the Issei and Nisei lose most of their prewar possessions, but they also earned only a fraction of what other Americans made during the war and what savings they carried into camp were almost entirely consumed. Few people who left on seasonal or indefinite leave found really lucrative positions, for they were usually employed in nonskilled or semi-skilled jobs.

Roger Daniels made some general observations about the Nikkei population of West Coast cities after the war that apply to San Francisco. "The day of the Issei had passed"; new Japanese American communities were led by Nisei and Sansei, and they predominated economically. The ethnic economy that Oscar Hoffman identified in prewar San Francisco had been destroyed. Japanese American businessmen had been forced out, losing either their leases or their property itself in the evacuation. The laundries and dry cleaning shops were gone; the Issei shopkeepers on Grant Avenue had been displaced by Chinese; the fishermen had sold out to Portuguese and Italians; the Japanese banks had closed. Even the ethnicity of Japantown had changed, for former Japanese residences were now occupied by African Americans. Nihonmachi, the Japantown of the Fillmore district, was no more. The early returnees who had worked for Issei or Nisei businessmen before the war had no jobs to return to, for their employers had been liquidated. In addition, Daniels noted, "culturally, there were no longer established ethnic institutions to shape their lives," for the Buddhist priests and Protestant ministers had been interned along with their flocks and most of their houses of worship had fallen to other owners.[17] The story of the Salvation Army of San Francisco, recounted earlier, merely illustrates the larger point.

The announcement of victory over Japan came quite suddenly, just days after the October 31 date announced for Topaz's closure. It broke down much of the resistance that remained among the Issei and the few Nisei still in camp. After Topaz closed, the cautious trickle of departing residents became a flood tide.

When the residents of the camps came back to San Francisco, they faced two critical problems—employment and housing. The latter was the most urgent, as personal reports from scouting expeditions and letters to remaining Topazeans made clear. San Francisco Nikkei who had either rented or leased housing before the war had nothing to return to, and those who owned property had let it to others and sometimes could not immediately repossess it. Since the area that was formerly Japantown was now predominantly African American, many Nikkei did not wish to live there. There was no overt hostility between the ethnic groups, but the Fillmore just was not the Nihonmachi they had known. Those who had money did not want to buy houses there, but they found that realtors would not sell them residences in "white" areas. Restrictive housing covenants, which limited an owner's right to sell to anyone he or she wished, circumscribed their options. Some found that realtors were willing to sell but banks would not loan them money for mortgages. Returning Japanese Americans established small communities all over the city rather than a single enclave, and they shared these areas with other minority groups. The dispersal that Roosevelt had desired for the Japanese population throughout the country was taking place in San Francisco as well.

The stories of the San Francisco and Bay Area Nikkei who were interviewed for this book provide a sense of the problems the returning residents faced. Although in 1990 some might agree with Leonard Arrington that the evacuation was a "blessing in disguise,"[18] hardly anyone would have accepted such a verdict in 1945. It was not easy to pick up the pieces of one's life, and it was impossible to go on as before.

Dave Tatsuno's experiences were far from typical in many respects, yet his return and eventual economic success were mirrored by many Nisei. Tatsuno had not found Topaz unbearable; in fact, he believed he had gained valuable business experience managing the dry goods section of the co-op. After farming on a seasonal leave and teaching at Topaz High School, he was eager to leave Utah. His younger brother had been drafted, and the incongruity of the situation struck Dave when his sibling, in an army uniform, came to camp to visit. Dave wrote to General Delos Emmons, who was in charge of the Western Defense Command at the time, complaining that "it doesn't make sense for my brother to be in the United States Army and for us to be locked up here." The Tatsunos were cleared to return to California just the day before the state was opened to resettlement.[19]

The Tatsunos had a home in San Francisco, which they had rented to a sympathetic Quaker, Caleb Foote, who had published some pro-Nisei articles during the war. Foote invited Tatsuno to return to the Bay Area on an exploratory trip and stay with him for a few months. Dave Tatsuno left Topaz in January for his home in the old Japantown and got along very well with the tenants. He was pleased with the friendliness of the new African American residents, who included businessmen and bankers. Since Tatsuno was the resettlement expediter for the Presbyterian Church, he checked on the property of other parishioners, many of whom had lost all their possessions. He was extremely fortunate to have suffered relatively little, only because he had discovered what was happening to his property before he left Tanforan for Topaz. Tatsuno returned to Topaz to move his family and his parents west, and ever the photographer, he filmed their journey. "I did a movie all the way back crossing the Great Salt Lake and coming back into California. We were met at the ferry building in San Francisco by friends and then [I watched them]

going up the stairs of the house of my father [on] May 5, 1945,"
he recalled.

The Tatsuno family was even fortunate with regard to the family
business. Although they had liquidated it before the evacuation,
they retained a small amount of stock. "That became seed money
for the reopening of our store," Dave said. The one store soon
became two, and the family hired assistants who still worked for
them forty years later. Tragedy struck their lives with the unexpected death of Dave's young son in 1947 following a tonsillec-
tomy; the store in San Jose became a memorial to him.[20] Dave
Tatsuno was not a bitter man, yet he knew relocation had been
unjust and that redress was warranted for the injustice done him
and so many others. The $20,000 the government agreed to pay the
survivors was "blood money" as far as he was concerned, but he
concluded philosophically, "It is better to light a candle than to
curse the darkness."[21]

Tomoye Takahashi, born and raised in San Francisco, wanted
nothing so much as to return home. After the Takahashi family left
camp, they took the train back to the Bay Area and crossed the bay
on the ferry. The view of the San Francisco skyline is always
dramatic, but it never looked lovelier than on the evening they
returned, with the sun setting behind the city. The sight was one
Mrs. Takahashi would never forget: "In the sky ahead of us, lav-
ender was sliding into pearly gray and the tinted pinks and oranges
couldn't have been more beautiful. I shall never forget it. I just stood
there and wept. It was the greatest happening; I was finally coming
home."[22]

The family had left their possessions locked in one room of their
home near Golden Gate Park; the house itself was rented, fully
furnished, for $45 a month. The locked room, in the basement,
contained special possessions that Tomoye treasured: wedding gifts
she had received, Japanese kimonos, silk parasols, crystal beads,
rose quartz necklaces from the family home in Yamanashi, records,
dolls, and family photographs. They found the room had been

vandalized; their trunks had been opened, and their personal letters spilled all over the floor. They later found some of the family photographs on the floor of the garage, but most of their heirlooms were irretrievably lost. The Takahashis knew where some of their possessions had gone, for they saw their neighbors using their furniture, a vacuum cleaner, and typewriters. Some chairs were missing but the pillows that matched them remained, for the people who had raided one room did not know what was in another. Tomoye went immediately to the Golden Gate Park Police Station to report her losses to the policemen, former classmates and other men whom she had known since childhood. Such ties counted for little: the policemen told her, "Have you ever heard of a China-man's chance? You don't have a Chinaman's chance. No court will listen to you and no lawyer would take your case." There was no point in filing a complaint, for the goods were gone forever.[23]

Finding a job in the city was just as hard. Tomoye Takahashi and her sister scoured San Francisco for jobs, only to be rejected. Finally her sister, a biochemist by training, got a job at the Emporium department store. She was put in a small back room to work alone checking sales slips, out of sight so the other employees would not be upset. After barely a week she received a better offer from the Western Regional Research Lab and quit, but the family always remembered with gratitude (and their continued patronage) that the Emporium had come through.[24]

The Takahashis became the exemplars of the Japanese American success story. They established a prosperous importing firm that was well known in San Francisco forty years later. Among their benevolences was a donation that helped to found the National Japanese American Historical Society.

Tsuyako "Sox" Kitashima returned to San Francisco, too, but since she had no housing, she and her husband had to search for a place to stay. Many people she knew went to army housing at Hunters Point, but with the help of a friend who had arrived before they did they found lodging at the Buddhist church. When the headquarters of the Buddhist Church in America returned to San Francisco, it provided space for many of the homeless Nikkei. "Sox" recalled, "We slept at the Buddhist church auditorium where they had just rows and rows of cots for single men. Married couples slept on the balcony. They had army blankets for partitions. We stayed there until someone threw a rock into the window and they felt it was too dangerous." Before that, she remembered, she and her husband had slept in the movie projection room in the church, where only the two holes cut in the walls for the cameras provided ventilation. The Health Department pronounced it unhealthy and chased them out. Sleeping in either location was not easy, she recalled: "There was somebody getting up all the time, going to the bathroom because it was cold. The snoring resembled an orchestra tuning up." She was just grateful that they had a roof over their heads. Next they moved into a Sunday school room, which they shared with two or three other families, but as people got up very early to do the cleaning, no one could sleep late.[25]

The Kitashimas soon moved to somewhat better lodgings, staying with a sister and three other families who shared food and cooking and pooled their food stamps. The next task was to get a job. "Sox" considered herself lucky, since she found employment right away. Although her husband had a harder time, he found a job working for the WRA at the warehouse where evacuees had stored their possessions before the evacuation. The WRA may not have given preferential treatment to Japanese Americans, but it did provide temporary work for many. The Kitashimas survived, and "Sox" reflected years later, "We were more frightened than we should have been. But you just [didn't] know how acceptance would be. We sort of tiptoed into town." She was amazed that many San Franciscans did not know that she and her family had been interned: "They wanted to know where we had been all those years." "Sox" was employed by the Veteran's Administration until she retired, and she was very proud of her position. Many Caucasians were then surprised that she, a Nisei and a citizen, would work all the rest of her life for the very government that had imprisoned her. "Sox" was a loyal American, and she had no hesitation about working for her government.[26]

"Sox" Kitashima's life illustrates another facet of the recovery of the Nikkei in the Bay Area. Civil service was quickly opened to Japanese Americans, and although the anonymous naval intelligence officer might have expressed doubts about their suitability, others found them very well qualified, well educated, reliable, and hardworking. Many of the Nisei who had been employed in the camp administrations received good recommendations from their employers, as "Sox" did from Claud Pratt. They were experienced, qualified, and like "Sox," they were proud to work for the federal or state government. They did not have to prove their loyalty; they were good citizens, diligent and competent, and they always had been. After her retirement "Sox" Kitashima worked at the Kimochi Senior Citizens' Center. She campaigned hard for redress, working with the National Coalition for Redress/Reparation, and she also helped advise Issei of their rights. She received one of the first redress checks.[27]

Many of the Nisei who had planned to enter college during the war years but had not been able to returned to the Bay Area to continue their education. Morgan Yamanaka was one of these people. His four-year hiatus was, as he described it, more "colorful" than most of his peers'; segregated from Topaz to Tule Lake, he ended up in the stockade. He stayed in Tule into 1946, while the camp remained open to take care of people who wished to leave for Japan. Morgan did not return to San Francisco until the fall of 1946, after a six-month residence in Chicago. The initial shock of reentry had passed by then. He contacted the dean of Lowell High School, who had provided him with a recommendation that netted him a job at the Topaz fire station, and asked the educator's opinion about continuing his education. Since by 1946 many GIs were also returning to college, the dean considered how Morgan could best compete. "Logically, you should go to Berkeley," he advised, but because of the four-year gap in Morgan's formal education, he advised him to go to San Francisco City College as preparation first. Morgan decided to major in psychology, sociology, or social work, for he wanted to help others, especially members of minorities. He completed a master's degree in social work, worked in Fresno, and returned to San Francisco to direct a settlement house in the Mission district. He found working with ethnic minorities gratifying. He was, in 1988, on the faculty at San Francisco State University.[28]

Morgan's residence in Marin County is a testimonial to his heritage and his American life. He and his Caucasian wife decorated the living room and study of their gracious home with beautiful Japanese art objects. Morgan has collected traditional Japanese swords, honed to a razor-sharp edge. The room, he told me, gave him much pleasure and also reminded his children of their Japanese heritage. The rest of the home is purely Californian.

※

Don Nakahata's family, including an aunt, his mother and her cousin, and his sister, went east when the war ended, and Don remained in Rochester, New York, throughout his high school years. But the family, like many other Japanese Americans, decided to return to California. For Don the reason went beyond simple homesickness: the California university system offered free tuition to residents, and such quality education was a bargain that could not be bypassed. His relatives packed up their belongings, and the family moved. Aunt Faith Terasawa was their pioneer: she went first to scout out a place to stay, for even in 1947 that was no sure thing. Years later Nakahata remembered what she found: "It was essentially one big room in a hotel at Turk and Fillmore run by some friends from prewar days that had a hotel." They stayed there for about a year, sharing a bathroom down the hall and all sleeping in the same room. Nakahata commented, "We were the nation's first boat people—except we didn't have to come by boat."[29]

Don and his mother eventually settled into the postwar economy of San Francisco. His mother, an Issei, returned to work as a domestic and then became a seamstress for the I. Magnin department store, where she remained for many years. Don and his sister followed the path of upward mobility that was so common among the Nisei. His sister, a graduate of the University of Rochester, was trained in the philosophy of history, not the most employable field at any time. She finally secured a position in the army's military traffic management system, shipping munitions overseas. The Korean War made her indispensable, Don Nakahata recalled, and she remained in that occupation for the rest of her career. Don studied first at the City College of San Francisco and then transferred to the University of California, majoring in biology. After graduation he moved to the UC campus in Davis, where he was a research assistant. From there he was drafted. After two years of military service, he returned to college on the GI Bill to obtain his professional education in dentistry. He had a practice in San Francisco, then joined the University of California, San Francisco, faculty in dentistry and consulted for a dental insurance company.[30]

Life in the East Bay slowly resumed the tenor of its prewar days. Tad Hayashi and his fiancee, Fumi Manabe, were married in Berkeley, their prewar home, where both their parents lived. They settled in the part of the city where many other Japanese Americans—including many campmates from Topaz—had found homes. Isao James and Chiyoko Yano lived nearby, as did Tad Fujita and Tad Hirota and their families. Tad Fujita and his wife had returned first to Los Altos, where they stayed in a Quaker hostel run by Josephine Duveneck and her family. Although they experienced discrimination in the community, they never lost faith that God would look after them, and they were convinced that He had. Chizu and Ernest Iiyama lived for a while in the Midwest, finally returning to California to live in El Cerrito. Harry Kitano, Chizu's brother, went to the University of California, received a doctorate in social welfare, and taught at the University of California, Los Angeles, where he became a specialist in the Japanese American subculture. In 1993 he held an endowed chair in Japanese American Studies. Chiz's sister Tish Yamasaki also returned to live in Berkeley with her family.

Further south, Kenji Fujii returned to the family business in Hayward after a stint in Detroit to make some money. The nursery was very dilapidated but, as Fujii said, "I expected it to be run down, and I knew the guy [who had leased it] made money on it, and I wanted him to make money on it, because it would have been run down *more* [otherwise]." The Fujii family spread out across the country after the war, again like many other Japanese American families. One of Ken's sisters stayed in the East, while another returned to Hayward after the war and attended college. Once her education was completed, she moved east to take a government job. Kenji Fujii said the Nikkei had a lot of fear of discrimination and hostility, but it seemed to be misplaced. It was not as bad as they had expected. His advice was not to look for trouble or anticipate hostile responses: "You don't take every little thing and imagine by it, otherwise you're out of distortion yourself." Fujii's friendly and open manner of dealing with people was one that would defuse all but the harshest animosity. "The hostility was in ourselves," he said.[31]

Fujii slipped back with little difficulty into the life he had led before the war. He was nearly drafted, but in 1952 the Korean War ended and to his great relief he was not called. In 1949 he married Allyce Hirabayashi, who had been interned at Poston, and they had two sons. Although there were hard times bringing up the children, everyone survived the boys' adolescence and "ended up still liking one another." Given the world his sons lived in, the era of the Vietnam War, protest, and drugs, that was no mean achievement. In 1987 Fujii was retired, and his sons were running the nursery. How has he told his sons about Topaz? "Piecemeal . . . when the time is right. They haven't asked—I think they're too busy dealing with today's social conditions."[32]

❧

Relocation might have remained a hidden story, its damage confined to the lives of the people who were immediately affected, were it not for the redress movement. Beginning in the early 1970s, this demand for an admission of error and some type of monetary compensation from the federal government grew slowly but inexorably. The report of the Commission on Wartime Relocation and Internment of Civilians, published in 1982 as *Personal Justice*

Denied, documented not only the events of the war years but also their continuing impact on the lives of the Issei and Nisei who had been held behind barbed wire. In 1988 Congress finally apologized, stating that relocation was "motivated largely by racial prejudice, wartime hysteria, and a failure of political leadership." It acted to approve redress, setting aside $500 million to be paid in $20,000 installments in 1991, $500 million in the 1992 fiscal year, and an estimated $250 million in 1993. As of 1990 there were an estimated 65,000 eligible recipients, with payments to be made to the oldest first. President Ronald Reagan signed the bill. On October 9, 1990, the first payments were made. Nine elderly Issei, six of them over a hundred years old, received checks and letters from President George Bush.[33] Bush's letter contained an apology acknowledging that money and words alone could not "right the wrongs of the past. But we can take a clear stand for justice and recognize that serious injustices were done to Japanese Americans during World War II."[34]

The Office of Redress Administration in the Department of Justice honored Japanese Americans who had worked to make redress a reality. In the Bay Area the honorees included Masi Nihei, once a resident of Delta, Utah, and Tsuyako "Sox" Kitashima, who was interned at Topaz. Kitashima spent more than ten years working for redress and sent 25,000 letters of support for the project during those years; she capped her personal campaign with 600 mailgrams, dispatched in the final months. When the press interviewed her about her activities, she expressed not only satisfaction that the movement had succeeded but also sorrow that, for many, the day of redress had come too late. "We lost so many people," she said, remembering her brother who had died just after Reagan signed the bill. Her check came later in 1990. "Hopefully for myself and thousands of others, this will unburden the stigma of disloyalty," she reflected.[35] Finally the memories of Topaz could be laid to rest.

✤

What of the Nikkei's sense of community? Certainly the old Nihonmachi was gone, replaced by a new, shiny one financed in part by Japan, which was as much a tourist attraction as a residential and business area. Nevertheless, in 1992 some of the old stores remained, such as Soko Hardware. Nichi Bei Bussan had been reborn. Japanese restaurants dotted the area, the national headquarters of the JACL was on Sutter Street, and homes for elderly Nikkei abounded. Yet Japanese Americans were to be found all over the city in virtually every occupation. They themselves decried the notion that they were a "model minority," so successful as to no longer warrant minority status. Many unmarried Issei did not share in the general prosperity. The fight over redress bore many similarities to the camp fights between the "accommodationists" and those who would resist, avoid the draft, and stay put until the camps closed. Some redress advocates, like William Hohri, wanted a much more radical approach with much larger financial compensation than the JACL supported. Others shied away from redress at all. They were loath to call attention to themselves, wanting only to blend into white culture and succeed on their own merits. The controversy caused many schisms among the camp survivors.

In many ways Topaz still survives. Its residents know one another, are friends and neighbors, and keep up with one another's lives. An annual picnic reunites members of the JACL in the Bay Area, and many of the attendees are former residents of Topaz. Even East Coast Nisei from Topaz occasionally come west, and some keep in touch by phone or letter. Perhaps the most persistent memories emerge in the reunions held periodically by the high school graduating classes, especially the last one, the Class of 1945. It was a closely knit group, and its members still keep in touch. An all-camp reunion was held in 1988 and proved so successful that camp residents held another one in 1992, the fiftieth anniversary of evacuation. Out of pain, grief, and suffering came bonds of shared memories and a sense of survival. Even the Caucasians who were the closest to the camp members participated, including Eleanor and Emil Sekerak and Paul Bell, the only white graduate of Topaz High. Jane Beckwith, a Delta High School teacher who taught her class about Topaz and served as a "local guide" to former inmates, also attended faithfully. She hopes to construct a small museum in Delta housing artifacts of the camp.

The site of Topaz is bleak today. Jane Beckwith can point out the former buildings, still in use in the Delta area, and the sharp-eyed can spot the concrete slabs that once held the barracks. Occasionally a few shells or part of a pot-bellied stove surfaces. For the former residents who have returned—and many have—the site is full of memories. One can only hope that seeing it again imparts a sense of closure, a personal ending to a national episode of shame.

Abbreviations

AWS	Tape transcribed by the American West Center, on file with Western Americana, Marriott Library, University of Utah, Salt Lake City.
BCA	Buddhist Churches of America.
CA Reports	West Coast Locality Study, Community Analyst Reports, War Relocation Authority, Topaz, Microfilm, National Archives.
JACL	Japanese American Citizens League.
JERS	Japanese Evacuation Research Study, Bancroft Library, University of California, Berkeley.
ML	Western Americana Section, Marriott Library, University of Utah, Salt Lake City.
RG 210	Record Group 210, National Archives.
RG 338	Record Group 338, 0410, National Archives.
WCCA	Wartime Civil Control Administration.
WDC	Western Defense Command.
WRA	War Relocation Authority.

Notes

Preface

1. Bell and Newby, *Community Studies*, 15–16.

2. Bender, *Community and Social Change*, 7–8. In *Imagined Communities,* Benedict Anderson uses the term to refer to nations as a form of community.

3. Miyamoto, *Social Solidarity*, 3. Miyamoto then discusses the Japanese cultural heritage, emphasizing the ethical system, family organization, and other facets of Japanese behavior that were manifest especially among the Issei and somewhat among the Nisei. This work was originally done in the mid-1930s as Miyamoto's master's thesis and was reissued in 1981 and again in 1984. As his revised introduction to the 1984 edition bears heavily on the concept of community in the prewar period, all references will be to that edition.

4. Modell, "Japanese of Los Angeles," 44.

5. Lukes and Okihiro, *Japanese Legacy*, 2–3.

6. Miyamoto, *Social Solidarity*, 64. More specific definitions of American communities have been the subject of much debate; Bell and Newby have catalogued no fewer than ninety-four different meanings of the term; *Community Studies*, p. 15 and chap. 2.

7. Chan, *Asian Americans*, 63.

8. Seattle: University of Washington Press, 1991.

9. The primary works on Japanese in Los Angeles and Seattle are still Modell, "Japanese of Los Angeles," and Miyamoto, *Social Solidarity*. Until the present work, little has been done on Japanese San Francisco.

10. The entire camp experience has been ably surveyed in such studies as Daniels, *Concentration Camps, U.S.A.*; Grodzins, *Americans Betrayed*; Girdner and Loftis, *Great Betrayal*; and Petersen, *Japanese Americans*. There have been histories of individual camps: Wakatsuki and Houston,

Farewell to Manzanar; Ishigo, *Lone Heart Mountain;*, and Nelson, *Heart Mountain.* There have been numerous memoirs by participants, notably Okubo, *Citizen 13660,* and Uchida, *Desert Exile.* (These two works are on Topaz.) There has also been a biography of the man responsible for running the camps, Dillon Myer: Drinnon, *Keeper of Concentration Camps.*

11. The WRA's "first 'Final Report'" was written by General John DeWitt in 1942. Ten copies were printed and bound and six were formally transmitted to the War Department on April 13, 1943. Assistant Secretary of War John L. McCloy told DeWitt to destroy them since they were full of errors, especially the assertion that evacuation was a military necessity. These copies were burned. The final version of this *Final Report* was submitted to the War Department by DeWitt on June 5, 1943, but it was not released until January 1944 (no day mentioned). These false reports were presented to the Supreme Court in the cases of Fred Korematsu, Gordon Hirabayashi, and Min Yasui. The Writ of Error (Coram Nobis) petition was filed in San Francisco in January 1983. As a result of the discovery of government misconduct, the convictions of the three men were set aside, not overturned. The federal government chose not to appeal. Clifford Uyeda, "The Big Lie," *Nikkei Heritage* I (Fall 1992): 4–9. Portions of the voluminous documentation, such as *Evacuated People,* were published separately after the war.

1. Japanese San Francisco

1. Ichihashi, *Japanese in the United States,* 240; Ichibashi cited Theodore Roosevelt's address to Congress December 3, 1907, in which he attempted to find a solution to U.S.-Japan tensions. Roosevelt noted that Japan had contributed $100,000 to sufferers of the 1906 earthquake (Richard, *Messages,* 743–46). Bronson, *Earth Shook,* 20, stated that the Japanese contribution was $244,960, of the total of $471,211 from foreign countries. The total cost was around $9 million.

2. Interview with Tad Fujita, Berkeley, October 28, 1987, AWC.

3. Tamotsu Shibutani, "The Social Organization of the Japanese Communities in the San Francisco Bay Region," JERS, 42.

4. Interview with Tomoye Nozawe Takahashi, San Francisco, November 2, 1987, AWC.

5. Daniels, *Politics of Prejudice,* 16.

6. Okihiro, *Cane Fires,* 20.

7. Shibutani, "Social Organization," JERS, 42.

8. Modell dated the approximate beginnings of the Los Angeles community somewhere in the early 1890s, "taking off" in 1893; "Japanese of Los Angeles," 44. Miyamoto stated that the Seattle community

was "incipient" from around 1900, although settlers in the Northwest arrived about the same time as the first arrivals in San Francisco; *Social Solidarity*, 10.

9. Takaki, *Strangers*, 45–46.

10. Daniels, *Politics of Prejudice*, 2–3; Daniels, *Asian America*, 100.

11. Okihiro, *Cane Fires*. See chapter 2 for a discussion of Japanese settlement in Hawaii. Okihiro cited census figures showing that migration from Hawaii to the mainland was 12,221 in 1906 but virtually ceased after President Theodore Roosevelt signed an executive order in March 1907 prohibiting aliens whose passports had been issued for travel to American territories or America's neighbors, Mexico and Canada, from entering the United States (p. 37).

12. Takaki, *Strangers*, 11.

13. Tom Kawaguchi recalled during our second interview, on March 7, 1990, in San Francisco, that agricultural laborers were still coming back into the city for the winter during the 1930s; notes in the possession of the author.

14. Oscar F. Hoffman, Community Analyst, to Dillon S. Myer, "An Interview on the Japanese Settlement in San Francisco," January 1945, CA Reports. These reports, which are extensive, advised Director Dillon Myer on whether the Japanese Americans interned in Topaz could rebuild their Bay Area community if they were allowed to return to the West Coast. They furnish invaluable, if biased, data on the condition of Nikkei life in San Francisco and its environs before the war. They were based on anonymous interviews with interned Japanese Americans from the particular trades of concern to the analyst and the WRA.

15. Miyamoto, *Social Solidarity*, 45.

16. See Taylor, *Advocate of Understanding*, 20–24.

17. Suzuki, *Ministry*, 13–14, citing Imaizumi Genkichi, *Miyama Kanichi and His Times* (Tokyo: Mikuni, 1940), 122 (in Japanese).

18. Ibid., 15.

19. Interview with Seizo Oka, San Francisco, March 9, 1990; notes in the possession of the author. Oka formerly ran the Japanese American History Room in Japantown. Suzuki, *Ministry*, 19.

20. Suzuki, *Ministry*, 15–19.

21. Interview with Tom Kawaguchi, San Francisco, March 7, 1990.

22. Suzuki, *Ministry*, 17, 42–43; conversations with Masamu Hayashi, Salt Lake City, January–March 1990, and information provided by the Institute of Buddhist Studies, Berkeley, Calif.

23. Interview with Tom Kawaguchi, March 7, 1990.

24. Ibid.

25. Daniels, *Asian America*, 103–4; see also the discussion of *shosei* in Hata, *"Undesirables,"* 49.

26. Interview with Seizo Oka, San Francisco, March 9, 1990.

27. The 1880 census is cited by Daniels in *Politics of Prejudice,* 3. James T. Conte, "Overseas Study in the Meiji Period: Japanese Students in America, 1867–1902," Ph.D. diss., Princeton University, 1977, as cited in Daniels, *Asian America,* 104.

28. Daniels, *Politics of Prejudice,* 1. At the time of their highest incidence the Japanese constituted .021 of the population of California and .001 of the population of the continental United States.

29. Miyamoto, *Social Solidarity,* Preface to the 1981 edition, vi.

30. Takaki, *Strangers,* 46.

31. Daniels, *Asian America,* 106.

32. Miyamoto, *Social Solidarity,* 30–31.

33. See Nakano, *Japanese American Women,* especially part 1, "The Issei."

34. Miyamoto, *Social Solidarity,* xii; the author is indebted to Fumi and Tad Hayashi for their hospitality and for sharing their Berkeley home with her, and to Michi Kobi and Jean Kariya for their hospitality in New York.

35. Nakano, *Japanese American Women,* 21. Information on Mrs. Manabe came from a brief interview and from a series of discussions with Fumi Manabe Hayashi in Berkeley in 1988 and 1990.

36. Nakano, *Japanese American Women,* 23–24; Takaki, *Strangers,* 46–47.

37. Interview with Robert Utsumi, San Francisco, May 11, 1988, AWC.

38. Issel and Cherny, *San Francisco,* 66. Japanese Americans today use the term Nihonmachi (Japantown) to refer to the area where they lived in the past as well as to the area of San Francisco beginning on Geary and running to Sutter between Fillmore and Buchanan, constructed primarily by money from Japan in the 1950s. Technically, Nihonmachi refers to the portion of any American or Canadian city that was all Japanese during the period of time when racial covenants prohibited people of Japanese origin from settling anywhere they desired or could afford. Seizo Oka prefered to use the term Nihonjinmachi to distinguish between the section of San Francisco now known as Japantown, primarily a cultural and business section of the city, and the prewar Japanese district. I am also indebted to Fumi Hayashi for her help in clarifying the distinctions between the two terms. However, in this work I use only the term Nihonmachi, to avoid confusing readers.

39. Shibutani, "Social Organization," JERS, 46.

40. Modell, "Japanese of Los Angeles," 65.

41. Interview with Tomoye Nozawe Takahashi, San Francisco, November 2, 1987; rough draft in possession of the author.

42. Hosokawa, *Nisei*, 90–91. Hosokawa pointed out that according to some sources, as many as 460 Issei had been naturalized, primarily in the eastern United States. The Supreme Court ruled after the *Ozawa* case that these earlier cases were in error, that even Issei who had served in the armed forces and been naturalized were ineligible for citizenship, since they were neither white nor of African descent.

43. Miyamoto, *Social Solidarity*, Preface to 1984 edition, x.

44. Daniels, *Politics of Prejudice*, 26, dated the origins to 1900 and attributed it to the plague scare of that year. See also Miyamoto, *Social Solidarity*, 60.

45. Chan, *Asian Americans*, 68.

46. Modell, "Japanese of Los Angeles," 142.

47. Daniels, *Politics of Prejudice*, 26.

48. Daniels, *Asian America*, 128–32.

49. The Japanese Association of San Francisco primarily served the city dwellers. Fumi Manabe Hayashi recalled that her family had little or no connection with it or any other Japanese Association, but they lived in Berkeley and her parents did not return to Japan after they immigrated to America.

50. See Levine and Rhodes, *The Japanese American Community*, chaps. 1, 2, 4–6; Kiefer, *Changing Cultures*.

51. Kiefer, *Changing Cultures*, 4–5. Kiefer used the term *ghetto* to refer to the ethnic communities within larger cities.

52. Daniels, *Asian America*, 109. Seattle was also a very important port of entry.

53. Issel and Cherney, *San Francisco*, 66.

54. Daniels, *Politics of Prejudice*, 12–13.

55. Yoneda, *Ganbatte*, 13.

56. Interview with Ernest Iiyama and Chizu Kitano Iiyama, San Francisco, May 13, 1988, AWC; telephone conversation with Chizu Kitano Iiyama, San Francisco, October 7, 1991. In 1991 Chizu's mother was 102 years old.

57. Oscar F. Hoffman, "Hotel and Apartment House Business in San Francisco," March 9, 1945, CA Report. The sources were interviews with four former owners and one Issei business leader of the district, plus several interviews with recent visitors, the *New World Sun Japanese Directory of 1941*, and the *1944 World Almanac*. Hoffman composed a series of locality studies between January and March 1945 for the WRA.

58. Yoneda, *Ganbatte*, 37. Yoneda passed through San Francisco in 1927 on his way to Los Angeles.

59. Daniels, *Politics of Prejudice*, 8.

60. Ibid., 11; Daniels's statistics came from *Reports of the Immigration Commission* 23:183–84.

61. Interview with K. Morgan Yamanaka, San Francisco, May 11, 1988, AWC.

62. Ibid; Shibutani, "Social Organization," JERS, 57.

63. Adachi, "History of Adachi Nursery," 15.

64. Ibid. Oscar F. Hoffman noted in "Domestic Workers in San Francisco," January 31, 1945, that the Nisei were not willing to take jobs as domestics after the war even in order to tide themselves over the immediate postwar readjustment period. Wages were too unattractive, and they "like most other Americans . . . prefer to be something more than house servants." CA Reports.

65. Oscar F. Hoffman, "Domestic Workers in San Francisco," January 31, 1945, CA Reports. This report was based on an interview with a former manager of "one of the leading and oldest Japanese employment agencies in San Francisco."

66. Daniels, *Asian America*, 111–12.

67. Shibutani, "Social Organization," JERS, 42.

68. Ichihashi, *Japanese in the United States*, 119–21, 129.

69. Daniels, *Politics of Prejudice*, 12.

70. Takaki, *Strangers*, 180.

71. Oscar F. Hoffman, "San Francisco and East Bay Cities Laundry Business," January 17, 1945, CA Reports.

72. Ibid.

73. Oscar F. Hoffman, "San Francisco Retail Dry Cleaning and Dyeing Business," January 17, 1945, CA Reports.

74. Ibid.

75. Interview with Kenji Fujii, Hayward, Calif., November 5, 1987; rough draft in possession of the author. Daniels noted in *Politics of Prejudice*, 63, that the law, which limited leases of agricultural land by Issei to maximum terms of three years, was easily evaded by the simple expedient of registering land in the name of American-born children.

76. Oscar F. Hoffman, "San Francisco Wholesale and Retail Art Goods Business," January 26, 1945, CA Reports. This report was based on interviews with five former merchants on Grant Avenue and one former leader in the Japanese colony in San Francisco.

77. Ibid. This was Hoffman's opinion.

78. Ibid.

79. Ibid.

80. Figures assembled in the West Coast Locality Study, presumably for the years before the evacuation, state that a small 24 × 50 store took in $5,000–$6,000 each month, while an average-sized store grossed more than $15,000 a month. The largest store, Nippon Dry Goods Company, did about $500,000 worth of business annually. Sources for these figures

are Hoffman's "San Francisco Wholesale and Retail Art Goods Businesses," January 26, 1945, CA Reports.

81. Oscar F. Hoffman, "San Francisco Fishing Industry," CA Reports.

82. Ibid.

83. Takaki, *Strangers,* 185.

84. Interview with Michi Onuma of the *Nichi Bei Times,* San Francisco, March 7, 1990; Thomas, *The Salvage,* 60–61; Hosokawa, *Nisei,* 181–82.

85. Hoffman, "Japanese Settlement in San Francisco," January 1945, CA Reports.

86. Ibid.

87. Conversation with Tad Hayashi, Berkeley, March 6, 1990; conversation with Tom Kawaguchi, San Francisco, March 7, 1990. The Scout troops before the war were all-Nisei, but after the war they included a few Caucasians. The basis of segregation appeared to be based more on residential area than on race.

88. Hoffman, "Japanese Settlement in San Francisco," January 1945, CA Report.

89. Interview with Chizu Kitano Iiyama, San Francisco, May 13, 1988, AWC.

90. Shibutani, "Social Organization," JERS, 43–45.

91. Yoneda, *Ganbatte,* 37.

92. Daniels, *Politics of Prejudice,* 16–17; Issel and Cherney, *San Francisco,* 125–26.

93. Takaki, *Strangers,* 201–2.

94. Daniels, *Politics of Prejudice,* 21, citing Phelan's remarks as quoted in the *San Francisco Examiner* and *San Francisco Chronicle,* May 8, 1900.

95. Miyamoto, *Social Solidarity,* xxiii.

96. Daniels, *Politics of Prejudice,* 16–24. Ichihashi also noted the connection with a bubonic plague outburst that began in Chinatown, and agitation to reenact the Chinese Exclusion Law; *Japanese,* 230–31. Takaki, *Strangers,* 200–202.

97. Daniels, *Politics of Prejudice,* 23.

98. Ichihashi, *Japanese,* 229–30.

99. Daniels, *Politics of Prejudice,* 34–43; Ichihashi, *Japanese,* 236–42; Takaki, *Strangers,* 201–3. There were ninety-three Japanese students in the San Francisco public schools at the time.

100. Daniels, *Politics of Prejudice,* 44.

101. Ibid., 44–45.

102. Ichihashi, *Japanese,* 277–78.

103. Lukes and Okihiro, *Japanese Legacy,* 58.

104. Taylor, *Advocate of Understanding,* 149–52; Daniels, *Politics of Prejudice,* 95–96.

105. Daniels, *Politics of Prejudice,* 94–98; Takaki, *Strangers,* 208.

106. Taylor, *Advocate of Understanding,* 160–61; Ichihashi, *Japanese,* chap. 19; Takaki, *Strangers,* 209.

107. Daniels, *Politics of Prejudice,* 102–3.

108. Hoffman, "Japanese Settlement in San Francisco," January 1945, CA Reports.

109. Takaki, *Strangers,* 213–14.

110. Daniels, *Politics of Prejudice,* 32–33.

111. Lukes and Okihiro, *Japanese Legacy,* 60–61.

112. Takaki, *Strangers,* 218.

113. Daniels, "Japanese America."

114. Modell, "Japanese of Los Angeles," 340–41.

115. "A Walk Through Japantown—1935."

116. Interview with Michi Onuma, San Francisco, March 7, 1989. Onuma, who has worked in the Japanese American newspaper business in San Francisco since the prewar years, said that this was not uncommon; it accounted for many businesses being able to reestablish themselves in the postwar community.

117. Ibid.

118. Ibid. Conversation with Tom Kawaguchi on March 7, 1989.

119. Interview with John Hada, San Francisco, November 2, 1987, AWC.

120. Hoffman, "Laundry Business," January 17, 1945, CA Reports.

121. Hoffman, "Retail Dry Cleaning and Dyeing Business," January 17, 1945, CA Report.

122. Hoffman, "Wholesale and Retail Art Goods Business," January 26, 1945, CA Reports.

123. Takaki, *Strangers,* 216. *Japanesy* is a term favored by the Nisei, who use it to refer to Japanese Americans who behave in ways more appropriate to natives of Japan than the United States.

124. Oscar F. Hoffman, "Southern Alameda County Farmers," June 6, 1945, CA Reports; Shibutani, "Social Organization," JERS, 57.

125. Miyamoto, *Social Solidarity,* 117.

126. Ibid.

127. Hoffman, "Southern Alameda County Farmers," June 6, 1945, CA Reports.

128. Ibid.

129. Interview with Kiyo Ito Kariya and Masako Tsuzuki Nakagawa, Leonia, N.J., June 14, 1988, AWC.

130. Ibid.

131. Oscar F. Hoffman, "Menlo Park—Atherton—Woodside," January 3, 1945, CA Reports.

132. Modell, "Japanese of Los Angeles," 269–72.

133. Interview with Lee Suyemoto, Newton, Mass., June 21, 1988, AWC.

134. Interview with Hiromoto Katayama, Berkeley, October 27, 1987, AWC.

135. Interview with Tomoye Nozawe Takahashi, San Francisco, November 2, 1987; notes in possession of the author.

2. From Pearl Harbor to Evacuation

1. Daniels, *Asian America*, 176.

2. Daniels, *Asian America*, 163–64.

3. Takaki, *Strangers*, 218.

4. Modell, "Japanese of Los Angeles," 340–41; the statistics are from Tupper and McReynolds, *Japan in American Public Opinion*, 283–84, and Cantril, ed., *Public Opinion*, 1081.

5. Takaki, *Strangers*, 221–23. Quote from p. 223.

6. The one biracial family I interviewed, who chose not to be identified by name, had succeeded because the white mother chose to identify with the Japanese and brought up her daughters as Japanese Americans.

7. Shibutani, "Rumors," 59.

8. Hosokawa, *Nisei*, 254. The weapons that were turned in were hunting rifles; farmers used dynamite to remove stumps.

9. Interview with Donald Nakahata, Mill Valley, Calif., May 12, 1988, AWC.

10. Shibutani, "Rumors," 58.

11. Shibutani, "Rumors," 66–67; *Nichibei Shinbun*, December 30, 1941.

12. Modell, "Japanese of Los Angeles"; see especially chap. 10.

13. Shibutani, "Rumors," 62.

14. Ibid., 61.

15. Masaoka, *They Call Me Moses Masaoka*, 65. Masaoka's autobiography, written with Bill Hosokawa, was published in 1987. Masaoka died in 1992.

16. Okihiro, *Cane Fires*, 124.

17. Daniels, *Concentration Camps, U.S.A.*, 67, 70–71; Takaki, *Strangers*, 386–91.

18. Shibutani, "Rumors," 65.

19. Daniels, *Concentration Camps, U.S.A.*, 74; Hosokawa, *Nisei*, 284.

20. The quote is from Hosokawa, *Nisei*, 291; see also Daniels, *Concentration Camps, U.S.A.*, 75–82.

21. Commission on Wartime Relocation and Internment of Civilians, *Personal Justice Denied*, 98.

22. Hosokawa, *Nisei*, 286–87.

23. Ibid., 198–99.

24. Daniels, *Asian America*, 182.

25. Hosokawa, *Nisei*, 203–5; Masaoka, *They Call Me Moses Masaoka*, 87.

26. Hosokawa, *Nisei*, 101, 290–91.

27. Masaoka, *They Call Me Moses Masaoka*, 87–93, 98.

28. Daniels, *Asian America*, 221–23; Masaoka, *They Call Me Moses Masaoka*, 91.

29. Shibutani, *Improvised News*, 150–51. Shibutani, a Nisei and JERS recorder, did a study of rumors in the California Japanese community, "Rumors in a Crisis Situation," as his M.A. thesis at the University of Chicago in 1944.

30. See Taylor, "The Federal Reserve Bank"; quotations from p. 30.

31. Interview with Kenji Fujii, Hayward, Calif., August 31, 1989; and with Tomoye Nozawe Takahashi, San Francisco, August 29, 1989.

32. Conversation with Grace Fujimoto Oshita, Salt Lake City, September 18, 1990.

33. Interview with Donald Nakahata, Mill Valley, Calif., May 12, 1988, AWC.

34. Conversation with Grace Fujimoto Oshita, Salt Lake City, September 18, 1990. Interview with Masako Tsuzuki Nakagawa, Leonia, N.J., June 14, 1988, AWC.

35. Uchida, *Desert Exile*, 60.

36. Shibutani, "Rumors," 92.

37. Oscar F. Hoffman, "San Francisco Fishing Industry," January 1945, CA Reports.

38. Oscar F. Hoffman, "San Francisco and East Bay Cities Laundry Business," January 17, 1945, CA Reports.

39. Oscar F. Hoffman, "San Francisco Retail Dry Cleaning and Dyeing Business," January 17, 1945, CA Reports.

40. Oscar F. Hoffman, "San Francisco Wholesale and Retail Art Goods Business," January 26, 1945, CA Reports.

41. Oscar F. Hoffman, "Hotel and Apartment House Business in San Francisco," March 9, 1945, CA Reports.

42. Oscar F. Hoffman, "San Mateo, Burlingame, Belmont," February 19, 1945, CA Reports.

43. *Personal Justice Denied*, 125.

44. Ibid., citing the testimony of Kinnosuke Hashimoto, New York, November 23, 1981, p. 123.

45. Interview with Hiromoto Katayama, Berkeley, October 27, 1987, AWC.

46. Oscar F. Hoffman, "Southern Alameda County Farmers," December 30, 1945, CA Reports.

47. Oscar F. Hoffman, "Alameda and East Bay," February 28, 1945, CA Reports.

48. Oscar F. Hoffman, "Japanese East Bay Floral Industry," February 16, 1945, CA Reports.

49. Oscar F. Hoffman, "Menlo Park—Atherton—Woodside," January 3, 1945, CA Reports.

50. United States Department of the Interior, *The Wartime Handling of Evacuee Property* (Washington, D.C., 1946), 3–4, as cited in Taylor, "Evacuation and Economic Loss," 163–67.

51. *Personal Justice Denied*, 133.

52. Daniels, *Concentration Camps, U.S.A.*, 83.

53. Uchida, *Desert Exile*, 58.

54. Arrington, *The Price of Prejudice*, 7–8, and "Utah's Ambiguous Reception," 92–99. See also Taylor, "Japanese Americans and Keetley Farms."

55. Interview with Nobu Miyoshi, New York, June 16, 1988, AWC.

56. Ibid.

57. Daniels, *Concentration Camps, U.S.A.*, 83–86.

58. Shibutani, *Improvised News*, 151, citing the *San Francisco Examiner*, April 12, 1942.

3. Life in a Racetrack

1. Daniels, *Concentration Camps, North America*, 87; Hosokawa, *Nisei*, 318–19.

2. Okubo, *Citizen 13660*, 54–55.

3. Uchida, *Desert Exile*, 64–67.

4. Conversation with Faith Terasawa, San Francisco, November 6, 1987; notes in possession of the author.

5. *Tanforan Totalizer*, May 23, 1942, as reported in "The First Month at the Tanforan Assembly Center for Japanese Evacuees," a preliminary report by Tamotsu Shibutani, Haruo Najima, and Tomiko Shibutani, JERS.

6. Kikuchi, *Kikuchi Diary*, 34. The history of JERS, the University of California project, is chronicled in Ichioka, *Views from Within*.

7. See the documents on this point assembled in Daniels, ed., *Archival Documents*; vol. 8 covers the Tanforan Assembly Center.

8. Miyamoto, *Social Solidarity*, xi; Modell, "Japanese of Los Angeles," 240.

9. Uchida, *Desert Exile*, 40–41.

10. Shibutani, Najima, and Shibutani, "First Month," JERS.

11. Uchida, *Desert Exile*, 70.

12. Shibutani, Najima, and Shibutani, "First Month," JERS.

13. Statement by Miné Okubo, drafted on June 4, 1988, from notes of an interview with the author held on October 4, 1987, in possession of the author. Okubo is still bitter about the effects of evacuation on her life; another brother was the first draftee from the city of Riverside, was widely honored, but then was interned at an army camp in Oklahoma. After Nisei were drafted, he was sent to Europe and air-lifted into Germany, where he was shot in the spine and liver. He never recovered from his injuries and was still in a veteran's hospital when Okubo wrote her statement.

14. Okubo, *Citizen 13660*, 35.

15. Shibutani, Najima, and Shibutani, "First Month," JERS.

16. Okubo, *Citizen 13660*, 50.

17. Shibutani, Najima, and Shibutani, "First Month," JERS.

18. Okubo, *Citizen 13660*, 63.

19. Interview with Midori Shimanouchi Lederer, New York, June 17, 1988, AWS.

20. Uchida, *Desert Exile*, 70.

21. Anonymous [name withheld from publication], "Diary," Tanforan, May–July 1942, JERS.

22. Okubo, *Citizen 13660*, 89; Shibutani, Najima, and Shibutani, "First Month," JERS.

23. John Yoshino to George A. Greene, May 18, 1942, RG 338.

24. "Mess Halls," 1942, Tanforan, JERS.

25. Uchida, *Desert Exile*, 76.

26. Shibutani, Najima, and Shibutani, "First Month," JERS.

27. "Tanforan: Visiting," May 7, 1942, JERS; Okubo, *Citizen 13660*, 79.

28. Shibutani, Najima, and Shibutani, "First Month," JERS.

29. Earle Yusa, "Internal Security Department," December 5, 1942, JERS.

30. Shibutani, Najima, and Shibutani, "First Month," JERS.

31. Uchida, *Desert Exile*, 76.

32. Earle Yusa, "Internal Security Department," December 5, 1942, JERS.

33. Uchida, *Desert Exile*, 76.

34. "Regulations Regarding Religious Practices and Assemblies," WRA, RG 338.

35. "Tanforan: Regulations," May 7, 1942, JERS.

36. Okubo, *Citizen 13660*, 87, 92–93; telephone conversation with Grace Fujimoto Oshita, Salt Lake City, September 18, 1990.

37. "House Managers," May 6–7, 1942, JERS.

38. Shibutani, Najima, and Shibutani, "First Month," JERS.

39. "House Managers," May 6–7, 1942, JERS.

40. Interview with Tad Fujita, Berkeley, October 28, 1987, AWS.

41. John Yoshino papers, June 9, 1942, RG 338.

42. Shibutani, Najima, and Shibutani, "First Month," JERS.

43. "Tanforan JACL Clique," June 1942, JERS.

44. Yoneda, *Ganbatte*, 111–19.

45. Interview with Kenji Fujii, Hayward, Calif., August 31, 1989; notes in possession of the author.

46. Yoneda, *Ganbatte*, 123.

47. "Tanforan JACL Clique," June 1942, JERS.

48. Interview with Ernest Iiyama and Chizu Kitano Iiyama, San Francisco, May 13, 1988, AWC.

49. Michio Kimutani, "Tanforan Politics," JERS; interview with Ernest Iiyama and Chizu Kitano Iiyama, May 13, 1988, AWC.

50. Kimutani, "Tanforan Politics," JERS.

51. Ibid.

52. "Tanforan Minutes of Committees," June 1 and 29, 1942, JERS.

53. Shibutani, Najima, and Shibutani, "First Month," JERS.

54. R. L. Nicholson to assembly center directors, May 31, 1942; RG 338.

55. "Instructions to Residents," July 30, 1942, JERS.

56. Telephone conversation with Grace Fujimoto Oshita, Salt Lake City, September 18, 1990.

57. Okubo, *Citizen 13660*, 54.

58. Shibutani, Najima, and Shibutani, "First Month," JERS.

59. Ibid.; Anonymous, "Family History," JERS.

60. "Report on Hospital and Health," September 15, 1942, RG 338.

61. James, *Exile Within*, 27.

62. Ibid.

63. Uchida, *Desert Exile*, 87–90.

64. Kikuchi, *Diary*, 134, 84, 243; see also Henry Tani, "The Tanforan High School," September 1942, JERS.

65. James, *Exile Within*, 30; Uchida, *Desert Exile*, 87–88; Kay Uchida and Grace Fujii, "The Preschool Program at Tanforan," late July 1942, JERS.

66. "Student Relocation," JERS; Uchida, *Desert Exile*, 85; Daniels, *Concentration Camps, North America*, 98–100.

67. Okubo, *Citizen 13660*, 92–93; Fred Hoshiyama, "Report on Recreation Program," September 1, 1942, RG 338.

68. Tomoye Takahashi, "Adult Education," June 30, 1942, RG 338.

69. Fred Hoshiyama, "Recreation," May 26, 1942, JERS; Hoshiyama, "Report on Recreation Program," September 1, 1942, RG 338.

70. July 2, 1942, RG 338.

71. Uchida, *Desert Exile,* 97.

72. Fred Hoshiyama, "Family Organization," October 1, 1942, JERS.

73. Spickard, *Mixed Blood,* 48–49. Spickard noted (p. 51) that most such marriages existed between Issei women and non-Japanese men, but that they were probably contracted when the men met the women in Japan or elsewhere. He concluded that most Issei who married out were those born before 1890, during the "restless, unsettled pioneer years." Very few of the Nisei who married out did so before World War II—3.1 percent of the men and 2.3 percent of the women; probably more would have if they had not been interned. Licenses for Caucasian-Japanese marriages were not issued legally in California at this time.

74. "Mixed Marriage Policy," July 16, 1942, JERS; Shibutani, Najima, and Shibutani, "First Month," JERS.

75. Okubo, *Citizen 13660,* 110.

76. Interview with Dave Tatsuno, San Jose, November 4, 1987, AWC.

77. Conversation with Faith Terasawa, San Francisco, November 6, 1987; notes in possession of the author. Toyo Suyemoto Kawakami, "Camp Memories," 28–29.

78. "Terminal Procedures for Closing," September 21, 1942, RG 338; "Moving to Topaz," October 9, 1942, JERS.

79. Adachi, "My Experiences in a Foreign Land," 153–55.

4. Welcome to Utah

1. Uchida, *Desert Exile,* 103–4; Anonymous [name withheld from publication], "Diary," October–November 1942, Topaz, JERS.

2. Suzuki, *Ministry,* 170.

3. Interview with Kenji Fujii, Hayward, Calif., August 31, 1989; notes in possession of the author.

4. Okubo, *Citizen 13660,* 117–20.

5. "Train Monitor and Car Capt. Suggestions," mimeographed sheet, Topaz; provided by Kenji Fujii to the author.

6. Interview with Tad Fujita, Berkeley, October 28, 1987, AWC.

7. War Relocation Authority, *Evacuated People,* table 5, page 17; *Topaz Times,* October 10, 1942; *Topaz,* 35; *Millard County Chronicle,* September 24, 1942. Figures on Santa Anita are from "The Number of Japanese Sent to Relocation Projects," December 5, 1942, JERS.

8. Interview with K. Morgan Yamanaka, San Francisco, May 11, 1988, AWC.

9. Anonymous, "Diary," October–November 1942, JERS; Topaz files, September 17, 1942, WRA, RG 210.

10. Kawakami, "Camp Memories," 27.

11. Okubo, *Citizen 13660*, 123.

12. Ken Verdoia, transcript of *Topaz*, a KUED-TV production (Salt Lake City, 1987), 23.

13. Conversation with Faith Terasawa, San Francisco, November 6, 1987.

14. Topaz files, September 17, 1942, WRA, RG 210.

15. Arrington, *Price of Prejudice*, 12; Roscoe E. Bell, "Relocation Center Life, Topaz, Utah, 1942–1945," ML.

16. Arrington, *Price of Prejudice*, 13.

17. *Millard County Chronicle*, October 15, 1942.

18. Interview by Wendy Walker with Roger Walker, January 1983, for Jane Beckwith's high school class, Delta, Utah; copy in possession of the author.

19. *Trek*, December 1942.

20. Claud H. Pratt, Ogden, Utah, "Topaz Relocation Center," April 1983, prepared for Jane Beckwith's high school class project, Delta, Utah; copy in possession of the author.

21. Uchida, *Desert Exile*, 110–11; Arrington, *Price of Prejudice*, 13.

22. Bell, "Relocation Center Life," ML.

23. As reported by Jane Beckwith, who interviewed Roper for a high school class project.

24. Verdoia, *Topaz* transcript, 25–26; Anonymous, "Diary," October–November 1942, JERS.

25. Telephone conversation with Evelyn Hodges Lewis, Wellsville, Utah, August 30, 1990.

26. Interview with Tom Kawaguchi, San Francisco, November 5, 1987, AWC.

27. Kawakami, "Camp Memories," 27.

28. Interview with Maya Nagata Aikawa, Oakland, November 4, 1987, AWC.

29. Interview with Lee Suyemoto, Newton, Mass., June 21, 1988, AWC.

30. Okubo, *Citizen 13660*, 127–32; Arrington, *Price of Prejudice*, 13. The Delta mortuary recorded 156 (including stillbirths). Okubo stated that the dead were cremated in Salt Lake City and the ashes held for burial after the war ended.

31. Uchida, *Desert Exile*, 110.

32. Topaz files, February 4, 1943, WRA, RG 210.

33. Anonymous, "Diary," JERS; Topaz files, September 17, 1942, WRA, RG 210; Yasuo William Abiko, "Central Utah War Relocation Project, Topaz Center, 1942–1945," copy of manuscript given to the author by Jane Beckwith.

34. Telephone conversation with Kenji Fujii, Hayward, February 26, 1990.

35. Comment by Jane Beckwith, Delta, July 21, 1987.

36. Arrington, *Price of Prejudice,* 43, compiled from the War Relocation Authority, *Evacuated People,* tables 3, 4, and 8. Table 37a on page 100 of *Evacuated People* lists a total of 8,232 and gives the breakdown by sex as of January 1, 1943. *The Topaz Times,* January 30, 1943, gives a slightly larger figure. Of the ten camps, only Granada was smaller, according to *Evacuated People,* 20.

37. Arrington, *Price of Prejudice,* 14.

38. Bell, "Relocation Center Life," ML; telephone conversation with Paul Bell, University Park, Pa., September 24, 1990, and with Roscoe Bell and Gladys Bell, Woodburn, Oreg., October 25, 1990.

39. Bell, "Relocation Center Life," ML.

40. Sekerak, "A Teacher at Topaz," 39; telephone conversation with Eleanor Sekerak and Emil Sekerak, Castro Valley, Calif., October 3, 1990.

41. Hochiyama, "Administration," JERS.

42. War Relocation Authority, *WRA,* 1.

43. Conversations with Paul Bell, University Park, Pa., September 24, 1990, and Eleanor Sekerak and Emil Sekerak, Castro Valley, Calif., October 3, 1990.

44. Pratt, "Utah Relocation Center." "Sox" Kitashima remembered how, in 1992, she still exchanged Christmas cards with him.

45. Hochiyama, "Administration," JERS.

46. Uchida, *Desert Exile,* 110.

47. Hochiyama, "Administration," JERS. The changed opinion of Ernst is documented in Hoffman's Community Analysis Newsletter No. 7 for week ending June 3, 1944, CA Reports.

48. Conversation with Eleanor Sekerak, Castro Valley, Calif., October 3, 1990.

49. Information on Ernst and Hoffman came from conversations with Roscoe Bell, Woodburn, Oreg., October 25, 1990, and Eleanor Sekerak, Castro Valley, Calif., October 3, 1990, and also from a letter to the author from Oscar Hoffman of Abilene, Kans., October 10, 1990.

50. Arrington, *Price of Prejudice,* 15.

51. Conversation with Eleanor Sekerak, Castro Valley, Calif., October 3, 1990, and letter from Oscar Hoffman, Abilene, Kans., October 10, 1990.

52. Hochiyama, "Administration," JERS.

53. Pratt, "Topaz Relocation Center."

54. Ibid.

55. Fumi Hayashi appended her comments to a rough draft of this manuscript, returned to me in October 1989, and Michi Kobi commu-

nicated her sentiments to me in a letter at the same time. Hoffman's letter of October 10, 1990, contained his assessment of the role. Neither Hoffman nor his predecessor, anthropologist Weston LaBarre, had misgivings about undertaking the position of community analyst, but later scholars have tended to see the analysts as "company spies," which many may have been, however inadvertently. See Oscar F. Hoffman, "Closing Report of the Community Analysis Section," September 1, 1945, CA Reports.

56. "Welcome to Topaz," printed at Topaz in 1942.

57. Section 3, "The Profile of the Community," from Hoffman, "Closing Report," September 1, 1945, CA Reports.

58. Verdoia, *Topaz* transcript, 30.

59. Conversation with Roscoe Bell, Woodburn, Oreg., October 25, 1990.

60. Papanikolas, *Peoples of Utah,* 336–37; Masaoka, *They Call Me Moses Masaoka,* chaps. 1–2.

61. Papanikolas, *Peoples of Utah,* 339.

62. Ibid., 337–40.

63. Ibid., 352.

64. Ibid., 343, 350, 352.

65. Conversation with Masi Nihei, San Francisco, September 1, 1989.

66. Papanikolas, *Peoples of Utah,* 352–53.

67. Ibid., 354–55. Eleanor Roosevelt persuaded the president to allow families to withdraw $100 a month, and this subsidy sustained Alice Kasai and her children.

68. Papanikolas, *Peoples of Utah,* 357.

69. In the Delta area water for irrigation was divided at the first of the year on the basis of a "call" system. The total amount available was divided on the basis of the number of shares an individual or company held. The water was stored in reservoirs until it was needed and then allotted by acre-feet to the shareholders. Topaz was supplied by the Abraham and Deseret Water Company shares. Telephone conversation with Roger Walker, Delta, Utah, November 27, 1990.

70. Interview by Jane Beckwith with Homer U. Petersen, Delta, Utah, May 1983; copy in possession of the author; *Millard County Chronicle,* May 28 and June 25, 1942.

71. Arrington, *Price of Prejudice,* 11; *Millard County Chronicle,* June 25 and August 2, 1942.

72. Verdoia, *Topaz* transcript, 19–20.

73. *Millard County Chronicle,* June 25 and August 6, 1942.

74. Anonymous, "Diary," October 2, 1942, JERS.

75. Suzuki, *Ministry,* 19.

76. Topaz files, September 11, 1942, WRA, RG 210.

77. Bell, "Relocation Center Life," ML.

78. Okihiro, *Cane Fires,* 214–24.

79. Bell, "Relocation Center Life," ML.

80. Arrington, *Price of Prejudice,* 14.

81. Topaz files, September 26, 1942, WRA, RG 210.

82. Anonymous, "Diary," October 2, 1942, JERS.

83. O'Brien, *College Nisei.*

84. War Relocation Authority, *WRA,* 30–31; Arrington, *Price of Prejudice,* 17.

85. Papanikolas, *Peoples of Utah,* 358.

86. Topaz files, October 7, 1942, WRA, RG 210; Ruth Griffin, "Relocation," *Trek,* June 1943, ML.

87. Topaz Files, October 7, 1942, WRA, RG 210.

88. War Relocation Authority, *WRA,* 37.

89. See Taylor, "Leaving the Camps," 4.

90. Drinnon, *Keeper of Concentration Camps,* 51.

91. Abiko, "Central Utah."

92. War Relocation Authority, *WRA,* 51–53; Warren Watanabe, "First Annual Report—September 1942–September 1943," November 20, 1943, JERS; and Drinnon, *Keeper of Concentration Camps,* 50–51.

93. Arrington, *Price of Prejudice,* 18.

94. "Relocation," *Trek,* June 1943, ML; Taylor, "Leaving the Camps."

95. Interview with Jane Beckwith, Delta, Utah, July 21, 1987; quotation from the *Millard County Chronicle,* October 15, 1942.

96. Jane Beckwith recalled that Yasuda paid $52 as monthly rent for himself and his family.

97. Anonymous, "Diary," October 2–December 9, 1942, JERS.

98. Watanabe, "First Annual Report," November 20, 1943, JERS.

99. *Salt Lake Tribune,* October 5, 1943.

100. Interview with Harry H. L. Kitano, Los Angeles, September 20, 1987, AWC.

101. George Sugihara, "Survey of Seasonal Work Leaves from Topaz," October 9–November 15, 1943, JERS.

102. War Relocation Authority, *WRA,* 52; Daniels, *Concentration Camps, U.S.A.,* 110–11; Drinnon, *Keeper of Concentration Camps,* 51.

103. Oscar F. Hoffman, "Resident Attitudes Toward Relocation," February 1, 1944, CA Reports.

5. The Jewel of the Desert

1. Warren Watanabe, "First Annual Report—September 1942–September 1943," November 20, 1943, JERS.

2. *Trek,* December 1942, 8.

3. James, *Exile Within,* 8.

4. Ibid., 38–41.

5. Topaz files, October 11, 1942, WRA, RG 210.

6. Uchida, *Desert Exile,* 116–20. Quotations from pages 117–18 and 120.

7. *Trek,* December 1942, p. 9.

8. Claud H. Pratt, Ogden, Utah, "Topaz Relocation Center," April 1983, prepared for Jane Beckwith's high school class project, Delta, Utah; copy in possession of the author; *Millard County Chronicle,* October 1, 1942.

9. Arrington, *Price of Prejudice,* 32.

10. *Trek,* December 1942, p. 9.

11. "Education in Topaz," Topaz files, January 1, 1944, WRA, RG 210.

12. Uchida, *Desert Exile,* 125–26.

13. "Education in Topaz," Topaz files, January 1, 1944, WRA, RG 210.

14. Ibid., 43–45.

15. Russell Bankston, "Annual Cabinet Meeting at Topaz," Historical Section Topaz, Project Report H433, 67/14 H. 2.07, as cited in James, *Exile Within,* 51.

16. "Education in Topaz," Topaz files, January 1, 1944, WRA, RG 210.

17. Sekerak, "A Teacher at Topaz," 38–43.

18. Paul Bell, "Views From an Inside Outsider," August 16, 1980, delivered to a reunion of the Class of 1945 in San Francisco, August 16, 1980. Copy given to the author by Paul Bell; telephone conversation with Paul Bell, University Park, Pa., September 25, 1990.

19. Note from Fumi Hayashi, Berkeley, undated, October 1989.

20. Kitano, *Japanese Americans: Evolution of a Subculture,* 38.

21. James, *Exile Within,* 46–61.

22. Miyamoto, *Social Solidarity,* 51.

23. Ibid., 63–65.

24. Conversation with Grace Fujimoto Oshita, Salt Lake City, September 10, 1990.

25. Topaz files, April 7, 1943, WRA, RG 210.

26. Kitano, *Japanese Americans: Evolution of a Subculture,* 36–37; Takaki, *Strangers,* 396.

27. Note from Fumi Hayashi, Berkeley, undated, October 1989; conversation with Grace Fujimoto Oshita, Salt Lake City, October 10, 1990.

28. James, *Exile Within,* 74.

29. Ibid., citing examples from R. A. Bankston, "First High School Commencement," Topaz Reports Division, Project Report H 441, RG 210.

30. Statements written by Hisako Hibi, San Francisco, given to the author November 2, 1987; in possession of the author. Deborah Gesensway and Mindy Roseman have compiled a moving collection of camp art, much of it from Topaz, in *Beyond Words*.

31. Topaz files, May 1, 1943, WRA, RG 210.

32. Interview with Abu Keikoan Guilday, Sacramento, May 14, 1988, AWC.

33. Interview with Maya Nagata Aikawa, Oakland, November 4, 1987, AWC.

34. Interview with Michiko Okamoto, New York, October 6, 1987, AWC.

35. Interview with Shigeki J. Sugiyama, Washington, D.C., June 9, 1988, AWC.

36. Ibid.

37. Interview with Robert Utsumi, San Francisco, May 11, 1988, AWC.

38. Interview with Lee Suyemoto, Newton, Mass., June 21, 1988, AWC. See also Kitano, "Japanese-American Crime and Delinquency," 161–70.

39. Kitano, *Japanese Americans: Evolution of a Subculture,* 36.

40. Daniels, *Asian America,* 234–35.

41. Ibid.

42. War Relocation Authority, *WRA,* 83.

43. Ibid., 86–87; Arrington, *Price of Prejudice,* 26–27.

44. War Relocation Authority, *WRA,* 86–87.

45. Ibid., 90; Watanabe, "First Annual Report," November 20, 1942, JERS; Arrington, *Price of Prejudice,* 26.

46. Weglyn, *Years of Infamy,* 120–21.

47. Daniels, *Asian America,* 235.

48. Watanabe, "First Annual Report," November 20, 1942, JERS.

49. Ibid.

50. Russell A. Bankston, "The Wakasa Incident," May 10, 1943, Topaz files, WRA, RG 210.

51. Telephone conversation with Evelyn Hodges Lewis, Wellsville, Utah, August 30, 1990.

52. Minutes of the Community Council, April 15, 1943, JERS.

53. Ibid.; *Topaz Times,* April 13, 1943.

54. Minutes of the Community Council, April 15, 1943, JERS.

55. Bankston, "Wakasa Incident," May 10, 1943, Topaz files, WRA, RG 210; Daniels, *Asian America,* 228–31; *Topaz Times,* April 12, 1943.

56. *Topaz Times,* April 12, 1943.

57. Minutes of the Community Council, April 16, 1943, JERS.

58. *Topaz Times,* April 12, 1943.

59. Ibid., April 16, 17, and 20, 1943.

60. Minutes of the Community Council, April 20, 1943, JERS.

61. Ibid.

62. Weglyn, *Years of Infamy,* 312.

63. *Topaz Times,* April 13 and 20, 1943.

64. Ken Verdoia, transcript of *Topaz,* a KUED-TV production (Salt Lake City, 1987). Verdoia states that this information came from the National Archives but gives no specific reference for it. He also states that the sentry testified at the court martial that he intended the shot that killed Wakasa as a warning shot. See pp. 33–34.

65. *Topaz Times,* April 22, 1943.

66. *Topaz Times,* April 20, 1943.

67. *Topaz Times,* April 16, 1943.

68. Okubo, *Citizen 13660,* 180.

69. Bankston, "Wakasa Incident," May 10, 1943, Topaz files, WRA, RG 210; Uchida, *Desert Exile,* 140.

70. Bankston, "Wakasa Incident," May 10, 1943, Topaz files, WRA, RG 210. The subject of the dog was widely disputed; Roscoe Bell thought Wakasa was walking a dog, but Bell's wife Gladys said he "liked to walk the dogs of the city" and was walking about five when he was killed. Roscoe Bell, "Relocation Center Life," and Gladys K. Bell, "Memories of Topaz, Japanese War Relocation Center, 1942 to 1945," ML.

71. Interview with Karl Akiya, New York, June 16 and 18, 1988; Akiya, testimony to the Commission on Wartime Relocation and Internment of Civilians, November 23, 1981, New York City, copy in the possession of the author.

72. Conversation with Evelyn Hodges Lewis, Wellsville, Utah, August 30, 1990.

73. Interview with George Gentoku Shimamoto, Fort Lee, N.J., October 5, 1987, AWC.

74. Drinnon, *Keeper of Concentration Camps,* 6.

75. Weglyn, *Years of Infamy,* 312.

76. Uchida, *Desert Exile,* 139–40.

77. Okubo, *Citizen 13660,* 180.

78. Conversation with Roscoe Bell, Woodburn, Oreg., September 25, 1990. Roscoe Bell, "Relocation Center Life," and Gladys Bell, "Memories of Topaz," ML.

79. Michi Kobi (Michiko Okamoto), interviewed in Verdoia, *Topaz* transcript, 32.

80. Hoffman to Myer, July 25, 1944, as cited in Drinnon, *Keeper of Concentration Camps,* 281. Drinnon incorrectly called Hoffman Louis instead of Luther.

81. Conversation with Jane Beckwith, Delta, July 21, 1987.

82. See Weglyn, *Years of Infamy,* 312 n.

83. Drinnon, *Keeper of Concentration Camps,* 281; Drinnon cited Jackman's article, "Collective Protest in Relocation Centers," *American Journal of Sociology* 63 (November 1957): 264–72.

84. Edward Ennis, interview in Verdoia, *Topaz* transcript, 35.

85. Daniels, *Asian America,* 261.

86. War Relocation Authority, *WRA,* 53–56.

87. Weglyn, *Years of Infamy,* 138.

88. Daniels, *Asian America,* 262–64; Russell Bankston, "Registration at Topaz," March 10, 1943, Topaz files, WRA, RG 210.

89. *Personal Justice Denied,* 195; see also War Relocation Authority, *WRA,* table 3, p. 199.

90. Bankston, "Registration at Topaz," March 10, 1943, Topaz files, WRA, RG 210.

91. Watanabe, "First Annual Report," November 20, 1943, JERS; Arrington, *Price of Prejudice,* 19–20; War Relocation Authority, *WRA,* table 3, p. 199; Bankston, "Registration at Topaz," March 10, 1943, Topaz files, WRA, RG 210.

92. Oscar F. Hoffman and Charles Ernst to Dillon Myer, October 12, 1943, CA Reports.

93. Interview with K. Morgan Yamanaka, San Francisco, May 11, 1988, and Mill Valley, Calif., March 9, 1990, AWC.

94. Arrington, *Price of Prejudice,* 20–21; Bankston, "Registration at Topaz," March 10, 1943, WRA, RG 210.

95. Interview with William Kochiyama, New York, October 6, 1987, AWC.

96. Drinnon, *Keeper of Concentration Camps,* 92.

97. Telephone conversation with Evelyn Hodges Lewis, Wellsville, Utah, August 30, 1990.

98. Watanabe, "First Annual Report," November 20, 1943, JERS.

99. Fumi Hayashi commented upon reading this section, "I think that it was a miracle that there wasn't more drinking and shouting in Topaz where the folks had so little to do and so little to console them." Her remarks say much about the persistence of the social mores of prewar Japanese America.

100. Hoffman and Charles F. Ernst to Myer, October 12, 1943, CA Reports.

101. Conversation with Roscoe Bell, Woodburn, Oreg., September 25, 1990.

102. Interview with Abu Keikoan Guilday, Sacramento, May 14, 1988, AWC.

103. Bankston, "Registration at Topaz," March 10, 1943, WRA, RG 210.

104. Kessler, "Fettered Freedoms."

105. Fumi Hayashi's comments on the rough draft of my interview with her, October 1989.

106. Oscar F. Hoffman, "Notes on Some Religious Cults at Topaz," June 15, 1946, CA Reports.

107. Suzuki, *Ministry,* 170–78, 191; Hoffman, "Notes on Some Religious Cults at Topaz," June 15, 1946, CA Reports.

108. See the cover of *Trek,* December 1942; Okubo, *Citizen 13660,* 156.

109. Interview with Tad Fujita, Berkeley, October 28, 1987, AWC; and Suzuki, *Ministry,* 189–90.

110. Hoffman, "Notes on Some Religious Cults at Topaz," June 15, 1946, CA Reports.

111. Suzuki, *Ministry,* 179–80; Roscoe Bell, "Relocation Center Life," ML; Arrington, *Price of Prejudice,* 33.

112. Arrington, *Price of Prejudice,* 22–23.

113. Russell Bankston, "Organization and Development of the Topaz Consumer Cooperative Enterprise," JERS; interview with Dave Tatsuno, San Jose, November 4, 1987, AWC.

114. Interview with Dave Tatsuno, San Jose, November 4, 1987; "Background to Topaz Films," statement prepared by Dave Tatsuno, in the possession of the author.

115. Statement by Chiyoko Yano and Isao James Yano, Berkeley, August 22, 1988, in possession of author; interview with Kazu Iijima, New York, October 5, 1987, AWC.

116. *Topaz Times,* April 1, 1943.

117. Conversation with Grace Fujimoto Oshita, Salt Lake City, January 25, 1993.

118. Reports from Topaz files, 1942–43, WRA, RG 210.

119. Conversation with Tom Kawaguchi, San Francisco, March 7, 1989; interview with Kazu Iijima, New York, October 5, 1987, AWC.

120. Drinnon, *Keeper of Concentration Camps,* 103–4.

121. Watanabe, "First Annual Report," November 20, 1943, RG 210.

122. Hoffman, "Notes on Some Religious Cults at Topaz," June 15, 1946, CA Reports.

123. Notes of interview with Faith Terasawa, San Francisco, November 6, 1987, in the possession of the author; interview with Kazu Iijima, New York, October 5, 1987, AWC.

124. Topaz files, November 16, 1942, WRA, RG 210. The complaints were listed in a grievance letter sent by the medical staff to the administration, dated November 16, 1942; the minutes of the Hospital Committee, January 20, 1943, also explain the situation. Both documents were given me by Kenji Fujii.

125. Topaz files, March 31, 1943, WRA, RG 210.

126. Interview with "Harry Ando," cited in Spickard, *Mixed Blood*, 52.

127. Several interviewees mention the sexual problem, and so does George Sugihara in "An Analysis of Delinquent Problems, Their Possible Causes and Cures," April 7, 1943, JERS; Bill Kochiyama made some reference to illegal drinking, as did Paul Bell. A report in the Topaz files, December 4, 1943, WRA, RG 210, refers to gambling.

128. Russell Bankston, "Labor Trouble in Topaz," October 2, 1943, JERS; Topaz files, November 5, 1943, WRA, RG 210; conversation with Roscoe Bell, Woodburn, Oreg., September 25, 1990.

129. Watanabe, "First Annual Report," November 20, 1943, WRA, RG 210.

6. Dissension, Departure, and Grim Determination

1. Daniels, Introduction, 33.

2. On the instructions given the community analysts, see Suzuki, "Anthropologists."

3. Letter from Oscar F. Hoffman, Abilene, Kans., October 10, 1990. Hoffman, who was ninety-four when he wrote to the author, commented that discussing his role at Topaz made him feel as if he were "already facing judgement day."

4. Oscar F. Hoffman, "Closing Report of the Community Analysis Section," September 1, 1945, CA Reports.

5. Oscar F. Hoffman, "Notes on Some Religious Cults at Topaz," June 15, 1946, CA Reports.

6. Topaz files, April 8, 1944, WRA, RG 210.

7. Topaz files, March 25, 1944, WRA, RG 210.

8. Topaz files, April 22, 1944, WRA, RG 210.

9. Hoffman to Dillon S. Myer, Washington, D.C., Newsletter No. 18, for the week ending October 28, 1944, CA Reports.

10. Newsletter No. 10, for the week ending July 29, 1944, CA Reports.

11. Topaz files, December 31, 1944, WRA, RG 210.

12. Ibid; James, *Exile Within*, 140–41.

13. Hiro Katayama, "The Reinstitution of Selective Service," prepared for Oscar F. Hoffman, to Dillon S. Myer, April 10, 1944, CA Reports.

14. Daniels, *Concentration Camps, North America,* 123.

15. Topaz files, January 20, 1944, WRA, RG 210; Katayama, "The Reinstitution of Selective Service," April 10, 1944, CA Reports.

16. Katayama, "The Reinstitution of Selective Service," April 10, 1944, CA Reports. Katayama estimated that 87 percent of the population favored this "conservative" approach, while only 13 percent supported more radical action.

17. Newsletter No. 2, for the week ending March 26, 1944, CA Reports.

18. Ibid.

19. Katayama, "The Reinstitution of Selective Service," April 10, 1944, CA Reports. Although these phrases originated in Hawaiian pidgin, many of the Nisei I interviewed reported their widespread use at Topaz; especially interviews with Mari Eijima, New York, October 5, 1987, and Fumi Hayashi, Berkeley, October 28, 1987.

20. Katayama, "The Reinstitution of Selective Service," April 10, 1944, CA Reports.

21. Hoffman, "Evaluating the Community Council's Role," April 3, 1944, CA Reports.

22. The ACLU was divided over the proper response to Japanese American internment. Peter Irons, who used the Freedom of Information Act to discover that the War Department had deliberately presented tainted records to the Supreme Court and suppressed crucial evidence, stated, "Leaders of the American Civil Liberties Union bear much of the blame for the outcome of the Japanese American cases." He found that ACLU lawyers were personally so loyal to Franklin D. Roosevelt that the National Board refused to challenge the constitutionality of Executive Order 9066, thus crippling the presentation of appeals to the Supreme Court. Irons, *Justice at War,* vii-xi.

23. Interview with Tom Kawaguchi, San Francisco, November 5, 1987, AWC.

24. Oscar F. Hoffman, Weekly Trend Report No. 23, for the week ending December 8, 1944, CA Reports.

25. Hoffman, Weekly Trend Report No. 24, for the week ending December 15, 1944, CA Reports.

26. Topaz files, December 3, 1944, WRA, RG 210.

27. Interview with Tom Kawaguchi, San Francisco, November 5, 1987, AWC.

28. Interview with Kenji Fujii, Hayward, Calif., August 31, 1989; notes in possession of the author.

29. Interview with Tad Hayashi, Berkeley, October 28, 1987, AWC.

30. Interview with Tomoye Nozawe Takahashi, San Francisco, August 29, 1989; notes in possession of the author.

31. Oscar F. Hoffman, Newsletter No. 6, for the week ending May 20, 1944, CA Reports; Topaz files, May 19 and Supplementary Newsletter, July 5, 1944, WRA, RG 210.

32. Minutes of a meeting between the Hospital Committee, headed by Kenji Fujii, and the assistant project directors, James Hughes and Lorne W. Bell, January 20, 1943; given to the author by Kenji Fujii.

33. Newsletter No. 9, for the week ending July 24, 1944, CA Reports.

34. Project Director Reports to Myer, Topaz files, September 22–30, 1944, JERS.

35. Newsletter No. 10, for the week ending July 29, 1944, dated August 10, 1944, CA Reports.

36. Newsletter No. 11, for the week ending August 12, 1944, CA Reports.

37. Newsletter No. 12, for the week ending August 26, 1944, CA Reports.

38. Newsletter No. 13, for the week ending September 9, 1944, and Newsletter No. 14, for the week ending September 19, 1944, CA Reports.

39. Newsletter No. 10, for the week ending July 29, 1944, CA Reports.

40. Newsletter No. 17, for the week ending October 21, 1944, and Newsletter No. 19, for the week ending November 4, 1944, CA Reports.

41. Oscar F. Hoffman, "Evaluating the Community Council's Role," Trend Report No. 40, for the week ending April 3, 1944, CA Reports.

42. Weglyn, *Years of Infamy,* 160–63. The strike was the beginning of serious trouble at Tule; within a month the army had been called in and the camp placed under martial law. Strikebreakers were eventually found, housed outside Tule Lake, and paid a dollar an hour. Topaz did not participate.

43. Hoffman, "Closing Report of the Community Analysis Section," n.d. (1945), CA Reports.

44. Ibid., 13–17; Project Director Reports to Myer, Topaz files, September 22, 1944, JERS.

45. Roscoe Bell to Myer, Topaz files, July 30, 1945, JERS.

46. Topaz files, December 31, 1944, WRA, RG 210.

47. If Japan had wanted to help its interned nationals, it could have used the American prisoners of war held in Japan as leverage. It did not; in fact, one former Nisei resident recalled that many former internees refused to greet Prince Akihito when he visited New York City years after the war—as an act of symbolic protest against the way Japan had aban-

doned them in their time of need. They did not wish that Tokyo had retaliated against American prisoners, only that it might have protested the treatment of the Issei. The situation of prisoners of war in Japan was far worse than that of the interned Japanese Americans, but the reasons for their incarceration were also vastly different.

48. Hoffman, "Closing Report of the Community Analysis Section," September 1945, CA Reports.

49. Interview with George Gentoku Shimamoto, New York, October 5, 1987, AWC; and Hoffman, "The New Council at Topaz," Trend Report No. 28, for the week ending December 28, 1944, CA Reports.

50. Sady, "Council History," CA Reports.

51. Trend Report No. 27, for the week ending January 3, and Trend Report No. 28, for the week ending January 6, 1945, JERS.

52. Daniels, *Concentration Camps, North America,* 138, 140–43; Irons, *Justice at War,* 99–103. Fred Korematsu, the subject of another landmark Supreme Court case, was also interned at Topaz after his conviction for refusing to obey the order to evacuate the West Coast. Unlike Endo, he applied for resettlement; in December he was working in Detroit, having been granted indefinite leave. Irons, *Justice at War,* 312.

53. Oscar F. Hoffman to Myer, Trend Report No. 25, for the week ending December 18, 1944, JERS.

54. Oscar F. Hoffman, "Resident Attitudes Toward Relocation," February 1, 1944, CA Reports.

55. Ibid.

56. Ibid.

57. Ibid.

58. War Relocation Authority, *Evacuated People,* 31.

59. Oscar F. Hoffman to Myer, Trend Report No. 22, November 21 and 25, 1944, JERS.

60. Weekly Trend Report No. 22, for the week ending November 25, 1944, CA Reports.

61. Newsletter No. 5, for the week ending May 6, 1944, CA Reports.

62. Oscar F. Hoffman, "Statement by Mr. S, a Resident Leader in Community Enterprises, on the History of Factionalism in His Organization," March 4, 1944, CA Reports.

63. Newsletter No. 4, for the week ending May 1, 1944, CA Reports.

64. Ibid.

65. Hoffman, "Closing Report," September 1945, CA Reports.

66. Newsletter No. 7, for the week ending June 3, 1944, CA Reports.

67. Newsletter No. 12, for the week ending August 26, 1944, CA Reports.

68. Newsletter No. 13, for the week ending September 9, 1944, CA Reports.

69. Newsletter No. 15, for the week ending October 7, 1944, CA Reports.

70. Weekly Trend Report No. 24, for the week ending December 9, 1944, CA Reports.

71. Oscar F. Hoffman, "Interview with Some Resident Teachers," Weekly Trend Report No. 1, for the week ending April 11, 1944, CA Reports.

72. Ibid.

73. Interview with Lee Suyemoto, Newton, Mass., June 21, 1988, AWC.

74. Oscar F. Hoffman, "Interview with Reverend T. Relative to the School Situation," May 24, 1944, CA Reports. James, *Exile Within*, 141, noted that resistance was "on the rise" in schools in all the camps in 1944, but apparently the technique of boycotting classes was most common in Topaz. James stated, "In short, students made it known that they were part of the politics of education in the camps. They sometimes drew the line and resisted openly when they did not like how they were being treated."

75. James, *Exile Within*, 45; Eleanor Sekerak vehemently denied that James's characterization applied to Topaz. She herself was scrupulously fair, as her former students have testified, and she said there was neither the turnover nor the turmoil that Hoffman reported. Conversation with Eleanor Sekerak, Castro Valley, Calif., October 3, 1990.

76. Oscar F. Hoffman, "Interview with Students at Topaz," Weekly Trend Report No. 1, for the week ending April 11, 1944, CA Reports.

77. Oscar F. Hoffman, "Thoughts of a High School Senior," April 26, 1944, CA Reports.

78. Of those I interviewed, Lee Suyemoto, Michiko Okamoto, Maya Nagata, and Bob Utsumi were very critical. Harry Kitano had high praise for Eleanor Gerard Sekerak, and Shigeki Sugiyama and Fumi Hayashi were relatively uncritical. Glenn Kumekawa remarked that in a sense, the students taught one another. Interview with Glenn Kumekawa, Wakefield, R.I., June 20, 1988; notes in the possession of the author.

79. Hoffman, Community Analysis Newsletter No. 4, April 22, 1944, CA Reports.

80. Oscar F. Hoffman, "Interview with the Student Relocation Counselor," April 26, 1944, CA Reports.

81. James, *Exile Within*, 129–31.

82. Newsletter No. 5, for the week ending May 6, 1944, CA Reports.

83. Oscar F. Hoffman, "Student Morale at Topaz," May 17, 1944, CA Reports; telephone conversation with Eleanor Sekerak, Castro Valley, Calif., January 29, 1993.

84. Hoffman, "Student Morale at Topaz," May 17, 1944, CA Reports.

85. Newsletter No. 9, for the week ending July 24, 1944, CA Reports.

86. Newsletter No. 10, for the week ending July 29, 1944, CA Reports.

87. Newsletter No. 12, for the week ending August 26, 1944, CA Reports.

88. Oscar F. Hoffman, "Profiles of the Centers: Central Utah," a paper given at a Community Analysis Conference, Denver, Colo., in "Monthly Narrative Report," September 30, 1944, CA Reports.

89. Newsletter No. 6, for the week ending May 20, 1944, CA Reports.

90. Hoffman, "Closing Report," September 1945, CA Reports.

91. Oscar F. Hoffman, "The School Situation at Topaz," June 17, 1944, CA Reports.

92. Newsletter No. 7, for the week ending June 3, 1944, CA Reports.

93. Weekly Trend Report No. 24, December 15, 1944, CA Reports.

94. Hoffman, "Interview with Rev. S.," October 11, 1944, CA Reports.

95. Ibid.

96. Weekly Trend Report No. 21, for the week ending November 19, 1944, CA Reports.

97. Newsletter No. 18, for the week ending November 3, 1944, CA Reports.

98. Sawada, "After the Camps."

99. Weekly Trend Report No. 20, for the week ending November 15, 1944, CA Reports.

100. Oscar F. Hoffman, "Atomization of Topaz Community," November 24, 1944, CA Reports.

101. Oscar F. Hoffman, "Relocation Prospects as of November 15, 1944," November 29, 1944, CA Reports.

102. Weekly Trend Report No. 25, for the week ending December 21, 1944, CA Reports.

103. Weekly Trend Report No. 26, for the week ending December 28, 1944, CA Reports.

7. An End and a Beginning

1. Oscar F. Hoffman, Weekly Trend Report No. 23, for the week ending December 8, 1944, CA Reports; Daniels, *Concentration Camps, North America,* 157. The announcement appeared in the *New York Times* on December 17, 1944.

2. Irons, *Justice at War,* 344–45.

3. Topaz files, December 27, 1944, WRA, RG 210.

4. Oscar F. Hoffman to Myer, Weekly Trend Report No. 57, for the week ending July 19, 1945, CA Reports.

5. Topaz files, January 18, 1945, WRA, RG 210.

6. Weekly Trend Report No. 26, for the week ending December 28, 1944, CA Reports.

7. Weekly Trend Report No. 27, for the week ending December 30, 1944, received January 5, 1945, CA Reports.

8. Weekly Trend Report No. 39, for the week ending March 27, 1945, JERS.

9. Weekly Trend Report No. 27, for the week ending December 30, 1944, CA Reports.

10. Weekly Trend Report No. 29, for the week ending January 18, 1945, CA Reports.

11. Ibid.

12. Ibid.

13. Weekly Trend Report No. 28, for the week ending January 11, 1945, CA Reports.

14. Ibid.

15. Topaz files, January 1, 1945: a series of letters and mimeographed forms regarding relocated residents from Luther Hoffman to WRA field offices, WRA, RG 210.

16. Topaz files, February 15, 1945, WRA, RG 210.

17. Drinnon, *Keeper of Concentration Camps,* 68. Drinnon considered the sign an example of Nisei self-hatred. I think that even though it may seem obsequious, it was more likely intended as a compliment, one that—with the passage of years—seems misguided as well as ironic.

18. Topaz files, February 26, 1945, WRA, RG 210.

19. Drinnon, *Keeper of Concentration Camps,* 163–66.

20. Weekly Trend Report No. 33, for the week ending February 14, 1945, CA Reports.

21. Weekly Trend Report No. 29, for the week ending January 18, 1945, CA; statement written by Chiyoko Yano, Berkeley, August 22, 1988, in the possession of the author.

22. Weekly Trend Report No. 33, for the week ending February 14, 1945, CA Reports.

23. Weekly Trend Report No. 32, for the week ending February 9, 1945, CA Reports.

24. Daniels, *Concentration Camps, North America,* 167.

25. Weekly Trend Report No. 34, for the week ending February 27, 1945, JERS.

26. Topaz files, March 21, 1945, WRA, RG 210.

27. Weekly Trend Report No. 40, for the week ending March 31, 1945, CA Reports.

28. Weekly Trend Report No. 33, for the week ending February 10, 1945, CA Reports.

29. Weekly Trend Report No. 34, for the week ending February 17, 1945, CA Reports.

30. Ibid.

31. Conversation with Clifford Uyeda, San Francisco, September 14, 1990; Suzuki, *Ministry,* 43 n. 11.

32. Topaz files, April 16, 1945, WRA, RG 210.

33. Weekly Trend Report No. 45, for the week ending May 5, 1945, CA Reports.

34. Weekly Trend Report No. 37, for the week ending March 10, 1945, CA Reports.

35. Ibid.

36. Weekly Trend Report No. 38, for the week ending March 17, 1945, CA Reports.

37. Weekly Trend Report No. 39, for the week ending March 24, 1945, CA Reports.

38. Weekly Trend Report No. 40, for the week ending March 31, 1945, CA Reports.

39. Hosokawa, *Nisei,* 437.

40. Girdner and Loftis, *Great Betrayal,* 389–93; Daniels, *Concentration Camps, U.S.A.,* 159.

41. Weekly Trend Report No. 31, for the week ending January 27, 1945, CA Reports.

42. Daniels, *Concentration Camps, North America,* 158.

43. Shibutani, *Improvised News,* 70.

44. Weekly Trend Report No. 41, for the week ending April 7, 1945, and Weekly Trend Report No. 42, for the week ending April 14, 1945, CA Reports.

45. Weekly Trend Report No. 43, "Dissemination of Information on Post-evacuation Policies and Procedures," for the week ending April 21, 1945, CA Reports.

46. Weekly Trend Report No. 40, for the week ending March 31, and Weekly Trend Report No. 43, for the week ending April 21, 1945, CA Reports.

47. Weekly Trend Report No. 44, for the week ending April 28, 1945, CA Reports.

48. Weekly Trend Report No. 45, for the week ending May 5, 1945, CA Reports.

49. Weekly Trend Report No. 41, for the week ending April 7, 1945, CA Reports.

50. Weekly Trend Report No. 45, for the week ending May 5, 1945, CA Reports.

51. Weekly Trend Report No. 46, for the week ending May 12, 1945, CA Reports.

52. Weekly Trend Report No. 48, for the week ending June 19, 1945; Weekly Trend Report No. 51, for the week ending June 16, 1945, CA Reports.

53. Oscar F. Hoffman, "Special Report of Nisei Exploring Resettlement Opportunities in San Francisco Bay Area—Jobs or Business, in Particular a House," May 25, 1959, CA Reports.

54. Weekly Trend Report No. 47, for the week ending May 19, 1945, CA Reports.

55. Weekly Trend Report No. 31, for the week ending January 27, 1945, CA Reports.

56. Weekly Trend Report No. 49, for the week ending June 2, 1945, CA Reports.

57. Acting director Roscoe Bell to Myer, Director's file, July 30 and August 11, 1945, JERS.

58. Weekly Trend Report No. 50, for the week ending June 9, 1945, CA Reports.

59. Weekly Trend Report No. 52, for the week ending June 23, 1945; Weekly Trend Report No. 53, for the week ending June 30, 1945; Weekly Trend Report No. 54, for the week ending July 7, 1945, CA Reports.

60. Weekly Trend Report No. 56, for the week ending July 21, 1945, CA Reports.

61. Hosokawa, *JACL,* 259–62.

62. Weekly Trend Report No. 55, for the week ending July 14, 1945, CA Reports.

63. Hosokawa, *JACL,* 259–62; Roscoe Bell to Myer, July 30, 1945, Topaz files, JERS.

64. Weekly Trend Report No. 56, for the week ending July 21, 1945, CA Reports; Roscoe Bell to Myer, July 30, 1945, Topaz files, JERS.

65. Roscoe Bell to Myer, August 11, 1945, Topaz files, JERS.

66. Weekly Trend Report No. 56, for the week ending July 21, 1945, CA Reports.

67. Weekly Trend Report No. 58, for the week ending August 4, 1945, CA Reports.

68. Oscar F. Hoffman, "Closing Report of the Community Analysis Section," September 1, 1945, CA Reports.

69. Director's report to Myer, September 5, 1945, JERS.

70. Topaz files, "Project Director's Final Report," December 1, 1946, WRA, RG 210; Luther Hoffman to Myer, September 5, October 1, 16, November 5, 1945, JERS.

71. Shibutani, *Improvised News,* 152.

72. Topaz files, "Project Director's Final Report," December 1, 1946, WRA, RG 210; Luther Hoffman to Myer, October 16, 25, 1946, JERS.

73. Luther Hoffman to Myer, October 16 and 25, 1946.

74. War Relocation Authority, *Evacuated People,* tables 3, 4, and 8; *Topaz Times,* January 30, 1943.

75. The figures vary; Alice Kasai of the JACL in Salt Lake City has a list of 156 names that she obtained from Nickle Mortuary in Delta, Utah. This larger figure includes stillbirths and several deaths with no statistics.

76. "Welfare Section Final Report," November 1, 1945, WRA, RG 210. It is not clear who wrote this report; many original administrators had left by the time the camp closed.

77. "Evacuee Property Office, Final Report," November 1, 1945, WRA, RG 210.

78. "Closing Report of Project Reports Division," December 10, 1945, WRA, RG 210.

79. "Closing Report on Education," December 10, 1945, WRA, RG 210.

80. "Closing Report, Community Activities Section," December 10, 1945, WRA, RG 210.

81. Memo from Fumi Hayashi, n.d.; Suzuki, *Ministry,* 193.

8. Nikkei Lives: The Impact of Internment

1. See Drinnon, *Keeper of Concentration Camps,* for Myer's career. Works that deal specifically with dependency and the American Indians include Jorgensen, *Sun Dance Religion,* especially the Introduction, and White, *Roots of Dependency.*

2. Sucheng Chan ably summarized the controversy over whether Japanese Americans should properly be termed a "model minority" in *Asian Americans.* She held that by 1970 Asian Americans had outpaced whites in family income; but total income did not take into account the number of family members working, the amount of education received by each individual, and their high concentration in urban areas; see pp. 167–71.

3. Okubo, *Citizen 13660,* 208–9.

4. Daniels, "Japanese Americans," 188.

5. See Taylor, "Evacuation and Economic Loss," 163–68.

6. Commission on Wartime Relocation and Internment of Civilians, *Personal Justice Denied,* 118.

7. Daniels, *Concentration Camps, U.S.A.,* 168–69.

8. Interview with George Gentoku Shimamoto, New York, October 5, 1987, AWC.

9. Note from Chizu Kitano Iiyama, July 10, 1990.

10. Interview with Faith Terasawa, San Francisco, November 6, 1987, notes in the possession of the author; and conversations with her nephew, Donald Nakahata of Mill Valley on May 12, 1988.

11. Memo from Fumi Manabe Hayashi, March 1990, and conversation with Chitose Manabe, Berkeley, October 28, 1987 (translated by Tad Hayashi).

12. The age breakdown of camp residents as of January 30, 1943, was as follows:

0–2 years	358
3–4 years	222
5–6 years	179
7–12 years	651
13–15 years	484
16–18 years	708
19–21 years	781
26–30 years	779
31–35 years	358
41–45 years	522
46–50 years	475
51–55 years	549
56–60 years	499
61–65 years	352
66–70 years	195
71–75 years	59
76–80 years	27
81–85 years	8
86–90 years	1

Topaz Times, January 30, 1943.

13. Interviews with Tomoye Nozawe Takahashi, San Francisco, November 2, 1987, and August 29, 1989; notes in the possession of the author.

14. Ibid.

15. Ibid.

16. Ibid.

17. Tatsuno's film of Topaz was used extensively by Ken Verdoia in the television documentary "Topaz," made for public television station KUED in Salt Lake City in 1987. It has been restored and colorized and was used to illustrate news broadcasts in the Bay Area when the first redress checks were mailed. The original film was donated to the Japanese American National Museum in Los Angeles in 1992. Telephone conver-

sation with Dave Tatsuno, San Jose, October 4, 1990; letter from Tatsuno to the author, January 7, 1993.

18. Telephone conversation with Dave Tatsuno, San Jose, October 4, 1990; letter from Tatsuno to the author, January 7, 1993.

19. Ibid.

20. Interview with Kenji Fujii, Hayward, Calif., August 31, 1989; notes in the possession of the author.

21. Ibid.

22. Dillon Myer, press conference, May 14, 1943, as cited in Drinnon, *Keeper of Concentration Camps,* 83; chapter 6 is entitled "Troublemakers."

23. Interview with Karl Akiya, New York, June 16 and 18, 1988, AWC; letters from Karl Akiya to Dillon Myer, January 15 and 27, 1943, copy in the possession of the author; Karl Akiya's testimony to the Commission on Wartime Relocation and Internment of Civilians, New York, November 23, 1981, copy in the possession of the author.

24. Interview with Karl Akiya, New York, June 16 and 18, 1988; Yoneda, *Ganbatte,* 112–13.

25. Interview with Karl Akiya, New York, June 16 and 18, 1988.

26. Ibid.

27. Interview with K. Morgan Yamanaka, San Francisco, May 11, 1988, AWC; "Morgan Yamanaka," in Tateishi, *And Justice for All,* 113–20.

28. Ibid.

29. Ibid.

30. Ibid.

31. Interview with Tsuyako "Sox" Kitashima, San Francisco, November 6, 1987, AWC.

32. Ibid.

33. Ibid.

34. Ibid.; letter to the author from Tsuyako "Sox" Kitashima, San Francisco, December 11, 1993.

35. I wish to thank Masa "Kitty" Tsuzuki Nakagawa for helping me place people in the proper high school classes. I have identified married women here by their maiden names only; elsewhere in the text their maiden and married names appear.

36. Mixed families such as the one referred to here were given the option of separating, the white parent remaining outside camp and the children and Japanese American parent being interned. This particular family chose to stay together. Information came from informal conversations with Fumi Hayashi and others associated with the JACL in San Francisco.

37. Interview with John Hada, San Francisco, November 2, 1987, AWC.

38. Ibid.

39. Interview with Robert Utsumi, San Francisco, May 11, 1988, AWC.

40. Ibid.

41. Interview with Tom Kawaguchi, San Francisco, November 5, 1987, AWC; "Tom Kawaguchi," in Tateishi, *And Justice for All,* 176–85.

42. Ibid.

43. Ibid.

44. Ibid.

45. Interview with William Kochiyama, New York, June 18, 1988, AWC.

46. Ibid.

47. Ibid.

48. Testimony of William Kochiyama at the Hearing of the Commission on Wartime Relocation and Internment of Civilians, New York, November 23, 1981; copy in the possession of the author.

49. Interview with Chizu Kitano Iiyama and Ernest Iiyama, San Francisco, May 13, 1988, AWC.

50. Ibid.

51. Interview with Midori Shimanouchi Lederer, New York, June 17, 1988, AWC.

52. Ibid.

53. Hohri discussed his redress plan in "Redress as a Movement Towards Enfranchisement," in Daniels, Taylor, and Kitano, eds., *Japanese Americans,* 196–99.

54. Interview with Shigeki J. Sugiyama, Washington, D.C., June 9, 1988, AWC.

55. Written statement by Kiyo Ito, November 21, 1988, to the author; interview with Kiyo Ito, Leonia, N.J., June 14, 1988, AWC. Kiyo Ito is now Jean Kariya.

56. Ibid.

57. Ibid.

58. Interview with Kiyo Ito, Kitty Nakagawa, and Mari Eijima, Leonia, N.J., June 14, 1988, AWC.

59. Ibid.

60. Written statement by Michi Kobi, January 25, 1988, and interview, New York, November 6, 1987, AWC.

61. Ibid.

62. Ibid.

63. Ibid.

64. Interview with Maya Nagata Aikawa, Berkeley, November 4, 1987, AWC.

65. Ibid.

66. Ibid.

67. Ibid.

68. Ibid.

69. Interview with Donald Nakahata and Alice Nakahata, Mill Valley, Calif., May 12, 1988, AWC; "Donald Nakahata," in Tateishi, *And Justice for All,* 32–38.

70. Ibid.

71. Ibid.

72. Ibid.

73. Ibid.

74. Ibid.

9. Coming Home, Wherever That Is

1. District Intelligence Officer, Twelfth Naval District, to the Director of Naval Intelligence, Counter-Intelligence Report on Recent Developments in Japanese Situation, Twelfth Naval District, March 25, 1945, San Francisco, quoted in "Army and Navy Intelligence Reports, 1944–1945," 6–9, in Daniels, ed., *Archival Documents.*

2. Ibid.

3. Ibid., 19–22.

4. Ibid., 9–12.

5. Ibid., 15–17.

6. Ibid., 17–19.

7. Ibid., 27.

8. Ibid.

9. Girdner and Loftis, *Great Betrayal,* 356.

10. Daniels, *Concentration Camps, U.S.A.,* 158.

11. Ibid., 4.

12. See Taylor, "Evacuation and Economic Loss," 163–67.

13. Daniels, *Asian America,* 292–93.

14. Ibid., 5–6.

15. Yoneda, *Ganbatte,* 170–71.

16. Daniels, *Asian America,* 290–92; Taylor, "Evacuation and Economic Loss," 163–67.

17. Daniels, *Asian America,* 286.

18. Arrington, *Price of Prejudice,* 42. The phrase refers to the fact that many Japanese Americans, displaced from the harsh lives they faced in rural California, returned to urban areas there or elsewhere, not only moving out of regions of strong discrimination but also achieving economic mobility. It does describe the situation of some, particularly the younger Nisei, but it ignores the plight of the elderly Issei, many of whom had lost everything. Men who had no families to care for them were left destitute after the camps closed; they were too old to begin again and spent

the remainder of their lives in poverty. As Harry H. L. Kitano remarked, no other ethnic group in America had to achieve upward mobility by losing its freedom, possessions, and livelihood; interview with Harry Kitano, Los Angeles, September 20, 1987, AWC. If this was a blessing, it was a very mixed, uneven one, and the phrase itself seems patronizing, since it assumes that Japanese Americans could have achieved upward mobility in no other way.

19. Interview with Dave Tatsuno, San Jose, November 4, 1987, AWC.

20. Ibid.

21. Telephone conversation with Dave Tatsuno in San Jose, October 3, 1990; letter from Tatsuno to the author, San Jose, January 7, 1993.

22. Interviews with Tomoye Nozawe Takahashi, San Francisco, November 2, 1987, and August 29, 1989; notes in the possession of the author.

23. Ibid.

24. Ibid.

25. Interview with Tsuyako "Sox" Kitashima, San Francisco, November 6, 1987, AWC.

26. Ibid.

27. *Rafu Shinpō,* October 9, 1990; *Hokubei Mainichi,* October 12, 1990; *Salt Lake Tribune,* October 9, 1990.

28. Interview with K. Morgan Yamanaka, San Francisco, May 11, 1988, AWC.

29. Interview with Donald Nakahata and Alice Nakahata, Mill Valley, Calif., May 12, 1988, AWC.

30. Ibid.; letter from Donald Nakahata to the author, Mill Valley, Calif., December 19, 1992.

31. Interview with Kenji Fujii, Hayward, Calif., November 5, 1987; notes in the possession of the author.

32. Ibid.; letter from Fujii to the author, Hayward, Calif., December 16, 1992.

33. *Salt Lake Tribune,* October 9, 1990; *Hokubei Mainichi,* October 10, 1990.

34. *Rafu Shinpō,* October 10, 1990.

35. Cited in *Rafu Shinpō,* October 9, 1990; *Salt Lake Tribune,* October 9, 1990.

Bibliography

Archival Sources

Japanese Evacuation Research Study, Bancroft Library, University of California, Berkeley. (Note: The files in this enormous archive are cited simply by name of person and date, not by file box and number.)

Files on Central Utah Project, Record Group 210, National Archives, Washington D.C. These files are also cited by name of writer or report (as in the case of the many Community Analysis Reports of Oscar Hoffman to Dillon Myer). They are not cited by individual file and box.

Oral Histories conducted from 1987 to 1991 with Maya Aikawa, Karl Akiya, Jane Beckwith, Mari Eijima, Tad Fujita, Abu Keikoan Guilday, Fumi Hayashi, Arthur Tad Hayashi, Hisako Hibi, Hiromoto and Eiko Katayama, Nobu Hibino, Chizu Kitano Iiyama, Ernest Iiyama, Harry Kitano, Midori Shimanouchi Lederer, Kiyo Ito (Jean Kariya), Masako Tsuzuki Nakagawa, Michiko Okamoto (Michi Kobi), Tom Kawaguchi, Tsuyako "Sox" Kitashima, Glenn Kumekawa, William Kochiyama, Chiyoko Manabe, Donald and Alice Nakahata, Masi Nihei, Miné Okubo, Shigeki Sugiyama, George Gentoku Shimamoto, Lee Suyemoto, Tomoye Takahashi, Faith Terasawa, Robert Utsumi, Isao and Chiyoko Yano. I also talked by telephone with Grace Oshita, Dr. Clifford Uyeda, Paul Bell, Roscoe Bell, Evelyn Hodges Lewis, and Eleanor and Emil Sekerak. I corresponded with Oscar F. Hoffman. I had extended but untaped conversations with Michi Onuma and Seizo Oka. Oral histories that were transcribed, edited by the subject, and revised are on file at the Western Americana, in the Marriott Library at the University of Utah. Interviews that were not edited and returned have been used in rough draft form without any direct quotations. In all such cases, permission to use the material was obtained verbally from the subject at the time of the interview and confirmed before publication. Sometimes written statements were substituted for the interview by the subject when he/she reviewed the unedited transcript; this is noted in the endnotes. Some people were interviewed but their words were not recorded owing to problems with the tape recorder; they include Jiro Nakaso, Jim Kajiwara, Tad Hirota, and Mike Suzuki. The author wishes to thank all who participated in this lengthy interview project.

Manuscripts

Roscoe Bell, "Relocation Center Life," Western Americana, Marriott Library, University of Utah

Newspapers

Hokubei Mainichi (San Francisco)
Millard County Chronicle (Delta)
Pacific Citizen (San Francisco)
Rafu Shinpō (Los Angeles)
Salt Lake Tribune
Topaz Times

Secondary Sources

Adachi, Fumino. "My Experiences in a Foreign Land." In East Bay Japanese for Action, ed. *Our Recollections*. Berkeley: Privately published, 1986.

Adachi, Wakako. "History of Adachi Nursery." In *Stories of Issei Women,* translated by Janey Egawa. Berkeley: Privately published, 1987.

Anderson, Benedict. *Imagined Communities: Reflections on the Origin and Spread of Nationalism.* London: Verso, 1983; revised 1991.

Arrington, Leonard. *The Price of Prejudice: The Japanese-American Relocation Center in Utah During World War II.* Logan: Faculty Association of Utah State University, 1962.

———. "Utah's Ambiguous Reception: The Relocated Japanese Americans." In Daniels, Taylor, and Kitano, eds., *Japanese Americans.*

Bell, Colin, and Howard Newby. *Community Studies: An Introduction to the Sociology of the Local Community.* New York: Praeger, 1956; reprinted 1974.

Bender, Thomas. *Community and Social Change in America.* New Brunswick, N.J.: Rutgers University Press, 1980.

Bronson, William. *The Earth Shook, the Sky Burned.* New York: Doubleday, 1959.

Cantril, Hadley, ed. *American Concentration Camps: A Documentary History of the Relocation and Incarceration of Japanese Americans, 1942–45.* New York: Garland, 1989.

———, ed. *Public Opinion, 1935–1946.* Princeton: Princeton University Press, 1951.

Chan, Sucheng. *Asian Americans: An Interpretive History.* Boston: Twayne, 1991.

Commission on Wartime Relocation and Internment of Civilians. *Personal Justice Denied.* Washington, D.C.: Government Printing Office, 1982.

Daniels, Roger. *Asian America: Chinese and Japanese in the United States Since 1950.* Seattle: University of Washington Press, 1988.

———. *Concentration Camps, U.S.A.: Japanese Americans and World War II.* New York: Holt, Rinehart and Winston, 1971. Reprinted as *Concentration Camps, North America: Japanese in the United States and Canada During World War II.* Malabar, Fla.: Krieger, 1981.

———. Introduction to Asael T. Hansen, "My Two Years at Heart Mountain: The Difficult Role of an Applied Anthropologist." In Daniels, Taylor, and Kitano, eds., *Japanese Americans.*

———. "Japanese America, 1930–1941: An Ethnic Community in the Great Depression." *Journal of the West* 21 (October 1985): 35–50.

———. "Japanese-Americans." In Richard S. Kirkendall, ed., *The Harry S Truman Encyclopedia.* Boston: G. K. Hall, 1989.

———. *Politics of Prejudice: The Anti-Japanese Movement in California and the Struggle for Japanese Exclusion.* Berkeley and Los Angeles: University of California Press, 1962; 2d ed., 1972; reprinted Gloucester, Mass: Peter Smith, 1966.

———, ed. *Archival Documents, 1944 and 1945.* Vol. 8 of *American Concentration Camps: A Documentary History of the Relocation and Incarceration of Japanese Americans, 1942–45.* New York: Garland, 1989.

Daniels, Roger, Sandra C. Taylor, and Harry H. L. Kitano, eds. *Japanese Americans: From Relocation to Redress.* Salt Lake City: University of Utah Press, 1986.

Drinnon, Richard. *Keeper of Concentration Camps: Dillon S. Myer and American Racism.* Berkeley and Los Angeles: University of California Press, 1987.

Gesensway, Deborah, and Mindy Roseman. *Beyond Words: Images from America's Concentration Camps.* Ithaca: Cornell University Press, 1987.

Girdner, Audrie, and Anne Loftis. *The Great Betrayal: The Evacuation of the Japanese-Americans During World War II.* New York: Macmillan, 1969.

Grodzins, Morton. *Americans Betrayed: Politics and the Japanese Evacuation*. Chicago: University of Chicago Press, 1949.

Hata, Donald T., Jr. *"Undesirables": Early Immigrants and the Anti-Japanese Movement in San Francisco, 1792–1893*. New York: Arno Press, 1978.

Hohri, William. "Redress as a Movement Towards Enfranchisement." In Daniels, Taylor, and Kitano, eds., *Japanese Americans*.

Hosokawa, Bill. *JACL in Quest of Justice*. New York: William Morrow, 1982.

———. *Nisei: The Quiet Americans*. New York: William Morrow, 1969.

Ichihashi, Yamato. *Japanese in the United States*. Stanford: Stanford University Press, 1932; reprinted New York: Arno Press, 1969.

Ichioka, Yuji. *Views from Within: The Japanese American Evacuation and Resettlement Study*. Los Angeles: UCLA Asian American Studies Center, 1989.

Irons, Peter. *Justice at War: The Story of the Japanese American Internment Cases*. New York: Oxford University Press, 1983.

Ishigo, Estelle. *Lone Heart Mountain*. Los Angeles: Anderson, Ritchie, and Simon, 1972.

Issel, William, and Robert W. Cherny. *San Francisco, 1865–1932*. Berkeley and Los Angeles: University of California Press, 1986.

James, Thomas. *Exile Within: The Schooling of Japanese Americans, 1942–1945*. Cambridge: Harvard University Press, 1987.

Jorgensen, Joseph G. *The Sun Dance Religion: Power for the Powerless*. Chicago: University of Chicago Press, 1972.

Kawakami, Toyo Suyemoto. "Camp Memories: Rough and Broken Shards." In Daniels, Taylor, and Kitano, eds., *Japanese Americans*.

Kessler, Lauren. "Fettered Freedoms: The Journalism of World War II Japanese Internment Camps." *Journalism History* 15, no. 2–3 (Summer–Autumn 1988): 70–79.

Kiefer, Christie W. *Changing Cultures, Changing Lives*. San Francisco: Jossey-Bass, 1974.

Kikuchi, Charles. *The Diary of Charles Kikuchi*. Berkeley and Los Angeles: University of California Press, 1973.

Kitano, Harry H. L. "Japanese-American Crime and Delinquency." In Stanley Sue and Nathaniel N. Wagner, eds., *Asian-Americans: Psychological Perspectives*. Palo Alto, Calif.: Science and Behavior Books, 1973.

———. *Japanese Americans: The Evolution of a Subculture*. Englewood Cliffs, N.J.: Prentice-Hall, 1969.

Levine, Gene N., and Colbert Rhodes. *The Japanese American Community: A Three-Generation Study*. New York: Praeger, 1981.

Lukes, Timothy J., and Gary Y. Okihiro. *Japanese Legacy: Farming and Community Life in California's Santa Clara Valley.* Local History Studies, 31. Cupertino: California History Center, 1985.

Masaoka, Mike (with Bill Hosokawa). *They Call Me Moses Masaoka.* New York: William Morrow, 1991.

Meyer, Dillon S. *Uprooted Americans.* Tucson: University of Arizona Press, 1971.

Miyamoto, S. Frank. *Social Solidarity Among the Japanese in Seattle.* Seattle: University of Washington Press, 1984.

Modell, John. "The Japanese of Los Angeles: A Study in Growth and Accommodation, 1900–1946." Ph.D. diss., Columbia University, 1969.

Nakano, Mei T. *Japanese American Women: Three Generations, 1890–1990.* Berkeley: Mina Press and San Francisco: National Japanese American Historical Society, 1990.

Nelson, Douglas. *Heart Mountain: The Story of an American Concentration Camp.* Madison: State Historical Society of Wisconsin, 1976.

O'Brien, Robert. *College Nisei.* Palo Alto: Pacific Books, 1949.

Okihiro, Gary Y. *Cane Fires: The Anti-Japanese Movement in Hawaii, 1865–1945.* Philadelphia: Temple University Press, 1991.

Okubo, Miné. *Citizen 13660.* Seattle: University of Washington Press, 1946; reprinted 1973 and 1983.

Papanikolas, Helen Z. *The Peoples of Utah.* Salt Lake City: Utah State Historical Society, 1976.

Petersen, William. *Japanese Americans: Oppression and Success.* New York: Random House, 1971.

Richardson, J. D. *Messages and Papers of the Presidents.* Washington, D.C.: Bureau of National Literature, 1911.

Sawada, Mitziko. "After the Camps: Seabrook Farms and the Resettlement of Japanese Americans, 1944–47." *Amerasia Journal* 13 (1986–87): 117–36.

Sekerak, Eleanor Gerard. "A Teacher at Topaz." In Daniels, Taylor, and Kitano, eds., *Japanese Americans.*

Shibutani, Tamotsu. *Improvised News: A Sociological Study of Rumor.* Indianapolis: Bobbs-Merrill, 1966.

———. "Rumors in a Crisis Situation." M.A. thesis, University of Chicago, 1944.

Spickard, Paul R. *Mixed Blood: Intermarriage and Ethnic Identity in Twentieth-Century America.* Madison: University of Wisconsin Press, 1989.

Suzuki, Lester E. *Ministry in the Assembly and Relocation Centers of World War II.* Berkeley: Yardbird, 1979.

Suzuki, Peter T. "Anthropologists in the Wartime Camps for Japanese Americans: A Documentary Study." *Dialectical Anthropology* 6 (1981): 23–60.

Takaki, Ronald. *Strangers from a Different Shore: A History of Asian Americans.* Boston: Little, Brown, 1989.

Tateishi, John. *And Justice for All: An Oral History of the Japanese American Detention Camps.* New York: Random House, 1984.

Taylor, Sandra C. *Advocate of Understanding: Sidney Gulick and the Search for Peace with Japan.* Kent, Ohio: Kent State University Press, 1984.

———. "Evacuation and Economic Loss: Questions and Perspectives." In Daniels, Taylor, and Kitano, eds., *Japanese Americans.*

———. "The Federal Reserve Bank and the Relocation of the Japanese in 1942." *The Public Historian* 5 (Winter 1983): 9–30.

———. "Japanese Americans and Keetley Farms: Utah's Relocation Colony." *Utah Historical Quarterly* 54 (1986): 328–45.

———. "Leaving the Camps: Japanese American Resettlement in Utah and the Intermountain West." *Pacific Historical Review* 60 (Spring 1991): 169–94.

Thomas, Dorothy Swaine. *The Salvage: Japanese-American Evacuation and Resettlement.* Berkeley and Los Angeles: University of California Press, 1952.

Thomas, Dorothy Swaine, and Richard S. Nishimoto. *The Spoilage.* Berkeley and Los Angeles: University of California Press, 1946.

Topaz: Fortieth Year Topaz Reunion. San Francisco, 1983.

Tupper, Eleanor, and George E. McReynolds. *Japan in American Public Opinion.* New York: MacMillan, 1937.

Uchida, Yoshiko. *Desert Exile: The Uprooting of a Japanese American Family.* Seattle: University of Washington Press, 1982.

United States Department of the Interior. *The Wartime Handling of Evacuee Property.* Washington, D.C.: Government Printing Office, 1946.

Wakatsuki, Jeanne, and James D. Houston. *Farewell to Manzanar.* Boston: Houghton Mifflin, 1973.

"A Walk Through Japantown—1935." *Hokubei Mainichi,* Supplement, January 1, 1989.

War Relocation Authority. *The Evacuated People: A Quantitative Description,* vol. 3. Washington, D.C.: Government Printing Office, 1946; reprint AMS Press, New York, 1975.

———. *WRA: A Story of Human Conservation.* Washington, D.C.: Government Printing Office, 1945.

Weglyn, Michi. *Years of Infamy: The Untold Story of America's Concentration Camps.* New York: William Morrow, 1976.

White, Richard. *The Roots of Dependency: Subsistence, Environment, and Social Change Among the Choctaws, Pawnees, and Navajos.* Lincoln: University of Nebraska Press, 1983.

Yoneda, Karl G. *Ganbatte: Sixty-Year Struggle of a Kibei Worker.* Los Angeles: Asian American Studies Center, 1983.

Index

Compositor:	Braun-Brumfield, Inc.
Printer:	Braun-Brumfield, Inc.
Binder:	Braun-Brumfield, Inc.
Text:	11/14 Sabon
Display:	Sabon